The Psychology of Speech and Language

THE PSYCHOLOGY OF

An Introduction to

CONSULTING EDITOR: Russel R. Windes, *California Western University*

SPEECH AND LANGUAGE
Psycholinguistics

JOSEPH A. DEVITO

Herbert H. Lehman College of
The City University of New York

Random House, New York

Preface

The Psychology of Speech and Language is intended for students of speech, linguistics, psychology, and, in fact, all who are concerned with speech, language, and behavior.

In purpose and in scope this book is an introduction to the field of psycholinguistics. Although much has been written in this area, little in other treatments is addressed to the beginning student. Here I have tried to right this imbalance. No pretense is made for original formulations or for new theories. My purpose is to present, in as clear and unbiased a form as possible, some of the major concepts and theories essential to an understanding of this complex discipline.

Despite the great amount of research being done in psycholinguistics, the field itself has not been given clear definition. "Psycholinguistics," noted Sol Saporta (1961, p. vi), "is still an amorphous field." And Susan Ervin-Tripp and Dan Slobin (1966, p. 435), summarizing the growth of the field, correctly observe that "psycholinguistics appears to be a field in search of a definition." My own preference, reflected in the topics considered here, is to view psycholinguistics broadly as the study of speech and language behavior and thus not to limit the field to too narrow an area.

In Part One, "Theoretical Foundations," I present the major approaches to the study of speech and language psychology. The first chapter presents a general overview of speech and language behavior that provides some basic insights necessary for later discussions. The next three chapters, covering linguistic, learning, and communication theories, provide the major theoretical formulations for the study of psycholinguistics.

In Part Two, "Speech and Language Behavior," I consider speech and language acquisition, breakdown, differences, and effects—four topics which are currently centers of great research activity.

The literature on speech and language psychology is growing so rapidly that no single work—of whatever length—could aspire to completeness. Some will undoubtedly object to the inclusion of certain topics and to the emphasis given them and to the omission of others. My intention here is to cover a limited number of topics in some depth rather than to range widely but superficially. The topics included are those which I have found most meaningful and useful to both undergraduate and graduate students beginning their study of psycholinguistics. The omission of various topics, for example, bilingualism, speech perception, and second-language learning, is due not to their irrelevance or unimportance but rather to practical limitations of space and time.

In the hope that the reader will wish to continue his study of speech and language psychology suggestions for further reading appear at the end of the text.

After reading this text I would hope that the student would have acquired some insight into the nature of speech and language behavior, some of the information essential for understanding and critically evaluating current research and theory, and, most importantly, some facility for asking new and meaningful questions about speech, language, and behavior.

In using this book the student should read Chapters 1 through 4 first since these provide the theoretical background for the topics considered in Part Two. The chapters in Part Two may be read in any order. As often as possible the student should consult some of the references for those topics which arouse interest or to get a point of view different from that expressed here.

Throughout the writing of this book I have profited by the suggestions and comments of a number of persons. Special thanks must go to my students who over the past years have provided the stimulation essential to this kind of task. My colleagues at Herbert H. Lehman College have been particularly helpful. Professors Luther Sies, Norma Stegmaier, Cj Stevens, and John F. Wilson all read portions of the manuscript; their comments were most helpful. John DeCecco, Professor of Psychology at San Francisco State College, read the entire manuscript; his extensive and incisive comments resulted in many improvements. Lastly, but most importantly, I would like to express my appreciation to Russel Windes, Professor of Communication Arts and Sciences at Queens College and Consulting Editor for Random House, for providing the initial encouragement to write this book and for his many comments and suggestions.

To Richard Kennedy, Judy Rosenberg, and others on the Random House staff I owe much; they have made the task of writing this book a most pleasant one.

Contents

List of
Figures and Tables

FIGURES

TABLES

Part I

In this section we present an introduction to the ways in which psycholinguistics may be approached.

In Chapter 1 we offer a general overview of speech and language behavior which serves to provide some common ground for the following chapters.

In Chapter 2, "Linguistic Theory," Chapter 3, "Learning Theory," and Chapter 4, "Communication Theory," we provide the general theoretical approaches for the study of speech and language psychology. Devoting a separate chapter to each of these areas should not imply that they are of equal influence or importance in the field today. In the original 1954 publication of *Psycholinguistics: A Survey of Theory and Research Problems* (Osgood and Sebeok, 1954) these three areas were each considered and regarded as essentially equal contributors to the development of this new field. In the last few years this situation has changed drastically. Linguistic theory, particularly generative grammar, now dominates the theoretical and experimental research. Learning theory, once the most valuable source of hypotheses about language and speech behavior, has been attacked as inadequate and incorrect in principle. Communication or information theory, the approach which provided the original impetus

THEORETICAL
FOUNDATIONS

for collaboration between linguistics and psychology, now has a peripheral position.

There were two major reasons for including linguistic, learning, and communication theories. First, each discipline has stimulated a great deal of research which is impossible to understand without some notion of the concepts and theories of these areas. Even the attacks on learning theory, for example, cannot be understood or evaluated without first understanding the general nature of learning theory and something of the specific theories to which objections are raised. Second, each area has the potential for contributing a great deal to the broad field of speech and language behavior. That these contributions have not been made is perhaps not the fault of the area but of its students and researchers.

In these four chapters I also weave in some discussion of relatively specific research methodologies, namely lexical and stylistic analysis, kinesics, semantic differentiation, proxemics, and cloze procedure. Although these methodologies are considered only briefly, these discussions should serve to introduce the reader to some of the more specific ways in which speech and language behavior may be studied and should provide a better understanding of research utilizing these approaches.

Chapter One

Speech, Language, and Behavior: An Introduction

In this chapter we first attempt to clarify the role of speech and language in human behavior and in human society. Second, we explain the general nature of speech and language, how language differs from speech and how speech differs from writing. Third, we explore the semantic or meaning dimension of speech and language: the meanings of meaning and their functions, levels, and styles. Fourth, we examine the pragmatic dimension of speech and language, that is, the relationship between speech and language on the one hand and behavior on the other.

THE ROLE OF SPEECH AND LANGUAGE

" Speech," wrote Thomas Mann, " is civilization itself." In this simple sentence Mann captured the essence of man's most distinctive feature. Take speech away and what would be lost? Leslie White (1949, pp. 33–34), the cultural anthropologist, presents a persuasive argument for Mann's assertion.

> Without articulate speech we would have no *human* social organization. Families we might have, but this form of organization is not peculiar to man; it is not *per se, human*. But we would have no prohibitions of incest, no rules prescribing exogamy and endogamy, polygamy or monogamy. How could marriage with a cross cousin be prescribed, marriage with a parallel cousin proscribed, without articulate speech? How could rules which prohibit plural mates possessed simultaneously but permit them if possessed one at a time, exist without speech?

> Without speech we would have no political, economic, ecclesiastic, or military organization; no codes of ethics; no laws; no science, theology, or literature; no games or music, except on an ape level. Rituals and ceremonial paraphernalia would be meaningless without articulate speech. Indeed, without articulate speech we would be all but toolless: we would have only the occasional and insignificant use of the tool such as we find today among the higher apes, for it was articulate speech that transformed the nonprogressive tool-using of the ape into the progressive, cumulative tool-using of man, the human being. In short, without symbolic communication in some form, we would have no culture. " In the Word was the beginning " of culture—and its perpetuation also.

The history of any animal species reveals a distinct sameness, an absence of change, in behavior. A bird building its nest today will do it in almost exactly the same way that birds did it yesterday, a year ago, even thousands of years ago. And one can be quite sure that birds will continue in this same way thousands of years from now. All animals, even the higher apes, closest to man in intelligence, show this sameness over vast stretches of time.

Man is different. Change is a general characteristic of human thought, human actions, and human development. A house built today is quite different from one that was built thousands of years ago or even a few decades ago. And we can be certain that a house built twenty or thirty years from now will differ greatly from one built today.

Alfred Korzybski (1921) described this uniqueness of man in terms of a hierarchy of capabilities of living things. Plants, at the lowest level, have the ability to combine chemicals, as in photosynthesis. At a higher level, animals, in addition to the ability to bind chemicals, can also bind space. A bird, for example, can build a nest by moving objects from different places to one particular site. Man, at the highest level, has not only the ability to bind chemicals and space but also the ability to bind time and it is this ability which enables him to grow and improve.

A bird cannot learn from past generations of birds, nor can a bird teach future generations. Man can. He can learn, at least theoretically, all that has been learned before his birth and all that he has learned can be taught to his offspring who will in turn become the teachers of future generations. The process is a never-ending one and is made possible by man's ability to communicate, by man's knowledge of symbols and symbol systems.

Man can learn all the inventions, all the theories, all the answers to questions which have preceded him. He can understand the mistakes of those who have gone before him and hopefully avoid them.

But knowledge not only brings wisdom. Seldom does it come without certain rather ironic side effects. Man, of all the animals in the universe, is the only one who knows that he will die. Man is the only animal who can fool himself completely, the only animal who can give himself a nervous breakdown, and probably the only animal who can lie. And there is at least some evidence which indicates that without language or some symbol system man would never be able to fool himself or develop schizophrenia or have hallucinations or contemplate suicide. At the same time, however, without language he would not be able to progress, to develop, to grow. He would remain at one level—never learning, never teaching.

THE NATURE OF SPEECH AND LANGUAGE

Although the term *language* is frequently used, it is also frequently confused. Few authorities agree with one another as to what constitutes language. Roger Brown (1958a, p. 260), for example, in his provocative *Words and*

Things, observes that language "is nothing less than an inventory of all the ideas, interests, and occupations that take up the attention of the community." Such a definition, however, fails to define language *per se* but merely equates it with almost everything else in the objective and subjective worlds in which we live.

Edward Sapir (1921, p. 7), in his classic *Language: An Introduction to the Study of Speech*, defines language as "a purely human and noninstinctive method of communicating ideas, emotions and desires by means of a system of voluntarily produced symbols." The problem with this definition is that it fails to take into consideration the important distinction between language and speech. John Hughes (1962, p. 6), also failing to differentiate speech from language, defines language as a "system of arbitrary vocal symbols by which thought is conveyed from one human being to another." Furthermore, if there were but one person living, according to this definition, there would be no language because thought could not be communicated from one person to another. These same basic problems are present in Joseph Bram's (1955, p. 2) definition of language as "a structured system of arbitrary vocal symbols by means of which members of a social group interact."

A Definition of Language

I define language as *a potentially self-reflexive, structured system of symbols which catalog the objects, events, and relations in the world.*

Symbols stand for other things but bear no real relationship to them. A symbol is an arbitrary "stand in" for the actual thing. The word *rain* is not the actual rain but serves as a symbol of rain. Its relationship to the actual rain is arbitrary—the word *rain* is not, for example, wet or even a little damp. In fact, the symbol *rain* is not any wetter than the symbol *dry*. Symbols do not possess any of the qualities or characteristics of the thing for which they stand. The word *small* is actually larger than the word *big* and the symbol *green*—on this paper—is just as black as the symbols *black* and *white*.

A *sign*, on the other hand, does bear a real relationship to the thing for which it stands. High fever, to use Aristotle's example, is a sign of sickness. Here there is a real rather than an arbitrary relationship between the thing (sickness) and the sign (fever). Similarly, dark clouds are a sign of rain; they are not the actual rain but their relationship to rain is not as arbitrary as the symbol *rain*.

The arbitrariness of symbols, however, does not leave the speaker a choice. As Saussure (1959, pp. 68–69) has phrased it, in a now famous passage, "the term [arbitrary] should not imply that the choice of the signifier [that is, symbol] is left entirely to the speaker. . . I mean that it is unmotivated, that is, arbitrary in that it actually has no natural connection with the signified."

Symbols can be made of any substance.   They may be made of rock as in the case of the pyramids, which were symbols of royalty or divinity; of cloth or color as in the case of wearing black for mourning or purple for royalty, of ink as in the case of writing; and, of course, of sound as in the case of speech.   It is these vocal symbols which constitute human *speech*. Speech, then, is the vocal manifestation of language symbols.

These symbols are used according to clearly defined rules, even though these rules may not be known consciously by native speakers of the language. All linguists, psychologists, communicologists, and in fact all who are concerned with language and language behavior, agree that language is a *structured system*.   Yet, exactly what this structure consists of has not been made entirely clear.   We know at least that language is not random— symbols are not combined in any order but only in certain ones.   These rules of constraints, consisting of both prescriptions and proscriptions, exist on all levels of language usage.   There are rules for the combination of individual sounds; for example, one can coin the word *synpax* but not the word *ngzt* simply because the English language has built into it certain rules for the combination of sounds which *synpax* does and *ngzt* does not observe. Similarly, one cannot say *two wuges* where the final syllable is pronounced as in *dishes* but must say *two wugs* where the final sound is pronounced as a "z."   The rules of English specify that in forming the plural of a word ending in a voiced sound—a sound made with vibration of the vocal folds of which "g" is one example—a "z" sound must be used.   Similarly, rules exist on the word level.   One cannot say *the of up* simply because this violates the grammar of English, but one can say "The blue matron rode the stationary fly."   Even though this sentence does not make much sense, if any, it is still recognized as a grammatical English sentence, that is, a sentence which follows the structural rules of the language.

Language symbols must be capable of referring to a wide variety of objects, events, and relations in the world.   By its nature language must contain symbols, for example, words, which *catalog the numerous objects, events, and relations in the world*.   This characteristic enables us to exclude "languages" which are constructed for very specific purposes such as the "language" of symbolic logic or the "language" of computers.   These "languages" permit communication about only a limited number of subjects and are not human language in the sense in which the term is used here.   This quality also enables us to exclude animal "languages" since these are for the most part rather specific and cannot be used to talk about "the objects, events, and relations in the world."

Language is *potentially self-reflexive* or capable of being used on at least two different levels.   It must permit reference to the real or object world, as already observed, and also must allow reference to itself.   Language is language only if it can be used for language analysis.   Many animals, for example, can communicate and, in the case of the honey bee (cf. Chapter 7), the communication systems are quite complex, permitting communication about many different things.   One essential difference between these forms of communication and human language is that animals cannot communicate about their communication.   A bee, for example, can communicate, by means of a dance, about nectar and pollen but it cannot dance about its dance.   Man, on the other hand, can talk about objects, in what is called an object language, and he can also talk about his talk, in what is called a metalanguage, that is, a language for talking about language.

In summary, these are the essential ingredients of language which distinguish it from other communication systems of animals or those which are invented to serve rather limited and specific purposes.   Note that we have not defined *a* language, that is, a specific language such as English or Chinese, but rather human language in a general and abstract sense.

Language versus Speech, Speech versus Writing

Two confusions, prevalent in the literature, need to be clarified here. The first is that language and speech are synonymous.   They are not.   What has been defined above is language, the abstract system which is manifested or actualized as speech, as vocal utterances.   People who, due to some physical or psychological abnormality, fail to develop speech may nevertheless possess language.   Many people, for example, who cannot speak can nevertheless understand speech and in order for them to do this they must possess this system of symbols and rules called language.   The converse of this does not hold.   That is, people who speak cannot be without language.   The ability to speak presupposes a knowledge of language, but a knowledge of language does not presuppose the ability to speak.

This distinction between language and speech was developed most clearly by the French-Swiss philologist, Ferdinand de Saussure (1959). Language, *la langue* in Saussure's terminology, is a social thing, possessed by the entire community.   Speech, *la parole* to Saussure, is an individual product.   Language is the *potential* vehicle whereas speech is the *actual* activity of communication.

There is also an important distinction between speech and writing. Speech is clearly the primary form of communication; writing is a secondary and derived system—a system developed in imitation of the spoken language. Speech is not spoken writing, nor is writing simply written speech.   Although it is true that speaking and writing have great similarities and that the same language may be spoken or written, these two modes of communication must not be regarded as isomorphic manifestations of language.

The differences betwen speech and writing are most obvious from a prescriptive point of view.   Speakers and writers are generally advised that the form of oral and written communications *should* differ because of significant differences in the processes of listening and reading.   Listeners cannot rehear an oral communication and so must get the meaning immediately or else lose it completely.   Readers, however, can and often do reread.

Another difference is in the psychological sets of listeners and readers. The former are generally more relaxed and are prepared to let the speaker do the work; the latter are expected and prepared to exert more effort. The speaker, furthermore, is pressured to avoid silence and maintain fluency whereas the writer is pressured with limitations in space. These differences will generally force the speaker to repeat, perhaps to give himself time to think of his next idea, to search for a particular word, to avoid the dreaded silence, or to maintain control of the speaking situation. The writer, on the other hand, systematically avoids repeating himself and is forced to find a single word to do the work of two or three.

Because of these basic differences communication teachers suggest that speech be instantly intelligible but writing only ultimately intelligible. The suggestions given speakers for making their messages instantly intelligible are many and include the use of short, familiar, and easy words, frequent repetition, and active rather than passive constructions. Writers, primarily because of limitations in space, are advised to avoid repetition and to pack as many thoughts as possible into the allotted space.

More important, however, are the purely descriptive differences, that is, the differences that do in fact exist between speech and writing (cf. DeVito, 1967d). Differences between speaking and writing exist on two levels— differences which might be regarded as all-or-none features (elements present in one system and absent in the other) and differences which might be regarded as more-or-less features (elements more frequent in one system than in the other).

Among the most obvious characteristics of speech not present in writing are silence or pause, pitch, volume, and stress. Speech also contains numerous forms of hesitations, for example, vocalized pauses such as *er, a, ah,* false starts such as " I saw the boy -er the girl go home," and stutters such as " the sssspeaker."

Variation in these and other vocal characteristics enable a speaker to communicate meaning and to reinforce or even contradict the literal meaning of the message. Thus, for example, the same sentence said with different stress will communicate different meanings. The sentence " Is this the face that launched a thousand ships?" when repeated, each time with stress on a different word, conveys distinctly different meanings. Sentences containing numerous hesitations will probably be perceived as less forceful and less convincing than sentences which flow more smoothly. For each of the characteristics of spoken language variations can be made and these variations communicate meanings just as surely as do the actual words.

In writing, strictly speaking, stress, pitch, pause, and hesitation are absent, even though these features can be represented graphically. As purely acoustic phenomena these characteristics clearly do not exist in writing. However, writing is no less varied than speech because of these absences and has numerous characteristics which speech lacks. Among these are punctuation marks, which correspond, though only partly, to intonation and stress; capital letters which indicate sentence beginnings or proper nouns; and spacing which corresponds closely, though again not iso-morphically, with pausing.   To these main features one might add such less frequently observed characteristics as color, size, shape, intensity, and posi-tion of type and symbols such as &, %, $, and #, which in the spoken language do not differ from their unabbreviated forms.

Among those features found more frequently in one mode of communica-tion than the other are the following: (1) Speech contains more easy, short, and familiar words, more personal pronouns, and more function words—words which indicate grammatical relations rather than make reference to the real world as do nouns, verbs, adjectives, and adverbs.   (2) Speech contains fewer different words.   (3) Speech contains more self-reference terms, more allness terms such as *never, all*, and *always*, more pseudo-quantifying terms such as *many, much*, and *very*, more qualification terms such as *but, however*, and *although*, and more terms indicative of consciousness of projection such as *it seems to me* and *apparently*.   (4) Speech is less abstract than writing, containing more concrete verbs and less abstract nouns than does writing.   (5) Speech contains more verbs and adverbs whereas writing contains more nouns and adjectives.

THE SEMANTIC DIMENSION OF SPEECH AND LANGUAGE

Semantics is the science of meaning and deals with signs and symbols in two principal ways.   First, semantics is concerned with how signs and sym-bols signify or refer to referents.   This we cover in our discussion of the meanings of meaning.   Second, semantics is concerned with the ways signs and symbols signify referents.   This we cover in our discussion of the func-tions, levels, and styles of speech and language.

The most obvious purpose of speech and language is to communicate meaning.   Meaning, however, is so complex and so little of a substantial nature is known about it that linguists, until recently, have all but abandoned its study.   Consideration of meaning, beyond the rather gross reference in determining whether two groups of sounds meant the same or different things, was largely ignored.   Without meaning, however, there would be no language and if it were not to communicate meaning, there would be no speech.

The Meanings of Meaning

I. A. Richards (Ogden and Richards, 1923) provides us with a simple theory of how symbols signify.   Suppose that you were to ask what I mean by *stuttering*.   To this question I may answer in a variety of ways.   (1) I might say that stuttering is an anticipatory, apprehensive, hypertonic, semantogenic, avoidance reaction (Johnson, 1946) and then define each of

the words in the definition.   (2) I may say that stuttering, being semantogenic, can so easily be avoided, and it is unfortunate that so many people
stutter.   (3) I may decide to take you to a speech clinic to observe a
stutterer or perhaps imitate the various behaviors which characterize
stuttering.

In each of these answers the word *meaning* was interpreted differently
and the three answers exemplify the three kinds of meaning considered by
Richards.   In the first instance, where stuttering was defined by Johnson's
definition, the word *meaning* was interpreted to refer to the word *stuttering*.
That is, it was assumed that the meaning of the word was unclear.   In the
second instance, where stuttering was defined by noting that it is unfortunate
that so many people stutter, *meaning* was interpreted to refer to my own feelings and thoughts about stuttering.   That is, it was assumed that how I felt
about stuttering was uncertain.   In the third instance, where an actual
stutterer was observed, the word *meaning* was interpreted to refer to the actual
thing.   That is, it was assumed that actual stuttering behavior was unknown.

In the first instance focus was on the word or symbol, in the second it
was on the thought or reference, and in the third it was on the actual thing
or referent.   Richards has exemplified these three elements or aspects of
meaning in the form of a triangle, presented in Figure 1.

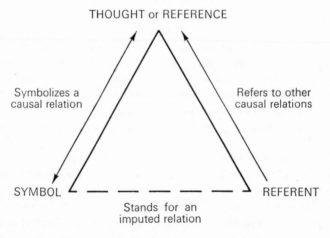

FIGURE 1. The Triangle of Meaning. *From C. K. Ogden and I. A. Richards,*
The Meaning of Meaning *(New York: Harcourt, Brace & World, 1923), p. 11.*

First note the three points of the triangle.   On the bottom left is the
symbol, generally a word or some linguistic form.   Richards limits the concept of symbol to words which refer objectively to things in the real world.
Words referring to feelings, emotions, fears, loves, hates, and, in general, to
the subjective world are not considered symbols.   The symbol, in Richards'

system, refers impartially to the thing—it is purely denotative or referential or factual.   Connotation refers to the communication of subjective feelings, emotions, and attitudes about a thing.   It is that aspect of meaning which is communicated in addition to the purely neutral denotation.

As purely abstract concepts denotation and connotation are polar opposites and mutually exclusive.   Seldom, if ever, are they truly separated in ordinary language.   As they appear in speech they are most often inter-related and overlapping.   The words *mother* and *father*, for example, are generally thought of as purely denotative though with even a minimum of reflection it becomes obvious that these terms also carry connotations which naturally vary from one communication situation to another.   In fact, almost all words, as they appear in normal everyday speech, have some connotative component.

In excluding connotative terms from his system of meaning, Richards is not assigning them a place of lesser importance in language but merely omitting them from this particular system.   Although many semanticists choose to deal solely with denotative language, a complete system of semantics would have to deal with connotation in some way.

At the apex of the triangle is the reference or thought.   This refers to the thought which the speaker or symbol user has of an object or event.   At the bottom right of the triangle is the referent, the actual thing of the real world.

In the three answers to the question about stuttering the definition was the symbol, the feelings about stuttering was the reference, and the actual stuttering was the referent.

The relationships are somewhat less obvious.   Between the reference and the symbol there is a causal relationship in both directions.   The symbol-user, in using the symbol *stuttering*, causes in the hearer a thought or reference similar to his own.   Likewise, the thought in the mind of the symbol-user causes the use of a certain word or symbol to refer to it.

Between the reference and the referent there is a causal relationship insofar as the referent, which has been experienced in some way, has stimulated the symbol-user and caused him to think about the source of the stimulation.   The referent has caused him to have a reference or thought about it. Seeing stuttering, for example, causes one to think about or have a reference of stuttering.   The causal relationship does not go from the reference to the referent.   The reference cannot cause the referent—thinking about something does not cause it to appear.

The last relationship is probably the most important and has already been explained in part in the discussion of symbols.   Between the symbol and the referent there is no causal relationship.   The symbol merely "stands for" the referent.   The symbol, in referring to the referent, must go through the thought or reference.   This is simply a diagrammatic explanation for the fact that meanings are not in the thing or in the word but rather in the thoughts of the symbol-user.

The Functions of Speech and Language

Although Richards' conception of the components and relationships involved in meaning has provided significant insights into the semantic dimensions of speech and language it is, nevertheless, incomplete. One of its most obvious insufficiencies is that it does not account for functions of speech and language other than the referential. (In this and in the following two sections these dimensions are considered as common to both speech and language. Following the distinction introduced earlier, however, functions, levels, and styles are to be viewed as actualized in speech and as potential in language.)

The functions of speech and language can be described from different points of view. In the literature of speech and linguistics classifications abound. Frank Dance (1967a), for example, distinguishes three functions of speech communication: (1) to link the individual with his milieu or environment, (2) to develop the higher mental processes, and (3) to regulate both the internal and external behaviors of oneself and others. Jon Eisenson (Eisenson, Auer, and Irwin, 1963) divides the functions into two major categories: noncommunicative purposes, which include oral pleasure and verbal contact, and communicative purposes, which include speech as social gesture, speech to disarm hostility, speech to ease anxiety, speech as aggression, and speech of concealment.

Joshua Whatmough (1956) has developed a four-fold classification. The informative or referential function is concerned with communicating facts; the dynamic with moulding or changing attitudes and opinions; the emotive with directing the behavior of others; and the aesthetic with giving the form of a message a certain distinctiveness. Stephen Ullmann (1966), utilizing the most elementary communication model possible—speaker-message-listener—notes that each element has a corresponding speech function. The expressive function is closely associated with the speaker, the communicative function with the message, and the effective function with the listener.

Roman Jakobson (1960) has proposed a classification based on the same general principle followed by Ullmann, namely, that each element in the communication process has a particular speech function oriented to it. Jakobson's system, however, is more complete and will be used here and as a basis for organizing the later discussion of communication models (Chapter 4). In this scheme six functions are distinguished, each of which is associated with or oriented to one of the six essential elements in communication: source, channel, message, code, receiver, and referent.

(1) *Emotive* speech, closely associated with the source or speaker, serves a psychological function and is seen most readily in speech used to express the feelings, attitudes, or emotions of the speaker. The clearest example of speech serving a psychological function is probably seen in

catharsis, a process whereby the speaker frees his mind of certain pressing problems.

(2) *Phatic* speech creates social relationships and may be considered identical to what Bronislaw Malinowski (1923) referred to as phatic communion. Phatic speech cannot be interpreted literally; rather, its meaning rests in great part on the immediate and specific communication situation. The greeting *How are you?* is in most situations phatic speech. The speaker does not expect or want the listener to tell him how he actually feels but rather is merely saying *Hello*. Another way of looking at this function is as speech whose purpose is to keep the channels of communication open and in good working order. Logically, this function is oriented to the channel.

(3) *Cognitive* speech makes reference to the real world and is frequently referred to as referential, denotative, or informative. It is most closely associated with the referent and is the function which Richards described.

(4) *Rhetorical* speech, also referred to as directive or conative, is probably the most complex of all the functions. Rhetorical speech seeks to direct or influence thought and behavior. It is the language of the clergy, of the politician, and of the salesman. It is the speech of persuasion and associated most directly with the receiver.

(5) *Metalingual* speech is used to talk not about the objects and events in the real world but about speech itself. It is a higher order or more abstract speech and is oriented to the code of communication.

(6) *Poetic* speech serves to structure the message, to which it has its primary orientation, so that it may be more appealing from an aesthetic point of view or more distinctive.

To this basic list other functions could be added. For example, one could consider speech which seeks to communicate aggression or speech which seeks to conceal facts. On closer inspection, however, it will be found that these functions can be viewed as subheadings under the six general functions discussed here, though it would be hazardous to claim that all conceivable functions could be included.

Any given utterance may serve any number of functions. This classification does not imply that only one purpose or function can exist at any one time. In fact, almost any speech sample will be found to serve a number of functions at the same time. One function, however, is likely to be more obvious or more dominant than others.

The Levels of Speech and Language

In addition to serving different functions speech and language can also be used on different levels of abstraction, ranging from the extremely concrete to the extremely abstract. Inspect Figure 2, which illustrates these levels.

The event level is represented by the largest circle. The circle is broken to indicate that the event level encompasses infinity. This is the

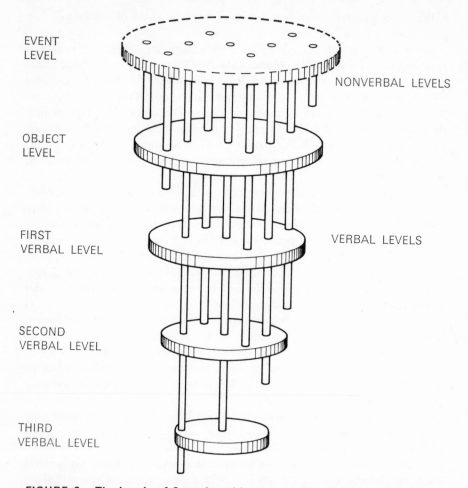

FIGURE 2. The Levels of Speech and Language This diagram is a modification of Alfred Korzybski's Structural Differential. *From Alfred Korzybski,* Science and Sanity *(Lakeville, Connecticut: International Non-Aristotelian Library Publishing Co., 1933), p. 393.*

level of the real world and appropriately called by J. Samuel Bois (1966) **WIGO**, the level of *what is going on*. This is the level of the atomic goings-on which we construct or infer out of what science as of this date tells us about the world. This level is not perceived directly but rather its existence and its characteristics are inferred from the information which physicists, chemists, biologists, and other scientists provide. The event level is characterized by (1) infinite complexity, (2) constant change, and (3) nonidentity—no two things are ever the same. The characteristics of the event level are represented by the tiny circles which are infinite in number.

From the event level our senses abstract certain characteristics—it is these characteristics that we see, hear, taste, feel, and smell. Characteristics which are abstracted are symbolized in the diagram by poles connecting the two levels. Those characteristics which are not abstracted are denoted by poles not penetrating the lower levels. The characteristics of this second level are finite in number, limited by the nature of our perceptual capacities. For example, science asserts that the event is composed of molecules moving around at varying speeds. This is what exists on the event level—molecules in motion. If one were to touch a substance composed of fast moving molecules one would abstract or feel heat, as well as perhaps smoothness or roughness, etc. If one were to touch a substance composed of slow-moving molecules one would abstract coldness as well as various other characteristics. The sensations of "hotness" and "coldness" do not exist on the event level —only molecules moving around at different speeds exist here. The perception of hotness or coldness is a result of the interaction of the speed of the molecules with our own nervous system. From the same event, therefore, different people will inevitably abstract different characteristics because of differences in their psychological and physiological make-up. This second level is called the object level; it is the level on which we live our lives, the level of sense perception.

Both the event and the object levels are nonverbal. These are the levels we would have been restricted to had we not learned symbolic systems; they are the only levels on which preverbal babies and animals function.

The third level, the first verbal level, is the level of concrete naming and descriptive statements. For example, it is the level of *John Smith* and of *John Smith is here*. This level, like the previous levels, contains a number of characteristics but as one goes from the event to the object to the first verbal level the number of characteristics decreases. The small circles on this first verbal level are intended to signify only those characteristics of the thing which are included in the actual verbal name or statement. Thus while many characteristics of John Smith may be observed, the statement, *John Smith is here*, does not include the type of clothes he is wearing or whether he is walking or sitting, etc.—all of which would be included in the actual perception of him, that is, on the object level. There are, of course, many more characteristics of John Smith which one does not perceive and which, therefore, exist on the event level but not on the object level.

The next level, the second verbal level, is the level of class terms, for example, *boys, Democrats*, and of inferential statements, statements which go beyond the actual facts of the situation. For example, *John Smith is here* is a descriptive, factual statement. If one went beyond this and said *John Smith is here to borrow money* this latter statement would be inferential since it does not restrict itself to the facts as observed but goes beyond these to draw inferences. This second verbal level is also the level of theories and generalizations, statements made on the basis of other statements. Another way of putting this would be to say that as one goes from the first to the second verbal level more of the observer and less of the observed is included.

The next level, the third verbal level, is the level of statements about statements about statements about the perception of the thing, for example, I saw John [first verbal level] who was sad [second verbal level] because he had failed his examination [third verbal level]. This third verbal level, then, is the level of inferences [that John failed his examination] about inferences [that John was sad]. There is actually no end to this process —one can always make statements about statements about statements about statements, etc.

The Styles of Speech and Language

Speech and language, then, may serve different functions and may be used on different levels of abstraction. But the most obvious way in which speech and language may vary is in style. Style is the way in which a speaker or writer utilizes the resources of his language—the choices he makes and the arrangements or patterns which result. The difference between "Sir, I don't have any paper" and "Ain't got no paper, man" is a stylistic one—the word choices and the arrangement of the words differ.

In this section some of the ways in which styles may be analyzed and classified are considered.

Whereas the classifications of the functions and levels of speech and language are relatively recent, the consideration of different styles has a long and eclectic history. Over two thousand years ago, for example, Cicero's *Orator* classified three styles: a plain style made use of pure and Latin terms, simply and clearly arranged; the moderate style was more forceful, possessing sweetness but little vigor; the grand style was ornate, sublime, dignified, copious, and graceful. With relatively little modification this classification persisted in the theories of rhetoric for centuries. Cicero's classification, prescriptive in purpose, was advanced as a means of training the orator in the art of persuasion. The more recent classifications, having been advanced through the "hands-off" policy of the linguists, are primarily descriptive.

Mario Pei (1956, p. 65), for example, considers five styles: (1) literary, poetical, super-erudite (for example, "Those individuals do not possess any"); (2) literary, prose, cultured (for example, "Those men haven't any"); (3) spoken standard (for example, "Those men haven't got any"); (4) colloquial lower class (for example, "Those guys haven't/ain't got any"); and (5) vulgar and slang (for example, "Dem guys ain't got none").

Probably the best-known linguistic classification is that proposed by Martin Joos in *The Five Clocks* (1962) and modified somewhat by Gleason (1965). Like Pei, Joos also distinguishes five styles. (1) Frozen style is the style of written prose and of social strangers. (Gleason, limiting this level to speech, refers to it as "oratorical.") There is no participation by the addressee here. The speaker speaks and the listeners listen; in fact, the speaker is hardly aware of the listeners' presence and in any case does nothing to alter his style on the basis of listener reactions.

(2) Formal style (called "deliberative" by Gleason), also not participated in by the listener, serves primarily an information function and is the style generally used in addressing a large audience. When used with only one listener it signals distance between speaker and hearer. At times the distance is one of deference and at other times it is one of contempt. This concept of distance as signaled in language has recently been elaborated by Wiener and Mehrabian (1968) in their theory of "immediacy." When formal style is used where casual style would be expected it signifies that something is wrong in the relationship. If a mother calls *John David Smith* when *Johnny* is the usual name she calls, the child knows that something is wrong and consequently modifies his response. The formal style signals distance or nonimmediacy. The speaker addresses his audience with a cohesive, carefully planned, and well-constructed talk. Sentences are varied and grammatical and the vocabulary is extensive; repetitions, sentence fragments, slang, and "in group" expressions are avoided.

(3) Consultative style, the style of business talks and small-group discussions, does involve participation by the addressee. Here the speaker supplies background information, the amount and kind of which is regulated by the listener. By his participation the addressee insures that the speaker does not provide unnecessary or already known information and that he does provide information which is essential to their interaction. In consultative style there is no extensive planning of what will be said or how it will be expressed. The continuous participation by the addressee makes such planning unnecessary and, in fact, impossible. Because of this lack of planning there will be a number of grammatical "errors," for example, run-on sentences, the use of *can* instead of *may* to indicate permission, and the "overuse" of certain terms such as *and, well,* and *on.*

(4) Casual style is the style in which friends and "insiders" speak. Background information and continuous participation by the addressee are absent; both are unnecessary in casual style and, in fact, might be insulting since they imply that speaker and listener do not share the same information. Casual style is characterized by the frequent occurrence of terms used in special senses and by ellipsis (the omission of various unstressed words or certain sounds). For example, in casual style *The coffee is cold* would be rendered *Coffee's cold* and *can* as *c'n.* Other casual expressions include *Don't care* for *I don't care, Got a flat?* for *Have you got a flat?* and *Want to come?* for *Do you want to come?* Determiners and auxiliaries, being unnecessary for communicating meaning, are omitted. Ellipsis, of course, does not occur in the first three styles.

(5) Intimate style is characterized by the use of the private and relatively permanent language code of the group and by extraction. In extraction some minimum pattern taken from a casual utterance serves as the entire sentence, for example, *Coffee's cold* would be said as *Cold.* In contrast to formal style which serves to inform the addressee about the outside world, intimate style serves to convey feelings, that is, to inform about the world inside the speaker's skin. One particularly interesting feature of this style

is that language itself can never be a topic of conversation. Any mention of grammar automatically removes the conversation from intimate style.

Whereas Joos has concentrated on speech, others have focused on the styles of writing and on speakers as they appear in literature or written prose. Walker Gibson (1966) offers an imaginative and provocative three-fold classification of styles into tough, sweet, and stuffy. The tough speaker is the man who has "been around," the hero of the modern novel; it is the style of Augie March and Winston Churchill's "We shall go on to the end." The tough talker tends to talk in terms of himself; it is I-talk. The sweet talker is a personable individual who claims unearned familiarity with his listeners, their needs, and their interests. Sweet talk is characteristic of advertisements, articles in fashion magazines, and airline instructions for emergency escape. The sweet talker tends to speak directly to the audience; it is you-talk. The stuffy talker is "a bloodless fellow" who speaks not for himself but for some organization and in his speaking keeps a healthy distance from his listeners. It is the style of scholarly articles and college catalogs. Stuffy style is not of the speaker or to the listener but from some third party; it is it-talk.

Gibson also proposes sixteen quantitative measures for indexing these styles and which can, in effect, serve as criteria for classifying the style of any given piece of prose.

In *word size* Gibson includes (1) the proportion of monosyllables (highest in tough and lowest in stuffy talk) and (2) words of three or more syllables (most frequent in stuffy and least frequent in tough style).

Under *substantives* are included (3) first person pronouns (highest in tough and absent in stuffy style), second person pronouns (highest in sweet and absent in stuffy style), and (4) whether the subjects of the sentences are people (as in one-half or more of the tough and sweet sentences) or neuter (as in two-thirds or more of the stuffy sentences).

Verb categories include (5) the frequency of finite verbs (highest in tough and sweet styles), (6) forms of the verb *to be* used as finite verbs (highest in tough style), and (7) passives (highest in stuffy and lowest in sweet style).

Modification includes (8) adjectives and (9) adverbs (highest in sweet and lowest in tough style) and (10) noun adjuncts, for example, *traveling expenses* and *foodarama living*, (most common in stuffy and least common in tough style).

Subordination includes (11) embedded clauses (longest in stuffy style), (12) the proportion of total words appearing in clauses (over 40 percent in stuffy, 33 percent or less in sweet, and 25 percent or less in tough), and (13) the number of words intervening between subject and verb (most in stuffy and least in tough style).

The last three indexes are included under *other effects of tone*. (14) The frequency of the determiner *the* is highest for tough talk and lowest for sweet talk. (15) Fragments and contractions are highest in sweet and entirely absent in stuffy style. Lastly, (16) certain punctuation marks (namely italics, parentheses, dashes, question marks, and exclamation points) are most frequent in sweet talk and least frequent in stuffy talk.

Any given passage will naturally contain elements of all three styles. Yet one style seems to dominate. Gibson's system is not an either-or classification but rather a more-or-less one. That is, it attempts to classify prose styles according to the dominant or primary tone.

Undoubtedly the most popular attempt to classify styles is that of Rudolf Flesch (1963) and the readability researchers (cf. Klare, 1963). The most well-known and most useful are probably Flesch's analyses of reading ease and human interest. Here styles are classified according to their degrees of difficulty and human interest. Both classifications are obtained by applying relatively simple formulas. Reading ease is measured in terms of the length of words in number of syllables and the length of sentences in number of words. The formula is: Reading Ease = 206.835 − .846 × (the number of syllables per 100 words) − 1.015 × (the average number of words per sentence).

The resultant scores are to be interpreted in terms of seven "styles" or levels of difficulty: 90 to 100 is "very easy" (for example, the style of comic books); 80 to 90 is "easy" (pulp fiction); 70 to 80 is "fairly easy" (slick fiction); 60 to 70 is "standard" (digests, *Time*, mass nonfiction); 50 to 60 is "fairly difficult" (*Harper's*, *The Atlantic Monthly*); 30 to 50 is "difficult" (academic and scholarly publications); and 0 to 30 is "very difficult" (scientific and professional journals).

The human interest score is a function of the number of personal words (personal pronouns, words having natural masculine or feminine gender, for example, *mother* or *brother* but not *doctor* or *teacher*, and the group words *people* and *folks*) and personal sentences (sentences addressed directly to the audience, exclamations, questions, commands, requests, sentence fragments, sentences marked by quotation marks or other indicators such as *he said*, and sentences whose complete meaning must be inferred from the context). The formula is: Human Interest = 3.635 × (the percentage of personal words) + .314 × (the percentage of personal sentences).

Like the reading-ease score this one will also range from 0 to 100 and is to be interpreted as follows: 60 to 100, "dramatic" (fiction); 40 to 60, "highly interesting" (*The New Yorker*); 20 to 40, "interesting" (digests, *Time*); 10 to 20, "mildly interesting" (trade publications); and 0 to 10, "dull" (scientific and professional).

The value of these several classifications depends on the purposes for which they are used. For example, if someone wished to judge the difficulty level of a reader proposed for an elementary school audience the Flesch reading ease formula would prove useful. On the other hand, if someone were interested in analyzing how the style of language used in comedy differs from that used in tragedy the classifications of Joos or Gibson might prove more satisfactory.

Naturally there are many other approaches to classifying and quantifying styles. These few, however, should provide some idea of the many possibilities which exist for the study of speech and language styles.

THE PRAGMATIC DIMENSION OF SPEECH AND LANGUAGE

Pragmatics is concerned with the relationship between symbols and symbol-users, between speech and language and behavior. To this relationship a number of researchers have addressed themselves. Here we focus on the contributions of Alfred Korzybski and the science of General Semantics since it provides essential insights into the structure and function of speech, language, and behavior. A sketch of the basic assumptions and point of view of General Semantics has already been presented in the diagram of the levels of speech and language (Figure 2).

Although man " created " language it would not be fair to say that he therefore understands language or that he is in control of language. Certainly, we are far from a complete understanding and perhaps even farther away from complete control. In fact the reverse may be, at least in part, the more accurate statement; the analogy with the typical science fiction story in which the robot achieves control over the scientist who created it, is perhaps not too far-fetched.

Despite the fact that man has been studying language for a good many years it was not until relatively recently that the influence which language exerts on thought and behavior was made clear. Korzybski, a mathematician and engineer, posed for himself a seemingly simple and basic question but one which took him and numerous others a lifetime of study and writing to even begin answering. Why is it, he wondered, that a bridge seldom if ever collapses and if and when it does, the cause of its failure is quickly determined and remedied? Why isn't this true of human institutions such as marriage? Why aren't the causes of emotional illnesses determined just as quickly and remedied just as surely? Why is it that a scientist functions efficiently and effectively in his laboratory but in the real world is subject to the same problems, maladjustments, and misevaluations that plague the rest of us?

The answer, Korzybski felt, rested at least in part on the language being used. The language used in the laboratory is well suited to the tasks at hand while the language of everyday living is perhaps not so well suited. Perhaps language, its structure and its vocabulary, force upon us modes of thinking and behaving which are not adequate to the purposes at hand. Perhaps the language we use fosters various misevaluations.

In *Manhood of Humanity* (1921) and *Science and Sanity* (1933) Korzybski explained his views on man, language, and behavior and developed the science of General Semantics, the study of word-referent-evaluation relationships. The nature of General Semantics may be clarified by comparing and contrasting it with other sciences of language, a method used by Anatol Rapoport (1952).

(1) Grammar is the science of language which deals with word-word relationships. It is concerned with relations within a sentence rather than with how one sentence is related to another sentence. (2) Logic deals with relations between and among sentences or assertions. The logician is concerned solely with validity, that is, given X does Y follow. It makes no difference what X and Y stand for as long as the relationships expressed are valid or internally consistent. (3) Semantics concerns itself with the relationship between words or assertions and their referents. In addition to being concerned with validity the semanticist is also concerned with truth. He is concerned with defining the conditions under which a proposition or assertion can be assigned a true or false label. At least to some semanticists, the statement *He is good* cannot be dealt with because *good* does not have an objective referent. Hence, many concern themselves exclusively with statements phrased in objective or referential language.

(4) General Semantics, not to be confused with semantics or thought of as a general approach to semantics, deals not only with the relationships among words in a statement or with the relations among statements or with the relations between statements and referents but also with one's evaluations to words and statements. General Semantics is concerned with the relationships among words, referents, and evaluations.

Whereas the semanticist asks "What does the word mean?" the General Semanticist asks "What does the speaker and listener mean and what are their evaluations?" Whereas the semanticist can study language apart from speakers and listeners the General Semanticist makes the user of language the central focus of his study.

Among the primary purposes of General Semantics is to make speech and language better reflect reality and to this end offer three "simple" laws or principles. The principle of *non-identity* states that no two things are ever the same, nor is one thing ever the same at two different times. The verbal level is not the referent, as both Richards' triangle of meaning and Korzybski's structural differential emphasize. The word is not the thing; the map is not the territory. The word and the map both omit many things in the real world they symbolize.

The principle of *non-allness* states that the word is not the whole of the thing; the map is not the whole of the territory. Non-allness is a principle of humility, a principle which holds that one can never know all about anything.

The principle of *self-reflexiveness* states that speech and language can refer not only to the real world but also to itself. Statements can be made about the real world and about themselves and in turn there can be statements about statements about statements, ad infinitum.

If the objectives of General Semantics had to be summed up in one basic purpose it would be to foster a more extensional orientation (note the "s" in extensional). Too often reactions are more to symbols, particularly linguistic, than to the real world. In reacting to words an *in*tensional orientation is displayed, instead of an *ex*tensional one in which reactions are primarily to the real world.

Extensional orientation is an outlook, a point of view, an awareness of things, events, and processes as they actually operate in the real world instead of as how they are talked about. The goal of extensional orientation can be achieved by a seemingly basic method, by "using" five extensional devices.

The *index* emphasizes that there are differences as well as similarities between things even though they may both have the same label: politician$_1$ is not politician$_2$. The *date* emphasizes that things, people, and events change. Change is one of the few constants in the world and although labels and assertions remain relatively static the real world to which these labels and statements refer is changing rapidly. Politician$_{1960}$ is not politician$_{1970}$. The *etc.* emphasizes that no statement can be complete; no statement can say all there is to be said about anything. There is always more to be said, *etc.*

These three devices, referred to by Korzybski as "working devices," are considered the most important part of General Semantics and are intended to reflect the three major properties of the event level: non-identity, constant change, and infinite complexity.

The "safety devices" are likewise means of keeping speech and language in line with the extensional world. *Quotation marks* serve to emphasize that terms are being used in a specialized or particular sense and that the reader should therefore be on the lookout. The *hyphen* is used to indicate that what may be separable verbally may not be separable on a nonverbal level. There are many things which can be discussed individually and discretely, for example, body and mind, cause and effect, space and time, structure and function. Although these can be separated verbally, it does not follow that they exist separately in reality. The problem of body and mind is not the same as the problem of body-mind; the latter more clearly indicates that both body and mind are interrelated and in reality inseparable.

In this chapter we have covered two of the three major areas of what Charles Morris (1955) refers to as semiotics, the science of signs. Signs, according to Morris, are things which serve as substitutes for other things.

The first area, semantics, concentrates on signs from two points of view. In its concern with the relationship of signs to referents it seeks to answer the question, What and how do signs signify? This we attempted to cover in the discussion of Richards' triangle of meaning. In its concern with the ways in which signs signify it seeks to answer the question, In what ways do signs signify referents? This we considered in our discussion of the functions, levels, and styles of speech and language.

The second area, pragmatics, focuses on the relationship of signs to sign-users, seeking to answer the question, What are the effects of signs on behavior? This is the question to which Korzybski and the General Semanticists have addressed themselves and one to which we return throughout the book.

The third area, syntactics, is concerned with the relationship of signs to other signs, concentrating on the question, How are signs patterned or arranged? This question is an extremely complex one and to this we devote the next chapter, "Linguistic Theory."

Chapter Two

Linguistic Theory

To understand the psychology of speech and language in any meaningful sense, it is first necessary to inquire into the structure of speech and language —the area Charles Morris denotes as "syntactics." This is surveyed in two parts. In the first we will consider some of the essential elements and relationships in speech and language, specifically the individual speech sounds and sound classes (phonetic and phonemic analysis), the units formed from the combination of these sounds (morphemic analysis and word analysis), and the larger units formed from the combination of morphemes and words (constituent analysis).

In the second section we will consider generative grammar—the approach to the structure of language which has the most relevance for a science of language and for speech. After providing a few basic distinctions for this type of grammar and linguistic theory, the three major divisions of a generative grammar—the syntactic, semantic, and phonological components—will be reviewed.

In the first section the discussion proceeds from the microscopic to the macroscopic, that is, from the smaller to the larger units. In the second section this pattern is reversed, the discussion beginning with the component concerned with the largest units and working down. These different orders will help clarify not only the basic elements but also the aims and methods of linguistic theories.

There were two main reasons for not omitting the more "traditional" approach considered in the first half of the chapter. First, much past and current research utilizes the concepts and the frame of reference provided by this first approach and it is therefore necessary to understand it if this research is to be meaningfully evaluated. Second, generative grammar seems more understandable, both in regard to its point of view and its justification, in terms of the ways in which it differs from "traditional" linguistic theory.

SOME BASIC ELEMENTS AND RELATIONSHIPS

The elements of language and the relationships existing among them are considered here so as to provide some understanding of how language is structured: what it consists of and how these constituent units are related.

Phonetic and Phonemic Analysis

Phonology, the study of speech sounds, may be pursued in a number of different ways. First, starting at the beginning of the speech act one can focus on the sound as produced by the vocal mechanism and analyze each sound according to the manner of production. Here the analysis would be primarily physiological, with the sounds being described in terms of the organs and processes of the body involved. The [p] sound, for example, can be described as one produced bilabially (by two lips), without voicing (without vibration of the vocal cords), as a stop (with closure of the lips prior to completed articulation), and so on. This particular analysis, called *articulatory phonetics*, provides the most commonly used system for sound classification.

Second, sounds can be analyzed as they pass through the channel or medium, the air. The description of the patterns of air produced by the various sounds is referred to as *acoustic phonetics*. This method of analysis relies heavily on the procedures of the physical sciences and is generally thought to provide the most objective and precise description of speech sounds.

A third approach focuses on the sound as received by the listener. This approach, referred to as *auditory phonetics*, may center on the physiology of the hearing mechanism in receiving sound or on the psychology of perception. Although for some time this approach has lagged behind the others and is, in many discussions of linguistics, completely ignored, there is at present much interest and research activity in speech perception.

Phonetic analysis allows for great precision in description. For example, in articulatory phonetics three tongue positions—high, medium, and low— are commonly distinguished. But some linguists, such as Block and Trager (1942), distinguish seven positions. Thus when tongue position is combined with various other characteristics, such as the tenseness or laxness in the tongue or the roundness of the mouth, or the manner of articulation, there are a tremendous number of possible designata. In fact, since such criteria are continuous rather than discrete variables there are actually an infinite number of possible tongue positions, degrees of tenseness or roundness and hence an infinite number of possible representations. Theoretically each and every sound uttered (called phones) would have its own unique representation.

Such precision is useful for many purposes, for example, evaluating articulatory proficiency and describing dialectal variation. However, despite such detail a phonetic analysis can never specify when sounds function differently or when different sounds function in the same way in a given language. In other words, phonetic analysis provides only a limited and specialized guidance in the study of the sound structure of a language.

In order to deal only with those sounds which are functionally significant in the language being studied one must turn to the second branch of phonology, phonemics. Phonemics is the science of speech which deals with meaningful sounds and sound features. It may be thought of as "functional phonetics." Insignificant differences, say in tongue position, are ignored and only significant differences (differences which make a difference to native speakers of the language) are considered. The basic unit in phonemic analysis is the phoneme, which now needs to be defined.

Consider the pair of words *tab* and *tap*. A native speaker of English recognizes these two complexes of sounds as different words; they differ in that one word ends in [b] and one ends in [p]. Looking more closely at these two words it can be seen that the difference between them is only that of one sound feature. That is, the final sounds are made in exactly the same way except that [b] is made with vibration of the vocal folds and [p] is made without vibration. Numerous other examples of pairs which differ in these very small ways can easily be found, for example, *tot-dot* and *game-came*. In each of these pairs the distinction between the words rests on the difference between two sounds or more specifically on the difference between the presence or absence of one sound feature, namely, voicing.

When words differ in this way they are called *minimal pairs*, denoting that the distinction between them is as small as it can possibly be. The sounds which distinguish minimal pairs are called phonemes. In writing, phonemes are placed in slash marks, for example, /p/ and phonetic symbols are placed in square brackets, for example, [p].

Observe the initial sounds in the words *keep* and *cool*. If one pays close attention to the way in which these sounds are pronounced one notes that the initial sound in *keep* is made with the tongue toward the front of the mouth whereas the initial sound in *cool* is made with the tongue toward the back of the mouth. These sounds, then, differ phonetically. But do they also differ phonemically? That is, are these two sounds different phonemes? To establish these two sounds as separate phonemes one would have to find minimal pairs—words which differ solely on the basis of the fact that one has a /k/ sound made toward the front of the mouth and one has a /k/ sound made toward the back of the mouth. In English one would not find such a pair of words and so it must be concluded that these two sounds are not separate phonemes but two variations of the one /k/ phoneme.

Such variants of a phoneme are termed *allophones*. Thus a back /k/ and a front /k/ are allophones of the /k/ phoneme. The variation which occurs here does not distinguish one word from another. In all the words in which these two sounds occur there are additional distinctions which separate the words; the difference between two English words never rests on the distinction between a front and a back /k/.

Allophones are said to be in *complementary distribution*. Note that the two /k/ sounds are not in the same phonetic environment; they precede different sounds. The front /k/ (in *keep*) precedes a vowel made in the front of the mouth while the back /k/ (in *cool*) precedes a vowel made in the back of the mouth. If one were to examine all the possible environments in which /k/ occurs in English it would be found that the front /k/ never appears in the same environment in which the back /k/ occurs. This is what is meant by complementary distribution; the sounds are never distributed in the same places. When sounds are in complementary distribution, they are allophones of the same phoneme.

If the word *keep* were uttered one hundred times, each utterance would be unique. Focusing specifically on the /k/ sound, there would be one hundred different pronunciations. Each production would vary somewhat from the next. This variation, however, does not distinguish one sound from another; in fact, in order to perceive the differences one would have to record the sound on a speech spectrograph and examine the graphs for each production. Furthermore, each of the one hundred productions would be accepted by a native speaker of English as the same; one would be regarded as a repetition or imitation of the other. The variation which does exist cannot be controlled by the speaker. These differing productions which cannot be controlled and which are perceived as the same by the speaker and listener are said to be free and the differences are said to be in *free variation*.

One further criterion needs to be mentioned. For sounds to be considered allophones of one phoneme they must be phonetically similar, that is, produced in essentially the same manner. Even if two sounds behaved as if they were allophones of the same phoneme, for example, if they were in complementary distribution, they would not be classified as belonging to the same phoneme if they were not phonetically similar.

Perhaps because of long training in the written language one tends to think of phonemes as similar to letters. There are instances in the analysis of speech when the tendency to think in terms of the written language can obscure important considerations.

Consider the following sentences:

The manager and the union leader signed the contract.
Rubber, when placed in a cold environment, will contract.

Focus now on the last words in each sentence. Are they the same or are they different? Clearly one would say they are different. But on what basis is this judgment made? Generally one would say that they mean different things and are different parts of speech, which of course is true. When questioned further it might also be noted that they sound differently;

there is a difference in stress or accent. In the first the accent or stress is on the first syllable whereas in the second the stress is on the second syllable. (Technically, these words also differ in the vowels of the first syllable.)

Because stress serves to distinguish between word pairs such as these it is generally regarded as phonemic. In English four kinds of stress are usually distinguished: primary stress, denoted by an acute accent, $/'/$, secondary stress, denoted by a circumflex accent, $/^/$, tertiary stress, denoted by a grave accent, $/`/$, and zero or weakest stress, denoted by $/˘/$ or left unmarked. All of these accent marks are placed above the character or phonemic symbol of the nucleus of the syllable and are appropriately called suprasegmental phonemes, phonemes which are placed on or superimposed above the basic segmental phoneme. Segmental (also called linear) phonemes are simply those arranged in sequential order.

Pitch variation can also change the meaning of a word or phrase. Pitch, or the relative highness or lowness of tone, is also regarded as phonemic. As in the case of stress, there are four pitch phonemes in English, designated by the numbers 1, 2, 3, and 4, from low to high. These are written in front of the phoneme and slightly raised.

The class of phonemes which is perhaps most difficult to recognize intuitively are the juncture phonemes. Juncture refers to the units of silence or pause inserted in the more or less continuous flow of speech. In English three juncture phonemes are generally distinguished. Close juncture is the normal rather rapid transition which would be used, for example, within a syllable between phonemes. Close juncture has no special symbol and is indicated simply by writing the phonemes together. Here is an example of open or plus juncture. Pronounce *a name* and *an aim*. In the first example the pause between *a* and *name* is open juncture as is the pause between *an* and *aim*. The position of juncture distinguishes these two phrases. Open juncture is designated $/+/$. Terminal juncture, as its name implies, is the pause which occurs when speech is somehow stopped. The silence, however, may be of varying length. Generally, single bar juncture or sustained terminal juncture is the silence which occurs following a somewhat level pitch as in the example ,"Mary, the young girl, walked . . ." Here the single bar juncture, designated $/|/$, would be the silence on either side of the phrase *the young girl*. Rising terminal juncture or double bar juncture, designated $/‖/$, occurs as the pause before a rise in pitch as in the sentence "John is $/‖/$ here?" Falling terminal juncture or double cross juncture, designated $/\#/$, occurs as the pause at the end of most English sentences or isolated words as in the reading of a word list.

The phonemes of English and the traditional symbols used to represent them are presented in Table 1.

Although all languages may be analyzed into phonemes, references to specific phonemes apply only to the particular language being considered. That is, the general concepts such as phoneme and allophone may be used in reference to all languages. Specific phonemes, however, differ from one

TABLE 1. The Phonemes of American English

Consonant Phonemes

p	(pass)	ð	(this)	n	(no)
b	(but)	s	(so)	ŋ	(ring)
t	(to)	z	(zero, boys)	l	(love)
d	(do)	š	(should)	w	(wish)
k	(kiss, calm)	ž	(azure)	hw	(when)
g	(go)	č	(church)	y	(yes)
f	(for)	ǰ	(Jim)	r	(run)
v	(value)	m	(more)	h	(how)
θ	(thing)				

Vowel Phonemes

i	(bit)	e	(bet)	æ	(map)
i	(children)	ə	(above)	a	(not)
u	(put)	o	(boat)	ɔ	(law)

Suprasegmental Phonemes

Stress phonemes	/	∧	\	∪
Pitch phonemes	1	2	3	4
Juncture phonemes	+	|	||	#

language to another. For example, in English there are no two words which are distinguished solely by the frontness or backness of /k/. However, this need not be true in all languages. In fact, in Arabic this difference does distinguish pairs of words and in Arabic these sounds are separate phonemes, to the same degree that /p/ and /b/ are separate phonemes in English. In other words, there is no such thing as a general /k/ phoneme; there is only an English /k/ phoneme or a French /k/ phoneme or a German /k/ phoneme, etc.

Before giving a complete definition of a phoneme an analogy which is often cited may be of some value. In a detective story when the murderer is present the butler never is and when the butler is present the murderer never is. The butler and the murderer may be said to be in complementary distribution; they never occur in the same environment. One then begins to suspect that they are one and the same. But before coming to this conclusion it is necessary that they be alike in essential respects, for example, sex, age, height, weight, and so on. That is, it must be established that the two sounds are phonetically similar before grouping them into the same phoneme. Slight differences such as the way in which the hair falls may be disregarded; this is the free variation.

A *phoneme*, then, is a group of sounds (or allophones) which are phonetically similar and which are in free variation or complementary distribution.

In analyzing languages the discovery of the phonemes or the phonemic system of the language is one of the first tasks of the linguist. And part of his procedure, as already indicated, is to find minimal pairs—words which are distinguished solely by one sound. The sounds which distinguish minimal pairs are given phonemic status in that particular language. In recording the language the linguist cannot assume that two sounds which he hears as different are actually different in the language he is studying, nor can he assume that sounds which at first sound alike are actually alike to the native speaker of the language being described. In order to counteract any tendency which the linguist might have for prejudging which sounds are phonemes and which sounds are not phonemes he records even the slightest differences by using what is called a narrow phonetic transcription. So in hearing the initial sound in the word *keep* he would attempt to record at approximately what position the tongue touched the roof of the mouth, how much aspiration or expelled breath was involved in the production, and so on. When he has this narrow phonetic transcription he then attempts to discover which differences actually make a difference and it is at this point that he begins his search for minimal pairs. Continuing with the above example, he notes that he observed two /k/ sounds—one made in the front of the mouth and one made in the back of the mouth; these differences he has recorded phonetically. Then he searches for minimal pairs. In Arabic he would find them and so would record these as separate phonemes; in English he would not find them and so would record these as allophones of the same phoneme.

Morphemic Analysis

If a language consisted of only phonemes a speaker would be able to talk about very little since there are only about forty to fifty phonemes in any language. Given an inventory of phonemes and a need to talk about many things there are two principal alternatives. First, the number of phonemes in the language could be increased. This, however, presents two major problems. The first problem is that even if the number of distinctive or meaningful sounds were increased there would still be relatively few—certainly not nearly as many as would be needed to talk about even a small portion of the universe. The second problem is that as the number of phonemes is increased so is the similarity among them. For example, /t/ and /d/ differ from one another in that the /t/ is made without vibration of the vocal folds and /d/ is made with vibration. If a phoneme between /t/ and /d/ were created, distinctions among amount of vibration would have to be made. As can easily be appreciated this would create a number of problems in the production and perception of sound. Slight changes in the condition of the vocal mechanism or slight distortions introduced by outside noises would make such small distinctions extremely difficult to maintain and perceive. To increase the number of phonemes does not appear a very practical decision.

The alternative decision is to use phonemes in combinations, the choice of all natural languages. They combine phonemes, not randomly but according to some system of rules. The rules for combining phonemes, called phonological rules, apply only to phonemes between pauses, not to phonemes across pauses, and naturally differ from one language to another. Certain phoneme combinations constitute morphemes and it is on these units that linguistic analysis next focuses.

A morpheme, analogous in many ways to a phoneme, can be defined as the smallest unit of meaningful speech. It cannot be divided without introducing a drastic change in its meaning or without actually destroying its meaning. Consider the word *meaning*. Is this a morpheme? To answer this question one must determine whether or not the word can be divided. If it can be divided but only at the expense of destroying or drastically altering its meaning then the word must be one morpheme. If it can be divided without such change then it is more than one morpheme. The word *meaning* can be divided most easily into *mean* and *ing*. Both parts have meaning related to that of the whole word. Therefore, *meaning* is not one morpheme; it is at least two morphemes—*mean* and *ing*. Now can *mean* or *ing* be further divided? Here no further division is possible, at least not without destroying their meanings. One can, of course, make such divisions as *me* and *n* or *i* and *ng* but these parts do not bear any relationship to the meaning of *mean* or *ing* or *meaning*. *Meaning*, therefore, consists of two morphemes—*mean* and *ing*.

What about the word *major*? This word can be divided into, for example, *ma* and *jor* or *maj* and *or*. No matter how it is divided, however, the parts do not retain the meaning of the original whole word. Therefore, *major* is one morpheme—a unit of speech which cannot be divided without losing its original meaning.

Morphemes are not identical with syllables. Morphemes may consist of one syllable, for example, *a* and *-ing*, of two syllables, for example, *major*, or of three syllables, for example, *Missouri*, or of any number of syllables. Also, a one syllable word may be more than one morpheme. For example, the word *it's* contains two morphemes—*it* and *is* (though in contracted form). The morphemic status of a speech unit bears no relationship to its syllabic status; morphemes and syllables are simply two independent units of analysis.

Similarly, morphemes are analyzed without regard to their phonemic status. For example, the /z/ phoneme in the words *boys* is clearly a morpheme indicating plurality. However, the /z/ phoneme in the word *zoo* is not a morpheme because this element taken alone does not have a meaning related to the meaning of the original word *zoo*. To complicate matters just a bit more, consider the phoneme /z/ in the word *stores*. Is this the same morpheme as the /z/ in *boys*? The answer depends on whether *stores* is a noun or a verb. If a noun the /z/ is the same morpheme as the /z/ in *boys* since both mean plural. If *stores* is a verb, however, then /z/ is not the same as /z/ in *boys* since it has the meaning "third person present tense singular." It is, however, the same morpheme as in the verbs *buys* and *loves*.

The fact that two speech segments sound alike does not signify that they mean the same thing.   This is true of morphemes whether they are one phoneme morphemes, as the /z/ phoneme in *boys* and *stores* or whether they are composed of more than one phoneme as in the case of *help* as a noun and as a verb or in the case of /roz/ which could be the morpheme naming a particular type of flower, the plural of *row*, the third person present tense singular of *row*, or the past tense of *rise*.   These similar sounding morphemes, called homophonous morphemes, should not cause any problem if it is recalled that in morphemic analysis it is meaning rather than sound that counts.

Morphemes are commonly divided into two classes—free and bound. A free morpheme is one which can stand alone, for example, *say, major, Missouri*.   A bound morpheme, on the other hand, cannot stand alone, for example, the {-z} morpheme meaning plural or the {-ly} morpheme meaning adverbial.   In writing, as these last examples illustrate, morphemes are placed in braces.

In the discussion of phonemes it was pointed out that variants of a phoneme, for example, the initial sounds of *keep* and *cool*, were allophones of the phoneme.   In morphemics the same concept of allo-, meaning a variant, is used.   An allomorph is a variant of a morpheme.   For example, in forming plurals, excluding exceptions such as *ox: oxen, man: men* and foreign plurals such as *alumnus: alumni*, there are three sounds used: {-s}, {-z}, and {-əz}.   {-s} is used after voiceless consonants, {-əz} occurs after groove fricatives and affricates, and {-z} occurs after all other sounds.   They all, of course, have the same meaning.   Now, just as the linguist uses the criterion of complementary distribution in defining phonemes and in determining when two sounds are one or two phonemes, he uses this same criterion in morphemic analysis.   The three sounds ({-s}, {-z}, {-əz}) all have definite contexts in which they appear; no two of them ever occur in the same environment.   They are, therefore, in complementary distribution. Since they are in complementary distribution and since they have the same meaning, they are classified as belonging to the same morpheme, plural. They are thus allomorphs of the plural morpheme, generally and arbitrarily symbolized {-əz}.

Word Analysis

The next largest unit in the analysis of speech is the word.   The word, commonly regarded as the most obvious linguistic unit, turns out to be the unit most difficult to define.   If the analysis of words were limited to the written language there would be relatively little problem; a word could simply be defined as letters or symbols set off at either end by a blank space or end punctuation mark.   Under this definition, *I, can't, anti-American, Dr.,* and *butterfly* would all be single words.   Since speech, however, is the primary concern and since linguists are often forced to deal with languages which have no written representation, this definition is less than adequate.

The alternative which suggests itself most readily, namely to use pause instead of "blank space" and define a word as a stream of speech separated by pause at either end, would not solve the problem.   Under this definition the "word" *Plato*, in many dialects, would have to be considered two words since there is a pause between *Pla* and *to*.   On the other hand, in the sentence, "I've run the race" there is no pause between *I've* and *run* and we would conclude that these were one word.

Linguistics now provides no universally accepted definition of "word" (cf. Greenberg, 1957; Chomsky and Halle, 1968).   Since, however, our primary concern is English which does have a written language we can use "word" to denote the smallest unit of written speech bounded by blank spaces or end punctuation marks (cf. Francis, 1958).

The failure of contemporary linguistic theory to provide a definition of "word" should not imply that this unit is not psychologically or linguistically significant or that it cannot be profitably analyzed.   The word is the one unit with which linguistically naïve speakers are most familiar and which they can manipulate and control with greatest facility.   And it is probably the unit most extensively investigated by students of speech and language behavior.

Because of its acknowledged importance and relevance, considerable time and energy has been devoted to the classification of words.   Probably most familiar to the reader is the classification of words as parts of speech. Here one finds that words naming persons, places, or things are nouns, that words denoting actions or states of being are verbs, etc.   That these simple statements are inadequate from a linguistic point of view can be made obvious by citing just a few examples.   *Red*, although clearly the *name* of a color, is in such phrases as *the red boat* classified not as a noun but as an adjective.   Adjectives are defined as words which modify nouns and yet *her* in the phrase *her house* is not classified as an adjective but rather as a pronoun even though it clearly modifies *house*.   A pronoun is defined as a word which "stands for a noun."   In the sentence "Jim and Bob had an early appointment so the boys took the train" it is clear that *boys* stands for *Jim and Bob*. Yet *boys* is not a pronoun but a noun.   These examples illustrate that the traditional criteria for classifying the parts of speech is woefully inadequate.

Charles C. Fries in *The Structure of English* (1952) proposes that words be classified according to the positions they may occupy in sentences.   This system has proved far superior to the traditional classification and has gained considerable though certainly not universal acceptance.   Words, in Fries' system, are first divided into two major classes: content words and function words.   *Content words* make reference to the real world, are words for which synonyms can be easily found, and have both connotative and denotative meaning.   Content words correspond to, but are not identical with, nouns, verbs, adjectives, and adverbs.   Fries has avoided using traditional names for these parts of speech and designates them simply as Class 1, Class 2, Class 3, and Class 4 words.   In order to facilitate classifying these words according to the positions they may occupy Fries has developed test frames. The words which can fit into the same position belong to the same part of speech. In classifying content words the following test frames are used:

The concert is/was good (always)/ Concerts are/were good (always).
The clerk remembered the tax (suddenly).
The team went there.

Class 1 words are ones which can be substituted for *concert, clerk, tax,* and *team* in these test frames. (A word can be "substituted" for another if it does not change the grammatical structure of the sentence; changes in meaning resulting from the substitution are of no importance here.) Thus *coffee, husband, boy, elephant, car, book, odor, article, thing,* etc., would all qualify as Class 1 words simply because they can appear in the stated positions.

Class 2 words can substitute for *is, was, (are, were), remembered,* and *went* in the above frames. Thus *saw, discussed, knew, understood, signed, stopped,* etc., are all Class 2 words.

Class 3 words behave as does *good* in the test frame and can serve as substitutes. Fries makes one change with this part of speech and suggests that the test frame "The good concert was good" be used. Class 3 words must be able to occupy both positions occupied by *good.* Thus *large, necessary, foreign, new, empty, hard, best, lower,* etc., would all meet the criteria for Class 3 words.

Class 4 words are those which can serve as substitutes for *always, suddenly,* and *there* in the test frames. Thus *here, then, sometimes, soon, now, generally, lately,* etc., would all qualify as Class 4 words.

Although these classes correspond closely to nouns, verbs, adjectives, and adverbs, respectively, they are not identical; if they are confused with these classes it will be impossible to deal correctly with the second major class, function words.

Function words include all those words not belonging to the four categories already considered. Function words do not make reference to the real world, synonyms cannot be easily found, and they generally do not have connotative meaning. Fries describes fifteen classes of function words which he labels Groups A through O.

Group A includes all the words which can be substituted for *the* in the sentence "*The* concert was good." These words are generally called "determiners" since they appear with Class 1 words.

Group B includes the words which can be substituted for *may* in the sentence "The concert *may* be good."

Group C includes only the word *not* as in the sentence "The concert may *not* be good."

Group D includes all the words which can be substituted for *very* in the sentence "The concert may be *very* good."

Group E includes all words which can substitute for *and* in the sentence "The concerts *and* the lectures are *and* were interesting *and* profitable now *and* earlier."

Group F includes all words which can be substituted for *at* in the sentence "The concerts *at* the school are *at* the top."

Group G includes only the word *do* and its variant forms *does* and *did* used as an auxiliary not as a synonym for *make*. Group G words can substitute for the first *do* in the sentence "*Do* the boys do their work promptly?"

Group H includes only the word *there* as in the sentence "*There* is a man at the door."

Group I includes all the words which can be substituted for *when* in the sentence "*When* was the concert good?"

Group J includes all the words which can be substituted for *after* in the sentence "The concert was good *after* the new director came."

Group K includes only the four words *well*, *oh*, *now*, and *why* when used at the beginnings of sentences as in "*Why*, the concert was good!"

Group L includes only the two words *yes* and *no*.

Group M includes the attention-getting utterances *look*, *say*, and *listen*.

Group N includes only the word *please* which most frequently appears at the beginning of requests as in the sentence "*Please* take these two letters."

Group O includes only the form *lets* which in a request sentence includes the speaker and is not the same as *let us* which does not include the speaker.

This approach to the parts of speech is not universally accepted. Generative grammarians in particular (cf. Lees, 1964) find this system inadequate and propose as an alternative (cf. Chomsky, 1965) a system based on semantic and syntactic "features." For instance, the word *cat* would be described as possessing the features Noun, Count Noun, Animate, Nonhuman, Concrete, and so on. Words having the same features would then be considered members of the same lexical class. Although this system has not been worked out in complete detail it will undoubtedly contribute greatly to the problem of word classification as well as to numerous other linguistic and psycholinguistic questions.

In addition to the purely linguistic classifications such as that proposed by Fries there are a number of other lexical classifications.

The eight word types suggested by Wendell Johnson (1946) and presented below should provide some indication of the wide range of possible classes which might be developed for specific purposes.

1. Self-reference words—generally first-person pronouns, but also such expressions as *the writer* and *the author*.
2. Quantifying words—precise numerical terms.
3. Pseudo-quantifying words—terms only loosely indicative of size or amount, such as *many*, *much*, *a lot*, or words used as qualifiers of other pseudo-quantifying terms such as *very* in the expression *very much*.

4. Allness words—extreme or superlative words such as *none, all, every, always, never*.
5. Qualification words—terms which serve to limit or qualify statements such as *if, however, but, except*.
6. Consciousness of projection words—terms which indicate that the observed is in part a function of the observer such as *apparently, to me, seems, appears*.
7. Negative words—terms expressive of negative evaluation such as *no, don't, terrible, unsatisfactory, hate*.
8. Positive words—terms expressive of positive evaluation such as *yes, beautiful, satisfactory, love*.

Simple frequency counts or ratios of one type to another can be computed. Comparisons can then be made of the same source's use of the different classes, of particular word types for different sources, communication situations, or subject matters, or for different messages regardless of source. Numerous other bases for comparison can easily be developed.

Probably the most often used of all language measures is the type-token ratio (TTR). The TTR is the number of different words (types) over the total number of words (tokens). Thus in the sentence "The boy hit the dog" there are four types and five tokens. The TTR is therefore 4/5 or .80. The TTR is a measure of language diversity; the larger the vocabulary used, the higher will be the TTR. Johnson (1946) has suggested four basic variations of this ratio.

The Overall TTR is simply the TTR for an entire language sample. The problem with computing such a measure is that the TTR varies inversely with the size of the sample and therefore language samples of different lengths cannot be compared (cf. Carroll, 1938). In the sentence used above the TTR was calculated as .80, which is extremely high. As that sentence is expanded, however, in, say, a composition about the boy who hit the dog, a number of terms would be repeated; these repetitions lower the TTR. Other things being equal, the longer the language sample the lower the TTR.

The Mean Segmental TTR is probably the easiest and the most useful TTR to compute. Since samples of different sizes cannot be compared, the samples must be made equal in size. Usually samples being compared are divided into segments of equal length (generally 100 words each), the TTR for each segment computed, and these several TTRs averaged. In this way the TTRs for samples of different sizes can be compared.

The Cumulative TTR Curve is the curve drawn from plotting successive TTRs as increments are added to the sample. For example, a sample of 1,000 words is first divided into ten segments of 100 words each. The values from these segments are then plotted to obtain the cumulative TTR curve. The first value is the TTR for the first 100 words, the second value is the TTR for the first 200 words, the third value is the TTR for the first 300 words, etc.

The Decremental TTR Curve is the curve drawn from the numbers of new types which occur in each successive sample.   In computing the decremental TTR curve for a 1,000-word sample it would again be divided into ten segments of 100 words each and ten values would be plotted.   The first value is the number of types in the first 100 words, the second value is the number of new types which occur in the second 100 word but not in the first 100 word segment, the third value is the number of new types occurring in the third but not in either of the first two segments, etc.

Other researchers have proposed other ratios.   For example, the verb-adjective ratio proposed by Busemann (1925) and utilized by Boder (1940) in a now classic study has been used as an index of emotional stability (cf. Chapter 7).   Dollard and Mowrer (1947) have suggested the distress-relief quotient, the ratio of distress expressing phrases to the sum of these plus relief expressing phrases, as a measure of disturbing drive states.

The number of possible ratios is obviously great; those noted here are merely suggestive of the many ways in which words may be analyzed and classified.

While most researchers in language focus on the linguistic units such as phonemes, morphemes, and words, a small but growing number have concentrated on defining and classifying the bodily motions which, like the linguistic units, also serve a communicative function.   This study, called *kinesics* by its founder Ray Birdwhistell (1952, 1960, 1967), now commands considerable attention in the fields of linguistics, psychology, and communication (cf. DeVito, 1968b).

Bodily motion appears to be analyzable in much the same way as is language.   Like speech, it is learned behavior and is thus dependent upon the particular cultural and social system into which the child is born.   As Pittenger and Smith (1957) point out, it is only when, for example, a person points with his nose or his lip instead of his index finger that the arbitrary relation which these movements bear to reality and the role played by the particular culture in conditioning these movements are realized.   These movements are learned without any specific effort on the part of the "learner" or the "teacher."   Perhaps the most important parallel between these movements and speech is that they too are patterned or structured, occurring consistently with the same meaning.   They are, therefore, subject to systematic and objective analysis in the same way as is speech.   Kinesic researchers have capitalized on these similarities and have analyzed bodily motions in much the same way that a linguist analyzes speech.   Movements are broken down into kines and kinemes, corresponding to phones and phonemes, and have been shown to combine into larger units in ways analogous to spoken language.

For convenience, the field of kinesics can be divided into three major areas (Birdwhistell, 1960): prekinesics, microkinesics, and social kinesics. These areas are interrelated and interdependent.

Prekinesics is concerned with the physiological aspects of bodily movements, much like phonetics is concerned with the physiological aspects of sounds. As phonetics provides a method for the description of all sounds, prekinesics provides a method for the description of all bodily movements. In phonetics not all of the described sounds are significant in the actual language—that is, not all of the individually produced sounds have different meanings. Similarly, in prekinesics not all of the possible bodily movements have meaning.

Microkinesics is concerned with bodily motions which communicate different meanings and is analogous to phonemics which describes the functionally different sounds in a language. In microkinesics the researcher is concerned with analyzing kines into classes just as the phonemicist is concerned with analyzing phones into classes of sounds or phonemes. The range of movements which are functionally important or which communicate different meanings are termed "kinemes" and are analogous to the phonemes which define the range of speech sounds which are functionally important in the language or which communicate different meanings. For example, although eleven positions of the eyelid can be distinguished not all of these function to communicate different meanings. In fact, only four positions have been found to communicate different meanings. The eleven discernible positions are kines whereas the four meaningful positions are kinemes. The kineme, like the phoneme, is defined for a particular language community. In other cultures only two or perhaps as many as five or six positions of the eyelid might be meaningfully different.

Social kinesics is concerned with the roles and meanings of different bodily movements. Whereas microkinesics seeks to explore the meaningful body movements, social kinesics seeks to explore the specific meanings which these movements communicate.

Of particular interest here are what Birdwhistell (1967) calls kinesic markers, those small bodily movements which accompany spoken language. At present these markers are classified according to the lexical items which they regularly accompany.

Pronominal markers, movements which are associated with or, in certain environments, substituted for pronouns, are head, finger, or hand motions which are directed toward the object or event to which reference is made. These movements accompany such verbalizations as *he, she, it, they, those, that, then, there, any,* and *some.* Proximal movements of these same body parts accompany such lexical items as *I, me, we, us, this,* and *here.*

Pluralization markers consist of slight sweeps of some body part during the production of terms indicative of plurality such as *we, these, those, them, our, you* (plural), *their,* and *us.*

Verboid markers serve to indicate the tense of the verb. Past tense verbs, for example, are generally accompanied by a distal movement to the rear of the body whereas future tense is accompanied by a distal movement to the front of the body.

Area markers accompany prepositions such as *on, under, behind, in front of*, and manner markers accompany such lexical items as *a long time, slowly, smoothly,* and *jerkily*.

Constituent Analysis

The structure of language represents a hierarchy of levels. On the lowest level or at the base phones are organized or classified into phonemes. On the second level phonemes are combined to form morphemes. On the third level morphemes are combined to form words. The fourth level is that of constituents or what traditional grammars call phrases. Constituents can exist at various levels and can be very small or very large.

Consider the sentence "The man lost his fortune." The *immediate constituents* would be the parts of the sentence which native speakers would agree could be most easily separated. In this example the immediate constituents would *the man* and *lost his fortune*, corresponding to what is generally referred to as subject and predicate. Constituent analysis further divides the sentence into *lost* and *his fortune*, corresponding to the distinction between verb and object. The next cuts would be made between *the* and *man* and *his* and *fortune*. Here the division separates modifier and noun. The ultimate constituents would correspond to the individual morphemes of the sentence and in this case would parallel the division of the sentence into words with one exception, namely, the word *lost* would be divided into its component morphemes—*lose* and "past tense."

Constituent analyses are most often represented in diagrammatic form as "boxes" or "trees." These two representations are presented in Figure 3. In Figure 3(**A**) each row represents a different level of constituent analysis. The bottom row is the largest constituent, the sentence. Each additional row represents a more refined analysis. The top row, the final step in constituent analysis, corresponds to the division of the sentence into its component morphemes. The tree diagram, Figure 3(**B**), is simply another way of representing constituent structure. Each level of branches corresponds to a level of constituent analysis and each node (that is, the origin of the branches, for example, verb phrase, noun phrase, verb) represents a different constituent.

GENERATIVE GRAMMAR

Originally linguists believed that the analysis of a sentence into its constituents was the final stage of grammatical description. Only relatively recently has this position, referred to as taxonomic syntactic theory (cf. Chomsky, 1966a), been shown to be insufficient for describing any of the more complex sentences. Among other things one would expect the grammar of a language to distinguish between sentences which are understood differently. The grammar should provide a different breakdown or analysis

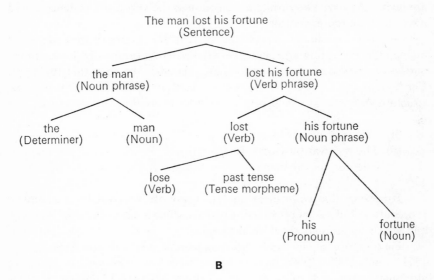

the	man	lose	past tense	his	fortune
the	man	lost		his	fortune
the	man	lost		his	fortune
the	man	lost		his	fortune
the	man	lost		his	fortune
the	man	lost		his	fortune

A

B

FIGURE 3. Two Representations of Constituent Structure

for sentences which may appear alike but which are understood quite differently. Consider, for example, the following, now famous sentences:

(1) John is easy to please.
(2) John is eager to please.

Although both of these sentences have the same basic surface structure they are understood differently, apart from their obvious semantic differences. Notice that (1) can be paraphrased as "It is easy to please John." When the same operation is performed on (2), however, the result is a drastic change in meaning—"It is eager to please John." Yet if these two sentences were analyzed according to their constituents and trees or boxes were drawn, the same picture would be constructed for both sentences. In other words, the important syntactic difference between these sentences cannot be explicated by constituent analysis.

One would also expect a grammar of a language to provide different structures or different analyzes for the same sentence which is understood in two different ways.   That is, a grammar should explicate syntactic ambiguity. Constituent analysis cannot always do this.   Consider sentence (3).

(3) The doctor's bills are high.

This sentence can be interpreted in two different ways.   It may mean that the doctor charges a lot for his services or that the bills the doctor has to pay are high.   Analyzed according to constituents, however, the sentence would have only one representation.

Another reasonable expectation is that the grammar provide some method for illustrating how sentences are related.   Intuitively, for example, one knows that sentences (4) and (5) are related in the sense that (6) is not. Yet (4) and (6), according to constituent analysis, would be given the same structure whereas (5) would be given a completely different structure.

(4) The man bit the dog.
(5) The dog was bitten by the man.
(6) The dog bit the man.

It appears that constituent analysis is not an incorrect but incomplete procedure.   It does not provide distinctions which a native speaker " knows " and which a grammar should make explicit.

For a more complete analysis of language, Noam Chomsky (for example, 1957, 1964, 1965, 1966a) and his associates have developed generative grammar.   Although this grammar is extremely complex some basic essentials can be explained without doing too much injustice to the detailed and sophisticated treatment provided by Chomsky.

Some Basic Assumptions of Generative Grammar

There are a number of basic assumptions underlying this new grammar. These assumptions can best be explained in terms of distinctions made between concepts and processes which are often confused in everyday language (cf. Thomas, 1965).   The distinctions most important for our purposes are those between (1) static and process descriptions, (2) competence and performance, (3) descriptive and prescriptive grammars, and (4) deep and surface structures.

STATIC AND PROCESS DESCRIPTIONS.   The dominating influence throughout much of the history of linguistics has been language change over time. In the twentieth century there was a change in emphasis; description was here given primary importance. Linguists at this time concentrated on describing the sound and structure of languages as they then existed.

Inevitably and perhaps unwittingly linguists became preoccupied with language as something static; the process character of language was largely ignored. Today the emphasis is still on descriptive (as opposed to historical) linguistics but the primary concern is on the description of processes and operations in language rather than on the description of states. This concentration on process description is most clearly seen in the emphasis generative grammar places on grammatical transformations—processes or operations by which strings of elements are altered or changed by addition, deletion, substitution, or permutation.

COMPETENCE AND PERFORMANCE. Earlier, the distinction between language and speech was introduced. It will be recalled that language, *la langue* in Saussure's terminology, refers to the abstract linguistic code; it is the rules which the native speaker possesses but which he may not be capable of explaining or even realizing. Speech, Saussure's *la parole*, refers to the actual utterances of the language; it consists of the actualizations or manifestations of the abstract code.

In a manner similar, though not identical, to Saussure's distinction between language and speech, Chomsky (1965) and the generative grammarians (cf. Fodor and Garrett, 1966) draw a distinction between competence and performance. Competence, similar to language, refers to the rules of grammar which the native speaker "knows"; that is, he can apply them and their operations can generally be brought to consciousness. Performance, similar to speech, is the actual vocal noises uttered and heard. Using an example cited by Katz and Postal (1964), competence can be conceived as analogous to a symphony whereas performance would be analogous to the symphony as played and heard. In only an idealized orchestra and audience would the symphony and the symphony-as-played-and-heard be identical. Similarly, only with an idealized speaker and hearer would language competence and language performance be identical. Performance is determined by many factors only one of which is competence. Many of the other influencing factors are extra-linguistic such as memory span, age of the speaker, nature of the audience, motivational state, and so on.

Linguistics is primarily concerned with competence. Linguists seek to discover the grammar which enables the native speaker to generate sentences that have phonetic representations and semantic interpretations. Ideally this grammar will generate all the grammatical sentences of the languages and none of the ungrammatical sentences. Although there are a finite number of linguistic elements and rules there are an infinite number of possible sentences. In any human language the number of possible sentences is infinite. A language (as opposed to language in general) can be defined as this infinite set of grammatical sentences. The grammar of a language can be viewed as the device for specifying or describing this infinite set of sentences.

Linguistics is also concerned with language in general, as opposed to *specific* languages. With the impetus supplied by Chomsky, linguists are now devoting considerable energy to the description of "universal grammar." That is, they are attempting to describe the form which a grammar of *any* human language must take. They attempt to define those features which all languages possess and which all linguistic descriptions must include. For example, all languages contain the basic grammatical relation of subject and predicate; this, therefore, will be part of universal grammar, a general grammar of human language. Grammatical universals may pertain to the phonetic, semantic, and syntactic levels (Greenberg, 1963; Chomsky, 1967).

DESCRIPTIVE AND PRESCRIPTIVE GRAMMARS. The distinction between descriptive and prescriptive grammars is an old one and especially to those unacquainted with the aims and methods of linguistic science, a confused and confusing one. Linguists and especially generative grammarians aim to describe the competence of the speaker. They do not aim to prescribe rules and instruct the speaker in the niceties of language usage. Scientific and descriptive grammars are generalized grammars which do not concern themselves with the nature and background of the specific user of the language nor do they concern themselves with concepts such as "right" and "wrong." Prescriptive and teaching grammars, on the other hand, must be designed with specific speakers in mind and do concern themselves with matters of rightness and wrongness, much to the displeasure of students.

DEEP AND SURFACE STRUCTURES. Chomsky makes a distinction or, more accurately, reintroduces a distinction once widely recognized, which holds that in addition to the surface or superficial structure of a sentence there is also a deep or underlying structure (cf. Chomsky, 1965; Postal, 1964a). The distinction can be clarified by considering a sentence such as "The criticisms of the student were negative." The surface structure can be viewed as a labeled bracketing of the sentence into its constituents similar to that presented in Figure 3(**B**). However, this sentence (as all sentences) also has a deep structure. In fact, this particular sentence has two deep structures. Because of this, it is an ambiguous sentence. One deep structure would resemble "The student gives negative criticisms" and the other "Someone gives the student negative criticisms." The generative grammarians argue that sentences are understood on the basis of their deep, rather than their surface, structure and have adduced numerous examples similar to the one given here to illustrate the existence and significance of deep structure (cf. Chomsky, 1968).

Another way in which the distinction between deep and surface structure becomes apparent is seen in sentences which are different on the surface but which have only one deep structure as in the following two sentences:

The boy hit the girl. The girl was hit by the boy. These sentences are understood in essentially the same way not because their surface structure reveals this similarity but because their deep or underlying structure is the same.

These four basic distinctions will be further illustrated and clarified in the discussion of the components of the grammar. In a generative grammar, three components are recognized: syntactic, semantic, and phonological. The general outline of a generative grammar is diagramed in Figure 4.

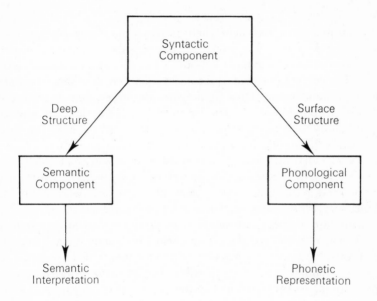

FIGURE 4. The Structure of a Generative Grammar

The remainder of this chapter is devoted to explaining the elements and processes included in this diagram.

Syntactic Component

The syntactic component is the generative portion of the grammar, that is, it generates the sentences or, more correctly, provides stuctural descriptions for the strings of elements, which will serve as input to the phonological and semantic components. The syntactic component consists of two parts or subcomponents: a base and a transformational subcomponent. Each of these may be thought of primarily as a system of rules.

THE BASE SUBCOMPONENT. The base section contains rules such as those presented in Figure 5, generally referred to as phrase-structure rules. The

(i)   S——→NP + VP
(ii)   NP——→ det + N
(iii) det——→ the, a
(iv)   N——→ boy, girl, man, dog, cat
(v)   VP——→ V + NP
(vi)   V——→ hit, love, bite
(vii) aux——→ past, will, should

FIGURE 5. Phrase-Structure Rules for a Simplified Grammar

rules given in Figure 5 and elsewhere in this chapter are for purposes of illustration and are therefore simplified considerably.   Note first the general form of these rules.   Each has a left- and a right-hand side, separated by an arrow.   The rule is to be read as the instruction to rewrite the left-hand side as the right-hand side.   Thus (i) provides the instruction to rewrite S as NP + VP, (ii) provides the instruction to rewrite NP as det + N, and so on. The symbols used in the rules are of two types.   First, there are the abstract symbols S, NP, VP, det, N, V, aux, and past, which are abbreviations for classes of grammatical elements or constituents: S = sentence, NP = noun phrase, VP = verb phrase, det = determiner, N = noun, V = verb, aux = auxiliary, and past = past tense.   Second, there are word-symbols, for example, *boy, girl, man, dog, cat, hit, love, bite, will,* and *should.*

These base- or phrase-structure rules produce what are referred to as *deep structures* (also called "deep P-markers" or "underlying P-markers") which provide a proper bracketing of the constituents of the sentence.   To provide an example, one of the possible deep structures derived from this sample grammar is presented in Figure 6.

Any group of symbols which is dominated by a single node, for example, the node NP or the node V, is a constituent of the sentence.   Thus from this

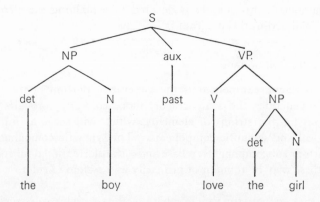

FIGURE 6.   Deep Structure Generated by Phrase-Structure Rules (i)—(vii)

diagram it can be seen that *the boy* is a constituent (since it is dominated by the single node NP) as is *love the girl* and *the girl*. But *love the* is not a constituent since it is not dominated by a single node.

These deep structures serve as the input to the semantic component of the grammar which provides a semantic interpretation or meaning for the sentence.

THE TRANSFORMATIONAL SUBCOMPONENT. The second set of rules contained in the syntactic component are the transformational rules, rules of substitution, addition, deletion, and permutation.   That is, transformational rules perform operations of substitution, etc., on deep structures, deriving what are referred to as *surface structures* (also called " derived P-markers " or " P-markers "). These surface structures then serve as input to the phonological component which assigns to them a phonetic representation.   In deriving a surface structure from the deep structure of Figure 6 only one such rule should be needed, namely the rule to transform *past love* into *loved*.

The formation of interrogatives, following Bellugi's (1965) explication, may be used to illustrate the nature of transformational rules in more specific terms.   This example will also serve to help illustrate the child's acquisition of transformations considered in Chapter 5.   The more formal statements of the various transformational rules [my own addition] are approximations intended to clarify the general nature and form of such rules rather than to provide the specific rules as they might appear in a completed grammar.

It would be wise to begin by considering how different types of questions might be derived from more basic structures.   Sentence (7) may be used as the starting point, though even this simple sentence has already undergone transformation.

(7) The boy played the game.

This sentence contains an NP, *the boy*, and a VP, *played the game*.   The VP can be divided into V, *played*, and another NP, *the game*.   Similarly, the V can be further divided into verb, *play*, and past tense and the NP into det, *the*, and N, *game*.   (When there are two constituents denoted by the same symbol subscripts may be used to distinguish them.   Thus NP_1 will refer to *the boy* and NP_2 to *the game*.)   From (7) one can derive a number of interrogative sentences, for example, (8) through (14).

(8) The boy played the game?
(9) Did the boy play the game?
(10) Didn't the boy play the game?
(11) Who played the game?
(12) What did the boy play?
(13) The boy played the game, didn't he?
(14) The boy didn't play the game, did he?

These questions differ in the ways they are formed and in the types of responses they require. Questions (8), (9), and (10) are *simple yes/no questions*, so designated because they require *yes* or *no* as answers. Questions (11) and (12) are called *wh*-questions because of the question words *who* and *what*. In (11) the *wh*-word substitutes for the subject of the sentence; it is the subject (*the boy*) that is questioned. In (12), however, the *wh*-word substitutes for the object; the object (*the game*) is questioned. Sentences of type (11) may be designated as *wh-subject questions* and those of type (12) as *wh-object questions*. Questions (13) and (14) are called *tag questions* since the interrogative element is "tagged" to the end of such sentences. In (13) the tag is negative and the main verb is positive and in (14) the tag is positive and the main verb is negative. These two questions are also of the yes/no variety but somewhat more complex than (8), (9), or (10). Questions (10), (13), and (14) may be further distinguished from the others by the presence of the negative *n't*.

The rules which are followed in forming these questions from the more basic structures can be specified, at least approximately. Here the discussion will be simplified by considering sentences (8) through (14) as being formed from (7); this is not entirely accurate, however. Sentences (8) through (14) are formed from deep structures which only resemble sentences such as (7). However, since deep structures are similar in form to the basic declarative such as (7) we will speak of (7) as if it were identical to the deep structure.

Declarative sentences of type (7) are characterized by an intonation contour designated by linguists as 2-3-1 which means that the sentence begins on a relatively even pitch (2), goes up (from 2 to 3), and then goes down (from 3 to 1), as the sentence is spoken. The simplest way to change a declarative into an interrogative is to change the intonation contour from 2-3-1 to 2-3-3, a contour characteristic of questions of this form. Questions such as (8) differ from the declarative only in intonation pattern; question words are not used, nor is the order or form of the words changed in any way.

The rule for forming questions such as (8) from declaratives such as (7) might be phrased as

$$S(2\text{-}3\text{-}1) \longrightarrow S\ (2\text{-}3\text{-}3)$$

This rule would read as the instruction to rewrite sentence with an intonation contour of 2-3-1 as sentence with intonation contour 2-3-3. In the remaining examples necessary changes in intonation contour will be assumed rather than explicitly stated.

In all questions except those formed by a simple change in intonation and *wh*-subject questions auxiliaries are used. When auxiliaries are already present in the declarative form, for example, as in "The boy can run fast," the auxiliary (*can*) and the subject NP (*the boy*) are interchanged in forming a question, yielding "Can the boy run fast?" More formally the rewrite rule might be stated as

$$NP + aux + VP \longrightarrow aux + NP + VP$$

Some declaratives, as, for example, (7), do not contain auxiliaries. In order to form questions from these it is necessary that an auxiliary, a form of *do*, be introduced. In the example "The boy played the game" the auxiliary *do* is added and placed in the position formerly occupied by NP, that is, in sentence initial position, and to it is added the tense morpheme formerly carried by the main verb. More specifically, the past-tense morpheme is deleted from *played* which becomes *play* and is added to *do* which becomes *did*. *Did* and *the boy* (NP_1) change places, yielding the question form "Did the boy play the game?" This rule would be stated as

$$NP_1 + V + Past\ tense + NP_2 \longrightarrow aux + past\ tense + NP_1 + V + NP_2$$

For questions which also involve negation as, for example, (10), (13), and (14), the negative element *n't* is tacked on to the past-tense form of the auxiliary; *did* becomes *didn't*. The relevant part of the rule here would read: aux + past tense + *n't*.

In forming interrogatives in which the subject is questioned, as in (11), the operations are relatively simple since these do not require auxiliaries. The question word *who* (or *what* if the subject is nonhuman) is introduced as a replacement for the subject NP. The rule here would be

$$NP_1 + V + NP_2 \longrightarrow Who + V + NP_2$$

Interrogatives in which the object of the sentence is questioned, as in (12), are formed by deleting NP_2 and introducing the question word *what* (or *whom* if the object is human) into sentence initial position. In describing this transformation, we may assume as completed those changes specified above for changing (7) into (9). Another way of describing this *wh*-object question transformation is to say that it applies to sentences of the simple yes/no type. The left-hand side of this rule may be taken as the same as sentence (9); the rewrite rule to form (12) would be

$$aux + NP_1 + V + NP_2 \longrightarrow what + aux + NP_1 + V$$

To form tag questions, for example, (13) and (14), the auxiliary is put at the end of the main part of the sentence (after the comma) and followed by the subject which is pronominalized, that is, the subject, *the boy*, becomes *he*. If the verb in the main part of the sentence is negative, as in (14), then no negative is used in the tag. For (13) the rule would be

$$NP_1 + V + \text{past tense} + NP_2 \longrightarrow NP_1 + V + NP_2 + \text{aux} + \text{past tense} + n't + \text{Pron}$$

For (14) the rule would be basically the same except for the change in the location of the auxiliary and the negative:

$$NP_1 + V + \text{past tense} + NP_2 \longrightarrow NP_1 + \text{aux} + \text{past tense} + n't + V + NP_2 + \text{aux} + \text{pron}$$

When sentences already contain auxiliaries, as in "The boy can run fast," this same auxiliary is repeated in the tag, yielding the question "The boy can run fast, can't he?" In sentences not containing an auxiliary the appropriate form of *do* is used and, as in other question sentences, also carries the same tense morpheme as the main verb.

Although these operations seem complex, it should be recalled that they must do a great deal of work. Assuming they are accurate and complete they describe the processes by which an infinite number of question sentences may be formed. When looked at in this way, the rules seem relatively few and simple.

Semantic Component

The semantic component of the grammar takes as its input the deep structures generated by the base rules of the syntactic component and provides semantic interpretations or meanings. According to Katz and Fodor (1963; Katz and Postal, 1964; Katz, 1966) the semantic component consists of two parts: a dictionary and a set of projection rules. It should be noted at the start that this theory has been severely criticized by linguists and philosophers (cf., for example, Weinreich, 1966; Bar-Hillel, 1967; Lackowski, 1968). At best, the theory is incomplete; at worst, it is incorrect. It is considered here because it is currently the major attempt to integrate semantics with the generative model of grammar developed by Chomsky and because it has stimulated much theory and research.

THE DICTIONARY. The dictionary contains entries for each lexical element in the language; for purposes of simplification these may be viewed as words though more correctly they are morphemes. A sample and much simplified dictionary entry for the word *man* is provided in Figure 7.

man → N	(i)	(animate) (human) (member of the human race) <SR>
	(ii)	(animate) (human) (male) (any male individual) <SR>
	(iii)	(animate) (male) (one who serves) <SR>
	(iv)	(inanimate) (conical heap of stones) <SR>
	(v)	(inanimate) (chesspiece) <SR>
→ VT	(i)	(to supply with men) <SR>

FIGURE 7. Simplified Dictionary Entry for *man*

Each entry consists of three kinds of information. (1) *Syntactic markers*, for example, N = noun, VT = verb transitive, denote the syntactic properties of the term which determine how the word functions. Thus, for example, nouns can be made plural, they can function as subjects of sentences, and so on. (2) *Semantic markers*, for example, animate, male, provide information relating to the general semantic properties of the term *man* which influence the way in which the term is interpreted and used. Thus, for example, the words *husband, boy, congressman, brother,* and *uncle* have the common semantic property of "maleness" and because of this common property these terms are treated in similar ways in the language, for example, they can all be replaced by the masculine pronoun *he*. "Maleness" thus denotes the similarity among these terms and also separates them from such terms as *wife, girl, congresswoman, sister,* and *aunt* which would have the common semantic marker "femaleness." (3) *Selection restrictions* (<SR>) function to limit the ways in which a particular term may be used. An example provided by Katz (1966) might make the nature of selection restrictions clearer. In the sentence "There is no school now" the term *school* is ambiguous; the sentence can mean that there is no school building or that school is not in session. However, in the sentence "The school burned up" there is no ambiguity; the term *school* must refer to the actual building. The reason for the absence of ambiguity in this second example is that the dictionary entry for the verb *burned up* contains the selection restriction which limits its use to physical objects. In such an entry the selection restriction <physical> would simply be inserted after the semantic markers.

PROJECTION RULES. The projection rules make use of two basic kinds of information. First, they utilize the information supplied by the deep structures, that is, the analysis of the sentence into constituents, and second, the information contained in the dictionary.

The projection rules deal first with the smallest units in the deep structures; that is, with the words. As noted earlier, the deep structure provides a labeling of all the constituents of the sentence; this information is used by the first projection rule to select the correct syntactic marker. For example, in the sentence "The man hit the boy" the deep structure would have *man* labeled as N. The projection rule would then eliminate those entries not syntactically marked by N. In Figure 7 it would eliminate the entry for VT.

Other projection rules (and there are as many projection rules as there are grammatical relations) then focus on increasingly larger constituents and on the basis of the syntactic information contained in the deep structure select the correct reading or meaning for *man*.

Although the nature and function of these rules are not very clear, an example of how they might operate may be ventured. Entry (i) would be eliminated on the basis of the fact that *man* is preceded by *the*. That is, the projection rule dealing with determiner-noun relations would reject (i) since this sense of *man* does not occur with a determiner. Another projection rule dealing with subject-predicate relations would reject (iv) and (v) since these cannot *hit the boy*. The projection rules would probably not be able to distinguish between (ii) and (iii). This, of course, is precisely the source of this sentence's ambiguity. That is, the sentence does not make clear whether the one who hit the boy is simply a human male or whether he is also a servant. The semantic component is not designed to resolve ambiguity but rather to reflect the way in which sentences are understood. Ideally, it would reflect only that ambiguity that native speakers perceive.

The projection rules continue to derive meanings for each of the constituents until the meaning for the largest constituent, the sentence, is derived. In our example, the meanings would first be for the individual words, then for the constituents *the man* and *the boy*, then for *hit the boy*. Finally, the meanings for *the man* and *hit the boy* would be combined to derive the meaning for "The man hit the boy." Notice that no meanings were derived for *man hit* or *hit the*. The reason for this is that these do not express grammatical relations contained in the syntactic component (that is, these are not constituents) and hence there are no projection rules for them.

Phonological Component

The phonological component of the grammar takes as input the surface structures generated by the syntactic component and derives, as output, a phonetic representation (Chomsky and Halle, 1968).

In generative grammar the phonetic representation is taken to be a two dimensional matrix such as that illustrated in Table 2. The rows specify the phonetic features such as consonantal as opposed to nonconsonantal, vocalic as opposed to nonvocalic, and so on. (These features, it should be added, are features of universal phonetics, the branch of linguistics which

TABLE 2.   Distinctive Feature Matrix for *boats*

	b	o	t	s
Vocalic	−	+	−	−
Consonantal	+	−	+	+
High	−	−	−	−
Back	−	+	−	−
Low	−	−	−	−
Anterior	+	−	+	+
Coronal	−	−	+	+
Round		+		
Tense	−			
Voice	+		−	−
Continuant	−		−	+
Nasal	−		−	−
Strident	−		−	+

specifies the possible phonetic representations of sentences in all languages. These features are not unique to English; rather, they apply to all possible human languages.)   The entries in the matrix (that is, the + or − signs) refer to whether the segments (that is, b, o, t, s) have (+) or do not have (−) the feature.   The columns refer to segments of the utterance.   The symbols (b, o, t, s), as used here, are *not* phonemes in the traditional sense; rather, they are informal abbreviations for the feature complexes.   The symbol *b*, in other words, is an abbreviation for nonvocalic, consonantal, etc. Matrices such as this, then, are the outputs of the phonological component of the grammar.

The way in which this phonological component derives a phonetic representation from the surface structure is by a system of rewrite rules. Specifically, these rules are of the form X⟶Y/A _____ B]n.   The symbols on the left of the diagonal have already been used so should present no special problem; here is simply the instruction to rewrite X as Y.   The symbols on the right are restrictions on the generality of the rule.   That is, they specify the conditions under which X can be rewritten as Y.   These restrictions are generally of two types.   The first restriction, symbolized by A _____ B, refers to the environment of X.   It states that X is to be rewritten as Y only when X occurs in the environment A _____ B, that is, when A is on the left and B is on the right.   In other words, it applies to the sequence AXB.   The second restriction, symbolized by *n* outside the bracket, refers to the lexical class to which the sequence belongs.   The *n* in this example would refer to the class of nouns.   The complete rule, then might be phrased as follows: X is to be rewritten as Y when X occurs in the environment A _____ B and when AXB is a noun.

Putting into this form a concrete example which has already been used might further clarify the nature of these rules.   Consider the following:

Plural ⟶ s/$\bar{V}$ _____ #]n

This rule states that "plural" is to be rewritten as *s* (that is, consonantal, nonvocalic, nonnasal, etc.) when it is preceded by a voiceless sound (denoted here as $\bar{V}$) and followed by a pause (denoted here as #) when the word is a noun, as, for example, cat:cats.   In the actual grammar a number of other considerations would have to be employed.   For example, since only nouns can be made plural the *n* is perhaps unnecessary.   Furthermore, the element which follows the plural seems to impose no restrictions; the phonetic representation of plural is determined solely by the preceding sound.

By this general system the phonological component derives phonetic representations from surface structures.   In a more complete account of this component other facts would have to be noted.   For example, there are cases in which readjustment rules are employed to alter the surface structure so that the phonological rules may apply.   Also, there are different types of phonological rules; one type applies to phrases and another only to words.

We might return briefly to the sentences presented at the beginning of this section and attempt to examine how generative grammar can handle each of these three "requirements." The difference between sentences (1) and (2) is in their deep structure (cf. Chomsky, 1968). In (1) *John* is the object of the verb whereas in (2) *John* is the subject. The deep structure of (1) would resemble "It is easy for someone to please John" whereas the deep structure of (2) would resemble "John is eager to please someone."

In providing different structures for ambiguous sentences such as (3) the generative grammar would simply note the different underlying or deep structures of the sentences. That is, a sentence which can be understood in two different ways is ambiguous because it can be derived from two different deep structures. Transformations applied to these two sentences have yielded a similar surface structure which causes the ambiguity. More specifically, the sentence "The doctor's bills are high" has two underlying structures: (a) the doctor gives high bills and (b) someone gives the doctor high bills. By specifying the deep structures of ambiguous sentences the grammar provides insight which constituent analysis cannot.

Lastly, generative grammar can explicate why sentences (4) and (5) are related in the sense that (6) is not simply by specifying the deep structures from which these three sentences were derived. Notice that the structure from which (4) was derived is the same as that from which (5) was derived —"the man bites the dog." The structure from which (6) was derived is quite different—"the dog bites the man."

Clearly, generative grammar is only one possible way of approaching language. There are numerous other ways which, for various reasons, could not be considered here. It seems to me, however, that generative grammar is at present the only workable candidate for a theory of language simply because it is the only grammar which provides a convincing account of the speaker's linguistic competence. This, naturally, is open to dispute. What is not debatable is that the influence of generative grammar on psycholinguistics has far surpassed the influence exerted by any other approach, and if the research in this area is to be meaningful then generative grammar must be understood.

Chapter Three

Learning Theory

Ideally, the relevant facts of language as detailed by linguists would be correct and complete. In practice, however, they may not be correct and inevitably are far from complete. Nevertheless, it is assumed that that portion of the grammar which has been written is correct, at least in its basic assumptions, and that whatever else is added will not negate or contradict the fundamental principles already proposed. On the basis of this assumption and whatever linguistic data are available, the psychologist attempts to build a theory to explain how these principles or rules are learned and used, or, as Osgood (1963b) puts it, to explain the processes wherein sentences are created and understood.

This chapter reviews theories which attempt to explain the process of language behavior. After a brief review of some basic assumptions underlying the work of behavioral psychologists in general and of learning theorists in particular we will consider three general models of language behavior: a functional analysis model developed by B. F. Skinner, an elementary mediation model proposed by O. Hobart Mowrer and Charles Osgood, and finally a three-stage mediational model developed by Charles Osgood. In Chapter 5 the more specific theories of how the child acquires language will be discussed.

SOME BASIC ASSUMPTIONS

Behavioral psychology depicts the interaction between organism and environment in terms of stimuli and responses. These stimuli or inputs and responses or outputs are the observables upon which psychologists focus. The aim of psychology is to explain the relations between stimuli and responses, that is, to establish principles of lawful relations between what impinges upon an organism and how the organism reacts. Ultimately the psychologist aims to predict the responses of an organism under certain stimuli and attempts to formulate statements of the form *given stimulus X, response Y will result.*

Although most behavioral psychologists agree that the formulation of such principles is their main concern they do not agree on the processes occurring within the organism. Assume, for the present, that the organism is a black box, a box into which there is no access. What goes on in the box cannot be observed but only inferred. This box is the individual's nervous system which controls the relations observed between stimuli and responses. Nineteenth century psychologists, still functioning largely as philosophers, attempted to explain the relations between stimuli and responses by postulating some causative factor within the organism. Osgood (1956, p. 169) eloquently describes this orientation:

> Whenever something needed explaining, a new explanatory device was stuck inside the black box, and it rapidly became chock-full of ill-assorted and ill-digested demons. For every nameable phenomenon of human behavior a different "faculty" would be posited to explain it; for every nameable motive, a different "instinct" would be listed as its explanation. And, at least for communicating with his patients, Freud had big, flat-footed superegos stomping around on red-slippery ids, while cleverly anxious little egos tried to arbitrate.

This form of theorizing, aptly termed "junkshop psychology," did not provide answers to the questions psychology set out to study. Rather, theory construction took the form of naming relations and putting labels on hypothetical entities presumed to inhabit the black box.

As a reaction against this form of theorizing early twentieth-century psychologists, particularly John B. Watson and later B. F. Skinner, argued that psychology should make no assumptions concerning what went on in the nervous system; the box was black and could not be opened. Even if it could be opened its contents were not the province of the psychologist but of the physiologist and neurologist. The task of psychology was to describe, predict, and control *observable behavior*.

Although this black-box view may seem strange today in light of the intensive work being done by psychologists on the nervous system, it did serve a useful purpose at the time. For one thing it served to counteract the form of "theorizing" which labeled without explaining. It also fostered a healthy suspicion of unobservable "explanatory" devices and led to increased concern for valid and reliable behavioral measurements. On the debit side, however, this "empty organism" approach severely limited the field of psychology. By keeping the box completely closed and restricting psychology to observable behavior it forced psychologists to concentrate only on those questions which could be answered within this narrow framework. And since observable behavior was regarded as the only concern of psychology it is not difficult to see why the white rat, less expensive and easier to control, soon replaced man as the object of study.

Many psychologists, however, recognized that this empty organism approach, although serving a number of useful and important purposes, did not provide the freedom necessary for investigating man. Thus many of them began to put things back into the box, being careful this time not to put back too much lest psychology reach the stage it occupied a century ago.

Using this basic idea of the empty and not-so-empty black box three major theories of language behavior which have had the most influence on psycholinguistic research are examined. Each of these theories derives from basic principles of learning (hence the title of this chapter) and are essentially behavioristic in point of view. Each differs in the amount of behavior it can explain, each varies in complexity, and each makes different assumptions about the contents of the black box.

A FUNCTIONAL ANALYSIS "THEORY"

A theory of functional analysis was proposed by B. F. Skinner (1957), perhaps most popular for his work on teaching machines and programmed learning. Skinner's approach is essentially "atheoretical" (Skinner, 1950). He prefers to by-pass theoretical explanations and so the title of this chapter is perhaps somewhat inappropriate, at least as far as Skinner is concerned.

According to Skinner, behavior is of two basic types: respondent and operant. Classical stimulus-response psychology once held that if there is no stimulus there is no response. And it held to this even though no single stimulus could be identified when certain responses occurred. It assumed that the stimuli were present and that the psychologist was simply not equipped to detect them. Skinner broke with this tradition and claimed that here facts were made to fit theories rather than theories made to fit facts. Such an assumption was both undesirable and unnecessary. Skinner therefore advanced a distinction between what he called respondent and operant behavior, a distinction which enables one to deal effectively with the problem of "no stimulus" responses. Although not all of Skinner's approach is accepted, his distinction between respondents and operants seems widely adopted.

Respondents are behaviors or responses which are *elicited* by known and clearly identifiable stimuli. For example, if light is shined in a person's eye his pupil will constrict; if his patella tendon is tapped his knee will jerk. The constriction and jerking are responses which the shining light and the knee tapping stimuli elicited.

Operants, on the other hand, are behaviors which are *emitted* and for which the original stimuli are not known and not clearly observable. An infant who crawls or touches his feet is engaging in operant behavior; no stimuli can be clearly and unambiguously located for these behaviors. Verbal behavior is perhaps the most obvious type of operant behavior.

According to Skinner, operant behavior, although not the only type of behavior, is by far the most important and the most human form of behavior. Operant behavior is learned or not learned on the basis of its consequences, which can be either rewarding or punishing. More formally one would say that operant behavior is governed or controlled by two basic classes of events—positive reinforcers and negative reinforcers. Behavior is reinforced by the application of rewards (positive reinforcement) and by the removal or termination of aversive stimuli (negative reinforcement). For example, a rat will learn to press a lever if this lever-pressing behavior results in some positive reinforcement (for example, food) or if it results in the termination of some aversive stimulus (for example, shock).

In his *Verbal Behavior* (1957), Skinner develops a model which he argues can account for the significant aspects of speech and language behavior. His model is often referred to as "single stage" because only stimulus and response events are considered. Skinner makes no assumptions concerning intervening variables; the box is black and cannot be opened. When dealing with language and speech behavior the task of the psychologist or psycholinguist is simply to observe the verbal behavior (that is, the responses), the conditions under which such behavior is reinforced, and to postulate functional relations between verbal operants and the conditions under which they are reinforced. For example, when a particular operant is emitted and then reinforced in some way, say hunger is satisfied, this operant will tend to be emitted again. The conditions under which an operant is reinforced in effect constitute the stimulus for the future emission of that operant. Being able to speak in terms of stimulus and response will facilitate the comparison of this model with the others and will not do any injustice to Skinner's basic system.

The task of accounting for verbal behavior is seemingly simple. "Our first responsibility," says Skinner (1957, p. 10), "is simple *description*: what is the topography of this subdivision of human behavior? Once that question has been answered in at least a preliminary fashion we may advance to the stage called *explanation*: what conditions are relevant to the occurrence of the behavior—what are the variables of which it is a function?" In this functional analysis Skinner has searched for the various stimuli or conditions which control verbal behavior. His analysis takes the form of a listing of verbal operants each of which is controlled by a different set of variables.

A mand—a term Skinner coined and justified on the basis of its similarity with such words as *command* and *demand*—is a verbal operant controlled by drive states such as thirst or hunger and functions to alleviate or lessen the drive. The verbal utterance *water* when said in response to the drive state of thirst, constitutes a mand and functions to alleviate the thirst by aiding in the securing of water. Thus one who is thirsty will have a higher probability of manding *water* than will one who is not thirsty. The drive state, in other words, controls the emission of this class of verbal operants.

Mands generally specify the behavior of the listener, the ultimate reinforcement, or both. Expressions such as *Listen!* or *Pay attention!* specify the listener's behavior whereas expressions such as *Water!* or *Food!* specify the ultimate reinforcement. At times both the behavior of the listener and the reinforcement are named by the mand as in, for example, *Pass the bread* or *Pour the wine.*

Two characteristics which distinguish the mand from the other verbal operants should be noted. First, the mand bears no relation to any prior stimulus. Although the drive state which governs the emission of mands may be thought of as a stimulus it is not objective and observable as are those controlling other verbal operants. Second, the mand functions primarily for the benefit of the speaker whereas other verbal operants seem to benefit the listener. The result of the mand *water*, for example, is clearly of benefit to the speaker; the mand helps the speaker secure the reinforcement, in this case, the water.

A tact—a term coined to suggest behavior which "makes con*tact* with" the nonverbal world—is a verbal operant best viewed as a labeling response for some physical object or event or for some property of the object or event. In the presence of water the likelihood of emitting the verbal operant *water* is increased.

Although the emission of a tact is controlled by the presence of the physical object or event the probability of its occurrence may be increased in a number of different ways. For example, if a listener were to ask the name of some particular thing tacting behavior would have a greater probability of occurring than if such a question were not asked. Similarly, if the object were especially novel to the speaker's audience tacting behavior would be more probable.

Whereas the mand and the tact are both controlled by the nonverbal, the former by a drive state and the latter by a physical object, echoic, textual, and intraverbal operants are all controlled by verbal stimuli. An echoic operant is controlled by previously heard speech. It is an imitation or "echo" of another verbal utterance. When a child hears someone say *dada* and repeats it, he is engaging in echoic behavior. This type of operant is frequently observed in conversation where a somewhat infrequent expression is used by one speaker and the other members continue using it. In its extreme and pathological form it is seen in echolalia where the individual echoes or repeats whatever he hears. Fragmentary echoic responses are seen in the tendency to supply "clang associates" on word association tests. When, for example, someone is asked to supply the first word he thinks of upon hearing *rickety* he would be likely to respond with *rackety* or some such partially echoic response.

A textual operant is controlled by a nonauditory verbal stimulus. Although the most common stimuli would consist of orthographic symbols, a "text" may also consist of hieroglyphs, pictographs, phonetic symbols, or similar nonauditory verbal stimuli. When, for example, in response to the symbols t-a-b-l-e the speaker says *table* he is engaging in textual behavior.

The basic difference between echoic and textual behavior is that in the former case the stimuli and responses are of the same modality (both auditory) whereas in the latter case they are of different modalities (visual and auditory). Another distinction is that in echoic behavior the speaker receives immediate and relatively precise feedback concerning the accuracy of his behavior. Upon hearing an utterance and then hearing his own he knows if he has echoed correctly.   In the case of textual behavior the feedback is relatively limited.   Upon seeing a word and saying it the speaker may recognize that it sounds correct but the feedback is clearly not as complete as with echoic operants.

An intraverbal operant is under the control of verbal behavior which is of a different form.   For example, the stimulus "How are you?" will lead to the response "Fine, thanks"; the stimulus "Four score" will lead to the, response "and seven years ago."   Clichés, much social conversation, and responses on word-association tests are some of the more familiar types of intraverbal operants.   Since there is no formal correspondence between stimulus and response they may differ also in modality.   That is, a written response may be given to either an oral or a written stimulus and similarly an oral response may be given to either an oral or a written stimulus.

The sixth and last functional relation Skinner defines is the audience which influences the form and content of verbal operants.   Most obviously the audience will influence the language one speaks; one does not, for example, speak Chinese to speakers of English.   Similarly, subgroups within a speech community will exert influence over verbal behavior.   Jargon, cant, and technical vocabularies are clearly influenced by the nature of the audience.   When a linguist talks about morphemes, deep structure, and distinctive features, for example, his audience is most likely composed of other linguists or at least persons interested in linguistics.   The audience also influences the content or subject matter of verbal behavior.   A speaker does not talk about the same things to different listeners; rather, the topics of conversations are influenced by the interests and backgrounds of the audience.

The way in which verbal behavior is controlled can now be made explicit.   As noted earlier, the occurrence and frequency of operant behavior is controlled by reinforcement.   For example, when a listener does what a speaker mands the speaker is reinforced; consequently the frequency of manding behavior will increase under similar circumstances.   If, however, the speaker was punished then the frequency of manding behavior would decrease.   The way in which the audience controls behavior is perhaps most obvious.   The speaker who speaks English to English speakers would be positively reinforced (he would be listened to, for example).   If he spoke Chinese to exclusively English speakers he would be extinguished.   The neighborhood intellectual who speaks to the street corner gang in "academese" would soon find himself ignored or punished in some other way and the frequency of "academese" with this audience would soon decrease. If he spoke in their particular cant then he would be more likely to receive positive reinforcement.   In much the same way the audience controls the speaker's behavior by reinforcing certain topics and punishing others. Similarly, when a speaker tacts something (for example, names a particular building) and the listener provides positive reinforcement (for example, by acknowledging the speaker's competence) the speaker's tacting behavior is positively reinforced and its frequency will increase.   Echoic, textual, and intraverbal behavior are reinforced in parallel ways.   If reinforced they will occur with increased frequency; if punished they will occur with decreased frequency, or not at all.

These six functional relations do not constitute a classification of responses.   One cannot classify operants according to this scheme simply because their form does not always provide clues of the class to which they belong.   Furthermore, most operants are the result of multiple causation. For example, if a child says *water* one cannot tell whether this was controlled by a drive state (a mand), or whether he saw water (a tact), or whether he heard the word (echoic), or whether he saw the word (textual), or whether someone else said some part of a nursery rhyme and the child filled in *water* (intraverbal), or whether he saw someone who always gives him water (audience).   Nor, of course, can one tell what combination of factors the response *water* represents.   Skinner's system is useful as a classification of the circumstances in which verbal operants are emitted, of the conditions which control verbal behavior.

Skinner's model is probably the most detailed and certainly the most provocative attempt to deal with verbal behavior exclusively in terms of observables.   Although in his *Verbal Behavior* Skinner does not cite experimental support for his functional analysis, his approach has generated a great deal of experimentation.   Of most interest here is the research on "verbal conditioning."   In the typical experiments subjects are asked to supply a list of some particular class of terms, for example, nouns or verbs or statements.   The experimenter then reinforces a certain subclass of these, for example, plural nouns or hostile verbs or statements expressing opinion. The types of reinforcements used have varied greatly from the classic *mmm-hmm* used by Greenspoon (1955) to *good, give another one, please,* smiles, head nods, etc.   The results are generally interpreted by psychologists (cf. Osgood, 1963c; Krasner, 1967) as confirming the effectiveness of reinforcement; that is, the reinforced response class increases in frequency and may, therefore, be said to have been "conditioned."

There are problems with these studies, however, which are crucial to an evaluation of Skinner's conception of verbal behavior.   First, studies yielding negative findings (that is, where the reinforced response class does not increase in frequency) seldom get published.   Thus it is not surprising that the published evidence clearly supports the effectiveness of reinforcement.   Second, when the subjects are separated on the basis of whether or not they were aware of the conditions of reinforcement it appears that only those who were so aware exhibit the predicted conditioning effects.   Charles Spielberger (1965, p. 197), after thoroughly reviewing the relevant research, concluded that " 'what is learned' in verbal conditioning is awareness of a response-reinforcement contingency . . . subjects will act on their awareness provided they are motivated to receive reinforcement."   If one accepts this conclusion, then at least two corollaries follow.   First, reinforcement is not as powerful a control of verbal behavior as Skinner's model asserts; if a speaker only becomes conditioned when he is aware of the reinforcement contingencies then he and not the listener is in control.   Second, and most important, is that some mediating or intervening process—namely, conscious awareness—is operating to influence verbal behavior.   Awareness, however has no place in a model such as Skinner's where only stimulus and response events are considered.   Of course, even if it were shown that verbal behavior can be conditioned it would not necessarily follow that conditioning is essential to verbal behavior (cf. Fodor, 1965).

By concentrating solely on stimulus and response events Skinner limits his analysis of verbal behavior to what is overt and is forced to omit con- siderations of meaning, probably the most important single factor in language behavior.   Experiments on semantic satiation and semantic generalization, as Osgood (1958) has observed, demonstrate that meaning significantly influences behavior and that any account which fails to deal with this issue is incomplete.

In studies of semantic satiation (see, for example, Lambert and Jako- bovits, 1960; Fillenbaum, 1967) it is found that after repeating a particular word over and over again this word loses some of its meaning.   For example, if one were to respond to the word *elephant* on the following scales it might be rated somewhat as follows:

```
good  ____:__X__:____:____:____:____:____  bad
large  _X__:____:____:____:____:____:____  small
strong  _X__:____:____:____:____:____:____  weak
active  ____:____:__X__:____:____:____:____  passive
```

However, after frequent and rapid repetition the meaning for *elephant* is closer to the neutral positions and might appear as follows:

```
good  ____:____:__X__:____:____:____:____  bad
large  ____:__X__:____:____:____:____:____  small
strong  ____:____:__X__:____:____:____:____  weak
active  ____:____:____:__X__:____:____:____  passive
```

A term, therefore, will lose some of its meaning under conditions of massed repetition.   Since there is no mechanism in Skinner's model which would enable one to deal with meaning, phenomena such as semantic satiation cannot be explained.

The importance of meaning is likewise demonstrated by studies on semantic generalization where it is found that responses generalize on the basis of similarity in meaning.   Suppose, for example, that a subject, with his hand on a wire grid, received a shock a few seconds after the word *smell* appeared on the screen. Under these conditions the subject would soon learn to remove his hand every time this word appeared. But his removal response would also be made to words of similar meaning, for example, *odor*. That is, the response generalizes on a semantic or meaning basis. The response does not generalize to words of similar form, for example, *swell*, a conclusion which would probably be more consistent with Skinner's model. Again, however, the absence of meaning makes it impossible to deal with this type of behavior.

Furthermore, as Osgood (1958) notes, the massed repetition of the nonsense forms *nuka* and *groni* have no influence on the meanings of *canoe* and *Negro*, despite the fact that under conditions of massed repetition *nuka* and *canoe* and *groni* and *Negro* have the exact same form. The only way in which they differ is in meaning and yet this cannot be accounted for.

At times the predictions which Skinner's model makes are not consistent with experimental findings. As has been noted, Skinner treats word associations as examples of intraverbal behavior. If such is the case then the association to *man* should be a word which frequently follows it in everyday language, for example, *is* or *works*. In actual fact, of course, the association to man is not a word such as *is* or *works* but rather *woman*.

Because of the failure to deal with such aspects of verbal behavior Osgood (1958) views the model as incomplete. According to Osgood the model is correct as far as it goes but in its failure to consider such factors as meaning it is insufficient as an account of verbal behavior.

Other researchers, for example Noam Chomsky (1959) and Jerry Fodor (1965), have taken a different position and argue that the model is not merely insufficient but rather is incorrect. First, verbal behavior is held to be stimulus-free in the sense that the conditions under which verbal behavior is emitted are too complex to ever be specified in any meaningful detail. "A striking feature of linguistic behavior," notes Fodor (1965, p. 73), "is its freedom from the control of specifiable local stimuli or independently identifiable drive states. In typical situations, what is said may have no obvious correlation with conditions in immediate locality of the speaker or with his recent history of deprivation or reward. Conversely, the situations in which such correlations do obtain (the man dying of thirst who predictably gasps 'water') are intuitively highly atypical." Any model, therefore, which attempts to account for verbal behavior in terms of the controlling conditions or stimuli is doomed to failure for it can never describe any significant portion of verbal behavior.

Second, the model provides no mechanism for identifying when responses are functionally similar or when they are functionally different. That is, it does not enable one to determine when given operants are the same or different verbal responses. For example, *bachelor* and *unmarried man* are functionally similar and yet the model provides no means whereby this functional similarity can be recognized. Similarly, responses of the same form may be functionally different as the word *lift* in the sentences "Lift the child" and "Take the lift to the second floor." As is obvious from these examples, functional similarities and differences cannot be accounted for on the basis of their physical form or phonetic shape.

AN ELEMENTARY MEDIATIONAL MODEL

Recognizing that a complete black box could not account for numerous aspects of verbal behavior some psychologists have incorporated into their models mediational processes, that is, internal processes which "go between" or "mediate" between stimulus and response events. One such model has been proposed by O. Hobart Mowrer (1954, 1960b).

According to Mowrer, a word acquires its meaning by being associated with the thing for which it stands. The process can best be explained in stages, labeled in Figure 8**A**. In this and in other models, lower case letters refer to mediational processes. (1) The thing or referent elicits in language users some reaction. Using Mowrer's example, Tom (the person) elicits in various other persons a total reaction (R_t). (2) Of this total reaction (R_t) some portion of it becomes detached; this detached component can be labeled (r_t). (3) Tom (the person) and *Tom* (the word) are often associated together; that is, there is a paired presentation of Tom (the person) and *Tom* (the word). (4) The word *Tom* acquires its meaning or is understood when it elicits r_t (the detachable portion of the total reaction, R_t). In other words, the meaning of *Tom* is understood when *Tom* comes to elicit a portion of the total behavior which Tom (the person) normally elicits.

Mowrer explains the learning of sentences with essentially the same principles. The meaning of the sentence "Tom is a thief" is understood

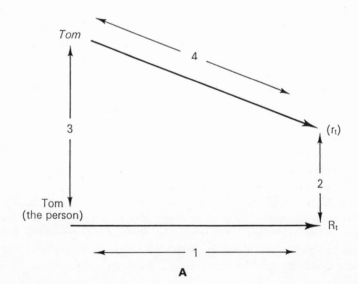

A

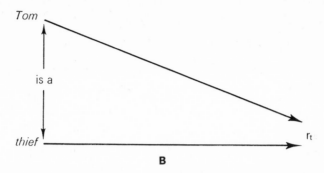

FIGURE 8. Mediational Theory of Language: **(A)** the Learning of Words; **(B)** the Learning of Sentences. *Adapted from O. Hobart Mowrer, "The Psychologist Looks at Language,"* American Psychologist, *IX (1954)* : **A**, p. 666; **B**, p. 664.

when the reactions elicited by the predicate (*thief*) shift to or become attached to the subject (*Tom*) and when one responds to *Tom* as one had previously responded to *thief*. The basic outline of this process is diagramed in Figure 8**B**.

Charles Osgood, in his early publications (for example, 1953, 1956), advanced a mediational model similar in many respects to that of Mowrer's. This model should also be examined since it will further clarify the nature of mediational theories and will simplify explaining the more advanced and complex model which Osgood has more recently proposed. The essential features of this theory can best be explained in terms of the diagram presented in Figure 9. Examples of the symbols have been added to simplify explanation.

Ṡ (for example, Tom, the person) is a stimulus which elicits a particular pattern of total behavior (R_t). That is, one responds to Tom in various ways and these responses are simply grouped together and symbolized R_t. $\boxed{S}$ (for example, *Tom*) is an originally neutral stimulus which is paired with Ṡ. That is, Tom (the person) and *Tom* (the word) are associated or experienced together. Part of the R_t becomes detached and is symbolized as r_m. This r_m is the representational mediation process. It is "representational" because the reaction made to the symbol $\boxed{S}$ is only part of or "represents" the behavior made to Ṡ. It is "mediational" because it functions to go between or mediate between the symbol $\boxed{S}$ and the responses to the symbol (R_x). Osgood symbolizes this process with *r* to emphasize that it has response properties; that is, it is an internal response to the symbol *Tom*.

This r_m then leads to or produces s_m which is "self-stimulation" and may be viewed as the conscious awareness of meaning. It is, in other words, an awareness of the r_m or of one's internal reactions to the symbol. Self-stimulation is symbolized with *s* to indicate that it possesses stimulus properties; it functions as an internal stimulus which leads to R_x. Finally, R_x

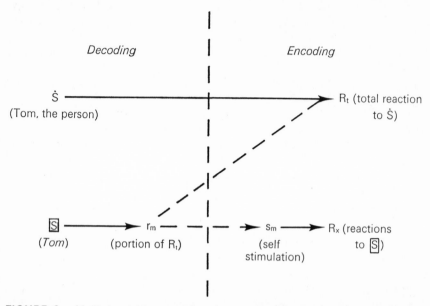

FIGURE 9. Mediational Theory of Language. *Adapted from Charles E. Osgood, "On Understanding and Creating Sentences,"* American Psychologist, XVIII (1963), 739.

simply denotes one's overt behavior to the symbol $\boxed{S}$. The vertical line dividing the model in half separates the two basic processes with which the model deals, decoding and encoding. In reacting to a symbol ($\boxed{S} \longrightarrow r_m$) one is decoding and in responding to some stimulus ($s_m \longrightarrow R_x$) one is encoding.

Working through an example might help make this model somewhat more concrete. Tom, the person ($\dot{S}$), and *Tom*, the symbol $\boxed{S}$, are paired. When we see Tom, for example, we also hear the word *Tom*. A portion of the reactions to Tom, the person (R_t), become separated (r_m). For example, R_t might be fear which is manifested by sweating, nervous and aimless activity, increased rate of heart beat, and r_m might be something like increased rate of heart beat; r_m is a part of R_t. The word *Tom* then comes to elicit that small portion of behavior (increased rate of heart beat) which has become detached from R_t and functions to stimulate or make us aware of the connection between Tom (the person) and *Tom* (the word). This self-stimulation (s_m) or awareness then leads to some overt behavior (R_x) which is appropriate to the original stimulus ($\dot{S}$), for example, some impression of our uneasiness or perhaps some fearful facial expression.

The elementary mediational model accounts rather directly for meaning and thus incorporates a mechanism to meet the major inadequacy of the single-stage model proposed by Skinner. Psychological phenomena such as semantic generalization and semantic satiation can, therefore, be explained. In semantic generalization, as previously noted, the response to a word such as *smell* generalizes to words of the same meaning, for example, *odor*. The model would account for this by noting that both *smell* and *odor*, because they have the same meaning, produce the same representational mediation processes which lead to a common self-stimulation which in turn leads to the same or similar responses. In other words, *smell* and *odor* produce the same r_m which leads to the same s_m which leads to the same R_x. This same overt response, of course, is exactly what is observed in semantic generalization, for example, the subject withdraws his hand from the grid upon seeing both *smell* and *odor*. Semantic satiation is accounted for by postulating that the representational mediation process (r_m) becomes temporarily inhibited and thus after mass repetition a word fails to produce the same self-stimulation and the same overt reactions as it had produced initially.

Donald Hebb (1949) has proposed that when a number of stimulus events or a number of response events occur together the occurrence of one of them will lead to the occurrence of the ones with which it was frequently paired. For example, if responses A, B, C, D, and E occur frequently together, the occurence of A will be sufficient to trigger the occurrence of B, C, D, and E. Examples of such behavior would include, in general, most rapidly executed motor behavior such as shoe-tying, typing, and, according to Osgood, human speech. However, a model which deals solely with stimulus and response connections, as does this elementary mediational model, cannot incorporate such behavioral phenomena. In order to remedy this failing Osgood (1963b) has revised his theory.

A THREE STAGE MEDIATIONAL THEORY

The three stage mediational model, presented in Figure 10 is the most detailed and sophisticated attempt to explain language behavior in a stimulus-response framework. The essential connections in Figure 10 are numbered for easy reference. The three levels (projection, integrational, and representational) and the three processes (decoding, association, and encoding) will each be explained in turn.

The projection level is essentially a neural relay system where a stimulus automatically leads to a response. This level has two defining characteristics: isomorphism and unmodifiability. *Isomorphism* means that there is a one-to-one relationship between the stimulation and the response. That is, if one knows the precise nature of the stimulation (say, the specific area of the nervous system that is stimulated) one can then predict the amount and the quality of the response (say, the specific muscles that will contract). The reverse also holds: knowing the precise nature of the response one can predict the type of stimulation. *Unmodifiability* means that what takes place in this projection system is not learned or influenced by past experience;

Levels   Processes

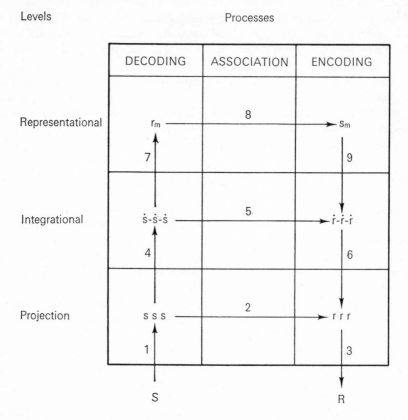

FIGURE 10. Three-Stage Mediational Theory of Language. *Adapted from Charles E. Osgood, "On Understanding and Creating Sentences,"* American Psychologist, *XVIII (1963), 740.*

that is, it cannot be modified. These connections between stimuli and responses can be thought of as "wired in." Unmodifiability coupled with isomorphism makes this system completely predictable, in an information theory sense. An example of the sequence of activity which might occur on this level (that is, from 1 to 2 to 3) will clarify this system. A flashing light (stimulus, S) is shined in someone's eyes and stimulates the organism (s s s). This stimulation automatically sets off certain neural responses (r r r). These responses in turn lead to some form of overt response (R), say pupil constriction and blinking. The behavior occurring at this level, then, is essentially reflexive.

The integrational level is the level designed to account for behavior involving, for example, rapidly executed motor skills which the elementary mediational model could not handle (cf. Osgood, 1957a). When either stimulus or response events are repeatedly experienced together, the nervous system groups them together or "integrates" them.

For example, suppose that stimulus events A and B set off responses *a* and *b*, respectively. Further suppose that A and B are experienced together over a long period of time. Now when A is experienced alone it would normally serve only as a stimulus for response *a*. However, because of A's frequent association with B, the experiencing of A will also cause response *b*. This is what is meant by integrations. A and B are frequently paired so that one of them experienced alone will serve to produce the responses generally produced by both of them.

Integrations of this form are produced in three different ways. In the above example one way was noted, namely, frequency. That is, when two stimuli, A and B, are frequently paired they and their responses will become integrated. Integrations can also be formed if stimuli are experienced closely in time, that is, by temporal contiguity. A third way is by redundancy; integrations will be formed if stimulus B or response *b* is redundant or completely predictable, given stimulus A or response *a*.

There are two basic kinds of integration: predictive and evocative. Predictive integration refers to the situation in which one can predict with only some degree of probability that given response *a* response *b* will follow. This would be the situation when the frequency of pairing, for example, is not extremely high. Predictive integration, then, refers to integrations which are probable but not definite.

Evocative integration, on the other hand, refers to situations in which the occurrence of one event (*a*) will be a sufficient cause for the occurrence of another event (*b*). That is, the occurence of *b*, given *a*, is definite. Such integrations are formed by extremely high frequency, high redundancy, or close temporal proximity of the stimulus or response events.

Behavior occurring at this level would follow the sequence 1-4-5-6-3. For example, someone says "How are you?" This utterance is the stimulus (S). This S stimulates the organism (s s s). At ś-ś-ś the message is received and at ṙ-ṙ-ṙ the organism responds physiologically. These physiological responses set off certain neural responses (r r r) which in turn lead to some overt response (R), for example, "Fine, thank you."

At this level we have such forms of behavior as tying one's shoe or tie or speaking, conceived of simply as rapidly executed motor behavior. At this level exist many grammatical rules which one may not know intellectually but to which one nevertheless conforms. For example, if given the statement "One pug plus one pug equals two_____," a native speaker of English would fill in *pugs*, pronouncing the final sound as [z]. This response involved no conscious thinking or intellectualizing; it was a response based on integrations.

The representational level has already been explained in the discussion of the more elementary mediational model. It is this level which is concerned with meaning.   We recall that r_m denotes the internal responses to S and s_m denotes the awareness of meaning.   The sequence of behavior involving "meaning" would be 1-4-7-8-9-6-3.   For example, someone yells "Fire!" in a theatre.   This utterance is the stimulus, S.   Traveling through paths 1, 4, and 7, it arouses in the organism some portion of the behavior which would be made to the fire itself.   These behaviors, for example, increased respiration rate, increased rate of heart beat, are symbolized by r_m.   These behaviors then give rise to some recognition of meaning (s_m); that is, one becomes aware of the significance or meaning of the word *Fire!* Traveling through paths 9, 6, and 3 this awareness leads to overt behavior (R), for example, looking around, getting out of one's seat, running to the door, which would be appropriate to the actual fire.

The processes of decoding and encoding have also been noted in the discussion of the elementary mediational model.   When dealing with language behavior the decoding process begins with the auditory or visual reception of language stimuli and ends with the internal responses (r_m) to these stimuli.   The encoding process beings with some recognition of meaning (say an "idea") and ends with some behavior, speaking or writing in the case of linguistic encoding, or some nonverbal behavior in the case of non-linguistic encoding.   The association processes are simply the connections between decoding and encoding, and, as the model and the examples illustrate, also exist on all three levels.

Although Osgood's conception of language behavior, like Skinner's, has come under attack it would be amiss if we did not first explain one of the major derivations of this theory—the semantic differential (Osgood, Suci, and Tannenbaum, 1957; Snider and Osgood, 1969).   No work in speech and language psychology can ignore this tool and here is perhaps the best place to consider it since it follows logically from the nature of meaning as conceived by Osgood.

The semantic differential is a tool for measuring the connotative meaning of terms.   In his various factor analytic studies Osgood has found that the meanings for a wide variety of terms in a wide variety of cultures cluster around three main factors or dimensions—evaluation, potency, and activity.   The semantic differential enables one to measure the evaluative, potency, and activity dimensions of various terms.   The actual semantic differential form consists of a series of seven-point scales each of which is bound by polar opposites.   A concept is placed at the top of the page, for example, and a series of scales appear below it.   The subject then indicates his meaning for this concept by placing an "X" on the appropriate scale.

The evaluative factor is measured by such scales as good-bad, beautiful-ugly, sweet-sour, clean-dirty, tasty-distasteful, valuable-worthless, and kind-cruel.   Potency scales include large-small, strong-weak, heavy-light, thick-thin, hard-soft, loud-soft, deep-shallow, and brave-cowardly.   Activity scales consist of fast-slow, active-passive, hot-cold, sharp-dull, and angular-rounded.

The seven points on the scale are to be interpreted as follows:

good————:————:————:————:————:————:————bad

| ex-tremely good | quite good | fairly good | neutral | fairly bad | quite bad | ex-tremely bad |

The actual form and the procedure used in semantic differentiation can probably be explained best by reference to a specific example. In the example presented below a subject has indicated his meaning for the concept *higher education*.

HIGHER EDUCATION

bad	:	X :	:	:	:	good
sharp	:	:	: X	:	:	dull
sweet	:	: X	:	:	:	sour
large X	:	:	:	:	:	small
passive	X :	:	:	:	:	active
ugly	:	:	: X	:	:	beautiful
hot	:	:	: X	:	:	cold
weak	:	:	:	: X	:	strong
light	:	:	:	: X	:	heavy

Notice that in using the semantic differential the three scales used to measure each dimension (and a larger number could have been used) are not grouped together since this would lead one scale to influence the others. Also, the positive and negative poles are randomized. This is to prevent a subject from developing a particular set and then simply checking down the column. The purpose of randomizing the scales is to force the subject to make each judgment an independent one. The differential is not a standardized test but is subject to concept-scale interaction (cf. Darnell, 1966).

In interpreting the results a number of things can be done. Generally, if one wished to make inferences or statements concerning the evaluation of higher education one would take the scores from the three evaluative scales and simply add them. (In calculating the scores the numbers from 1 to 7 are used to stand for each of the seven scale positions. Generally 1 is used for the negative end and 7 for the positive end.) In the example the subject would have a score of 12 for evaluation (the sum of his scores on the good-bad, sweet-sour, and beautiful-ugly scales). Similarly, the potency and activity scale responses would be totaled. This subject would have a score of 19 for potency (the sum of his scores on the large-small, strong-weak, and heavy-light scales) and 8 for activity (the sum of his scores on the sharp-dull, active-passive, and hot-cold scales). (Remember that since the polarity of the scales is randomized the positive pole will sometimes be on the right and at other times on the left.)   Although the proper use of these scores necessitates some sort of comparison, say with other concepts or with other subjects, for purposes of illustration it can be said that this hypothetical subject's meaning for *higher education* was quite potent, neutral in evaluation, and somewhat inactive or passive.   The semantic profile, then, provides a measure of an individual's connotative meaning for *higher education*.   His meaning is, in effect, located somewhere in semantic space, quantified by his responses on these various bi-polar scales.

With the semantic differential meanings can be compared for different concepts, for the same concepts at different times, and for different concepts or the same concepts as viewed by different subjects.

The evaluative dimension, it should be mentioned, is taken by Osgood to serve as a measure of what is normally referred to as attitude and it is in its capacity as a device for measuring attitude that it has found its widest use among communication researchers (cf. Chapter 8).   Martin Fishbein (1963; Fishbein and Raven, 1962), however, has argued against this position as it is made to apply to attitude change especially.   According to Fishbein, attitude change is not solely a function of one's evaluation of the object. Rather, attitude, and consequently attitude change, is a function of beliefs about an object, (for example, beliefs in the probability-improbability that an object bears a specific relationship with another given object or value or characteristic) and evaluations of those beliefs (for example evaluations toward the related object, value, or characteristic).   Fishbein, therefore, has constructed semantic differentials for measuring attitude so conceived. Attitude, according to Fishbein, then, consists of two dimensions which he labels attitude (that is, evaluations of beliefs) and belief (that is, beliefs about objects having certain relationships).   This instrument, commonly called AB (Attitude/Belief) scales, consists of ten individual scales, five for attitude and five for belief.   Attitude is measured by the scales beneficial-harmful, good-bad, healthy-sick, wise-foolish, and clean-dirty; belief is measured by the scales true-false, possible-impossible, probable-improbable, likely-unlikely, and existent-nonexistent.   From an examination of these scales it is perhaps easier to see that under belief the concern is with the degree to which one thinks that a particular characteristic is associated with the concept being measured and under attitude the concern is with one's evaluations of the characteristics.

Because of the ease with which semantic differential tests may be administered, the high validity and reliability of the scores, and the potentiality for investigating meaning in so many different areas of interest, a number of other researchers, following Osgood's lead, have constructed semantic differentials for more specific purposes.

John Carroll (1960b), for example, has developed a semantic differential for investigating style. Utilizing the factor analytic techniques used by Osgood, Carroll found that style contained five basic dimensions or factors. All of these dimensions, except the general stylistic evaluation factor, can be further indexed by various objective measures.   (1) *General stylistic evaluation* is measured by such scales as good-bad, pleasant-unpleasant, strong-weak, interesting-boring, graceful-awkward, and varied-monotonous. (2) *Personal affect* is measured by such scales as personal-impersonal, intimate-remote, emotional-rational, and vigorous-placid and objectively by a high proportion of pronouns, a high proportion of personal pronouns, and inversely by the number of syllables per word. (3) *Ornamentation* is measured by florid-plain, wordy-succinct, lush-austere, affected-natural, and complex-simple and objectively by long sentences, long clauses, wide variation in sentence length, high proportion of common nouns modified by adjectives or participials, long paragraphs, high proportion of nouns with Latin suffixes, a low proportion of verbs of physical action, a high proportion of dependent clauses, and a high proportion of descriptive adjectives. (4) *Abstractness* is measured by such scales as subtle-obvious, abstract-concrete, profound-superficial, complex-simple, hazy-clear, original-trite, and remote-intimate and objectively by a low proportion of numerical expressions, determining adjectives, participles, and pronouns, and a high proportion of noun clauses. (5) *Seriousness* is measured by earnest-flippant, serious-humorous, masculine-feminine, meaningful-meaningless, and profound-superficial and objectively by a low proportion of indefinite articles and a high proportion of indefinite and quantifying determining adjectives, and determiners. (6) *Characterization* (as opposed to narration) did not yield a high factor loading on any particular scales and therefore this dimension is postulated as a probable aspect of style whose meaning needs to be more fully investigated. It would be indexed objectively by a high proportion of transitive verbs and proper nouns.

Raymond Smith (1959, 1961, 1962) has constructed semantic differentials for use with speech-related concepts—general speech, theater, and speech correction. These scales are presented below; the general factor or dimension is given in italics with the relevant scales below.

GENERAL SPEECH CONCEPTS	SPEECH CORRECTION CONCEPTS	THEATER CONCEPTS
Optimism optimistic-pessimistic negative-positive	*Interestingness* boring-interesting empty-full narrow-broad	*Manner* excitable-calm hot-cold
Seriousness light-heavy serious-humorous	*Pleasantness* lenient-severe pleasurable-painful relaxed-tense	*Seriousness* serious-humorous tense-relaxed heavy-light
Honesty honest-dishonest true-false	*Honesty* honest-dishonest true-false	*Esthetic Value* beautiful-ugly pleasing-annoying pleasurable-painful
Value worthless-valuable meaningless-meaningful	*Difficulty* difficult-easy	*Ethical Value* valuable-worthless true-false honest-dishonest
Poise (*manner*) calm-excitable hot-cold		

Another semantic differential which should be mentioned here is one constructed by David Berlo, James Lemert, and Robert J. Mertz (1966) to measure speaker credibility. These researchers found three dimensions of credibility: (1) *safety*, measured by the scales safe-unsafe, just-unjust, kind-cruel, friendly-unfriendly, and honest-dishonest; (2) *qualification*, measured by the scales trained-untrained, experienced-inexperienced, skilled-unskilled, qualified-unqualified, and informed-uninformed; and (3) *dynamism*, measured by the scales aggressive-meek, emphatic-hesitant, bold-timid, active-passive, and energetic-tired.

That the semantic differential has found such wide acceptance (though see Weinreich, 1958; Osgood, 1959a; Carroll, 1959b) and application speaks clearly for the heuristic power of the mediational theory from which it was derived. It does not, however, argue its basic validity which, as in the case of Skinner's model, has been questioned. In fact, one of the major controversies in psycholinguistics today centers on the value of learning-theory approaches to language behavior (cf. Dixon and Horton, 1968). Since Skinner's model seems to have been abandoned by most psycholinguists, the current attack now focuses on mediational theories. On the one hand, psychologists such as O. Hobart Mowrer (1960b), Charles Osgood (1963b, 1966, 1968), Arthur Staats (1968), and D. E. Berlyne (1966), maintain that the general mechanism of behavioristic learning theories can account for language behavior or at least can be improved to the point where they will prove adequate. On the other hand, linguists and psychologists such as Noam Chomsky (1959), Jerry Fodor (1965, 1966a), David McNeill (1966c, 1968), Thomas Bever (1968), and Merrill Garrett (Garrett and Fodor, 1968; Bever, Fodor, and Garrett, 1968) argue that behavioristic learning theory accounts are *in principle* inadequate to the task.

One of the theory's assumptions is that the learning of words takes place through association with the actual object. Mowrer (1960b, p. 144), for example, states that "some part of the total reaction elicited by real thieves is shifted to the word 'thief'." Yet it is obvious that the meanings of many words are learned and understood without their being associated with the actual object. "Most well brought up children," Fodor (1965, p. 78) argues, "know what a thief is long before they meet one, and are adequately informed about dragons and elves though encounters with such fabulous creatures are, presumably, very rare indeed. Since it is clearly unnecessary to keep bad company to fully master the meaning of the word 'thief' a theory of language assimilation must account for communication being possible between speakers who have in fact learned items of their language under quite different conditions." This objection is at least not beyond the theory's capacity to handle (cf. Osgood, 1953). There is nothing inherent in the model which demands that the actual object be paired with the word. The original stimulus (Ś) can be one which has acquired a certain meaning and which can then function in much the same way that other stimuli (that is, actual objects) do. Thus, for example, the word *mermaid* can be learned from being associated with various other stimuli, such as pictures, verbal descriptions of tails and torsos, etc., and not necessarily from association with actual mermaids.

Another objection Fodor raises is that mediational models make no provision for the belief or disbelief one might have regarding a sentence. There are many sentences, for example, to which one does not respond in the manner the model states simply because the sentences are not believed. In a previous example the word *Fire!* served as a stimulus which set off various behavioral responses. But it would only do so if one believed there was an actual fire present. If this statement were not believed, one would obviously not respond in ways which are appropriate to the actual fire. Again, however, it appears that the model can incorporate belief, as an aspect of meaning, in the representational mediation process and the self-stimulation. Although the specific manner in which this would be done is not clear, a mechanism for handling belief does not seem inherently incompatible with a model such as Osgood has proposed.

Other objections raised may not be so easy to answer, however. For example, Fodor (1965) has pointed out that mediational models attempt to explain the learning and understanding of different types of words by the same basic process. In the sentence "Tom is a thief," the process of learning and understanding both *Tom* and *thief* is assumed to be basically the same. But clearly there are differences. Any native speaker knows that he can say "Who is Tom?" but not "Who is thief?" "What is a thief?" but not "What is a Tom?" and "What does *thief* mean?" but not "What does *Tom* mean?" In other words, there are basic differences in the way these words function but learning theories fail to explain what these differences are or how these differences are acquired by native speakers. Attempting to answer this argument Berlyne (1966, p. 410) says: "It is not conceivable that names and predicates might be different with respect to the wording of the questions by which we inquire into their meaning and yet similar in other respects, including those with which Mowrer is concerned?" Although this situation is certainly conceivable it is, nevertheless, begging the question. There is little value in building a theory which avoids the facts of language (by considering only similarities, for example) it was originally designed to explain.

The major objection to S-R theories derives from the distinction between surface and deep structure in contemporary linguistic theory. As has been noted (see Chapter 2) many sentences can only be understood on the basis of their deep structure. For example, in the sentence "The teacher's marks were low" an ambiguity is perceived because the sentence can have either one of two deep structures. In one *the teacher* is the subject (The teacher gives low marks) and in the other *the teacher* is the object (Someone gives the teacher low marks).

Furthermore, it has been shown that sentences whose surface structures more directly reflect their deep structure are easier to handle, for example, to recall or remember (cf. Miller, 1962; Garrett and Fodor, 1968; DeVito, 1969a).   Consider sentences (1) and (2).

(1) John is eager to please.
(2) John is easy to please.

As was noted in the previous chapter, *John* is the subject of the verb in the surface structures of both of these sentences.   In the deep structures, however, *John* is the subject of the verb in (1) but the object of the verb in (2). In other words, the surface structure of (1) more closely resembles its deep structure than does the surface structure of (2).   In an experiment on the ability to recall sentences of these types Blumenthal and Boakes (1967) found that when the first noun (*John*) is given as a prompt, sentences of type (1) are easier to recall than are sentences of type (2).   Yet the only way in which these sentences differ is in the relation between their surface and deep structures.   This example as well as various others which could be cited (cf. Garrett and Fodor, 1968) illustrate that the deep structure of sentences influences various behavioral phenomena.   Deep structure, in other words, has a psychological reality.

The objection, then, to behavioristic learning theory models is simply this: how does a model which deals only with observables account for the learning of linguistic facts (for example, those of deep structure) which are never observable?   This appears to be the crucial argument.   It seems clear that speakers learn and understand linguistic data which exist only in deep structure, data which are never overt in language usage.   Theories based solely on overt stimuli, as are S-R theories, seem incapable of dealing with such data.

Some psychologists appear content to pursue the application of such learning-theory models in those areas where they seem adequate, for example, in experiments dealing with nonsense syllables or word lists.   Although this research may be of some value it is clearly not concerned with language behavior in any meaningful sense.   Learning theories must confront squarely the relevant facts of language and language usage and this includes relations between deep and surface structures.

At this point it would seem premature to abandon such learning-theory models of language behavior, as some linguists have advised.   At the same time, however, it would be equally premature to dismiss the possibility that they may be inadequate "in principle."   More evidence seems needed before any definite conclusions are drawn.   What does seem clear is that there are certain aspects of language behavior for which learning-theory models cannot at present offer convincing explanations and these constitute definite inadequacies.

Charles Osgood (1968, p. 519) has, I think, expressed a reasonable direction for psycholinguistics: "None of us is very close to an understanding of how people create and understand sentences.   We will be wise to learn what we can from each other."

Chapter Four

Communication Theory

Some twenty years ago Claude Shannon published two papers on the mathematical theory of communication (Shannon and Weaver, 1949). In these papers Shannon proposed a method for quantifying information which has revolutionized the entire field of communication. The purpose of the theory and methodology was to provide answers to practical problems in electronic communication with which Shannon and Bell Telephone were primarily concerned.

Communication theory's principal contribution to the psychology of speech and language, at least as viewed here, is to provide methods for conceptualizing, understanding, and investigating the structures and functions of communication. For this reason our discussion avoids the specific mathematical formulas for quantifying information. Primary attention is focused on the elements or variables involved in communication (Communication Concepts) and the different ways in which the communication process may be viewed (Communication Models).

COMMUNICATION CONCEPTS

The model presented in Figure 11 represents *some* of the elements and *some* of the processes relevant to communication. The purpose of this diagram is to provide a visualization of some of the more important concepts essential to an understanding of speech, language, and communication as developed in this book. Other models are discussed in the second half of this chapter to clarify additional and more specific questions and to illustrate different approaches and points of view.

Like the actual communication act the model appears in a context which may be viewed as the specific communication situation. All communication takes place in some context, which, at the least, entails psychological, sociological, and physical dimensions. The psychological context is perhaps the most difficult to isolate but would involve, for example, the various attitudinal and motivational states of the communicators as well as their past histories, experiences, and knowledge. This psychological dimension might

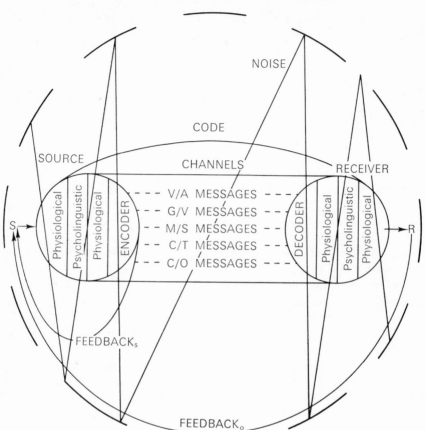

FIGURE 11. A Model of Communication Concepts

be described along such continua as friendly-hostile, formal-informal, serious-humorous, negative-positive, and optimistic-pessimistic. The sociological context would include, for example, the status relationships among speakers, their roles, and the norms and cultural mores of their society. The physical context is the actual place in which communication occurs such as a class-room, a lecture hall, a dimly lit nightclub, a park bench. It would also refer to such physical components as lighting and temperature.

All communication takes place in a context which exerts a powerful, but sometimes unperceived, influence on both the form and substance of the communication act; one does not communicate with a professor in a class-room and with a friend in a bar in the same way or about the same things. The psychological, sociological, and physical contexts are not independent of one another; rather they interact freely and continuously. If, for example, a room becomes extremely hot this might well lead to a more informal atmosphere and a breakdown in the roles people would normally be expected to play. When New York City experienced an electric power failure, the formal nature of communication which normally characterizes the interaction of strangers became much more informal, status relationships became less important, and numerous other changes were introduced because of this change in one contextual factor. The context in the diagram is represented as a broken circle to indicate that it is constantly changing. Numerous contextually relevant elements may be added, eliminated, or modified during the communication act.

The communication interchange begins with the stimulation of one of the parties. The stimulus (S) may be of various kinds; it may be external and physical such as a sound, a touch, or a visual object, or it may be some form of internal psychological stimulation such as an idea or a feeling.

This stimulation is perceived in some way by the source's or communicator's physiological system—he may feel, hear, see, taste, or smell the particular stimulus. This stimulation is then transmitted to the brain of the source which can best be viewed as his psycholinguistic system, that is, the system concerned with transferring physiological stimulation into thought and some form of linguistic representation. This thought or idea serves as a stimulus to his physiological system, again, and the source responds in some way.

In electronic communication the source is the speaker and the encoder is the device which transfers the linguistic symbols which the speaker emits into wave disturbances or electrical impulses. In telephone communication, for example, the encoder is the mouthpiece into which one speaks. In face-to-face communication, source and encoder refer to two different systems within the communicator. "Source" refers primarily to the communicator's conceptual system whereas "encoder" refers to his sound-producing system, that is, his vocal mechanism—diaphragm, lungs, larynx, articulators. The concept of source is often extended, and rightly so, to any person or group of persons who initiates communications. Thus a source could be a single individual speaking or writing or it could be a politician's speech-writing team, the staff of a newspaper, a political party, religious organization, union, or any such group that produces messages.

After the encoder processes the message, turning it into signals, these signals are sent across one or more channels. In human communication three primary channels are utilized. The most obvious and the most important is the Vocal/Auditory channel which carries sound and sound waves from mouth to ear. The Gestural/Visual channel, used primarily as an auxiliary channel, carries light waves from movements, signals, print, and the like to the eye of the receiver. A third channel, the Manipulative/Situational, carries messages resulting from the manipulation of various objects. The clearest example of this is probably the "language" of flowers developed into a sophisticated art form by the Japanese.

The Cutaneous/Tactile and the Chemical/Olfactory channels are also used in human communication, though to a lesser degree and in more subtle ways. The makers and users of hand lotions and nail files would testify to the importance of the former and producers and users of perfumes and deodorants would testify for the latter. These channels are of primary importance in many animal-communication systems and though they may serve only a limited function in most human communication they cannot be ignored.

The important point to note about these channels, which might better be thought of as bands within one large channel, is that they communicate information simultaneously and, therefore, one channel can add to or contradict information carried by another channel. For example, when someone pounds his fist to make a point more emphatic, the Gestural/Visual messages add to and supplement those from the Vocal/Auditory channel. When a person winks while speaking to indicate that he does not believe what he is saying or is just trying to fool the listener, the Vocal/Auditory messages are contradicted by the Gestural/Visual ones. In direct face-to-face human communication it is impossible to use only one channel and the communicator's task is to combine the information conveyed by these different channels in ways which are most effective for the given situation.

Edward T. Hall (1959, 1963, 1966), in the study he calls proxemics, has provided much new and significant insight by demonstrating how messages from these different channels may be analyzed and by relating them to the spatial dimension of communication. More formally, proxemics may be defined as the "study of how man unconsciously structures microspace—the distance between men in the conduct of their daily transactions, the organization of space in his houses and buildings, and ultimately the layout of his towns" (Hall, 1963, p. 1003).

Like verbal behavior proxemic behavior communicates; space speaks just as surely as do words. A speaker who stands close to his listener with his hands on the listener's shoulders and his eyes focused directly on those of his listener clearly communicates something completely different from the speaker who sits crouched in a corner with his arms folded and his eyes to the floor.

Like verbal and kinesic behavior, proxemic behavior is learned without any conscious or direct teaching by the adult community. The child is merely exposed to certain spatial relations and unconsciously internalizes them much as he seems to acquire the particular codes of speech or body motion. Probably the best way to explain proxemics is to briefly present the general classes of proxemic behaviors and their more specific categories as systematized by Hall (1963).

Postural-sex identifiers refer to the posture and sex of the communication source and receiver. Hall has divided this class into six possible categories: man prone, woman prone, man sitting or squatting, woman sitting or squatting, man standing, woman standing.

Sociofugal-sociopetal orientation, referring to the physical directness of the communication, specifies the relationship of one person's shoulders to the other person's. These positions are categorized on a nine-point scale ranging from face-to-face communication in which the shoulders of both parties are parallel through the situation in which the shoulders of the two parties form a straight line to the situation in which there is back-to-back communication and the shoulders are again parallel. The nine positions, then, are parallel face-to-face, 45° angle, 90°, 135°, 180°, 225°, 270°, 315°, and parallel back-to-back communication.

Kinesthetic factors refer to the closeness of the two persons involved in communication and the potential that exists for the holding, grasping, or touching of each other. The four major categories are within body contact distance, within touching distance with the forearm extended, within touching distance with the arm extended, and within touching distance by reaching. More specific degrees of closeness which lie between any two of these four major classes, for example, just outside body contact distance, might also be recorded.

Touch, referring to the amount and type of physical contact between the two parties, is quantified along a seven-point scale: caressing and holding, caressing and feeling, extended holding, holding, spot touching, brushing or accidental touching, and no contact.

Vision, the extent of visual contact between the two persons, is divided into four categories: sharp, focused looking at the other person's eyes; clear, focused looking at the person's face or head; peripheral, looking at the person in general but not focused on the head; and no visual contact.

Thermal factors, the amount of body heat of one person perceived by the other, are categorized into four types: detection of conducted heat, detection of radiant heat, probable detection of some kind of heat, and no detection of heat.

Smell, or olfactory communication, refers to the smelling of a person's body or breath odor. A five-fold categorization is proposed here: detection of differentiated body odor, detection of undifferentiated body odor, detection of breath odor, probable detection of some odor, and no detection of odor.

Loudness, or vocal volume, is described on a seven-point scale: silent, very soft, soft, normal, somewhat above normal, loud, and very loud.

These categories may appear at first to be somewhat rigid or too finely delineated. In analyzing proxemic behavior, however, adjacent categories can be combined to form more general ones or, if additional distinctions are needed, the categories may be further divided. Hall has presented this system as a tentative strategy for analyzing proxemic behaviors; certainly changes will be needed as research uncovers additional evidence bearing on the communicative function of space.

Despite the fact that little research has been conducted on proxemics its contribution is already great. It has succeeded in demonstrating the importance of nonverbal messages, in clarifying the nonobvious ways in which these messages may be communicated, and in providing a preliminary methodology for their analysis.

Returning to the signals, it should be noted that only part of them pass completely through the channels to the receiver. A small portion are fed back to the source. This information, called feedback, is in many ways similar to the more familiar feedback which comes to the source from the receiver. Both kinds are indicated in the model by arrows returning to the the source and both serve as additional stimuli for the source.

Feedback, although often neglected by inept writers and speakers, is probably the one element which can most successfully control behavior. Because of its importance in behavior control and in understanding communication some clarification of this concept is needed. As has been noted, feedback can come from oneself or from the receiver. The former may be designated as self-feedback (feedback$_s$ in the diagram) and the latter as other-feedback (feedback$_o$). Another way in which feedback can be distinguished is between positive and negative. Positive feedback is that which supports or reinforces behavior along the lines it is already proceeding in; negative feedback redirects the source's behavior or more specifically serves to correct his behavior.

The often cited example of the thermostat will serve to clarify the feedback concept (cf. Weinberg, 1959). In a home in which the thermostat is set for 72° information will be sent to the thermostat (from the heat of the room) when the temperature rises above or falls below this desired level. If the temperature falls due to a sudden snowfall, for example, then information in the form of temperature is sent to the thermostat which relays this information to the boiler. The boiler then increases the amount of heat it is producing. When this increased heat causes the temperature to reach the predetermined level of 72° then the thermostat "shuts off," to be reactivated only when the temperature again falls below or rises above 72°. The thermostat is a negative feedback mechanism; the information sent to the thermostat and by the thermostat to the boiler serves a corrective function, specifically to bring the temperature to 72°. It is *negative* in that it redirects or changes the activity of the source, in this case the boiler.

Suppose, however, that the thermostat went wild and that every time the temperature rose above 72° the thermostat would send information to the boiler which would effect an increase in its activity. This increase in the amount of heat the boiler was producing would raise the temperature of the room which would then lead the thermostat to signal the boiler to increase its heat production. This in turn would further increase the temperature of the room which would lead the thermostat to signal the boiler to further increase its production of heat which would naturally lead to a still further increase in the temperature of the room, etc. The process would continue indefinitely or until the house burned down or blew up. This thermostat-gone-wild is a positive feedback mechanism; the information fed back serves to increase the activity of the source along the lines it is already going; that is, increasing heat production.

Both negative and positive feedback are found in human communicative behavior. For example, a speaker addressing an audience might perceive yawning, wandering attention, and bored looks. This information is fed back to him, hopefully leading him to redirect his energies along different lines. The audience responses are examples of negative feedback. On the other hand, the speaker might perceive looks of acknowledged acceptance or pleasure while he is praising a particular political system, say, and this feedback may lead him to dwell on this point a bit longer, to claim the merits of this system more strongly, and so on. This is positive feedback—feedback which leads to behavioral activity along the lines already being followed.

Most often, however, positive feedback has a negative effect, as for example in stagefright, or at least in one theory of stagefright. Here a speaker is standing before a group and perhaps is somewhat fearful. He begins to feel his knees shaking. This information is fed back (that is, perceived by the speaker) and he begins to fear his shaking. This in turn leads him to shake all the more which then leads him to become more fearful of his shaking which then leads him to shake still more which then leads him to become still more fearful, and so on. If allowed to continue this positive feedback will generally result in some sort of breakdown.

The importance of feedback, however, is not limited to speaking situations such as those described in these examples. Rather, it is essential to all types of communication; without feedback communication as we know it could not exist. An example of the delayed auditory feedback experiment will illustrate this point (cf. Fairbanks and Guttman, 1958). In the typical experiment the speaker is equipped with earphones and speaks into a microphone both of which are connected to a specially adjusted tape recorder. In normal communication the feedback from hearing oneself is immediate. In this experiment, however, the feedback is delayed approximately one-fifth of a second by having the sound pass through a loop of tape before it returns to the speaker through the earphones. The effects from this brief delay are extreme. Speakers stutter, repeat, hesitate, lower their pitch, and increase their volume when reading even the simplest material. Generally after only a few minutes they will take off the earphones, amazed that this could prevent them from speaking coherently and fluently. Disturbances in drawing are also observed when the visual feedback is delayed (Smith, McCrary, and Smith, 1960).

Feedback is so vital to performance that it is seldom consciously recognized. A simple experiment the reader can perform which will illustrate the importance of feedback, in this case visual, is to stand on one foot noting how steady one's position can be maintained. Then note what happens when the eyes are closed.

Figure 11 shows that after the message is transmitted into signals and sent over the various communication channels the signals enter the decoder where they are changed into physiological or neurological impulses. These impulses are then sent to the brain or psycholinguistic system where they are given meaning. These meanings are then changed into physiological impulses which result in some kind of response.   The response need not be an overt behavioral one, of course.

The code, represented by a connecting line between source and receiver, refers to the rules or grammar of communication which override or govern the form of the various messages.   In the case where source and receiver are native speakers of English and communicating orally, the code is the grammar of spoken English.

Although the code for speech is the most important and the most carefully researched, it is not the only code used in communication.   There are in fact codes for all types of messages.   Gestural and spatial communication, as has been already indicated, are likewise governed by highly structured codes.   In much the same manner as the grammar of English, these codes influence both the transmission and reception of messages.   Messages which are not formed in accordance with the rules of the code will be misunderstood to the degree that they deviate from these rules.

To the extent that the codes of source and receiver differ, miscommunication will result.   The source and receiver who speak different dialects or even different languages will miscommunicate to the extent that their codes differ.   Put positively, they will communicate successfully to the extent that their codes overlap.   In the case of dialects the misunderstanding may be minimal; in the case of different languages it will be great.

Noise, another essential concept in this elementary model of communication, is denoted by lines running through each of the elements in the model. This particular representation of noise makes the model somewhat cluttered, unclear, and in general less aesthetically appealing than it might otherwise be.   Many communication models represent noise by a small box with an arrow entering the channel—a more artistically satisfying representation but probably much less accurate.   In this diagram noise distorts the model; this is precisely what noise does to communication.

For our purposes noise may be viewed as anything which distorts the message—that is, anything which interferes with the receiver's receiving the message as the source intended the message to be received.   Noise is present in the communication system to the degree that the message received is not the message intended.

Noise may originate from any of the elements in the communication act. It may originate in the source as a lisp or stutter, in the context as the sounds of a blasting radio or passing train, in the channel as faulty telephone wiring, or in the receiver as a hearing loss or visual defect.   Noise may even refer to the stereotypes in the minds of the source and/or receiver which prevent accurate communication exchange.   In written communication noise may refer to the print which shows through from the back of a page, misprints, blurred type, and the like.

Noise is always present.   Regardless of how ideal the communication situation may appear, noise will be present in some form and will distort the message to some extent.   Although noise can never be totally eliminated, it can be combatted and its effects reduced. One of the clearest and most often used defenses against noise is to introduce redundancy, another concept which needs more precise definition. But before defining redundancy, it is necessary to define more specifically what is meant by information, a term which has already been used but which has not been given a precise enough meaning.

In everyday language "information" and "meaning" are often used as closely related or even synonymous terms. In their more technical senses they are quite different. Information theory says nothing about meaning or meaningfulness. Nor does information refer to truth as opposed to falsity, to factual as opposed to inferential knowledge, or to whether there is belief or disbelief concerning the message.

In the sense in which it is used here and in communication theory "information" refers to amount of choice (cf. Miller, 1953). An example will help clarify this relationship. Suppose a machine were created which produced "information" in the form of answers to questions. Suppose further that Machine A would always give *yes* as an answer. Regardless of the question the machine would always respond *yes*. This machine has no choice; it must respond *yes* simply as a result of the way it was programed. The answers are completely predictable; one can predict with 100 percent accuracy how the machine will respond. This machine communicates no information because there is no choice. Put another way, it communicates no information because its responses are completely predictable.

Machine B, on the other hand, can answer *yes* or *no*. The probability of getting a *yes* is equal to the probability of getting a *no*—that is, each is 50 percent probable or each has a probability of .50. Intuitively it can be appreciated that in answering a question with either *yes* or *no* this machine will communicate at least some information. Machine B has choice and is not completely predictable. Machine C is still more versatile. Instead of being limited to *yes* and *no* this machine can respond *yes*, *no*, or *maybe*, each of which, it is assumed, has an equal probability of occurrence. Machine C will communicate more information than Machine B because it has more choices and because its answers are less predictable. Machine D, which can give any one of ten possible responses, communicates more information than all previous machines because its responses, being selected from a pool of ten, are less predictable than responses selected out of a pool of two or three.

The amount of choice which the machine has determines its information capacity. A machine which has no choice (A) has an information capacity of zero; a machine with two choices (B) has some information capacity; a machine with three choices (C) has a greater capacity; and a machine with ten choices (D) still greater capacity. The information capacity of a machine or of any system (mechanical or human) varies proportionally with its amount of choice.

Continuing with this example, suppose that another machine were to receive the output from Machines A, B, C, and D. That is, one machine would produce a symbol and this would serve as input to another machine. Let Machine B (which can produce either *yes* or *no*) be received by Machine X. Machine X can predict this response with 50 percent accuracy. Since there are only two choices it has a 50–50 chance of guessing correctly. Machine Y, which receives the answers from Machine C, can predict with 33 percent accuracy and Machine Z, receiving the answers from D, can predict with only 10 percent accuracy. When dealing with Machine D there is greater uncertainty than when dealing with Machines B and C. Similarly, there is greater uncertainty when dealing with C than with B. With Machine A there is no uncertainty.

The answers or responses from Machines B, C, and D all reduce uncertainty but since there is more uncertainty with D than with C, and more with C than with B, the response from D reduces more uncertainty than does the response from C which in turn reduces more uncertainty than the reponse from B. In other words, the more uncertainty that is reduced the more information is communicated. Machine D, then, communicates more information than Machine C since it reduces more uncertainty. Similarly, C communicates more information than B since it reduces more uncertainty. Machine A communicates no information since it does not reduce uncertainty; there was, in fact, no uncertainty to begin with.

On the production end, information is best viewed as the amount of choice in a system; the more choice the system has the more information its responses communicate. On the receiving end, information refers to uncertainty and its reduction. When the uncertainty is high a response will communicate much information; when the uncertainty is low a response will communicate little information.

Suppose, now, that a language were created which contained sixty-four sounds, labeled for convenience with the numbers 1 to 64. If a machine were programed to speak this language each sound, when produced, would communicate a certain amount of information. Assume further that the machine first gave clues as to which sound it was going to produce. If the machine said that the sound was going to be from the first half, that is, from numbers 1 to 32, it would have cut the number of alternatives in half and would have increased our ability to predict the sound to be produced. When the alternatives are cut in half, as in this example, one bit of information is communicated. ("Bit" is an abbreviation for binary digit and is also referred to as "binet" or "bigit.") Similarly, the machine would have communicated one bit of information if it had said that the sound would be from the second half, that is, from numbers 33 to 64, or that it would be an even number, or an odd number. In each of these conditions the number of alternatives is cut in half and our ability to correctly predict the sound is increased.

If the machine had said that the sound was going to be an even number from the upper half, that is, from numbers 34, 36, 38, ... 64, this would communicate more information than the clue given above since it reduces more uncertainty. This clue divides the number of alternatives in half twice. The information that the sound was going to be from the upper half cut the alternatives in half (from 64 to 32) and these alternatives were then cut in half again (from 32 to 16) by the information that the sound was denoted by an even number. This information, since it divided the number of alternatives in half twice, consisted of two bits. In order to predict the exact sound six bits of information would have to be communicated. Each bit would divide the alternatives in half until only one "alternative" is left. The production of a given sound, then, communicates the amount of information which would be necessary to specify it by successive halvings of the alternatives. In the case of a language consisting of sixty-four alternatives, each sound would communicate six bits of information since six bits are needed to locate or specify the sound by repeated halvings of the initial sixty-four alternatives.

In the familiar game of twenty questions in which yes/no questions are asked in order to guess a particular object, the assumption made is that any object in one of the three kingdoms (animal, vegetable, mineral) can be specified in twenty successive halvings. Twenty halvings would enable one to specify one out of an initial class of 1,048,576 objects, that is, 2^{20} (cf. Bendig, 1953).

The example selected is a very simple one and in cases in which there are more alternatives than sixty-four, where the alternatives cannot be evenly divided by two, and where each alternative has a different probability of being selected, the computation of the amount of information which each item communicates becomes more involved. What is important to note is that information, conceived in this way, can be measured precisely.

One of the implications of this theory is that information is always lost in transmission—the more systems or channels it passes through the more information is lost. Thus in the transmission of rumor, for example, where information passes through numerous sources, channels, and receivers a great deal of information is lost. In human communication information is not lost randomly. Much as there is selective learning and retention there is selective loss of information which is influenced by numerous psychological factors. The attitude of the receiver, one of the most potent influences, might serve as an example. Levine and Murphy (1943) divided their subjects into two groups, anticommunist and procommunist, and presented them with anticommunist and procommunist messages. The subjects, it was found, learned more information that was in accordance with their attitudes than information which was contrary to these attitudes. In a later study, Taft (1954) had both favorable and unfavorable items concerning Negroes read to both Negro and white students. The results showed that Negroes learned and retained, after a period of three days, more favorable items and forgot, after three days, more unfavorable items than did the white subjects.

The point made by these and similar studies is simply this: humans are not machines and consequently they do not take in, process, or give out information as do machines. Humans are extremely subjective creatures and their responses to information are likewise subjective. Machine analogies are useful for clarifying the abstract characteristics and relationships of communication systems but can mislead when carried too far.

In any communication system, then, there is a certain amount of unpredictability or uncertainty or entropy. (*Entropy* is a measure of the amount of uncertainty in a system.) When information is communicated this entropy is reduced and has led to the definition of information as negative entropy or negentropy. Although it is probably difficult at the present time to appreciate the importance of this simple equation, according to Ruesch and Bateson (1951) the recognition of this relationship between information and entropy marked the greatest single shift in human thinking since Plato and Aristotle.

Opposed to entropy is redundancy. In English composition redundancy refers to repeating oneself, using too many words to express an idea, or saying things twice. Expressions such as *yellow jaundice*, we are told, are redundant since "jaundice" means "yellow" and in using this expression we are actually saying *yellow yellow*. In communication theory redundancy has a similar meaning though it is made somewhat more precise. Redundancy is defined as the degree to which a message unit is predictable. A highly predictable signal will be of high redundancy and a signal of extremely low predictability will be of low redundancy. In English orthography, for example, the letter *u* must follow the letter *q*. Given the letter *q* the *u* is completely predictable and hence totally redundant.

As has already been pointed out, language signals cannot be arranged randomly—there are structure and rules which must be followed. These rules increase the predictability and redundancy of language signals. For example, the rule stating that *u* must follow *q* makes the *u* completely predictable or redundant. Machine A, discussed earlier, which had only one answer to give to every question, was totally redundant. There was no uncertainty; its responses were totally predictable. The responses did not reduce entropy since they communicated no information.

All natural languages have redundancy built into them. The clearest example in English is the q-u sequence. But there are numerous other instances where some degree of redundancy is present. For example, not all letters or phonemes can follow an initial *t*; another *t* cannot be used, nor can a *k* or a *g*. Similarly, for each letter and phoneme there are certain letters and phonemes which cannot immediately follow or immediately precede. Because of these restrictions predictability is increased since the language code has already excluded a number of possibilities. Other examples which might be cited are that the phoneme /ŋ/ cannot begin a word or syllable and /h/ cannot end a word. These rules, again, serve to increase predictability and reduce entropy.

Another characteristic of language which serves to introduce re-

dundancy is the fact that each sound has a different probability of occurrence. For example, /e/ is used more often than /z/; hence /e/ is more
redundant, more predictable, reduces less entropy and, therefore, communicates less information than /z/. It might help to visualize a crossword
puzzle at this point. If it is known from filling in some of the words that the
word one is looking for begins with /e/ this is of some help since all words
not beginning with /e/ are excluded as possibilities. But it would be easier
to fill in the word if one knew that the word began with /z/. There are fewer
words beginning with /z/ than with /e/ and consequently knowing that the
word begins with /z/ greatly reduces the number of possibilities. Since the
number of words beginning with /e/ is relatively large this information (that
the word begins with /e/) would not reduce uncertainty to as great an extent
as would the information of the /z/.

The amount of information which a particular speech signal communicates, then, depends partially on the nature of the language code. To
illustrate further, try to read the following mutilated sentence in which
every third letter has been omitted

Na_ur_ ha_gi_en _o m_n o_e t_ng_e, b_t t_o e_rs, _ha_ we _ay _ea_
fr_m o_he_s t_ic_ as _uc_ as _e s_ea_.

Even though one-third of the letters are missing one can still make some sense
out of this statement. In the next example deletions of a different type were
made:

Th_ tr__ _s_ _f sp__ch _s n_t s_ m_ch t_ _xpr_ss __r w_nts _s t_ c_nc__l
th_m.

The second sentence, in which all the vowels were omitted, was probably
easier to reconstruct. The uncertainty created by the omission of vowels
is not as great as the uncertainty created by the random omission of sounds
or letters. In the case of vowel omission one has a fairly good chance of
selecting the right one since there are relatively few vowels from which to
choose. If this was all the information one had available, it would still be
difficult to complete a mutilated sentence such as that given here. Since we
are dealing here with letters the probability of correctly guessing the missing
letter would be one-sixth since there are six vowels from which to choose.
There are, however, additional clues in the sentence which increase the
probability of correct guesses. For example, the vowel sound which follows
th and precedes a space can only be *e* since the other vowels (a, i, o, u, and y)
would not form an acceptable English word. (*Thy* is probably rare enough
to be disregarded in such a sequence.) So in this case there was no real
uncertainty, no entropy, and hence the letter *e* was completely predictable.

The two extremes of vocabulary redundancy in English prose are
probably passages written in Basic English (a language consisting of only

850 words) and James Joyce's *Finnegans Wake* which supposedly contains the largest vocabulary of any English work. The former would be highly redundant while the latter would be low in redundancy. The redundancy in Basic English would be reflected in the tremendous expansion necessary to write a passage of normal English into Basic English. For example, the single words *descend*, *leave*, and *enter* would be rendered in Basic English as *go down*, *go out*, and *go into*. *Finnegans Wake*, in drawing from an extremely large vocabulary, would be capable of compressing ideas into relatively few words (cf. Miller, 1951).

Utilizing this basic notion of relative redundancy Wilson Taylor (1953, 1956) developed a research tool which he calls "cloze procedure." Because this methodology has been used extensively in communication research and because it clarifies the concepts of redundancy and information, it would be well worth considering.

"Cloze" is derived from the Gestalt notion of closure—the tendency to perceive as complete (or closed) forms which are actually incomplete. It is, for example, the tendency to perceive broken or incomplete circles as whole circles. Even though much of a circle is missing it is perceived as a whole because the part which remains recalls a pattern which is so familiar.

Cloze procedure can best be thought of as the application of closure to language. For example, in the sentence "Adults sigh but babies_____" the word which is missing is obviously *cry*. Filling in the word *cry*, however, depends not only on a knowledge of babies and their behavior but also on a knowledge of the language. A speaker of English knows that the missing word must be a verb since it follows a noun. He knows also that the verb must be *cry* (rather than *cries*) since its noun is plural.

In using cloze procedure a written or oral message of approximately 250 words is mutilated by deleting every fifth word. This mutilated version is then given to a group of receivers to complete. One point is scored for each fill-in which is exactly the same as the deleted word. The total number of points is the "cloze score." From these scores two general types of inferences can be drawn. First, the difficulty of the message can be inferred —easy messages will contain a high percentage of correct fill-ins whereas difficult messages will contain a low percentage of correct fill-ins. Second, one can infer the degree to which the receiver understood a message given in mutilated form. In drawing inferences concerning the difficulty of the message we have what is more commonly referred to as a measure of readability; in drawing inferences concerning the receiver's understanding we have essentially a measure of comprehension.

In order to demonstrate that cloze procedure could serve as a measure of readability Taylor (1953) applied cloze to various passages for which Flesch and Dale-Chall readability scores were available and found that cloze procedure ranked the passages in exactly the same way as did these standard formulas. Taylor also demonstrated that readability formulas would break down when forced to deal with certain types of messages whereas cloze procedure would not. He selected passages from Erskine Caldwell, James Joyce, and Gertrude Stein. Intuitively, we know that Caldwell is the easiest, despite his use of long sentences, that Joyce is difficult, primarily because of the unfamiliar vocabulary, and that Stein is the most difficult because of her peculiar arrangement of common words. Flesch and Dale-Chall readability scores as well as cloze procedure scores were computed for these passages. Flesch ranked Caldwell and Joyce as equally difficult whereas Dale-Chall ranked Caldwell as easier than Joyce. Both formulas ranked Stein as the easiest, something we " know " is not true. However, cloze procedure ranked the passages in the same order that we arrive at intuitively, thus giving cloze findings greater face validity.

Cloze procedure, then, provides accurate rankings in terms of difficulty where other approaches fail. The reason for this is that cloze takes into consideration *all* language factors influencing readability. The Flesch formula accounts for sentence and word length only and the Dale-Chall formula accounts for sentence length and difficulty of vocabulary only. Since the difficulty of Stein depends primarily on the arrangement of words, neither formula can provide an accurate measurement.

In order to test the validity of cloze procedure as a measure of comprehension Taylor (1957) obtained two carefully matched comprehension tests which were both based on the same article. He then took samples of the article and made them into cloze tests by deleting certain words. Before the subjects read the article they were given a before-comprehension test and a before-cloze test. After reading the article they were given an after-comprehension test and an after-cloze test.

The before and after cloze scores correlated highly with the before and after comprehension scores, respectively, demonstrating that cloze results serve as valid comprehension scores. Furthermore, since IQ scores were available for these subjects Taylor also correlated the IQ scores with the comprehension-test and cloze scores. Cloze scores, it was found, correlated more highly with IQ than did the comprehension-test scores.

Variations in the methods of deletion and scoring can, of course, be employed. This flexibility which the general methodology allows increases the potential applications of this tool to a broad range of psycholinguistic problems and questions (cf. Osgood, 1959b; DeVito, 1967a). For example, although words are most commonly deleted it is possible to delete other linguistic units such as morphemes, constituents, or even transformations. One might devise a cloze test in which only certain syntactic or semantic markers are omitted, for example, references to tense or sex. Or one might delete only evaluative terms or only references to motivational states. Similarly, instead of scoring only exact fill-ins as correct, alternative procedures might be used. For example, any word or linguistic unit of the same form class or part of speech as the deleted unit might be scored as correct. The range of possibilities seem limited only by the number of linguistic units.

The concepts considered in this section are certainly not the only ones important in communication theory.   They are, however, some of the more useful terms for conceptualizing and for talking about communication. Some of these will become clearer and more meaningful when viewed in the various communication models which have been proposed.

COMMUNICATION MODELS

We live in two different worlds—a real world of people, objects, and events and a symbolic world of words, visual symbols, gestures, and a myriad of other forms and actions representing, signifying, and symbolizing reality. When compared with the infinite complexity, constant change, and non-identity of the real world, the symbolic world is indeed a simple one.

Because of the real world's complexity it is extremely difficult to deal with it without some framework, without some abstract conception of what one is looking for.   And although creating an abstraction is not always profitable, in the study of communication, man's most complex activity, it is probably a useful procedure.   With such an abstraction one can examine essential elements, exclude irrelevant ones, and visualize important processes more easily than would otherwise be possible.   One of the best ways of achieving this abstraction is to construct a model.

The most familiar models are probably miniature replicas of cars or airplanes—miniatures which are like the original in most essential respects. With communication, however, a model cannot be of this type simply because communication is not solely a physical thing.   Furthermore, it would be impossible to construct a model which included all the elements and pro-cesses which exist in the actual communication act, simply because we do not know what all these features are, how they function, or what their relationships might be.   But even if completeness were possible, it would not necessarily be desirable.   The purpose of a model is not to include *all* features of *every* communication act but only those common to all acts of communication.   In other words, a model should include only the univer-sals of communication.

Before presenting any communication model, the general purposes or functions which such models serve should be considered.   Our discussion will follow Deutsch's (1952) general outline.

One of a model's primary functions is to organize the various elements and processes of the communication act.   Before the model is constructed it may not be clear which elements are important, which elements influence each other, which processes are essential, or where these processes operate. The model makes these explicit.   Although it is not possible for any model to organize all available data, one can expect a reasonably good model to organize some of the facts in a relatively concise and meaningful way.

A model also serves a heuristic function; it aids in the discovery of new hypotheses, new facts, and new ways of looking at communication. The heuristic function is a research-generating function; the model generates questions which can be researched and perhaps answered, at least in part.

Third, models enable one to make predictions concerning what will happen given some change in the basic processes or elements. For example, a model which explicated the various channels through which communication could take place, would enable one to make predictions concerning the relative amounts of information which might be communicated by different media, for example, television as opposed to radio or radio as opposed to face-to-face communication. A model which failed to incorporate multiple channels could not make such predictions.

Another function is to provide measurements of the elements and processes involved in communication. Such a model would contain explicit statements concerning, for example, the relative importance of different communication channels and the means by which the information each transmits could be quantified.

One can then evaluate models in terms of their ability to serve these four major functions. The better a model serves to organize the relevant elements and processes, to generate research, to predict, and to measure, the more valuable is the model. In addition one would also employ the more traditional criteria for evaluating theories, namely, simplicity, originality, and realism.

Models should be, to some degree at least, original. That is, models may be expected to organize the relevant variables in a manner which is not totally obvious or self-evident. If a model is not original, at least to some extent, then it fails to provide any new information and really serves no useful function.

One would also expect a model to explain communication with some degree of simplicity. Given two models each of which meets all the other requirements equally, the simpler of the two would be regarded as the better. This criterion is not used solely for the ease it may afford in communicating the knowledge or insight but rather is based on the premise that the simpler the model the more general it will be. With increased generality comes increased applicability.

Lastly, a model of communication should explain the process with some degree of realism. The assumption made here is that the more realistic a model is, that is, the more it conforms to reality, the more of a chance it has of accurately representing significant variables and relationships.

Because of the significant insights into the structure and function of communication provided by models, a number of useful and provocative models are examined here. As already noted, one of the functions communication models serve is that of organizing complex data. However, in the past few decades there have been so many models proposed that *en masse* they appear to have added complexity to an already complex subject.

Some system or scheme, therefore, seems necessary for organizing these models. A number of such systems have been proposed. One system classifies models on a continuum of abstractness; here there are iconic or physical models at one extreme and symbolic or mathematical models at the other. Another classification is based on the functions of models previously discussed. In this system models which organize would be grouped into one class, models which predict into another class, and so on. Still another system classifies models according to their form, for example, physical models, verbal models, pictorial models.

None of these classifications, however, seems suitable for organizing or providing a typology of the numerous communication models. Such classifications either emphasize characteristics which are extraneous to the actual workings of the model (as in the case of abstractness and form) or set up categories which are not separate and distinct but rather interrelated and interdependent (as in the case of function).

The classification adopted here attempts to avoid these problems and utilizes a system based on the communication variable and language function the model focuses on or to which it has its primary orientation. The classes are then labeled according to the discipline or area of study most concerned with the specific variable or language function. This classification is based on the functions of language proposed by Roman Jakobson (1960) and already considered in the discussion of "The Functions of Speech and Language" (Chapter 1).

Metalinguistic Models

This first category includes those models which have as their primary orientation the code, that is, the syntax or grammar, of communication and which thus focus on language in its metalingual aspect. Metalinguistic models are higher order or more abstract models which serve as means for conceptualizing or talking about lower order or more concrete models. Jakobson's model may be considered the archetype of this class.

Models having a similar orientation are also grouped here and would include those which are clearly research-oriented. These are the models which serve to present in general and abstract terms the areas for communication research and study. One of the most famous of these models was proposed by Harold Lasswell (1948). The model, presented in Figure 12, lists in sequential order the essential components of the communication act with their corresponding research areas. George Gerbner (1956), in the Lasswell tradition, advances a similar model of communication components and their areas of study (Figure 13).

Other models in this class and which the reader may wish to consult include Osgood and Sebeok's (1954) model of the essential communication act, which describes the disciplines concerned with human communication and their provinces or areas of interest, and Franklin Knower's (1963)

Communication Component	Research Area
WHO	CONTROL ANALYSIS
SAYS WHAT	CONTENT ANALYSIS
IN WHAT CHANNEL	MEDIA ANALYSIS
TO WHOM	AUDIENCE ANALYSIS
WITH WHAT EFFECT	EFFECT ANALYSIS

FIGURE 12. A Metalinguistic Model of Communication. *Adapted from Harold D. Lasswell, "The Structure and Function of Communication in Society," in Lyman Bryson, ed.* The Communication of Ideas *(New York: Harper, 1948), p. 37.*

model for a communicology, which describes the essential aspects of communication as well as the related disciplines which rely on and contribute to the insights of communication. Westley and MacLean's (1957) and Schramm's (1954) communication models would also be included here since these are primarily research oriented, providing convenient schematic representations of the aspects for communication research and study.

Communication Component	Research Area
SOMEONE	COMMUNICATOR/AUDIENCE RESEARCH
PERCEIVES AN EVENT	PERCEPTION RESEARCH AND THEORY
AND REACTS	EFFECTIVENESS MEASUREMENT
IN A SITUATION	PHYSICAL/SOCIAL SETTING RESEARCH
THROUGH SOME MEANS	MEDIA INVESTIGATION
TO MAKE AVAILABLE MATERIALS	ADMINISTRATION; DISTRIBUTION
IN SOME FORM	STRUCTURE; ORGANIZATION; STYLE
AND CONTEXT	COMMUNICATIVE SETTING
CONVEYING CONTENT	CONTENT ANALYSIS; STUDY OF MEANING
OF SOME CONSEQUENCE	OVERALL CHANGES STUDY

FIGURE 13. A Metalinguistic Model of Communication. *From George Gerbner, "Toward a General Model of Communication,"* Audio-Visual Communication Review, *IV (1956), 173.*

Metalinguistic models, then, can all be viewed as abstract conceptions of communication, having the code of communication as their primary emphasis and metalingual concepts as their principal product.

Mathematical Models

The second class of models focuses on the message—its analysis and quantification. These models, often grouped together as information-theory models, are not concerned with messages in terms of meaning, persuasive appeal, or truth value but simply with the information carried.

In considering this communication variable Jakobson observes that its orientation is to poetic language; and in the context of literature and style, in which the model was developed, this would be accurate. However, more generally, the defining feature of this language function is the importance of its form as opposed to meaning or content. The models in this second category are all concerned with the message in terms of form. Information theorists and mathematical models concentrate on the message conceived as linguistic units, each with varying degrees of predictability or information content. Mathematical models are concerned solely with form, or more specifically, with the selection and arrangement of linguistic units measured in terms of their relative entropy.

The best known example of this category is the Shannon and Weaver (1949) mathematical theory of communication. A diagram of the essential features of this model is presented in Figure 14.

Communication, according to this model, follows a simple left to right process. The information source, say a speaker, selects a desired message from all possible messages. The message is sent through a transmitter, for example, a microphone, and is changed into signals. In telephone com-

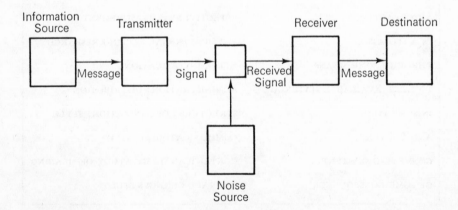

FIGURE 14. A Mathematical Model of Communication. *From Claude E. Shannon and Warren Weaver,* The Mathematical Theory of Communication *(Urbana: University of Illinois Press, 1949), p. 5.*

munication these signals would be electrical impulses and would be sent over a communication channel such as a wire. The signals are received by a receiver, for example, an earphone of some kind, changed back into a message, and given over to the destination, say a listener. In the process of transmission certain things are added to the signal which were not intended by the information source and these added distortions constitute noise.

This model, and the theory on which it is based, allows for great precision in the measurement of information. This model has been generalized by numerous writers and probably underlies most of the communication models we now have. Its great weakness is that it describes communication as a simple linear process going from speaker to listener. Because of the presence of feedback human communication is more a circular process than a linear one.

Other models which have followed in this tradition such as those of Colin Cherry (1957), Norbert Wiener (1954), and J. R. Pierce (1961) would also be included here.

Rhetorical Models

Models oriented to the receiver, particularly in terms of attitude and behavior changes, are clearly within the province of what is usually referred to as rhetoric.

Aristotle's *Rhetoric* and, in fact, every communication-skills textbook constitutes a rhetorical model of communication. David Berlo (1960) has advanced a model, presented in Figure 15, which might be used to illustrate this particular class. The principal function of this model is to identify those elements or variables which are important in the process of communication. In fact, Berlo labels it "a model of the ingredients in communication."

Source	Message	Channel	Receiver
COMMUNICATION SKILLS	ELEMENTS	SEEING	COMMUNICATION SKILLS
ATTITUDE	STRUCTURE	HEARING	ATTITUDES
KNOWLEDGE	CONTENT	TOUCHING	KNOWLEDGE
SOCIAL SYSTEM	TREATMENT	SMELLING	SOCIAL SYSTEM
CULTURE	CODE	TASTING	CULTURE

FIGURE 15. A Rhetorical Model of Communication. *From David Berlo,* The Process of Communication *(New York: Holt, Rinehart and Winston, 1960), p. 72.*

In this model there are four major components: source, message, channel, and receiver. Each of these can be looked at as containing elements or variables essential to communication. That is, each of these four components contains subcomponents which must be considered in describing the communication process.

In regard to the source or speaker one must consider such factors as communication skills (speaking and writing abilities), attitudes, knowledge, social system (for example, the roles he fulfills, the functions he is expected to perform, the prestige which people attach to him), and cultural system (for example, the beliefs and values which are dominant in his culture and the various acceptable and unacceptable forms of behavior). Similarly, one needs to consider the identical factors in discussing the receiver except that under communication skills the focus would be on listening and reading abilities.

There are three main factors in the message: content, treatment, and code. The content consists of such things as the assertions the speaker makes, the information he presents, the facts and opinions he advances. The treatment refers to the way or style in which the content is presented; it is, in a sense, the form given to the content. When a speaker encodes a message he has various choices available; his decisions at these choice points define his treatment for the content. The code refers to the language used and its rules, for example, English.

Each of these three components consists of elements and structure. The elements of the content are the individual ideas or facts and the structure is the pattern of these ideas or their organization. The elements of the treatment are the individual choices the speaker makes and the structure is the pattern of these choices. The elements of the code are the phonemes, morphemes, words, etc., and the structure is the grammar of the language. The elements and structure of the code exist on different levels. For example, at the most microscopic level the elements are the phonemes of the language, at a higher level the elements are morphemes, and at a still higher level the elements are words and constituents. When phonemes are the elements, structure refers to the rules of phoneme arrangement; when the elements are morphemes, structure refers to the rules for morpheme arrangement.

Messages can come through any of the five senses or channels—sight, hearing, touch, smell, and taste.

As an explanation of the ingredients of communication, this model serves its function only partly. It fails to incorporate a number of essential factors such as the beliefs of the speaker and listener, their psychological motivation, feedback, and noise. The model's principal weakness appears to be its failure to specify relationships existing among the various elements or subcomponents. For example, it includes the code as part of the message when in fact the message is a manifestation of the code.

A model of a somewhat different type, though also receiver oriented, is

Herbert C. Kelman's (1961) theory of compliance, identification, and internalization as the three basic processes by which people respond to social influence and by which opinions are changed.

These models, in focusing on the reception of messages, generally include only those factors which are of consequence in describing and controlling changes produced in the receiver. Rhetorical models concentrate on directive or conative language—language which has no necessary truth value but rather serves to command, to influence, to persuade.

Psychological Models

Communication models oriented to the source are many and varied. However, these models are all held together by one common and primary purpose—the understanding of the source and the analysis of the language as a means to that end. Whereas the models of Skinner, Mowrer, and Osgood, considered in the previous chapter, are general models of behavior which are applicable to language, the models considered here are of more limited scope and focus almost exclusively on only one aspect of behavior, namely communication.

A model developed by Joseph Wepman and his associates (Wepman, Jones, Bock, and Van Pelt, 1960) from their work on aphasia (see Chapter 6) may be used to illustrate this class. The model, presented in Figure 16, focuses solely on the source, though an identical model placed to the

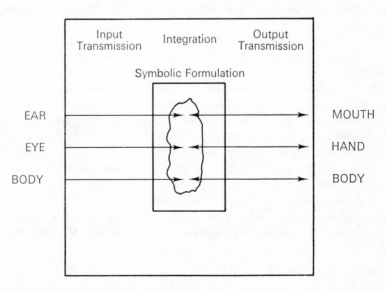

FIGURE 16. A Psychological Model of Communication. *From Joseph M. Wepman, Lyle V. Jones, R. Darrell Bock, and Doris Van Pelt, "Studies in Aphasia: Background and Theoretical Formulations,"* Journal of Speech and Hearing Disorders, *XXV (1960), 325.*

immediate left with connecting channels, would give us the traditional two-person communication system.

There are in this model three basic processes: (1) input transmission of signals to the end organs of the ear, eye, and body to the brain; (2) their integration into some meaningful symbolic formulation; and (3) their output transmission from the end organs of mouth, hand, and body. The end organs for input and output transmission serve to define the three major channels in this model. The ear-mouth organs define the auditory-verbal channel, the eye-hand organs the visual-graphic channel, and the body-body organs the tactual-gestural channel.

Although basic, this model adequately serves its purpose, namely, to elucidate what are to Wepman the three major types of language disturbance: agnosia and apraxia are disruptions involving input and output transmission, respectively, and aphasia is a disruption involving the integration of symbols. The language is analyzed as a means of providing insight into the workings of the communication source.

Other psychological models have been proposed by Jurgen Ruesch and Franklin Fearing. Ruesch (1953, p. 215) has advanced "a communication model suitable for the study of the psychiatrist's operations" as an aid "to improve the communication methods of the patient." Although Ruesch necessarily considers many of the elements and processes included in the other models, his focus is on language as an indicator of the communicator's psychological states, his needs, his values, his attitudes. Insofar as language serves this "indicator" function it may be termed emotive—regardless of the conscious attempts of the communicator to inform, to persuade, or to create bonds with others.

Another similar model, developed by Franklin Fearing (1953, p. 71), places human communicative behavior "in the context of the current formulations regarding cognitive-perceptual processes conceived as dynamically related to the need-value systems of individuals." When these need-value systems interact with the environment instabilities and disequilibria result. One's values may be changed or one's needs shown to be impossible to fulfill, for example. Because these disequilibria are productive of tension the environment is so structured by the cognitive-perceptual processes so as to reduce this tension. The communication theory proposed, then, is an attempt to formulate more clearly those relationships, elements, and processes necessary for a better understanding of the "how and why of human loquacity (and related processes)." The emphasis here also is on the source and on language as an indicator of psychological processes.

Semantic Models

Models focusing on the referent and the referential function of language are clearly semantic in their emphasis, giving primary attention to the relationship between symbols and referents and between symbol users and referents. Although not generally thought of as communication models, they do define essential variables in the communication act and add considerably to our understanding of the communication process.

Most prominent among the semantic models are I. A. Richards' triangle of meaning and Alfred Korzybski's structural differential which have already been considered (Chapter 1). Another semantic model, developed by Wendell Johnson (1951), is presented in Figure 17. Although this model

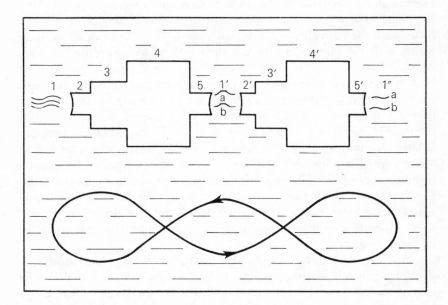

FIGURE 17. A Semantic Model of Communication. *From Wendell Johnson, "The Spoken Word and the Great Unsaid,"* Quarterly Journal of Speech, *XXXVII (1951), 421.*

may at first seem complex it is actually quite simple. The enclosing rectangle indicates that communication takes place in a context external to the actual communication process as well as to speaker and listener. The curved loop indicates the functional relationships of the various stages involved in the communication act; the stages, rather than being discrete events, are interrelated and interdependent.

Although a basic left to right model of communication, Johnson's conception, unlike the information theory model, takes into consideration a number of other important factors. The communication process begins at 1 which signifies the occurrence of an event. This "event" refers to anything that a person can perceive; it is the stimulus. Although not all communication occurs with reference to such external stimuli, according to Johnson, communication makes sense only when it does in some way relate to the real world.   At 2 the observer is stimulated through one or more of his sensory channels.   The opening at 2 is illustrated as relatively small to emphasize that out of all the possible sources of stimulation in the world only a small part of these actually stimulate the observer.   In General Semantics terminology, at 2 the observer is abstracting certain characteristics of the world.

At 3 organismic evaluations occur.   Here nerve impulses travel from the sense organs to the brain which effect certain bodily changes in, for example, muscular tension.   At 4 the feelings which were aroused at 3 are beginning to be translated into words, a process which takes place in accordance with the individual's unique language habits.   Individuals speaking widely differing languages translate their feelings in very different ways. An Arab, for example, in referring to a horse would be very specific since his language contains many specific terms for horse and yet no general ones. An English speaker, on the other hand, would translate his feelings more generally into *horse*.   If necessary he could, of course, modify or qualify this noun in various ways.   The point made here is simply that the language habits of the individual control to some extent the way in which his feelings are translated into linguistic symbols.   At 5 he selects from all the possible linguistic symbols certain ones which he will use and arranges them into some pattern.   The actual words he selects are extremely few when compared to the large number of possible words and are dependent in part upon his unique language habits and in part upon the restrictions his grammar imposes.

At 1' the words which the speaker utters, by means of sound waves, or the words which he writes, by means of light waves, serve as stimulation for the hearer, much as 1 served as stimulation for the speaker.   At 2' the hearer is stimulated, at 3' there are organismic evaluations, at 4' his feelings are beginning to be translated into words, at 5' certain of these symbols are selected and arranged, and at 1″ these symbols, in the form of sound and/or light waves, are emitted and serve as stimulation for another hearer   The process is, of course, a continuous one.

Johnson's model emphasizes in relatively simple terms the importance of the individual's verbal habits and internal reactions and clarifies the nature of abstracting in general communication.   Most important, however, and the reason for its being included as a semantic model, is that it makes clear that the words selected, at stage 4, are selected by a functioning organism and that they consequently refer to the reality only through the speaker.   This is the same point made in Richards' triangle of meaning.

Sociological Models

One of the most controversial of all models, and most clearly sociological or channel-oriented, is Marshall McLuhan's (1964) "medium is the message."   According to McLuhan, the medium or channel through which information is conveyed is the most influential communication component and shapes both the content and the receiver's perceptions.

McLuhan classifies media as either hot or cold. Hot media, best characterized by print, require little audience participation whereas cool media, best characterized by speech or television, require much participation. The medium, not the content, according to McLuhan, is most influential— it is, in fact, the message. Or, as phrased in the title of one of his books, *The Medium is the Massage* (McLuhan and Fiore, 1967). The medium is not something through which information merely passes on its way from source to receiver; rather, the medium does something to the message as well as to the receiver. The medium shapes the message and the receiver's responses; it forces him to participate; it "massages" him.

In its emphasis on the degree of audience participation the different channels demand, this model focuses on language in its phatic aspect, language which serves to keep the channels of communication open and functioning.

Another model concentrating on the channels of communication is Elihu Katz's (1957) two-step flow hypothesis. According to this view communication does not travel from the source directly to the receivers. Instead, this model hypothesizes, messages from mass communication systems such as radio, television, and newspapers travel to a relatively small and select group of persons who function as opinion leaders. These opinion leaders in turn transmit the messages to the general population. A visualization of this hypothesis is presented in Figure 18.

Although this model has been applied with considerable success to rhetorical theory and directive language, its primary contribution to communication theory is in its emphasis on the channels through which information passes on its way from source to receiver. The model, consequently, focuses on phatic language since communication channels remain open and operative only to the extent that the language serves a phatic function.

Insofar as the models of interpersonal relationships described by such sociologists as George Homans (1950) and Theodore Newcomb (1953) emphasize the channels of communication and the function of language in keeping these channels operative, they too would be included in this class.

Naturally, no communication model focuses solely on one component; if one did it would not be a communication model but rather a channel model or a code model, for example. Similarly, and as emphasized earlier, no sample of language serves only one function—this, for some reason, appears impossible. The scheme discussed here is simply an attempt to put some order into a field which has paid little attention to it. Hopefully objections will be raised to this scheme and a better one developed out of it.

Communication theories have been derived from numerous and diverse sources, from engineering and mathematics at one extreme to rhetoric, psychology, and sociology at the other. All, however, share common purposes—to make clear what communication is, what it does, and how it

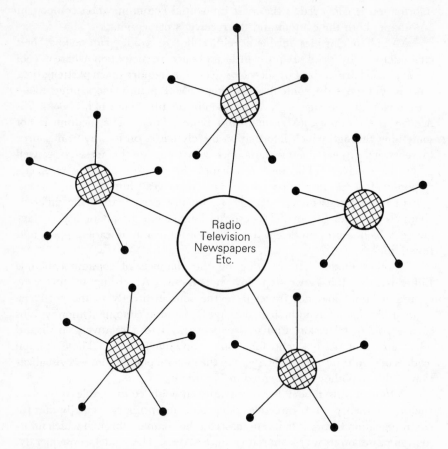

FIGURE 18.   A Sociological Model of Communication.   The transmission of information from the mass media to opinion leaders (crosshatched circles) to general population (darkened circles).   Author's Note: *I have based this diagram on Elihu Katz's
"The Two-Step Flow of Communication: An Up-to-Date Report on an Hypothesis,"*
Public Opinion Quarterly, *XXI (1957), 61–78.*

does it.   That answers to these questions have not been attained, at least not
to complete satisfaction, should not obscure the wealth of insights already
obtained.   Many of the important concepts have been identified and given
definitions which make predictions and measurements possible.   The
theories which have been advanced have clarified some of the essential
relationships among communication components, defined relevant processes,
and, most important, have succeeded in generating hypotheses for research.
This research will then lead to modifications and improvements in the
theories which in turn will generate more and improved research.   The
process from theory to research and back again is a never-ending one and
probably best typifies man and his time-binding capacity.

In this chapter I have attempted to accomplish two related goals.   First, I tried to explain some of the essential concepts for understanding, conceptualizing, and talking about communication.   Second, I tried to present some of the many approaches to the study of communication processes. Though each of the models discussed is valid and useful for various purposes, all have inadequacies.   Hopefully the reader will recognize some of these inadequacies and attempt to build his own model of the communication process.

Part II

In this section we consider four general areas of speech and language behavior.

In Chapter 5 we explore speech and language acquisition or what David McNeill (1966c) has referred to as "developmental psycholinguistics," an area which is central to the entire field of psycholinguistics. In fact, some researchers characterize the entire discipline of psycholinguistics as the study of this one question (cf. Smith and Miller, 1966; Fodor, Jenkins, and Saporta, 1967; Dixon and Horton, 1968).

In Chapter 6 we consider speech and language breakdowns or what might be referred to as "pathological psycholinguistics" and concentrate on two communication breakdowns—aphasia and stuttering. These particular pathologies seem to have the most important implications for a science of psycholinguistics.

In Chapter 7 our concern is with differences in speech and language which have some relationship to cognitive and/or behavioral differences. Although much research has been conducted in this area, which we might label "differential psycholinguistics," little has been done to unify and relate the varied approaches and findings. Here we make some attempt in this direction.

In Chapter 8 we focus on the effects of speech and language, an

SPEECH AND
LANGUAGE BEHAVIOR

area which might be called "rhetorical psycholinguistics." It should be noted that some researchers would regard this area as peripheral or even totally unrelated to the main concerns of psycholinguistics. Fodor, Jenkins, and Saporta (1967, p. 161), for example, note that the fact that verbalization appears as a variable in a psychological study does not qualify it as psycholinguistic. In many such studies it is immaterial whether the communication utilizes language or "lanterns in the belfry window." These researchers prefer to limit psycholinguistics to the study of the "acquisition, production, and comprehension of language." My own preference is not to limit the field to so narrow an area of study, at least not at this early stage of its development. It seems to me that any meaningful and significant theory of a language processing organism must go beyond comprehension and deal with effects. One of the best ways to approach this question is by considering the effects of communication in general.

In each of these chapters an attempt is made to present the relevant theories and research and to offer some evaluative comments. The field is too young to offer definitive conclusions or to present definitive syntheses. Consequently, these chapters present questions rather than answers and different points of view rather than *the* point of view.

Chapter Five

Speech and Language Acquisition: Developmental Psycholinguistics

Currently commanding the center of attention in speech and language psychology is the question of how the child acquires the ability to understand and generate sentences. In this chapter we consider this general question. In the first section we consider those factors supposedly related to speech and language development, primarily to provide some background on the nonlinguistic aspects of speech and language acquisition. In the second section the various stages in speech and language development are surveyed to provide some general picture of the events leading up to the emergence of speech and language behavior. The third section focuses on the actual development of the major aspects of speech and language— phonological, syntactic, and semantic. Here the concern is with *what* is acquired. In the final section we consider a number of different attempts to answer the question of *how* the child acquires speech and language.

The term "language" is used here to refer to the competence of the speaker, that is, the child's knowledge of linguistic rules. "Speech" refers to his actual, concrete utterances. Although both speech and language are considered, primary interest is in the child's acquisition of *a language*. By "a language" is meant an infinite set of sentences, each having a phonetic representation (that is, actualized in speech) and a semantic interpretation (that is, has some meaning). The correspondence between its representation and interpretation is specified by the rules of syntax (cf. Chapter 2). In other words, primary concern is with how the child acquires the ability to generate and understand an infinite number of sentences.

FACTORS INFLUENCING SPEECH AND LANGUAGE ACQUISITION

In his *Language and Communication* George A. Miller (1951, p. 157), after summarizing the data on speech and language development in the child, concluded:

> If we tried to picture the most precocious child orator, we should think of a blind girl, the only daughter of wealthy parents. The child with the greatest handicap would be a hard-of-hearing boy, one of a pair of

twins, born into a large family with poor parents who speak two or three languages.

Although it would be unfair to hold Miller to this statement today, it does provide a starting place for examining those factors which might contribute to the acquisition of speech and language in the child. In Miller's summary five general factors are considered: physiological condition (for example, blindness, hearing impairment), sex, number of siblings, bilingualism, and economic level. Since economic level is tied so closely to one's social level these might be considered together. Also, the factor of intelligence should be added since this is widely assumed to exert significant influence.

Physiological Condition

In the literature on speech and language development one of the most widely acknowledged influences is sensory impairment. Blind children, it is reasoned, develop speech and language abilities more rapidly than sighted children because they are so dependent upon them. Deaf or hard-of-hearing children, it is thought, fail to develop as quickly since these abilities depend so much on babbling and imitation; the deaf child is seriously handicapped because he cannot hear himself babble, does not derive any pleasure from hearing his own speech, and therefore, ceases this activity rather quickly. Furthermore, since he cannot hear his own sounds or the sounds of others, he fails to imitate his own sounds (lallation) and the sounds of others (echolalia).

Here the confusion between speech and language is particularly blatant. Certainly speech development depends in great part on hearing abilities and in the case of the deaf child it is reasonable to assume that speech development will be delayed or retarded and much research can be adduced to prove this point (for example, Fry, 1966). However, with language the relationships are not so obvious. Evidence provided by Eric Lenneberg (1962, 1967), for example, indicates that deaf children develop language despite their lack of ability to hear. Whereas language ability or competence is a prerequisite for speech development, it would not be accurate to assume that the reverse also holds, namely, that speech is necessary for language. The deaf child, it would seem, will learn the abstract rules of language much as he learns other abstractions. Speech, a manifestation or actualization of the language code, is naturally greatly dependent upon muscular control, hearing ability, proper development of the speech mechanism, and numerous other such physiological factors.

It is similarly difficult to demonstrate the influence of blindness on language development. Although blind children may be more verbal, because of their greater reliance on speech, it does not necessarily follow that they have any greater language competence than sighted children.

The relationship, then, between physiological factors and language development remains to be proven.   The relationship between such factors and speech development, on the other hand, seems logical and justified.

Sex

A number of research efforts have been directed at determining whether there is a difference in the speech and language development of boys as opposed to girls.   Statements attesting to the superiority of girls over boys can be found in numerous texts and articles.   For example, it is noted that girls begin talking at an earlier age than boys and that their speech is in general more intelligible (cf. McCarthy, 1954; Templin, 1957; Berry and Eisenson, 1956).

Among the reasons given are that girls identify with and imitate the mother who is always present.   Boys, on the other hand, identify with the father who is not often present and consequently do not have a readily accessible model to imitate.   Another reason given is that girls play verbal games whereas boys play games which involve mechanical noises but not actual verbal utterances.   Today both of these reasons seem somewhat dated.   Mothers work a great deal now and the difference between the presence of the male and the female parent may not be substantial.   Furthermore, boys' games are much more verbal today than they were ten or twenty years ago.   Boys do in fact play with dolls—though they may be called soldiers or space men.   Educational toys, almost all of which are verbal, are played with by boys as well as by girls.   Television certainly has an influence and is probably watched at least as much by boys as by girls.   So it would appear that the differences in environment may not be as great as commonly assumed.

The evidence presented on the superiority of girls seems confined to speech proficiency.   Those few studies which have focused on language, such as those by Berko (1958), Shriner and Miner (1968), and Menyuk (1963b), for example, have found no differences between the sexes.

Until further evidence is advanced on this issue it would seem that language acquisition is unrelated to sex, despite the fact that women are more loquacious than men.

Siblings

The number of siblings, the order in which they are born, and whether they are twins or not, have also been assumed to influence speech and language development.   The evidence for this assumption seems to be based largely on the fact that twins or siblings very close in age will develop an ideoglossia—a language developed by the children to serve their own needs and purposes and which can only be understood by the rest of the community with great difficulty, if at all.

Unfortunately, very little is known about ideoglossia; what information is available stems largely from subjective and anecdotal clinical reports which are always difficult to interpret. When focusing on performance ideoglossia differs greatly from the normal speech of the adult community; consequently it is difficult, if not impossible, to understand. However, the words created by these children, while not standard English words, may nevertheless follow the rules of English phonology and morphology. For example, if they use the term *mip* for *milk* this would make comprehension extremely difficult but at the same time this neologism clearly follows the rules for the combination of English phonemes and it is therefore possible that the children have learned the basic structure of English phonology and morphology. Furthermore, it is likely that the basic structure of ideoglossic speech is the same as that of standard English and that the differences are confined primarily to the lexical level.

If such distinctions are valid it would appear that these children are not retarded or delayed in language but only in their learning of the speech of the adult community. Additional support for this belief comes from the attempts of some clinicians to assess competence as opposed to performance. From these attempts it appears that these children understand language as well as other children their age.

Still other research indicates that first borns and only children will develop language faster than will those born later or children born into larger families. Again, however, this evidence is largely based on performance rather than competence.

Given the present state of research it would be unreasonable to conclude that any definite relationship exists between siblings, twinning, and order of birth, on the one hand, and language development, on the other.

Socioeconomic Level

Research seems to indicate that the higher the socioeconomic level the faster the speech and language development. For example, it is reported that children from the upper classes will have larger vocabularies and will have attained a higher degree of articulatory proficiency than will lower-class children (McCarthy, 1954; Irwin, 1948b; Berry and Eisenson, 1956). The reasons given for this seem logical enough. The upper-class child lives in a more verbal environment, he is around adults more often and is therefore presented with better models. Furthermore, his attempts to communicate are more often positively reinforced.

Again, however, the data are restricted to speech performance despite the fact that the term *language* is often used in reporting such data. No one appears to have shown, for example, that upper-class children learn various transformations earlier than lower-class children. And it is precisely this kind of information which we would need to draw conclusions about language. In fact, Shriner and Miner (1968), in their comparison of morphological competence among upper- and lower-class children, were unable to find any significant differences.

Though the evidence might appear to support the hypothesis that upper-class children are superior in speech performance even this should not be taken without question. As in the case of sex, the environments of children from different status groups do not seem to differ as significantly in regard to linguistic factors as they may have twenty years ago. Even the poorest homes have television or at least the children have ready access to one. They therefore appear to be exposed to as much verbalization as are the upper-class children. The results of previous studies, conducted before the widespread access to television, do not seem applicable today. Naturally, however, if standards used to judge articulation, for example, are drawn from the speech of the upper class, it is obvious that upper-class children will score higher on this factor.

Even if it were shown that their verbal environments did differ this would not be evidence for claiming that the child in the more verbal environment will develop language faster. Most any environment seems to provide ample opportunity for the child to acquire the basic rules of his language. This argument would also apply to the case of the environments of boys and girls.

It is true that institutionalized children appear to progress more slowly in both speech and language. It appears that an extremely impoverished environment does exert a delaying influence. But this is only temporary; when an institutionally reared child is put into a linguistically rich environment he soon begins to function at the level appropriate to his age.

Therefore, it appears that within normal limits socioeconomic level has no clear and proven influence on language competence and probably little on speech performance. When the environment is extremely impoverished, as in the case with children in orphanages, its influence is to delay speech and language development but to exert no permanent damage.

Bilingualism

As suggested by Ervin and Osgood (1954) bilingualism can be differentiated on the basis of the modes of acquisition. *Compound bilingualism* develops when an individual learns the two languages under essentially the same conditions as, for example, when the parents speak both languages interchangeably. *Coordinate bilingualism* develops when the two language experiences are kept distinct, when they are seldom interchanged, as, for example, when one language is learned at home and the other at school.

Compound bilinguals, it is thought, have the same meaning for terms in both languages whereas coordinate bilinguals have different meanings. Because the compound bilingual was exposed to both languages at the same time and in the same circumstances he develops the same meaning for interchangeable symbols. The coordinate bilingual, having learned the language in distinct contexts, develops different meanings for interchangeable terms.

For some time the bilingual child was thought to be retarded in speech and language development because of his bilingualism. This conclusion, however, was probably more a function of inadequate testing procedures than of the effects of bilingualism. The testing was generally done on coordinate bilinguals in an attempt to assess the child's ability to use the language of the school (in most cases English). Since English was his second language and since he was seldom tested in both languages, it is not strange that the bilingual child scored poorly on language tests. Furthermore, the differences in cultural background would make it difficult for the bilingual child to understand certain culture-bound concepts or vocabulary items. Whereas a middle-class American child would be familiar with such terms as *violin* and *concert*, the bilingual child, often from the lower classes, would not.

When, therefore, vocabulary knowledge or articulatory proficiency in the second language is tested bilinguals will score lower. When, however, one tests for the ability to understand language—regardless of what that language is—these children would probably not differ significantly from monolinguals.

It is true that the bilingual child has an added task; he must learn two phonological systems, two syntactic systems, etc. This, however, is probably not as difficult as it may first appear. When it is realized that children acquire language over a period of approximately two and a half to three years—from the time they first string words together until the time they acquire most of the basic syntactic structures—without any explicit tutoring, the task of an additional language seems a relatively minor one. At this early age, when children can become true bilinguals, they are such expert language-acquiring organisms that the task of two languages hardly presents a challenge.

Intelligence

The factor of intelligence seems a logical inclusion in any discussion of influences on cognitive activity or capacity, especially speech and language. As in the case of bilingualism, however, the researcher is again faced with problems of measurement. The most reliable and most often used intelligence tests rely heavily on verbal knowledge; consequently, it is extremely difficult to draw any valid conclusions concerning the influence of intelligence. Generally, however, it is thought that intelligence and speech and language development are positively related; the more intelligent child will speak earlier and better than the less intelligent child. The intelligent child will have clearer articulation, use sentences earlier, use longer and more complex sentences earlier and more frequently, and command a more extensive vocabulary than the less intelligent child.

This evidence, however, pertains to speech performance and says relatively little about language competence. According to most recent research conducted by Eric Lenneberg (1967) the development of language competence is influenced by intelligence only when it varies drastically from the norm. It is only in cases of severe mental retardation that language development appears to be impaired. Despite its enormous complexity language seems to require relatively little intelligence.

The major differences observed between the speech and language development of the below-normal and normal child appear to pertain largely to factors which are technically outside linguistic competence. For example, the below normal child will be unable to generate or understand long sentences. This, however, is probably due to deficiencies in memory capacity rather than to failure to have acquired the basic structures of language. All children, except the extremely retarded, appear to acquire the basic structure of language, the rules of phonology, morphology, transformation and so on, much as does the normal or even the intelligent child.

These six factors, then, appear to have varying influences on speech development, though probably much less than was previously thought. When it comes to language competence, however, they appear to have relatively little, if any, influence. If language were a purely learned behavior one would expect it to be influenced greatly by these and numerous other factors. On the other hand, if it were largely innate, it would be expected to demonstrate relative independence of these factors. Clearly it is the latter position which appears to be supported. This independence is probably as good an argument as any for the innate-nativistic theory considered in the last section.

STAGES IN SPEECH AND LANGUAGE ACQUISITION

In acquiring speech and language all children pass through a number of stages which are relatively independent of the factors considered above and of the specific language being acquired. Although these various stages are separated, each considered discretely, in actual fact they constitute a continuous progression and overlap considerably. The ages at which these stages are reached naturally vary from one child to another; those given here are general averages.

The *first sounds* the child makes, upon being slapped by the physician, are clearly reflexive in nature, despite the claims of some psychoanalytically oriented researchers that the birth cry is a response to the child's felt inferiority when faced with such a complex world of sight and sound. What actually happens seems quite simple. When the umbilical cord is severed the oxygen supply to the infant is cut off. This increases the amount of carbon dioxide in the blood which causes the lungs to expand. The lung expansion results in air being drawn rapidly over the vocal cords which produces sound.

These cries are generally high pitched, indicating some degree of muscular tension. There is little obstruction of the breath stream during this period and consequently the cries are vowel-like in character.

The cries covering the first few months of life might be divided into undifferentiated and differentiated. During the first month or so the cries are undifferentiated; the infant cries in the same manner for numerous and different reasons. At about the second month the cries appear to become differentiated on the basis of causes. Although mothers will often claim the ability to pinpoint with amazing specificity the reason for the crying, it is more likely that the crying is only grossly differentiated and that the mother is actually inferring the causes from various nonlinguistic cues such as the time of day, the time since the last feeding, and so on.

For the first four or five months the child engages in more-or-less *reflexive and random vocalization*. Much as the child will play with his feet and his hands he also plays with the various organs of his speech mechanism— jaws, lips, tongue, and so on. When air is drawn over the vocal cords various sound patterns are produced. These sounds bear no relationship to the sounds contained in his linguistic environment. His "speech" at this stage seems to contain all the sounds he is capable of producing.

Paralinguistic features, such as volume and pitch, begin to be varied depending upon the child's particular internal state. There is still, however, no real understanding or comprehension. The sounds are for the most part random, having no symbolic meaning for the child.

At around the fifth month of life the child begins *babbling*. In this stage vocalizations become more and more syllabic in nature. Here intonation rather than phonetic form appears to dominate vocal behavior. Intonation is regarded by many investigators as the first significant stage of language development since it is the first linguistic feature which the child achieves control over and varies to express different internal states (cf. Lieberman, 1967).

Frequently, though not always, these vocalizations include repetitions of various sound combinations such as *baba* and *dada*. Although these are often interpreted by overanxious parents as true speech they appear to have no real meaning for the child. During these months the sounds occurring in the child's environment begin to increase in frequency while the "foreign" sounds decrease. Vowel-like sounds, although still predominant, begin to decrease in frequency while consonant-like sounds increase. More technically, these sounds only resemble the vowels and consonants of adult speech. From analyses of speech spectrograms it has been shown that the sounds of adult speech and children's babbling differ both acoustically and functionally.

At the babbling stage the child learns to combine phonation and articulation to produce sounds and comes to achieve some degree of control over his motor system.

During the sixth month of life the child reaches the *lallation* stage; he begins to imitate his own sounds. He appears to derive definite pleasure from these vocalizations and will generally produce these even when no one else is present, indicating that it is not social reinforcement which maintains this behavior. Often the child will continue lallation even when adults appear; although aware of their presence he apparently "prefers" his own vocalizations to those of others.

At this stage, sometimes called the "lalling period," a kinesthetic-auditory feedback loop is developed. Kinesthetic stimuli, received from articulatory and phonatory movements, become associated or connected with auditory stimuli. This feedback loop is commonly regarded as one of the major criteria for speech and language learning. Upon reception of the auditory stimulus the previously associated (and therefore appropriate) muscular movements can be recalled. It is generally thought that the failures of deaf children to develop speech normally is due to their inability to develop this feedback loop.

After devoting some two or three months to the imitation of his own vocalizations the child begins, at about nine months of age, to imitate the sounds of others, a stage referred to as *echolalia*. He appears particularly adept at imitating those voices which are closest to his own in terms of quality. He therefore finds it easier to imitate his mother's voice than his father's since his vocal mechanism at this stage of development is more similar to the mother's.

Naturally the child does not devote all his vocalizations to the imitation of others. This period is simply characterized by this echolalic process; in actuality such imitation may occupy relatively little of the child's total vocalization time.

At around twelve months of age (Darley and Winitz, 1961) the child begins to use vocalization as a means of *communication*. The utterances appear to have definite reference to the real world or at least to the world of the child. These vocalizations may refer to inner states of the child or to the outside world but in either case they are clearly meaningful in the sense that they are arbitrary symbols used in place of or as substitutes for some referent in the nonsymbolic world.

There is relatively little controversy concerning these stages; most researchers agree that these stages are followed by all children in their development of speech and language. There is much less agreement on what happens after the child passes these elementary stages. It is to this issue which most researchers have addressed themselves and it is to this that we now turn.

SPEECH AND LANGUAGE ACQUISITION

Accurate description of speech and language development has been beset by a number of serious problems. Among the most pervasive is the inadequacy with which data have been recorded. Unfortunately, many researchers interested in speech and language development have had little, if any, knowledge of linguistics, particularly phonemics and syntax.

Consequently their reports are largely subjective reactions to what they think the child has said rather than objective reports on what has actually been said. Second, since it is only relatively recently that significant gains have been made in understanding language and language structure, much previous research contributes little to our central concern since the questions these researchers have asked have often been trivial and their methods of analysis less than rigorous. Third, many researchers have failed to distinguish between performance and competence. As will be illustrated, it is often difficult, and at times impossible, to ascertain the relevance of reported data to language or competence development.

During the last decade or so great gains have been made in our understanding of both language and language development and it appears likely that the next few years will witness even greater gains in our ability to describe the processes of language acquisition in the child. Unfortunately, this optimism does not extend to understanding *how* language acquisition takes place but is limited to *what* is acquired and the general pattern that language acquisition follows.

The one process which appears to characterize speech and language development in all its aspects is that of gradual differentiation. That is, the child seems first to acquire gross or general rules of language—phonological, syntactic, and semantic—and gradually differentiates these into more refined and specific ones until the level of differentiation which characterizes adult speech and language is reached.

This is not to say that differentiation is the only process involved or that differentiation can account for all examples of language development   Other processes may well be involved and examples may be adduced which pose various problems for such a hypothesis (cf. McNeill, 1967a). All that is claimed here is that differentiation appears to characterize the vast bulk of available data and appears to be a reasonable pattern to follow in presenting the evidence on the various levels of analysis.

Phonological Level

On the phonological level there are two basic questions which research has attempted to answer. The first question concerns the sounds or phones that the child utters as he comes to master language. On this there is much data. M. M. Lewis (1963), for example, claims that the sounds the child makes can be related to and explained by his state of discomfort or comfort. The stages of early utterances for both comfort sounds and discomfort cries are given in Table 3.

Discomfort sounds, according to Lewis, are the child's vocal manifestations of his total reaction to whatever is disturbing. Such manifestations would involve a contraction of the facial muscles and a narrowing of the mouth cavities. These changes lead the child to produce vowels which are narrow and tense rather than relaxed and open. Similarly, the tension

TABLE 3. The Stages of Early Spontaneous Utterance

Stage	Discomfort cries	Comfort sounds
I. Vowel-like	(i) Onset: immediately after birth	(i) Onset: when the discomfort-cries have already begun to appear
	(ii) Narrow vowels: e, ɛ æ, a	(ii) Open vowels: not clearly defined, a, o, u
	(iii) Often nasalized	(iii) Rarely nasalized
II. Earlier consonantal	Sounds made by partial closure: w, l, ŋ, h	Mostly back consonants: ɠ, g, x, k, r
III. Later consonantal	Front consonants, usually nasal: labial, m dental, n	Front consonants, usually oral, sometimes nasal: labial, p, b, m dental, t, d, n

From M. M. Lewis, *Language, Thought and Personality in Infancy and Childhood* (New York: Basic Books, 1963), p. 17.

normally raises the pitch and in an attempt to increase volume the nasal passages would be employed, producing nasalized vowels. The emergence of [w], [l], [ŋ], and [h], at the second stage, results from the intermittent closure of some part of the child's vocal mechanism during his crying. The [w], for example, is produced when the lips are brought together. The third stage, during which the child utters the nasals [m] and [n], results from the anticipatory sucking movements made when hungry. When these movements are made during nasalized crying the resultant sounds are [m] and [n].

The comfort sounds are similarly part of the child's total reaction to his inner state. When the child is content, his vocal mechanism is relaxed and the sounds produced are therefore back vowels such as [a], [o], and [u]. As in the case of the second stage of discomfort cries, the second stage of comfort sounds results from the child's partial closure of his vocal mechanism during the making of the back vowels characteristic of the first stage. The labial and dental sounds of stage three are produced by sucking movements made after being fed. That is, after the child has been fed he perseverates and continues making sucking movements. When made in a state of relaxation [p], [b], [t], and [d] are produced and when coupled with nasalization [m], and [n].

The value of Lewis' approach is not entirely clear. One might argue that the explanation is ad hoc; alternative explanations are surely possible. Two points which this approach and explanation make, however, should be noted. First, these sounds are simply physiological reactions of the child to his inner state and have no meaning in the normal sense of the term. Second, these vocalizations are better described as noises than as sounds. At this stage of development they are not features of the language the child eventually acquires. Although they may resemble the sounds of adult language they are, to the child, simply noises and any similarity to the allophones of adult speech is imposed by the adult and not by the child.

Another type of study attempts to provide data relating to the age at which certain sounds are mastered. An example from a widely cited study is presented in Table 4. From this one learns that by the age of three-and-a-half the child has mastered the sounds [b], [p], [m], [w], and [h]. By four and a half he has added the sounds [d], [t], [n], [g], [k], [ŋ], and [y], and so on.

TABLE 4.   Age at Which Various Sounds Are Mastered

Age	Sounds Mastered
$3\frac{1}{2}$	b, p, m, w, h
$4\frac{1}{2}$	d, t, n, g, k, ŋ, y
$5\frac{1}{2}$	f
$6\frac{1}{2}$	v, ð, ž, š, l
$7\frac{1}{2}$	s, z, r, θ, hw

From Irene Poole, "Genetic Development of Articulation of Consonant Sounds in Speech," *Elementary English Review*, II (1934), 159–161.

As Roger Brown (1965) has pointed out, such research tells nothing about the development of language. In fact, it is not even clear what these data mean in regard to the child's speech since there are probably wide variations in the production of any of these sounds which are not recorded. Although the three-and-a-half-year-old child may be able to produce [b] and [p], for example, it is not clear what this means in terms of *his* language. More specifically, the [b] and [p] sounds, although produced by the child and recognized by the adult community as [b] and [p], may well be allophones of one phoneme to the child. That is, the child may be using these sounds interchangeably and may not be able to distinguish *pin* from *bin* either in production or in understanding. He may be using these sounds randomly.

Although data such as these are often interpreted to pertain to the development of phonemes, they actually say nothing about this level of language development. What one needs to know is when these sounds achieve phonemic status in the language of the child, when these sounds serve to make minimal pairs in the child's language. If one simply relies on recording the sounds heard there is no way of knowing when these sounds are in free variation in the child's language, just as aspirated and unaspirated [t] are in adult language, or when they are actual phonemes and serve to distinguish minimal pairs.

Despite the paucity of substantial research on the child's learning the phonemes of his language, it appears that he learns distinctive features and by a gradual process of differentiation acquires the entire stock of adult phonemes. In English, as in every natural language, phonemes are distinguished from one another by a series of contrasts; in some cases only one contrast serves to distinguish one sound from another; in other cases the number of contrasts is much greater, say three or four. For example, /b/ and /p/ are distinguished from each other by the feature of voice; /b/ is voiced and /p/ is voiceless. In all other respects the sounds are identical. Similarly, /f/ differs from /θ/ in that /f/ is made with the lips and teeth (that is, labiodentally) whereas /θ/ is made with the teeth and tongue (that is, dentally). More removed from one another are /d/ and /p/ which differ on the basis of voiceness (/d/ is voiced and /p/ is voiceless) and manner of articulation (/d/ is apical and /p/ is labial). The phonemes of a language can then be classified and analyzed according to their distinctive features (cf. Chapter 2). A distinctive features diagram of eight consonants is illustrated in Figure 19.

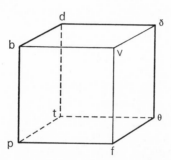

FIGURE 19. Distinctive Feature Matrix for Eight Consonants. The top-bottom contrast is between voiced and voiceless sounds: the front-back contrast is between labials and apicals: and the right-left contrast is between fricatives and stops. *From Roger Brown,* Social Psychology *(New York: Free Press, 1965), p. 266.*

In the child's acquisition of the sound system of his language it appears that he first acquires general or gross phonemes such as a dental phoneme or a labial phoneme. This dental phoneme, for example, does not exist as such in adult language. It is rather a general phoneme in the child's language which includes all those phonemes made dentally without regard for the manner in which the air is emitted or whether they are voiced or voiceless. This phoneme would then contrast with, say, a velar phoneme which again does not exist in adult language but which includes all those phonemes produced by the articulation of the tongue with the velum.

At this point one may say that the child has a language or a phonological system consisting of two phonemes, a dental phoneme and a velar phoneme. At a later stage these phonemes are further differentiated, perhaps on the basis of whether they are voiced or voiceless. When this distinction is acquired the child's phonological system would consist of four phonemes—a voiced dental, a voiceless dental, a voiced velar, and a voiceless velar.

In other words, it appears that the child does not learn phonemes as we may conceive of them (as bundles of distinctive features) but rather learns distinctive features such as voicelessness and voiceness and velarness and dentalness which permit him to gradually differentiate his initial general phonemes.

If the child does acquire the phonological system of his language by learning the distinctive features, certain predictions about the acquisition of phonology can be made. For instance, it would be expected that when a distinctive feature is acquired it will be applied to all cases rather than confined to, say, one or two phonemes. From the analyses of child language it appears that this does occur, although the evidence is at best meager. Velten (1943) found that his daughter at twenty-two months of age learned the contrast between /b/ and /p/ and at the same time the contrast between /d/ and /t/. Both of these pairs of sounds are distinguished from one another on the basis of the feature of voiceness. Had the child learned the individual phonemes there would be no reason to expect that they would all be acquired at the same time. In fact, one would expect the sounds to each be acquired at different times.

Also, it seems reasonable to predict that if distinctive features, rather than individual sounds, are learned that they are learned relatively independently of the specific language the child will acquire. In other words, the acquisition of distinctive features seems to depend principally on the clarity of the contrast, the ease with which it may be heard and produced, regardless of the specific language spoken. This prediction is supported at least from the preliminary data available. Menyuk (1968), for example, found that the order in the acquisition of distinctive features by both English- and Japanese-speaking children was identical. The order, from the earliest mastered, was: nasal, grave, voiced, diffuse, continuant, and strident. This suggests that there may be some universal pattern in phoneme acquisition.

From an analysis of the most frequent errors in the production of sounds made in the course of normal language development comes additional evidence for the distinctive features hypothesis. The most frequent errors involve substitutions of one distinctive feature change (Menyuk, 1968). The child who says *dis* for *this*, for example, is substituting the noncontinuant /d/ for the continuant/ð/. At this stage of development the child has not yet mastered the distinction between continuant-noncontinuant. Since these sounds are identical except for this one feature this should be a difficult contrast for the child to learn and one which will be learned later than others. This, it appears, is exactly what happens. Note that the child does not say *gis* or *mis* for *this*. These initial sounds involve a number of differences; even his gross differentiation has already enabled him to keep these phonemes separated.

Throughout the discussion of linguistics and speech and language acquisition the distinction between competence and performance has been emphasized. Few studies have attempted to assess the development of phonological competence. One recent study, however, did attempt such a task and is worth reviewing, not because it answers the question of how the child learns phonology but because its methodology provides insight into the study of competence and because its results are pertinent to an understanding of sound development in the child. This experiment, conducted by Stanley Messer (1967), began with the claim by Benjamin Lee Whorf (Carroll, 1956) that by a very early age the child has mastered the sound system of his language. As already noted, the rules of English phonology specify that only particular combinations of phonemes are permissible. The entire list of permissible sequences was analyzed by Whorf and put in terms of a formula for generating all and only those permissible sequences. It is this formula which the child acquires as part of his phonological competence.

The purposes of Messer's study were (1) to determine if children, between the ages of 3.1 and 4.5, could discriminate between monosyllables composed of nonpermissible phoneme sequences and permissible phoneme sequences and (2) to determine if children could pronounce these two types of monosyllables with equal facility. According to the Whorf theory it would be hypothesized that children could in fact so discriminate and that they would be better able to pronounce permissible sequences than nonpermissible sequences.

Twenty-five pairs of words were developed. One list consisted of words generated by Whorf's formula (that is, permissible words) and one list consisted of words which violated the formula. Fifteen words on this second list violated the formula once and ten words violated the formula twice. All the words were non-English or nonsense syllables. The children were told that they would be playing a new kind of game and that they were to tell the experimenter which of two words best described a specific piece of wood, which word sounded like something they had heard before, or sounded better. The subjects responses were recorded and later transcribed to include all mispronunciations. The results clearly demonstrated that the children had acquired the formula; they selected the permissible English word significantly more often than the nonpermissible word. Though not statistically significant they also tended to select more frequently the English permissible word when it was paired with a word which violated the formula twice than when it was paired with a word which violated the formula only once.

As hypothesized, the subjects mispronounced the nonpermissible words more often than the permissible words. What is particularly pertinent is that these mispronunciations were not random but rather appeared to be based, at least in part, on some sort of distinctive features analysis. In those cases in which mispronunciations consisted of substitutions, which Messer analyzed in detail, the children substituted for the sound which violated the formula a sound which was one distinctive feature removed from the original sound. In other words, he made a minimal change.

Clearly, there are many more unanswered questions concerning the acquisition of phonology than there are answered ones.   It does appear, however, that we at least have a useful hypothesis and some supporting evidence that the child acquires the phonemic system of his language by learning distinctive features which enable him to gradually differentiate his gross phonemes until they reflect the distinctions appropriate to his language environment.

Syntactic Level

Following the general outline provided by Chomsky (1957, 1965) the acquisition of syntax may be discussed in three parts: phrase-structure rules, transformational rules, and morphological rules.

PHRASE STRUCTURE RULES.   One of the most striking characteristics of early language is that one word is used to mean a number of different things. These one-word sentences—called holophrases—contain the meaning of what adults would normally express in an entire sentence.   The word *mama*, for example, might mean "Mama, I'm uncomfortable"or " Mama, come here."   The child's grammar at this stage could be expressed as the phrase structure rewrite rule S $\longrightarrow$ W, that is, rewrite sentence as word.

Most researchers in child language point to the development of what Martin Braine (1963a, 1963b) has referred to as pivot words.   These words, few in number, are used by the child as pivots or fixing points around which his sentences become organized.   For example, the word *it* might be a pivot word and to it the child will attach other terms, called open-class words, to produce such sentences as " Eat it," " Drink it," " Have it," " Want it," etc.   The pivots, then, are the cores around which the child builds his earliest sentences.

The pivot words and the open-class words, or nonpivots, are breakdowns from the initial one-word sentences.   The single word, used previously as an entire sentence, is here differentiated into pivots and nonpivots.   The rewrite rule which might be used to express the grammar would be S $\longrightarrow$ P + O or S $\longrightarrow$ O + P, that is, rewrite sentence as pivot plus open-class or open-class plus pivot.

At the next stage there is further differentiation of the open-class word, generally into a modifier, as yet undifferentiated as to type, and a noun. The rule of the child's grammar here would be S $\longrightarrow$ P + M + N, that is, rewrite sentence as pivot word plus modifier plus noun.   With this grammar the child would produce such sentences as " It a boy," " It a sock," and " It a dogs."

The verb forms are omitted here and are acquired at a later stage. Notice that there is a failure on the child's part to differentiate modifiers into those which can be used with plural nouns and those which can be used with singular nouns.   This results in the ungrammatical (in adult grammar) *a dogs*.   At a later stage of development these modifiers are differentiated and the ungrammatical sentences gradually diminish in frequency.

TRANSFORMATIONAL RULES. The next aspect of the child's acquisition of language involves the mastery of the transformational rules which enable him to produce complex structures from the more basic ones generated by the phrase structure rules. Although little work has been done in this area, Ursula Bellugi has made a significant beginning in identifying the stages in the acquisition of interrogatives (Bellugi, 1965) and negatives (Klima and Bellugi, 1966). Summarizing some of her findings on interrogatives will illustrate some of the processes involved in the acquisition of transformations. (You may need to review the section dealing with transformational rules in Chapter 2 before continuing here.)

Bellugi collected data from three children, primarily from their conversations with their mothers but also from small experiments designed to secure more specific information. Two of the children, called Adam and Eve, talked a great deal and were readily intelligible. Their fathers were Harvard graduate students and their homes were especially verbal. The third child, called Sarah, came from a very different language environment and had parents who had not graduated from high school.

The data, collected over a period of months by Bellugi and her associates, were divided into three periods or stages for purposes of describing the significant changes in the structure of the sentences, especially interrogatives.

At Stage 1 Eve was 18 months old; Adam, 28 months; and Sarah, 27 months. All were at approximately the same stage of language development as determined by their mean sentence length which appears to be the best available index. Their sentences, approximately two morphemes in length, consisted predominantly of nouns and verbs which were unmarked as to tense and number. The other parts of speech, pronouns, auxiliaries, articles, and modifiers, were absent.

The only transformation characteristic of adult grammar present at Stage 1 was that of intonation contour which marks yes/no questions. Sentences such as "Baby cry?" and "Kitty gone?" would illustrate the application of the basic rule S (2–3–1) ⟶ S (2–3–3). (Hereafter notation of the intonation contour will be omitted.)

Only a few *wh*-questions were produced and these appeared to be crude approximations of adult forms. For example, the children produced such sentences as "Where horse go?" and "Who that?" which seem governed by the very general rule S ⟶ *Wh* + S. The major difference between these questions and those of adults is that the children's do not contain auxiliaries. The absence of auxiliaries also accounts for their yes/no questions lacking the characteristics of adult grammar.

Some negative questions were present but, like the *wh*-questions, were approximations. In these the negative, generally *not* or *no*, preceded the sentences as in "No, my kitty?" A rule such as S ⟶ Neg (*not* or *no*) + S might describe this stage. There were no tag questions during this period.

At Stage 2 Eve was 22 months old; Adam, 32 months; and Sarah, 32 months. By this stage their speech evidenced a number of important changes. Pronouns, articles, and modifiers, present progressive and plural morphemes, some irregular past tense verbs, and some verb phrases which included prepositional phrases were now present. Still absent were auxiliaries, essential for forming interrogatives, as well as indefinite pronouns, clauses and other evidence of embedding. ("Embedding" denotes the grammatical operation by which one sentence is fit into another. For example, the sentence "The boy who is ten years old is tall" contains the embedded sentence "The boy is ten years old.")

Two forms, *don't* and *can't*, were present prior to the development of auxiliaries and were used in front of verbs. These were probably single morphemes in the children's grammar. For two of the children (Eve and Sarah) the yes/no questions were signaled by intonation only; since there were no auxiliaries there could obviously be no auxiliary inversion. With the forms *don't* and *can't* they produced sentences which had some characteristics of adult negative yes/no questions. In adult grammar these questions involve inverting the order of subject NP and auxiliary, for example, "You can't fix it" becomes "Can't you fix it?" In the children's speech at this stage, however, the only change was in intonation contour; the order of the declarative sentence was retained, yielding such questions as "You can't fix it?" Adam was somewhat different at this stage. His speech contained the form *D'you want* which was used in front of his yes/no questions, as in, for example, "D'you want me get it?" As in the case of *don't* and *can't* this functioned as a single morpheme.

Wh-questions were used in some instances. In these cases the *wh*-word, consistent with adult grammar, always appeared in sentence initial position but was not used to replace other elements. The children seemed merely to use these forms as question introducers, following the basic rule S ⟶ *Wh* + S.

Negative questions were formed generally by placing *why not* in front of sentences, for example, "Why not he eat?" "Why not me sleeping?" following the basic rule S ⟶ *Why not* + S.

At this stage there were still no genuine tag questions although some approximations to these did appear. Tags such as *huh* and *all right* were at times used to signal questions; they were placed at the ends of sentences and contained the rising intonation.

At Stage 3 Eve was 25 months old; Adam, 38 months; and Sarah, 38 months. The most significant change here was the presence of auxiliaries. Their speech also contained third-person-singular present-tense and regular past-tense morphemes. The sentences were more complex, containing clauses and other evidence of embedding, as in, for example, "I told you I know how to put the train together."

In addition to the appropriate intonation contour their yes/no questions now contained the auxiliary which, following the rules of adult grammar, was inverted with the subject NP. The negative *n't* was added to the auxiliary in a number of instances and appeared appropriately used. At times the main verb was left in the past tense and used in conjunction with the past form of *do*, yielding such sentences as "Did I lost you?" and "Did I caught it?" Here their rule was S ⟶ aux + past tense + (*n't*) + NP + V + past tense + NP.

The *wh*-questions seemed to follow the rule S ⟶ *Wh* + NP + aux + VP which would produce such sentences as "What he can ride in?" instead of the adult rule S ⟶ *Wh* + aux + NP + VP. That is whereas in adult grammar the auxiliary and the subject NP are inverted, in the child's grammar they are not. Furthermore, in sentences containing no auxiliaries the children failed to supply the appropriate form of *do*. In these cases the main verb was used to carry the past-tense morpheme, as in "What you took out?" Tag questions were still absent from the children's speech.

In yes/no negative questions the auxiliary and the subject NP were inverted. In *wh*-negative questions, however, they failed to make the required inversion and produced such sentences as "Why the kitty can't stand up?" From this it appears that there is a limit to the number of transformations which the child is capable of performing at any one time. For example, in the *wh*-negative questions the child does not invert NP and aux though he does apply the intonation transformation and introduces the *wh*-question word. He appears capable of applying two transformations but no more. In the yes/no negative questions there is only one other transformation which needs to be applied, namely, the intonation transformation. So in both the yes/no and the *wh*-negative questions he applies two transformations; in the former case this is sufficient to yield a grammatical question but in the latter it is one short of adult grammaticality. This, it might be added, provides some evidence for the psychological reality of transformations. It appears that the transformations, although all present in the child's competence, each take up a certain amount of room or storage space in his memory and he therefore can deal with only a limited number of them at any one time.

These examples all refer to performance development; evidence on the development of competence is much more difficult to obtain. Bellugi, however, was able to make some seemingly valid inferences concerning competence of the *wh*-object question from the ways the children responded to their mother's questions, a method which needs to be employed more extensively in future research. For example, if the mother said "What do you want?" and the child answered "Ice cream" this would provide evidence for assuming that the child understood, and hence had in his competence, the *wh*-object question. If, on the other hand, the child answered "Want" or "Me" this would lead to the conclusion that he did not understand and probably did not have the *wh*-object question in his competence.

At Stage 1 the child seems not to understand *wh*-object questions; his responses are incorrect. At Stage 2 he does understand and when asked, for example, "What do you have?" correctly responded "Have sugar." At this stage, however, the child did not produce grammatical *wh*-questions.

Comprehension, it appears, far exceeds speech performance. At Stage 3 the child continued to respond correctly but with more complex sentences. When asked "What do you want to do?" one child responded "I know what I should do; play with some more toys."

The detail with which Bellugi has analyzed the development of interrogatives should not obscure the more general pattern of differentiation which appears to be followed. The development began with the gross distinction between falling intonation, characteristic of declaratives, and rising intonation, characteristic of questions. Later the distinguishing characteristic of question-words was introduced and still later the process of inversion was added. Here, as in the case of other linguistic levels, a particular grammatical structure is first produced—or a particular grammatical rule is first acquired—with only general and gross features. As the child develops, the features become more and more finely discriminated until they parallel the level of adult grammar.

Throughout the period during which the child is learning syntax and especially transformations, his speech will contain both grammatical sentences and restricted sentences, that is, sentences which are restricted to the language of children and are ungrammatical by adult standards. For example, he may use such sentences as "Mommy was mad so he spanked Blacky," "I write that numbers," and "I see a dog what's white," illustrating pronoun, adjective, and relative pronoun restrictions, respectively (Menyuk, 1963a).

The specific forms of the various transformations are, of course, features which vary from language to language. It is necessary, therefore, for the child to learn these transformations from his linguistic environment. Although it is not entirely clear how the child secures the data on the basis of which he acquires the necessary rules, it appears that part of the data comes from the mother's expansions of his own sentences. Roger Brown and his colleagues (Brown and Bellugi, 1964; Brown and Frazer, 1963; Brown, 1965) have provided considerable insight into this question (see also Slobin, 1968). In this normal course of language development mothers expand the child's sentences approximately 30 percent of the time. In so expanding his sentences the adult provides the child not only with examples of transformations but also with data on the basis of which he can revise or reject his tentative rules or theory of language structure. In Table 5 are presented examples from Brown and Bellugi (1964). Although there are many possible expansions it appears that those sentences which the mother chooses to expand are expanded correctly—no doubt on the basis of numerous nonlinguistic cues.

On the basis of data such as these and probably much else the child acquires his transformational rules and is able to test whatever theories of language structure he may have developed. Although it is not known how he does this we do know that ultimately he settles on that theory which enables him to understand and generate all the grammatical sentences of his language.

TABLE 5.   Expansions of Child Speech Produced by Mothers

Child	Mother
Baby highchair	Baby is in the highchair
Mommy eggnog	Mommy had her eggnog
Eve lunch	Eve is having lunch
Mommy sandwich	Mommy'll have a sandwich
Sat wall	He sat on the wall
Throw Daddy	Throw it to Daddy
Pick glove	Pick the glove up

From Roger Brown and Ursula Bellugi, "Three Processes in the Child's Acquisition of Syntax," in Eric H. Lenneberg, ed. *New Directions in the Study of Language* (Cambridge, Mass.: M.I.T. Press, 1964), p. 144.

MORPHOLOGICAL RULES.   As in the acquisition of phonology and aspects of syntax already considered, the child, in his development of morphology, also acquires rules and not a simple list of permissible and nonpermissible sequences.   The latter alternative would clearly be a monumental task since this list would be exceedingly long.   Evidence for the first alternative comes from two related sources.   First, children can be observed to inflect forms, for example, apply the rules of morphology for past tense or plural, which they have never seen or heard before; their inflections clearly follow the rules of English morphology.   Thus when confronted with a novel "word," say *rit* the child knows that more than one of them is /rits/ and not /ritz/ or /ritəz/.   Second, and perhaps more convincing, children frequently follow these rules in inflecting irregular forms.   For example, when they say *drinked* instead of *drank* they are clearly following the morphological rules of English though in this particular case an "incorrect" structure is produced.

Though native speakers would have great difficulty if asked to state these rules, they are actually quite simple.   The morphological rules for the formation of the regular plural, possessive, and the third-person singular of the verb are identical and are phonologically conditioned, that is, they depend on the final sound of the stem.   When this sound is a groove fricative or affricate, the allomorph {-əz} is used; when it is a voiceless consonant, the allomorph is {-s}; in all other cases, that is, for voiced consonants, vowels, and semivowels, the allomorph {-z} is used.   The allomorphs for the formation of past tense are also phonologically conditioned: {-əd} is used after stems ending in /t/ or /d/; {-t} is used after stems ending in voiceless sounds, except /t/; and {-d} is used after stems ending in voiced sounds, except /d/.   An example of a morphologically conditioned plural is *ox*: *oxen* where the plural allomorph {-ən} is used not because of the sound preceding it (cf. *box*: *boxes*, *fox*: *foxes*) but because of the peculiarity of the morpheme {ox}.   Exceptions such as *ox*: *oxen* must, of course, be learned individually and not by some general rule.

Jean Berko (1958) presented children with various nonsense forms and pictures and asked them to supply the missing word in a sentence. The missing word required the child to inflect a form he had never heard before. For example, in testing for the plural morpheme the child was shown a picture of a bird and told that this was a *gutch*. When shown a picture of two of them he was asked to complete the statement "There are two _____." Here the stem ends in a groove fricative necessitating the allomorph {-əz}. In an item involving past tense the child was shown a picture of a man with a steaming pitcher on his head and told that this was a man who knows how to *spow* and that he had done the same thing yesterday. He was then asked to complete the statement, "Yesterday he _____." Since the stem ends in a voiced sound the correct allomorph is {-d}.

With this general procedure Berko tested two groups of children: one group ranged in age from four to five and the other group from five-and-a-half to seven. Both groups included boys and girls. Investigated were the rules for the formation of plurals, possessives, third-person singular of the verb, past tense, progressives, and comparative and superlative adjectival endings.

The older children, as expected, did significantly better than the younger children on almost half the items. Most children were able to supply the allomorphs {-s} and {-z} in forming plurals, possessives, and third-person-singular verbs but were unable to utilize the {-əz} allomorph. In the formation of the past tense most children were able to supply the {-t} and {-d} allomorphs but were unable to supply the {-əd} allomorph.

Most children were able to supply the progressive allomorph {-ing} though since only one test item was included it is difficult to draw any general conclusions. Of eighty children tested only one child was able to supply the correct comparative and superlative endings for the adjectives. When the children were given the comparative form and asked to supply the superlative (for example, "This dog is quirky. This dog is quirkier. This dog is _____.") 35 percent were able to do so correctly.

It appears that the hypothesis for the gradual differentiation of language rules is again supported though indirectly. That at this stage of development these children had allomorphs which were not as finely differentiated as they are in adult morphology is obvious from the evidence on the plural, possessive, third person singular verbs, and past tense morphemes. That is, the children had only two allomorphs for each of these morphemes where adult speakers have three. If younger children were tested they would probably possess only one allomorph for the plural, for example, which they would use indiscriminately.

This study focused solely on active control of language rules, which probably lags behind passive control. In active control the subject can actually apply the rules; the rules are manifested in his performance. In passive control the subject can detect the correct rule, that is, has it in his competence but cannot apply it himself. In some situations, for example, the child may not yet have mastered the production of a particular sound distinction but yet may be fully able to hear it and recognize it. Many parents have probably had conversations with their children similar to that described by Berko and Brown (1960): "That's your fis?" "No, my fis." "That's your fish." "Yes, my fis." Here it is apparent that the child has passive but not active control over the formation of the word or more specifically over the /š/ sound. In a similar manner it may be that children at the ages tested by Berko could tell the difference between *gutches* and *gutch* or *gutchs* but simply did not produce the forms correctly inflected.

On the basis of Berko's results it can be concluded that those allomorphs which the child correctly produced were part of his competence. However, one cannot conclude the reverse, namely, that those allomorphs which were not produced were not part of competence. The subject's passive control over these morphological rules was not tested and hence no conclusions concerning this aspect of language development seem warranted.

Semantic Level

Although the importance of semantic development cannot be denied, very little is known about the *what* and the *how* of the acquisition of semantics. By comparison, our knowledge of phonological and syntactic development is substantial. The acquisition of the semantic system seems to involve at least two processes: the acquisition of vocabulary items and the acquisition of semantic markers (cf. Chapter 2). The acquisition of semantic markers will be considered first since it ties in more closely with the previous discussion of syntax. It should be clear, however, that in the process of language acquisition vocabulary items are learned first and only then are the semantic markers learned.

In the discussion of linguistic theory it was noted that the semantic component of a grammar consisted of a dictionary and a set of projection rules. About the latter we can say nothing; about the former only a little and only in general and highly tentative terms. One thing which is known is that the acquisition of the semantic system differs greatly from that of the syntactic system. The most obvious difference is that of time. Whereas the child by the age of four or so has acquired his syntactic system and, as already pointed out, has in his competence and performance most of the syntactic structures he will use as an adult, it is not until the child is considerably older, say around eight or nine, that his semantic system reaches a comparable stage of development. In fact, semantic development continues throughout the school years and in many cases throughout life. The process of semantic as opposed to syntactic development, then, is an extremely slow one. The reasons for this are not entirely clear though David McNeill (1967b) has ventured some interesting hypotheses. First, the semantic system is probably much more complex than the syntactic system. Athough the syntactic rules which the child must master are many, they are in all likelihood far fewer than the semantic rules.   Second, the semantic markers which are to be learned are fewer than the number of words and consequently must be applied to many different cases before any single marker can be regarded as part of competence.   This naturally takes time.   The major reason for the slower learning, according to McNeill, appears to be that with syntax acquisition the child is presented with concrete examples of the rules he will master.   For example, although plurality is an abstract concept the child is constantly presented with concrete instances of this concept; the plural allomorphs are overt linguistic structures.   With semantics the picture is quite different.   To learn that *boy* and *girl* both have the semantic marker "human" cannot be found in the concrete utterances of adult speech.   Therefore, it is difficult to determine how the child acquires semantic markers since they are not manifested overtly in the child's linguistic environment.

We might venture two other possible reasons.   First, the semantic markers which are learned are applicable to linguistic units which bear no structural similarity to each other; there is nothing in the structure of a particular class of words which would enable one to identify them as members of the class.   Although certain parts of speech, most notably adverbs, do bear structural similarities with one another, not even an adult speaker could tell from hearing the isolated *toves* whether it was a noun, a verb, or a possessive.   Similarly, novel words such as *gan* and *ron* could belong to any part of speech.   Yet the child must learn that certain semantic markers apply only to nouns, others only to verbs, and so on.   Perhaps more importantly, he must also make distinctions within classes.   Thus, for example, he must learn that certain nouns are abstract and others are concrete, certain ones are animate and others are inanimate, certain ones are human and others are nonhuman.   And he must learn these distinctions without the aid of any structural clues in the words themselves.   On the basis of structure, there is no way he can distinguish the abstract *faith* from the concrete *school*; yet he must and does learn that he can say "I go to that school" but not "I go to that faith."

Second, it seems reasonable to hypothesize that many of the semantic markers which the child learns soon prove irrelevant and incorrect.   In the case of syntax, it is true, the child will often utter sentences which are not grammatically correct.   Yet the situations are different in that his utterances, although often ungrammatical, are nevertheless permissible by the grammar.   Therefore, although he may say "The man not going" in which he omits the auxiliary verb, he will not say "The going not man."

The child obviously acquires such relevant and correct semantic markers as "animate" and "human" which impose certain restrictions on the ways in which the terms may be used.   But it is likely that he also acquires "markers" which are totally irrelevant to his linguistic tasks and markers which are simply incorrect.   For example, it is easy to conceive of the child acquiring the semantic marker—if it may be called that—of "playful" for

Daddy. This, however, is irrelevant to the linguistic task and would seem to increase the time the child must spend learning relevant markers. Further-more, many markers which the child acquires are probably incorrect. For example, movable objects seem in the child's behavior to be equipped with a will of their own. Thus the ball rolls under the table because it wanted to and consequently is a "bad ball" and perhaps should even be spanked. This marker of, say, "will possession" will not only lead him to produce numerous semantically anomalous sentences but will also complicate his learning task since he must unlearn such markers as well as acquire new ones.

We can explain what appears to happen in the acquisition of semantics by reference to a hypothetical dictionary entry for a term which appears early in the child's language, *Daddy* (Table 6), and suggest how the entry

TABLE 6. Hypothetical Development of a Dictionary Entry for the Word *Daddy*

Stage 1	Stage 2	Stage 3	Stage 4
(large)	(large)	(large)	(large)
	(animate)	(animate)	(animate)
		(human)	(human)
			(male)

might look at different stages of development. It is postulated here that what the child acquires in his acquisition of semantics is a set of semantic markers such as "large" and "animate" which, in one sense, define the term for the child. In the early stages of language acquisition *Daddy* may mean nothing more than a large object, not distinguished from *Mommy* or *doggie* or even *table*. At Stage 2 the child has added the marker "animate" and here *Daddy* is distinguished from other large objects such as *table* but not from *doggie* or *Mommy*. At Stage 3 is added "human"; here *Daddy* is distinguished from *doggie* and at Stage 4, when "male" is added, *Daddy* is distinguished from *Mommy*. Although the addition of semantic markers is the more obvious process, it is likely that the child also eliminates certain acquired markers as he develops. Thus at a certain stage the semantic marker "large" may be dropped. The acquisition of these semantic markers, then, permits the child to gradually differentiate generally defined concepts into more specific ones.

These semantic markers do not only function to define the term but rather to indicate the way in which the word may or may not be used in a sentence. For example, assume that at one stage of development the child's dictionary for *Daddy* and *doggie* consisted solely of the markers "large" and "animate." This information would permit the child to construct sentences in which *Daddy* and *doggie* can be interchanged. This is not to say that the child at this stage does not perceive these two objects as different, but only to suggest that this is one reason why the child will produce sentences which are semantically doubtful such as "Doggie goes to work" and more generally why the actions of one are assumed to be doable by the other and why attributes of one are taken to be attributes of the other.

When it comes to the child's acquisition of vocabulary items it appears that the hypothesis of gradual differentiation meets with considerable problems. The hypothesis assumes that the child's vocabulary development must proceed from the abstract to the concrete, from the general to the specific. There is, however, considerable evidence to illustrate that the process actually goes in the opposite direction. For example, the word *Daddy* appears in the child's vocabulary much earlier than do the words *people, men, human beings,* and various others more abstract than *Daddy*. Here appears to be evidence that the child's vocabulary builds from the concrete to the abstract. On the other hand, there appears evidence that abstract terms are learned first. For example, the child will learn the word *car* before the words for various specific kinds of cars such as *convertible, station wagon, sedan,* and numerous others.

Roger Brown (1958b) has clarified much of this apparent rather than real confusion. According to Brown the child's language does in fact proceed from the abstract and general to the concrete and specific; the child learns his vocabulary by a process of differentiation. The examples which may be adduced and which at first seem contradictory are actually not so when they are considered from the child's rather than the adult's point of view. Specifically, the word *Daddy* is not, for the child, a concrete term but rather an abstract term which denotes all large things or all human beings or perhaps all males or all adults. To the child, then, this term is actually quite general; adults perceive it as specific because they give it their own meaning or assume it possesses the same semantic markers for the child that it does for them.

The learning of names, as Brown points out, probably reflects the adults' practices in supplying names for the child rather than the child's cognitive development. Adults, Brown argues, provide the child with that name for a thing which will be of greatest utility to him—a name which will enable the child to make the distinctions he needs to make. Thus at certain stages a dime may be referred to as *money* and not distinguished from nickels or pennies simply because these distinctions are not yet required by the child. The class term *money* provides all the essential information for the child and serves adequately to separate this item from items which are to be eaten or thrown away. When the child gets older and finer distinctions are needed, as when he begins to buy things, this initial general term will be differentiated into pennies, nickels, dimes, etc.

Although children do learn their vocabulary from the abstract to the concrete in most cases, they are rarely if ever given the most abstract terms for a class of things. Consequently, these extremely abstract terms, such as *quality, concept, mineral,* etc., are not learned in the early stages of language development but only when the child reaches school age and begins to learn vocabulary in more formal and, it might be added, more artificial ways.

It appears, then, that the child learns naming vocabulary by a process of differentiation, from the general to the specific. Although verbs, adjectives, and adverbs are more difficult to study they too are probably learned by this same general process. The child, for example, does not at first distinguish all the colors for which adults have names but rather considers only dark and light colors or perhaps only bright and nonbright colors. Here again the distinctions appear to be gross and general ones which only later are differentiated.

The acquisition of naming behavior differs in important ways from the acquisition of phonology and syntax. In the case of naming behavior the child is tutored directly and explicitly by an adult speaker. He is told that "This is a chair" or that "This is Uncle James." Furthermore, the child can often be observed to ask many questions concerning the appropriate names for things. With phonology or syntax, on the other hand, the child is not taught explicitly nor does he appear to ask questions concerning appropriate sounds or sentence constructions. Therefore, information concerning the child's learning of names, for example, while interesting and essential to a complete understanding of language development will probably not provide significant insight into the acquisition of other aspects of language.

This review suggests that the child acquires language—in all its aspects —by first acquiring general and rather abstract classes and by a gradual process of differentiation comes to make the distinctions appropriate in adult grammar. Obviously much more must be learned before the complete picture can be sketched. The role of distinctive features in the acquisition of phonology needs to be researched in much more detail. The specific function of phrase structure, transformational, and morphological rules needs to be more clearly defined and analyzed, especially in children acquiring widely differing languages. Only by such cross-linguistic investigations will it be possible to distinguish the universals from the particulars of language acquisition. The acquisition of the semantic system is perhaps the least well understood and it is to this that future research needs to give priority. How and when (or if) the child acquires the various semantic markers will undoubtedly have implications for much more than language acquisition.

Very likely the process of differentiation, seemingly confirmed on the different levels of language, will prove to be only part of the complete picture. Other processes, such as reclassification (cf. McNeill, 1967a) may well be involved and may, when more fully developed, provide a more general and more valid hypothesis.

THEORIES OF SPEECH AND LANGUAGE ACQUISITION

The task which a theory of language acquisition faces is, indeed, a formidable one. It must account for a child's knowledge of the major portion of his language by the age of about four—a task which would take an intelligent adult years to accomplish and even then only with numerous imperfections in sound, structure, and meaning. The child, by this very young age, has mastered language to the extent that he can understand and generate sentences which he has never heard before, theoretically an infinite number.

More specifically, this knowledge involves phonological, syntactic, and semantic competencies. Discussion of the last two follows Garrett and Fodor (1968). Among the child's phonological competencies is the ability to distinguish permissible from nonpermissible phoneme sequences. Thus he knows that whereas in English (1) is permissible (2) is not.

(1) glo
(2) nglo

Second, he is able to recognize when forms are terminal and when they are not, that is, when forms can have allomorphs added to them and when they cannot. For example, he knows that (3) is a terminal form but (4) is nonterminal and therefore the allomorph for past tense or progressive may be added.

(3) drank
(4) drink

Among his syntactic competencies he is, first, able to distinguish grammatical from ungrammatical utterances. Thus he knows that whereas (5) is an acceptable sentence (6) is not.

(5) The dog jumped on the man.
(6) The dog jumped the man on.

Second, he has the ability to distinguish the ways in which sentences can be given different syntactic descriptions. He knows, for example, that (7) can be interpreted as either (8) or (9) but not (10).

(7) The doctor's bills are high.
(8) The doctor charges a lot.
(9) Someone charges the doctor a lot.
(10) The doctor is high.

Third, he possesses the ability to relate sentences to each other on the basis of their deep structural similarity or difference. He knows that (11) and (12) are related but that (13), although similar in surface structure to (11) is not related.

(11) The man rode the horse.
(12) The horse was ridden by the man.
(13) The horse rode the man.

Among his semantic competencies he possesses, first, the ability to detect when sentences are semantically anomalous that is, when they are, meaningless. He knows, for example, that (14), although grammatical, is semantically meaningless.

(14) The blue man rode the stationary wind.

Second, he can detect sentences which are ambiguous and the different semantic interpretations they may be given. Thus he knows that (15) may be paraphrased as either (16) or (17).

(15) The dog smells.
(16) The dog is smelling (say, for a bone).
(17) The dog has a foul odor.

Third, he can tell when one sentence is a paraphrase of another and when sentences are synonomous. He knows, for example, that (18) and (19) are paraphrases of one another and that they have the same meaning.

(18) The boy hit the ball.
(19) The ball was hit by the boy.

We might add that a theory of speech and language acquisition must account for such abilities as these without any explicit or direct instruction by parents or other adults since these speakers are unable to verbalize what they know about their language. For example, most adult speakers are unable to state why (20) is ungrammatical whereas (21) is grammatical.

(20) The fortune lost the old man.
(21) The old man lost the fortune.

Nor are most adults able to explain why (22) may be an acceptable sentence of English whereas (23) could not be.

(22) Foggles danked by the wif will raddle.
(23) Foggles rin the wif will by raddle.

Still another problem is that the theory must account for the child's knowledge of grammar despite the fact that much of what he hears is ungrammatical; somehow he learns the phonological, syntactic, and semantic systems of his language even though what he hears is often contrary to these systems' principles or rules.

How such a young and unintelligent being, incapable of caring for his own most basic needs, masters a language which linguists have been unable to describe in complete detail, is surely not an easy question to answer.

Any theory of speech and language acquisition must answer the question of how the human organism, whose input is a finite corpus of utterances, develops the linguistic competence which enables him to perform at least the various decoding and encoding processes already noted. At present one of the major controversies in psycholinguistics centers on the relative influence of the corpus as opposed to the innate capacities of the organism in contributing to competence (cf. Fodor, 1966b).

At one extreme it might be assumed that the corpus the child hears is identical with his competence. If this assumption is made there is little reason to postulate any more than relatively simple principles of learning. If the corpus contained all the information which the child must acquire as his competence then the environment may be considered the sole determinant, or nearly so, and the specific nature of the language-acquiring organism need not be of any great concern.

At the other extreme it might be assumed that the corpus contains no information which will constitute the child's competence; that is, the corpus and the child's competence are completely different. If this were the case then the environment or the nature of the corpus could be disregarded and sole consideration given to the nature of the organism.

Clearly both extremes are untenable. For example, the corpus the child hears does not contain the abstract syntactic categories and rules which he eventually masters but rather only their manifestations or actualizations coupled with numerous and frequent violations. The base structures are never present in overt form in the corpus. Furthermore, a finite corpus could not account for the child's competence in dealing with sentences he has never heard before. Therefore, it is clear that the whole story cannot be contained in the corpus.

The other extreme is equally fallacious; the corpus obviously does bear a real and important relation to his language competence. This is most obvious from the simple fact that when the corpus is English the child eventually learns English, not French or Bantu. If the corpus bore no relationship to competence and if competence were completely innate, then all children would speak the same language.

The actual argument does not, of course, take this extreme form. The dichotomy was set up to put the issue into clearer perspective. It seems agreed that the innate capacities of the organism *and* some information contained in the corpus are essential if language is to be mastered. The more valid question is to what extent and in what ways language is innate and to what extent and in what ways it is dependent upon the linguistic environment.

At present there are two major ways to account for or describe how the child acquires language. The first type of theory, which assumes that the corpus or linguistic environment is the more important component, is derived from traditional behavioristic psychology and attempts to account for language acquisition by some principle of learning theory. The second type, which assumes that the organism is the more important component, argues that learning theories are inherently inadequate to the task. Relying heavily on data from evolutionary theory and the biological sciences, this biological theory holds that the child has an innate capacity to acquire language. The nativistic theory extends this argument and assumes that the child comes equipped with certain linguistic universals. The child, according to this theory, can hardly be prevented from acquiring language; mere exposure forces him to acquire the correct rules and structure of the language.

Learning-Theory Approaches

MOWRER'S AUTISTIC THEORY. One approach to language acquisition based on principles of stimulus-response learning theory has been proposed by O. Hobart Mowrer (1950, 1960b). The basic outlines of this autistic theory are stated by Mowrer (1950 p. 699):

> On the basis of many converging lines of evidence, it now appears that the most plausible explanation of the *first* stage of language learning lies along lines quite different from those usually suggested—lines which can be clearly traced only against the background of modern behavior theory and clinical theory. The essence of the hypothesis here proposed is that babies . . . first learn to reproduce the conventionalized noises which we call words, not because they can either understand or use those words in any ordinary sense, but because of what is, at first, a purely *autistic* function. . . . babies, according to this hypothesis, . . . make their first efforts at reproducing words because these words *sound good to them.*

The reason that these words "sound good" to the child, according to Mowrer, is that they have in the past been associated with pleasurable situations. The sounds which the mother has made have become in the mind of the child associated with pleasure; the mother's talking when feeding or fondling the child are clear cases in which the sounds of speech may be associated with pleasure.

The child, as has been mentioned, engages in random vocalization simply from playing with his speech mechanism. When these random sounds approximate those made by his mother, the child derives pleasure since they recall for him the pleasant situations of feeding or fondling, for example. When feeding, a primary reinforcer, is associated with certain sounds or words, these sounds or words come to acquire secondary reinforcing properties. That is, the sounds themselves become reinforcing or rewarding. Naturally, the child will derive more pleasure when the sounds he makes approximate those of his mother more closely. Therefore, he attempts to speak more and more like his mother and engages in what appear to be rehearsal and correction procedures.

The child soon controls a certain set of words which at first are meaningless to him. They are uttered merely because of their secondary reinforcing value, because they give the child pleasure.   Meaning for these words is learned when the word and the object are associated.   For example, when the child utters the word *doll* or some approximation and the mother produces the doll, the word and the thing become associated and the child, after a few such pairings, learns the meaning of the word.   On future occasions, when he wants the doll, for example, the child will say *doll*.   Sentences, it will be recalled, are explained in essentially the same way.   The sentence "Tom is a thief" is understood because the reactions learned to *thief* are transferred to *Tom*.   The sentence, which is essentially a conditioning device, is understood when the reactions appropriate to the predicate (*thief*) become attached to the subject (*Tom*).

As was mentioned in our discussion of learning theory, Mowrer's approach fails to take into consideration a number of facts essential to any viable description of language and language behavior.   Special note should be made here of the failure of the theory to deal with base structures and transformations—omissions which render this theory incapable of dealing with sentences in any meaningful way.

Mowrer's theory relies almost solely on the concept of reinforcement; words, for example, are established because they are reinforced.   However, even if verbal behavior can be conditioned it has not been demonstrated that conditioning is essential for verbal behavior (cf. Chapter 3).   Such a demonstration, it seems, would have to be offered before even the learning of words can be accounted for by a simple reinforcement theory.

The major problems, however, center on the theory's attempt to deal with sentences.   A reinforcement theory such as Mowrer's relies on mechanisms (for example, the concept of reinforcement) which can deal only with those linguistic facts which appear in the surface structure; it can only deal with overt linguistic data.   Clearly, however, this is not enough.   The base structures and rules for transformations which do not appear in the surface structure are nevertheless mastered by the child and account in no insignificant way for his capacity to generate and understand an infinite number of sentences.

Furthermore, if the sentence were a conditioning device then repetition would be expected to make a sentence more readily available, to aid in comprehension, and to increase its meaning.   In actual fact, however, repetition is unnecessary for creating and understanding sentences since all sentences, with only trivial exceptions, are uttered and understood as novel sentences.   And, rather than increase meaning, repetition leads to a loss in meaning, that is, semantic satiation.

Unfortunately, Mowrer too quickly dismisses the insights of linguistics and because of this his theory fails to answer the very questions which a theory of language acquisition must answer.

JENKINS AND PALERMO'S MEDIATIONAL THEORY.   Recently James J. Jenkins and David Palermo (1964) proposed a mediational theory which, although they no longer hold to it today, raises a number of pertinent questions. According to this theory, the child learns language by learning the grammatical classes of words. The child, for example, learns that *doll* and *bottle* belong to the same grammatical class from hearing them in equivalent contexts, for example, "Here is the doll" and "Here is the bottle." Sentences such as these, which occur frequently in the child's linguistic environment, "teach" the child that *doll* and *bottle* belong to the same class and can therefore appear in the same contexts. Thus upon hearing the new sentence "I want the doll," the child now knows that "I want the bottle" is permissible in his language. With additional examples the child comes to develop a rule which might be phrased as S $\longrightarrow$ *here is the* + any noun, where "noun" might be conceived of as any word which can appear in the same linguistic contexts as *doll* and *bottle*.

This conception of language learning at first appears quite logical and reasonable. When it is forced to deal with more complex sentences, how-ever, it proves inadequate. Note that this theory conceives of a grammar learning organism as generating sentences from left to right. The child, according to this theory, learns the transitions existing between words; in the above example, he knows that after *here is the* any noun can follow. The problem with this theory is simply that not all English sentences can be generated by observing only left to right processes, that is, not all sentences can be produced with only a knowledge of the dependencies existing between one word and the word immediately following. For example, in the sentence "The boy who fell into the water so many times is ten years old" the dependency relationship existing between *boy* and *is* spans eight words. The singular form of the verb (*is*) is not dependent upon *times* which immediately precedes it but rather upon the singular subject (*boy*).

Any theory, therefore, which attempts to account for the learning of language by the learning of transitions is inadequate simply because the number of permissible transitions is too great to ever be learned in such a short time. In fact, Miller and Chomsky (1963) have estimated that the child would have had to learn more than one transition for every second he has lived.

BRAINE'S CONTEXTUAL GENERALIZATION THEORY. Another theory, similar in many respects to that of Jenkins and Palermo, has recently been set forth by Martin D. S. Braine (1963a, 1963b, 1966). This theory, referred to as contextual generalization, is succinctly explained by Braine (1963b, p. 323):

When a subject, who has experienced sentences in which a segment (morpheme, word, or phrase) occurs in a certain position and context, later tends to place this segment in the same position in other contexts, the context of the segment will be said to have generalized, and the subject to have shown contextual generalization.

Contextual generalization occurs when a child who has learned, for example, "Go up," "Go out," "Go in" and various other phrases in which *go* appears in initial position, generalizes this initial position for *go* to other contexts and produces such sentences as "Go bed," "Go bye-bye," and so on. The word *go*, as noted earlier, is called a pivot word, a word which serves as a kind of hitching post for other words. Although relatively few in number these pivots account for most of the sentences produced by the child during his first stage of language learning. Most of the child's early sentences are produced by attaching newly learned words to pivots.

Whereas Jenkins and Palermo claim that the child generalizes to form grammatical classes Braine argues that the child generalizes position. Although this at first appears to be an insignificant difference it leads to different conclusions. For example, Braine's theory is clearly the more powerful since it can account for the numerous novel sentences understood and produced by the child. Furthermore, it accomplishes this by postulating relatively simple learning. Whereas the learning of all possible transitions, as required by Jenkins and Palermo's theory, would be monumental, the learning of position would easily be within the grasp of the child.

There are, however, a number of objections which might be raised to this theory (Bever, Fodor, and Weksel, 1965a, 1965b; McNeill, 1968). The most obvious objection is that Braine's theory of contextual generalization says nothing about transformations. Yet transformations are essential in accounting for the tremendous productivity in language competence and performance. Without coming to grips with transformations the theory which Braine proposes, like Mowrer's and Jenkins and Palermo's, cannot account for the child's ability to understand and generate sentences involving transformations. Similarly, it cannot deal with base structures. Contextual generalization can only deal with surface structures since these are the only structures which the child comes into direct contact with; no one hears or produces base structures. In concentrating solely on surface structures it, in effect, ignores the existence of base structures and of transformations and thus severely limits its explanatory power.

There is, however, one alternative which Braine (1965) has argued for and this is to rewrite the grammar so that surface structures and base structures are the same. That is, Braine claims that the grammar of the language should be rewritten to exclude certain differences between base and surface structures in the earliest sentences of the child. In this way contextual generalization would be able to account for at least the first stages of language learning. This argument raises an important and often misunderstood question in psycholinguistics. The point at issue is whether the psychologist, in his attempts to describe the way language is acquired, can rewrite the grammar so that his theories would prove adequate and sufficient. Put another way, can the psychologist simplify the description of a language to the point where his theories can account for language acquisition? The answer to this is a definite no. It is the job of the psychologist to construct theories that take into consideration the data provided by the linguist. The psychologist must deal with language as it is and not as he would wish it to be. Clearly, if there were no transformations and base structures in English it would be a relatively simple problem to account for the child's acquisition of language. But doing away with such linguistic facts does not solve the problem; it merely poses a different and irrelevant one.

There appear to be two main conclusions one might draw from this review of learning-theory approaches. One conclusion, argued by many linguists, is that learning theories are inherently incapable of dealing with this question (for example, Chomsky, 1959; Fodor, 1965; McNeill, 1968). Their reason for this extreme statement is simply that linguistic knowledge involves information which is never made overt in the speech with which the child comes into contact. Base structures, for example, which they hold the child must acquire, never appear in overt form; rather only surface structures are heard. Learning theories, they argue, can only deal with overt, surface linguistic data.

The other conclusion, argued largely by psychologists (for example, Osgood, 1963b, 1966, 1968; Staats, 1968), is that learning theories are not inherently incapable of dealing with language acquisition but rather in their present state of development may be insufficient.

Although it is premature to render a judgment on this question, it appears that the objections raised by linguists or linguistically oriented psychologists, are serious ones which have not been fully answered by current learning theories. Whether and in what way these objections will be met is not yet clear.

Biological-Nativistic Approach

In contradistinction to the learning-theory approaches is the biological-nativistic theory of language acquisition. Eric Lenneberg (1967) has provided much of the ground work for demonstrating that human beings are biologically constituted to acquire language; they have an innate capacity to become language-understanding and language-generating organisms. David McNeill (1966d, 1967a, 1968) has attempted to extend this basic approach and to specify the nature of this innate capacity.

Before explaining the nature of this capacity it would be wise to sketch some of the arguments which gave rise to and add support to such a position. Lenneberg (1960, 1964a) has attempted to demonstrate that language more closely resembles innate behavior, such as bipedal gait, than it does such clearly learned behavior as writing. His argument is a four-pronged one: language, like bipedal gait and unlike writing, shows evidence of (1) little variation within the species, (2) specific organic correlates, (3) heredity, and (4) no history within the species. These four characteristics, argues Lenneberg, can define or characterize innate behavior and are applicable to language.

(1) VARIATION WITHIN THE SPECIES. Although the vast differences in languages are easily appreciated there are also numerous similarities— similarities which appear too great to be accounted for by chance alone. For example, although human beings are capable of producing a vast number of sounds all languages make use of a relatively small number of phonemes—about forty to fifty. All human languages have a phonology even though man is quite capable of utilizing sounds which are imitative and nonphonemic. Animals taught to speak, such as parrots, do not acquire a phonemic system as does the child. The difference is most clearly seen when a child and a parrot are put into different (that is, foreign) language environments. The child will speak with an accent; he will have retained his basic phonemic system and the second language is, in a sense, filtered through the phonemic system of his first. The parrot, of course, will not speak with an accent. The parrot's speech is purely imitative; it does not acquire a phonemic system.

In addition to the universality of phonemic language, all languages employ concatenation; all languages are spoken by stringing together phonemes and morphemes. Nowhere does man speak in single-word utterances. Furthermore, in all languages this stringing together is done according to some system of rules; all languages have syntactic structure. In no language are words put together in random sequence.

These universals of language lead to one of two possible conclusions. First, it might be concluded that all languages, by chance, adopted the same properties; all languages independently adopted a phonemic system, communication by concatenation, and syntactic structure. This, Lenneberg argues, seems highly unlikely. The other alternative is to conclude that somehow man is predisposed to acquire language which is phonemic, utilizes concatentation, and is governed by syntactic rules. That is, there is some innate capacity for language.

(2) SPECIFIC ORGANIC CORRELATES. Like bipedal gait and unlike writing, language development seems to be dependent upon specific organic correlates. (Of course, writing is also dependent upon organic development and a person without the requisite motor skills could not learn to write. The absence of writing, however, does not indicate that there is an absence of organic development.) Children appear to acquire the phonemic system, to concatenate, and to utter grammatical utterances, independently of their learning experiences. Rather, the appearance of these features seems correlated with the development of specific organic capacities. Children acquire phonemes or, more correctly distinctive features, according to an almost universal timetable, regardless of the specific language environment. From evidence such as this it seems likely that there is a special time in the life of the child when he is biologically constituted to acquire the phonemic patterns of a language and other times when he is incapable of such acquisition.

In the same way, a child does not concatenate before a certain age. It is not that the child does not have enough vocabulary to form connected utterances but rather that he is not biologically ready for this feat. But when he reaches the age of say two or three it is impossible to prevent the emergence of concatenation. Similarly, the child appears to learn grammar according to his developmental level and not as a result of parental training.

Second-language learning provides additional support. A three- or four-year-old child, for example, when put into a foreign-language environment will learn that language extremely quickly and without an accent. These abilities, however, rapidly decline with age. By the time a child reaches his teens, for example, it is almost impossible for him to learn to speak a second language without an accent and without stylistic peculiarities which identify him as a nonnative speaker.

Aphasia provides still further evidence. When aphasia is acquired during the period propitious for language acquisition, say around three or four years of age, the damage may well erase all the child's language abilities; recovery, however, is generally very rapid and the child will again go through the various stages of language development at an accelerated rate, quickly attaining normal language ability. When aphasia is incurred between the ages of four and ten recovery, although a long process, will in most cases be complete. When aphasia is acquired after twelve it generally leaves permanent traces and when acquired after eighteen recovery is extremely rare.

Language, therefore, seems dependent upon the maturational development of the child rather than upon his individual learning experiences.

(3) HEREDITY. Language, like bipedal gait, will develop even when the conditions are most unfavorable. Deaf children, for example, still develop grammar and learn to write even though they fail to develop vocal communication at the normal rate. Children who cannot verbalize because of various physiological abnormalities still understand rather complex instructions, indicating that they have acquired linguistic competence.

This is not to say that environmental factors exert no influence on the speech and language development of the child. Certainly they do. The point which Lenneberg is making, however, is not that speech and language development will be uninfluenced but rather that the *capacity* for language acquisition will not be severely damaged despite environmental deprivation. As has been noted, institutionalized children will not develop communication skills as rapidly as will those normally raised. Yet soon after the institutionalized child is put into a normal language environment he functions at a level appropriate to his age. His capacity or potential for language remains unimpaired. This same pattern appears in motor development as with children who have their legs in casts during the period when they would normally "learn" to walk. When the casts are removed they function at their normal age level with little difficulty.

It appears, then, that language is a peculiarly human ability and that the capacity for language acquisition is dependent upon maturational level. The environment functions primarily to help actualize this potential.

(4) NO HISTORY WITHIN THE SPECIES. If language were a purely learned phenomenon it should be possible to trace it to some primitive stage of development. All learned behaviors can be traced, at least theoretically, to some less well-defined stage. Language (or bipedal gait), however, cannot be traced to a more primitive stage. Nowhere can evidence of an aphonemic, aconcatenative, or asyntactic system of language be found. Because of this Lenneberg concludes that such a stage probably did not exist and that therefore language is not a purely learned form of behavior but rather is a development of man's innate capacity.

It should be apparent that each of these arguments can be refuted on purely logical grounds. The argument from "variation within the species" can be challenged by noting that the features of language selected as evidence (that is, phonemic, concatenative, and grammatical universals) are all rather abstract characteristics. Writing, for instance, can be shown to have the same qualities. Furthermore, these characteristics may well have been developed on the basis of utility—the alternatives to a phonemic system of language, for example, are clearly cumbersome and needlessly complex and it does not seem unreasonable to assume that the phonemic system may have become universal simply because it best served man's purposes.

The argument from organic correlates is probably the most difficult to refute. However, no causal relationship between organic development and the emergence of certain language abilities is demonstrated by the high correlations.

The argument from inheritance is logically weak. Although deaf children will learn to write and speak they are generally taught rather specifically, and even though their teachers may not know the rules well enough to verbalize them they nevertheless know them well enough to inform the child when a sentence is grammatical and when it is not. Furthermore, there is little evidence available to demonstrate conclusively that this "feeling" for grammar will develop regardless of the environment.

The argument from history within the species is the weakest of all. Even if a time in history when man did not possess a more primitive form of language could not be found, this would not mean that such a time and such a stage of language did not exist. The time in the history of man of which we have some knowledge is admittedly a short one and it is precisely the period on which there is no data that one would expect such a primitive language to exist if, indeed, one did exist. For example, if one were to observe man from the age of, say, twenty to fifty and had no other evidence on which to base conclusions on the nature of man, one would have to conclude that man underwent little change. Yet the period before twenty, if it could have been observed, would have convinced anyone that man did change considerably in his development.   The same is true of the history of the species.   The period for which there is no evidence is precisely the period which would logically be expected to show evidence of primitiveness.

The important thing to note about these arguments and possible counterarguments is that although the evidence is not conclusive, the bio-logical theory has much to recommend it.   That is, although logically the arguments are not conclusive, the theory can nevertheless be defended in terms of its ability to come to grips with the basic data on the nature of language provided by linguistic science.   Whereas the learning-theory approaches present seemingly insurmountable obstacles, the biological theory presents a framework which is compatible with the basic linguistic facts.

David McNeill (1966d, 1967a, 1968) has recently attempted to specify the nature of this capacity for language acquisition in his nativistic theory. Whereas the nativistic theory assumes a biological theory such as Lenneberg has presented, the biological theory does not support or refute the nativistic theory.   The biological theory, postulating an innate *capacity* for language acquisition, is independent of any attempt to specify the linguistic informa-tion with which the child might be born.   Although this nativistic component is by no means clearly defined it appears to be assumed that it consists of at least two related aspects.   First, there is some preliminary linguistic infor-mation.   This information is not unique to any given language but rather is universal.   It facilitates and is applicable equally to the acquisition of Bantu, English, Russian, Chinese, and any other natural language.   This information pertains to the base rather than to the surface structure of lan-guage since it is the former which is universal and the latter which is language specific.

McNeill has postulated that this preliminary linguistic information probably contains the basic grammatical relations of subject and predicate of the sentence, the modifier and head of the noun phrase, and the main verb and the object of the verb phrase.   These concepts are all in the base structures of sentences.   Some evidence or support for the inclusion of these concepts in the child's capacity comes from the fact that these appear in the child's earliest sentences—before he has learned the various language specific rules for constructing sentences according to the specific grammar he eventually acquires.

The second component is even less clear.   It appears that the child comes to the learning task with some procedures for the analysis of grammar or grammars.   That is, the child is presented with a corpus of speech from the surrounding adult community and from this he must acquire the gram-mar by which these sentences could be constructed.   According to Jerry Fodor (1966b) the child may go through a number of possible syntaxes, discarding those that prove inadequate and eventually settling on the one which enables him to understand and generate grammatical sentences.   In other words, the child has a sort of discovery procedure which he uses to determine the correct grammar of the language with which he comes into contact. What the specific nature of this analysis procedure might be or exactly how the child goes about using it is not clear.

The question of how the child acquires language will probably remain unanswered for quite some time. Part of the problem and part of the reason for the pessimism is that a complete theory of language development can only be developed on the basis of a complete description of the grammar. At present the description of English grammar is far from complete.

Furthermore, if the biological-nativistic theory is pursued, it must eventually specify the physiological and neurological dimensions of language acquisition. Such an explanation will have to wait for considerable advancements in the understanding of the brain.

Although it appears from recent writings in psycholinguistics that the biological-nativistic theory is favored over the learning theory approaches, this may well be due to the fact that the former is still in its infancy and extremely general. In fact, it is so abstract that it is difficult to disprove it or to even offer arguments against it. The learning-theory approaches, on the other hand, have made specific assumptions and predictions, and although they have in many cases been shown to be incorrect they have served a useful function in directing research to the discovery of new facts about language and language behavior.

At the present stage of theory construction in the area of speech and language acquisition the arguments have been needlessly extreme—whether advanced for or against any particular point of view. Too few researchers have attempted to combine the different approaches. Such attempts seem badly needed.

Chapter Six

Speech and Language Breakdown: Pathological Psycholinguistics

In this chapter we concentrate on two communication breakdowns: aphasia and stuttering. These specific breakdowns were chosen for a number of reasons. First, they represent two different types of etiology; aphasia is a symptom of a physiological condition, but stuttering seems the result of psychological or learning processes. Second, aphasia represents a language pathology of deep structure; that is, the basic code of communication is disrupted. Stuttering, on the other hand, appears to represent a speech disorder of surface structure, a disorder in which the message rather than the code is disturbed. Third, these two pathologies have been the center of a great deal of research based on the latest theories and findings in the areas of linguistics, learning, and communication. They thus allow us to focus on the contributions which these areas may make to an understanding of language and speech problems and in turn the contributions which research on these pathologies may provide for speech and language psychology.

In this discussion we concentrate on reviewing recent research and theory pertaining to aphasia and stuttering. In aphasia research two basic questions are asked most often: What is aphasia? and, How might aphasia best be studied? These two questions we consider in our review of "contemporary theories of aphasia" and "new directions in aphasia research." In stuttering research the basic questions are: What is stuttered? and, What causes stuttering? These two questions we explore by reviewing data on "the properties of stuttered elements" and "contemporary theories of stuttering." Our purpose here is to further understanding of normal speech and language and consequently we do not consider how these breakdowns can be treated.

APHASIA

In an article entitled "Historical Highlights in the Study of Aphasia during the Past Fifty Years," Jon Eisenson (1959, p. 45) concludes:

We shall increase our understanding of the modifications that accompany the over-all behavioral changes in aphasics as a result of the thinking and analytic investigations of linguists, psycholinguists, semanticists, and psychologists.   Names such as Roger W. Brown, John B. Carroll, John W. Gardner, Roman Jakobson, Floyd G. Lounsbury, Jacques Maritain, G. A. Miller, C. W. Morris, Charles Osgood, Uriel Weinreich, and Joshua Whatmough may have to be considered along with the neurologists and even the speech pathologists whose research and thinking have provided a better understanding of aphasic language disturbances and aphasics as persons and patients.

Although this statement was written in 1959, it seems that even then Eisenson was underestimating these contributions to the understanding of aphasia in particular and speech and language breakdown in general.   To Eisenson's list many more names could and in fact must now be added— Noam Chomsky, James Jenkins, Eric Lenneberg, O. Hobart Mowrer, and B. F. Skinner are just a few of the more obvious ones.

Roman Jakobson (Jakobson and Halle, 1956, p. 55) puts this issue into proper perspective:

> If aphasia is a language disturbance, as the term itself suggests, then any description and classification of aphasic syndromes must begin with the question of what aspects of language are impaired in the various species of such a disorder.   This problem . . . cannot be solved without the participation of professional linguists familiar with the patterning and functioning of language.   To study adequately any breakdown in communications we must first understand the nature and structure of the particular mode of communication that has ceased to function.

It should be added that, as in the case of language acquisition, after the linguistic code has been described the insights of psychology must be applied in constructing a behavioral model.

Aphasia is a language rather than a speech pathology and is to be clearly distinguished from disturbances whose overt manifestations may be similar, such as abnormal intellectual functioning or paralysis of the speech musculature.   Aphasia, as considered here and as viewed by most contemporary researchers, involves language disturbances in decoding, manipulating, and/or encoding symbols whose etiology is to be found in brain damage. Brain damage may be incurred in various ways.   Vascular disturbances such as hemorrhages, thromboses, and embolisms appear to be the major causes, though diseases such as meningitis, encephalitis, and multiple sclerosis also result in aphasia in some cases.

Although aphasia is primarily a language disorder, its symptoms are not limited to language.   Rather, aphasics exhibit a number of other changes as well.   Joseph Wepman, in his *Recovery from Aphasia* (1951), for example, lists thirty-four nonlanguage deviations.   Among the most obvious modifications are an increase in the degree of egocentricity, a heightening of emotional behavior, and a lessening of attention and memory spans. Also, aphasics appear inconsistent in their behavior, responding appropriately at one time and failing to respond at all or only inappropriately at another time.   Still another modification in behavior is the tendency to perseverate.   The aphasic who perseverates generally responds, linguistically and/or motorically, without regard for changes in circumstances.   He may, for example, say what he had for breakfast and then when asked what he had for lunch again respond with what he had for breakfast.   Other deviations include poor organizing ability and judgment, feelings of inadequacy, social withdrawal and seclusiveness, reduced initiative and spontaneity, anxiety and tension, convulsive seizures, and the emergence and submergence of various personality characteristics.

Contemporary Theories of Aphasia

In keeping with the orientation of the entire book we shall here concentrate only on those approaches which have emphasized the contributions of linguistic, psychological, and communication theories and which will, at the same time they throw light on aphasia, advance our understanding of language and speech behavior in general.

JAKOBSON'S TWO-FOLD DISTINCTION.   According to Roman Jakobson (1957, 1968, Jakobson and Halle, 1956), language shows a basic two-fold character, consisting of the (1) selection of various linguistic elements and (2) arrangement of these elements into units of greater complexity.   This two-fold process is most obvious on the lexical or word level where a speaker *selects* certain words out of his storehouse of vocabulary and *arranges* or combines these words into phrases and sentences according to the rules of grammar.

Aphasia, according to Jakobson, can be analyzed as a disorder involving selection or arrangement.   Disorder in the selection of linguistic elements is referred to as selection deficiency or similarity disorder and disorder involving impairment of the ability to arrange or combine linguistic elements is referred to as contiguity disorder.

The aphasic suffering from *similarity disorder* is almost totally unable to function linguistically without the aid of some context, verbal or nonverbal. For example, he is unable to begin a conversation but once a conversation has been started he is able to participate.   He has difficulty starting a dialogue but is able to respond to a person who addresses him and is able to do this even when the addressor is an imaginary individual or when he imagines himself to be the addressor.   He cannot utter the sentence " It rains " unless he actually sees it raining.   The more his utterances are dependent upon context the better he is able to function.   Words which are grammatically dependent upon other words, as a verb form is dependent upon the subject, are affected only slightly by this disturbance.   Subjects of sentences, however, since they are not grammatically dependent upon other elements, are often lost in this type of aphasia.   Function words are preserved in the speech of the aphasic with similarity disorder whereas content words cause him great difficulty.   These patients have difficulty using synonyms and are unable to select equivalent terms.   To the question "What is an unmarried man called?" they are unable to give the equivalent form *bachelor* even though they may be able to use this word in connected discourse.

What seems to be lost in *contiguity disorder*, on the other hand, are the rules of grammar, and the disorder is therefore frequently referred to as "agrammatism."   It causes the degeneration of the sentence into what Hughlings Jackson called a mere "word heap."   Function words, retained in the speech of the aphasic with similarity disorder, are most difficult for the speaker with contiguity disorder.   Connectives, auxiliaries, prepositions, and articles disappear from this patient's speech with the result that his utterances resemble so-called telegraphic speech.   He will say, for example, "Man run hill" for "The man runs down the hill."   In advanced stages of this disorder the speech deteriorates into one-word sentences with only a few of the longer stereotyped sentences surviving.

Both of these disorders, as explained by Jakobson, represent extremes. Few cases, if any, could be found in which an aphasic shows the complete loss of his ability to select linguistic units while his ability to combine is totally unimpaired or vice versa.   Most aphasics represent conditions somewhere between these polar opposites.

Goodglass and Mayer (1958) attempted to determine whether Jakobson's dichotomy of aphasias was in fact a valid one.   The major purpose of their study was to identify those syntactical operations which distinguish contiguity disorder or agrammatism from noncontiguity or nonagrammatic aphasia.   Ten patients were selected for study: five agrammatic and five nonagrammatic.   The criteria used for the agrammatic group were that there was a loss of fluency in connecting words and phrases, a loss of syntactical words and inflectional morphemes, and a loss of normal speech rhythm and melody.   Subjects in the nonagrammatic group retained these abilities. Both of these groups were equated on the bases of severity of aphasia and memory span.   The subjects were administered two series of tests: a sentence repetition test consisting of sentences of varying levels of difficulty, ranging from simple phrases to sentences involving interrogatives, passives, and other complex structures, and a ten-item synonym-finding task in which each patient was asked to supply a word which could be used in place of the stimulus word.

The agrammatic group, it was found, made significantly more abortive starts (opening sentences with irrelevant words), more often failed to invert the interrogative-word sequences, and more often omitted the coordinating and subordinating construction of the sentence.   Other findings, although not statistically significant, are clearly in the predicted direction.   For example, the agrammatic group omitted more grammatical morphemes, more often changed the verb to a simplified form (omitting the inflectional verb morphemes), paraphrased incorrectly, and used stereotyped repetitions of the same errors.   They also had a greater number of total grammatical errors. In the synonym-finding task the results showed a tendency for the nonagrammatic group to have greater difficulty than the agrammatic group, as would be predicted. According to Goodglass and Mayer (1958, p. 111) "the results . . . serve to justify Jakobson's choice of 'contiguity disorder' and 'similarity disorder' as a significant basis for a dichotomy of types of aphasia."

Jakobson's distinction between selection and arrangement is probably correct. Language does involve processes of selection and combination and since aphasia is a linguistic disorder aphasic symptoms can be logically classified according to this basic two-fold distinction. The weakness of his classification is not that it is based on incorrect theory or that its basic assumptions are incorrect but rather that it is based on an incomplete theory and consequently the classifications offered are too gross for most purposes. There are in reality many more processes involved in language usage and an adequate classification of aphasic symptoms must be more specific than Jakobson's system would allow. The approach of Goodglass and Mayer, whereby the specific linguistic factors are analyzed in a controlled situation, illustrates the heuristic value of Jakobson's hypothesis and also demonstrates a methodology for concretizing and quantifying the more specific linguistic processes which might be subsumed under the two general processes Jakobson has defined.

Another hypothesis advanced by Jakobson and which permeates the research literature, is that aphasia follows the normal pattern of language development in reverse. Aphasic regression is viewed as the mirror image of the child's acquisition of language. Those features which the child learns last, that is, the more complex features, are lost first; those features which the child learns earliest, that is, the simplest features, are retained the longest. According to Luria (1958), however, the stages of speech development are never reproduced when the physiological conditions necessary for speech processes are broken down.

Although experimental evidence on this argument is not extensive some work has begun. Goodglass and Hunt (1958), for example, used this basic theory as the starting point for the hypothesis that with two inflectional morphemes the more complex will be absent from the speech of aphasics more often than will the less complex. The morphemes designating plural and possessive were selected for study. As already pointed out these two morphemes are phonemically similar and are phonologically conditioned by the same rules. The possessive morpheme was judged the more complex; therefore, the authors hypothesized that in both expressive and receptive processes subjects would make more errors with the possessive than with the plural. The expressive task was to have the subject answer questions which required the use of both morphemes. For example, the experimenter said " My sister lost her gloves." To elicit the possessive form he asked "Whose gloves were they?" The receptive task consisted of thirty correct and incorrect sentences arranged in random order. The patient was to indicate whether each sentence was correct or incorrect.   In all, twenty-four subjects were used, ranging in age from twenty-five to seventy and evidencing from severe to mild disturbances.

On the expressive task subjects made significantly more errors with the possessive than with the plural.   The total number of errors for the possessive was sixty-six but only thirty-seven for the plural.   On the receptive task subjects also made significantly more errors on the possessive (twenty-six) as compared with the plural (ten).

Although these results offer some support for Jakobson's hypothesis they do not, of course, "prove the theory."   The authors were probably justified in hypothesizing that the possessive is the more complex and is learned later than the plural.   However, it would not be fair to conclude that complexity was the causal factor in the significant results obtained.   It may well be that another factor contributed to the asymmetrical results.   For example, plurals occur more frequently than possessives and it may be that frequency rather than complexity actually accounts for the greater ease aphasics have in dealing with plurals.   Another possibility is that plurality is more concrete than possession; aphasics may, therefore, have performed better on plurals not because they are easier or acquired earlier but because they are able to deal with concrete categories but not with abstract ones.

While this study does not necessarily support the influence of complexity on aphasic disturbances it does demonstrate, again, the heuristic value of Jakobson's approach and illustrates a methodology by which this hypothesis might be further tested.

The experimenters also computed the correlations between the test scores, even though the expressive and receptive tasks were not parallel. Extremely low correlations were obtained.   This provides some support for the traditional distinction between expressive and receptive aphasia.   This distinction is contrary to the hypothesis advanced by Schuell and Jenkins (see below) which holds that aphasia results in a general language deficit affecting both expressive and receptive abilities.

BROWN'S CATEGORY THEORY.   A theory utilizing the data from both linguistics and psychology has been proposed by Roger Brown (1958a). According to Brown, aphasic symptoms can be described and classified in terms of category theory (see Brown, 1956).

For example, one common type of aphasic impairment is the loss in ability to deal with abstractions while ability to deal with the concrete remains intact.   This would be described as a loss for abstract categories and categorization and an intact ability for dealing with concrete categories.

Another type of impairment is the loss in the ability to recategorize. Brown notes that such a patient may be able to sort yarns into certain classes, for example, according to color with all the reds together and all the blues together and so on, but may be unable to recategorize these yarns into other classes, say bright colors or cold colors or warm colors.   Such "categorical rigidity" extends to nonlinguistic behaviors as well and characterizes the aphasic's general inability to switch mental sets. This is simply another way of viewing perseveration.

The inability to use proper names, especially first names, represents still another symptom. This particular loss is described by almost all researchers in aphasia and is probably one of the most often experienced symptoms. In more traditional terminology this loss is referred to as *anomia*. According to Brown, this symptom can be looked at in terms of the arbitrariness-nonarbitrariness dimension of categories. As has been noted, all words are arbitrary in that there is no real or inherent relationship between the word and the thing. Nevertheless, some words may be logically viewed as more arbitrary than others. For example, the word *man* is arbitrary and yet it is applied to many creatures all of whom possess certain characteristics in common; there is "manness" in all men. On the other hand, the name *Sam*, as applied to many individuals, refers to no common characteristic which all "Sams" possess or which are unique to "Sams"—there is no "Samness" in Sams. Furthermore, as Brown notes, many persons have had experience in naming babies or animals and consequently the separability of proper name and referent is probably felt more clearly. We are not, however, namers of chairs or tables, nor do we supply the names for the general classes of people as in the case of *man*. In aphasia it appears that the more arbitrary the category the earlier and more frequently it is lost.

Another symptom can be viewed in terms of the number of categories needed to make the word available. In this connection Brown recalls the case of Lanuti who was unable to make correct identifications; when shown an egg he called it a ball, when shown a match he called it a stick, when shown a lemon he called it a carrot. Now the egg resembles a ball, the match resembles a stick, and the lemon resembles a carrot. Each item shares properties with the item with which it is confused. In terms of Brown's approach there are categories under which both of the confused items could be logically put, for example, the category of thin, wooden objects includes both the match and the stick. When Lanuti was allowed to break the egg, however, he correctly named it as he correctly named the match when allowed to light it, and the lemon when allowed to taste or smell it. Although the normal person is able to function effectively with relatively few categories Lanuti needed additional categories, "break-ableness" in the case of the egg, "lightableness" in the case of the match, and particular taste or smell in the case of the lemon. Thus, according to Brown, the number of categories needed for correct identification may serve to characterize this type of aphasia.

This approach provides an interesting way to talk about aphasia. It seems, however, that its major weakness is that it is based solely on the lexical system of language. Aphasia, as Jakobson and others have pointed out, involves the grammatical system of language as well. Brown's approach concentrates almost exclusively on the selection process, concerning itself only indirectly with the process of combination. Because category theory provides such a limited approach to language, it is unlikely that it will prove viable in the analysis and classification of such a complex communication breakdown as aphasia.

SKINNER'S FUNCTIONAL RELATIONSHIP APPROACH. According to B. F. Skinner, aphasic symptoms can be described simply and clearly as losses in the functional relationships controlling verbal behavior in general. Skinner's position in regard to aphasia is clearly and succinctly explained in his *Verbal Behavior* (1957, p. 190):

> The pathological condition of verbal behavior called aphasia often emphasizes functional differences which are hard to understand in terms of the traditional account. The aphasic may not be able to name an object, though he will emit the name immediately in manding it; or he may be able to name an object although he cannot repeat the name after someone else or read it from a text as he once was able to do. But it is only traditional theory which makes this surprising. The aphasic has lost some of the functional relationships which control his verbal behavior. A response of a given form may no longer be under the control of one functional relation, although it is still under the control of another.

A patient may, for example, lose his ability to ask for a cigaret when he wants one (that is, he has lost his ability to mand) but he may be fully capable of saying the word *cigaret* if shown one and asked to name it (that is, he has retained his ability to tact or label).

The aphasic symptoms, according to Skinner, can be discussed in terms of the notion of difficulty which is inherent in all verbal operants. The order of damage generally follows the order of difficulty, a position similar, though not identical, to Jakobson's. Intraverbals and tacts, being the more difficult operants, are probably the least resistant to damage. Textual and echoic behaviors, being the least difficult, are the most resistant to damage. Manding behavior, since it is established through positive reinforcement, is also resistant to damage. On the other hand, behavior which has been punished (for example, untrue statements) will be weak and consequently will be easily susceptible to loss.

This approach to aphasic symptoms seems at first glance to be a relatively sophisticated one and, indeed, there seems to be much to recommend such an analysis. The problem with Skinner's approach to aphasia is the same problem which confronts his general "theory" of verbal behavior. Specifically, it is unable to account for numerous forms of verbal behavior and consequently is at best insufficient. One great advantage of Skinner's approach is that it is explicit in its claims and therefore its hypotheses and predictions can be tested experimentally. In regard to aphasia this necessary experimentation has not been conducted and it remains for researchers to supply the data on the basis of which such an approach may be evaluated more objectively.

OSGOOD'S MEDIATION-INTEGRATION THEORY. Earlier Osgood's theory of language behavior was presented (Chapter 3). It will be recalled that this model includes three basic processes: decoding, associative, and encoding. Decoding processes include the reception of input signals, their projection, their integration, and the actual decoding of their significance. Associative processes include associations among the representational mediators, associations between motor and sensory integrations, and wired-in associations as in the case of reflex behaviors. Encoding processes include the intentional selection of various linguistic units, their integration, and their expression.

This model of language behavior, as all such models, makes certain assumptions concerning communication breakdowns (Osgood and Miron, 1963). And it is to the credit of Osgood's model that the assumptions are explicitly stated in a form in which they can be tested experimentally. Specifically, the theory states that aphasias can be differentiated into two basic classes, one involving processes and the other involving levels. Aphasia may, therefore, be manifested in decoding or associative or encoding impairments and in impairments which involve grammatical aspects (that is, damage to the integration level) and impairments which involve the semantic aspects (that is, damage to the representational level). Since the projection level does not deal with language behavior it may be omitted when considering aphasia.

It would be rare to find a patient who manifests damage in only one of these six language areas. More often aphasics are found to evidence disturbances involving more than one area. Nevertheless, the theory clearly states that aphasia, in being a language disturbance, can be analyzed according to this model and that one can expect to find some patients who evidence difficulty with the grammatical system or with the associative processes or with semantic encoding, and so on.

In order to test the validity of the model as applied to aphasia, Osgood analyzed thirty-nine cases from the literature. Contingency and factor analyses were performed to test the adequacy of this theoretical model. In the contingency analysis reported disturbances were analyzed to determine which mechanisms were essential for normal performance. For example, labeling requires visual and motor sensory integration and representational encoding and decoding. Thus if two performances are dependent upon the same mechanisms, as, for example, labeling an object and pointing to an appropriate picture both require visual and motor sensory integration, then an impairment in one would presuppose an impairment in the other. The degree to which this was found to be the case was much greater than that expected by chance. Although this does not support Osgood's specific model it does indicate that distinctions between integrational and representational levels and between decoding, associating, and encoding processes appear to be valid ones.

In the second part of this analysis all of the performances were subjected to factor analysis in order to determine which performances clustered together. No factor was found to account for an extremely great portion of the variance which would be expected if there were a general language deficit running through all performances, as Schuell and Jenkins have proposed (see below). The first factor distinguished between representational and integrational performances—activities involving significance and comprehension; for example, written-sentence comprehension, spoken-word significance, and spoken-sentence comprehension clustered together. The second factor distinguished between decoding and encoding processes, the third between vocal and manual performance, and the fourth between sentence comprehension and word significance. These factors fit well within the framework of Osgood's model and add support to his theoretical analysis.

It should be noted, however, that analyzing thirty-nine cases from the literature, the reports of which must have varied greatly in detail and accuracy, is certainly less than rigorous. Clearly one should demand a more thorough and objective testing before accepting any particular theory of aphasia. This model, however, has served as the basic theory for the Illinois Test of Psycholinguistic Abilities (ITPA), which is now being widely used in diagnosing language impaired subjects and in analyzing language abilities in general. Although it is too early to generalize, research seems to indicate that both the model and the ITPA are accurate within limits (cf. Bateman, 1965). It appears that the value of this approach to the study of aphasia will be determined only after its adequacy for dealing with language behavior in general has been ascertained.

WEPMAN'S CONCEPTUAL MODEL. Joseph Wepman (1951; Wepman, Jones, Bock, and Van Pelt, 1960; Jones and Wepman, 1965) has proposed a model of aphasia which is in many ways similar to that proposed by Osgood. In the Wepman model there are also three levels of functions. The first, a reflexive level, does not involve language behavior but simply functions to translate received stimuli into motor acts automatically. This is similar to Osgood's projection level. The second, a perceptual level, similar to Osgood's integration level, involves imitative responses, responses which are not dependent upon understanding. At this level occurs such behavior as reading aloud without understanding. The third and highest level is the conceptual level which involves language and thought and is similar to Osgood's representational level. At this concept-formation level, the stimulus seems to arouse associations stored in the "memory bank" which together form a state of meaningfulness. At this meaning level Wepman postulates three types of aphasic symptoms corresponding to the three-fold distinction of Charles Morris's semiotics.   First there is aphasia involving the selection of language symbols to represent the reality (semantic aphasia). Second, there is aphasia involving the arrangement or combination of language symbols into patterns of various types (syntactic aphasia). Third, there is aphasia involving the interpretation of symbols as they relate to the objective reality (pragmatic aphasia).

The first two of these three types of aphasic symptoms correspond to the two-fold classification proposed by Roman Jakobson; the semantic corresponds to selection disorder and the syntactic to contiguity disorder.   The third disorder, pragmatic aphasia, is seldom mentioned in the classifications of aphasic symptoms, though it corresponds to what Luria (1961) describes as a breakdown of the regulatory role of speech.   The pragmatic aphasic has lost his ability to derive meaning from a symbolic or nonsymbolic stimulus and make use of it in the process of symbol formulation.   The meaning dimension, rather than the ability to select words or the ability to combine them, is most severely disturbed in pragmatic aphasia.

Wepman's theory views the central nervous system as consisting of three levels of functions—reflexive, perceptual, and conceptual.   Each of these functions in turn involves three processes: (1) a transmission process which involves the reception of stimuli by the brain, (2) an integration process which involves the comprehension of language symbols, and (3) another transmission process which involves encoding the brain's messages into output signals.   A diagram of this model appears in Chapter 4, Figure 16.

According to Wepman, "aphasia" should be limited to disturbances in the integration process at the conceptual level.   "Agnosia" should be used for disturbances in the reception of stimuli and "apraxia" for disturbances in the production of responses.   With this model Wepman argues that it is easier to delineate and separate the symbolic problems, those involving the integration processes, from the nonsymbolic disturbances, those involving the mere reception and transmission of symbols.

Studies conducted by Wepman and his associates (for example, Jones and Wepman, 1961, 1965; Spiegel, Jones, and Wepman, 1965) have, in general, supported this theoretical analysis.   Like Osgood's model, however, its value in the study of aphasia depends upon its accuracy in describing the normal processes of language behavior.   Little seems to have been done in this direction.

SCHUELL AND JENKINS' UNIDIMENSIONALITY THEORY.   Whereas most researchers, especially those with a linguistic or psycholinguistic orientation, view aphasic symptoms as varied disturbances involving different language levels or processes, Hildred Schuell and James J. Jenkins (1959; Jenkins and Schuell, 1964; Schuell, Jenkins, and Jiménez-Pabón, 1964) propose that research on aphasia should begin with the most elementary hypothesis possible.   They therefore advance the theory that "all aphasias are part of a general hierarchy of language deficit" (Schuell and Jenkins, 1959, p. 50).

Although aphasia often involves visual and motor disturbances, hearing loss, and other sensory deficits, they hypothesize that when such problems are screened out, the remaining language disturbance will be found to be unidimensional.

In order to test this hypothesis of unidimensionality Schuell and Jenkins (1959) utilized the Guttman scale analysis technique. According to this technique, (1) if aphasia is unidimensional (that is, varying only in amount of deficit and not in kind), and (2) if performance on language tests involving different language skills such as comprehending, writing, and labeling, is a function of the amount of general impairment, and (3) if the tests vary in terms of difficulty, then it would be expected that if two patients differ in their overall scores the patient with the higher score must have passed all the tests passed by the person with the lower score as well as at least one additional test. Furthermore, the easier tests must be passed by all patients who passed a more difficult test. Therefore, if the severity of aphasia in a given patient is known, the tests he will pass and the tests he will fail can be predicted. Alternatively, if the difficulty of a given test is known, the aphasics who will pass it and who will fail it can be predicted. The percentage of correct predictions provides what is called a "reproducibility index." An index of around .90 indicates extremely high accuracy. When such a high index is found it generally means that there is a unidimensional continuum.

The results of the Schuell and Jenkins (1959) study yielded a reproducibility index of .92, which they interpret as evidence for their theory that aphasia represents a general language deficit rather than deficits of various and different kinds.

As Osgood (Osgood and Miron, 1963) has pointed out, the validity of this conclusion is based on two assumptions: (1) that the test items were broad enough to allow for the recording of different types of aphasias if they did exist and (2) that the sample of aphasics was broad enough to allow for the inclusion of different types of aphasias if they did exist. In the Schuell and Jenkins procedure for establishing the final test battery a number of preliminary tests were eliminated. That is, those tests which did not correlate highly with the entire test battery were eliminated, leading to a final test battery which excluded items testing for other dimensions of aphasia if they were present. Such elimination functions to purify and specialize the language deficit being tested. Over 50 percent of the subjects used had incurred aphasia as a result of cerebrovascular accidents. There does not at present, however, seem to be evidence which indicates that using patients over fifty years of age and suffering from cerebrovascular accidents altered the obtained results in any significant way. Should such evidence be found the results of this study would require considerable reinterpretation.

Schuell and Jenkins do not argue, as some have assumed, that there is only one type of aphasia. Rather, they claim that there is a general language deficit common to all aphasias which is not modality specific but instead cuts across all modalities. Schuell and Jenkins clearly recognize that aphasics often have various perceptual or sensory-motor problems which affect certain aspects of language behavior more than others.   Furthermore, they do not claim that a recognition of this general language loss will solve the problems of diagnosis, treatment, or prognosis but only that such a recognition is an essential part of the whole solution.

The implications of the numerous studies conducted by these researchers can be summed up briefly:

> Simple expressive-receptive, motor-sensory, or other elementary clas-
> sifications of aphasia are inadequate.   There is a general language
> deficit in aphasia which is nonspecific to modalities, tasks or functions.
> This general deficit must be recognized in any description of the disorder.
> (Jenkins and Schuell, 1964, p. 93.)

It appears from an analysis of their results that there is in fact a general language loss, most clearly demonstrated in their factor analytic work (Schuell, Jenkins, and Carroll, 1962).   Acceptance of this position, however, does not mean that the other positions must be discarded.   The theory of unidimensionality appears to complement rather than refute other theories. Some of the most recent studies discussed under "New Directions in Aphasia Research" (see below) have rather clear implications for this theory.

LEE'S "GENERAL SEMANTICS IN REVERSE."   Although this next approach is not of wide currency and has not given rise to systematic programs of research, it is still profitable to investigate this application of General Semantics thinking to aphasia.   In her writing on aphasia Laura Lee (1958, 1959, 1961) has concentrated on the treatment of aphasia rather than on an analysis of the actual linguistic and psycholinguistic problems involved. Nevertheless, her program of therapy makes certain assumptions about the nature of aphasia and its various manifestations.

Basic to Lee's theory is the recognition of the distortions which language fosters and which General Semantics' training is aimed at correcting: (1) similarities, rather than differences, are labeled; (2) permanence, rather than change, is labeled; (3) inferences and descriptions are not differentiated in their linguistic representations; and (4) low order and high order abstrac-tions are not differentiated.

To Lee the aphasic exhibits the extreme opposite of these distortions and in order to get them to function like normals it is necessary to apply General Semantics' goals in reverse.   For example, aphasics are not able to note similarities but only differences; they have great difficulty in generalizing. Their language is extremely concrete; they do not perceive people-in-general but rather person$_1$, person$_2$, etc.   And although General Semantics' training is aimed at getting normals to see differences and not to concentrate on similarities, in the case of aphasics the goal is the opposite—to get them to concentrate on similarities, to teach them to generalize.

Second, aphasics see things as different from one time to another.   Things do not remain static as they seem to for normals; everything is in a state of flux. Again, normals must be trained to orient themselves to a process world where everything is constantly changing.   In the case of aphasics the goal is to get them to see permanence and to see that many things, at least for purposes of communication, do remain static.

Third, aphasics have great difficulty in making inferences.   They seem unable to say that something will happen, for example, if they do not know that it will in fact happen.   They function relatively close to the descriptive level.   Therapy is here aimed at getting the aphasic to make inferences, to anticipate what will happen, to make predictions about the future, about what they have not seen and not heard.

Fourth, aphasics find great difficulty in creating abstractions.   Consequently, they must be trained to see gross similarities and bases for categorizing unique things together and using the same label for things which admittedly are different and yet which our language groups together.

As Lee has defined it, aphasia may be seen as the extreme form of extensionalization and, in a sense, resembles a child, who, before learning language, perceives everything on the object level and everything as unique and different from everything else.   The aphasic has lost his ability to group, to categorize, to generalize, and consequently can be viewed as a person living in an almost preverbal world.

As an approach to the problem of aphasic symptoms this analysis is not original.   Rather, it restates in General Semantics terminology what Goldstein (1948) and various other writers on aphasia have already noted, namely, that the ability for abstract symbolizing is lost in aphasia.

Since any plan for therapy must be based, at least in part, on an analysis of the various aphasic symptoms, the therapeutic procedures are only as good as the classification on which they are based.   And the classification here seems too simplified not only in terms of its approach to this particular form of brain damage but also in terms of its view of language.   Language does not consist solely of different levels of usage but also of complex processes of selection, arrangement, transformation, and so on.   Without an adequate consideration of such processes involved in the generation, transmission, and understanding of language it is impossible to thoroughly analyze a breakdown.   An analysis such as Lee's, therefore, while it may be of some merit in dealing with certain language problems, cannot be viewed as a complete analysis of aphasia.

New Directions in Aphasia Research

Although the contributions of the neurologists and physiologists were not considered specifically in this discussion it should not be concluded that their contributions are not significant or that their approach is inadequate. Rather, they were omitted because the insight they provide for general language and speech behavior would be little in return for the great amount of space which would have had to be devoted to this area.   However, any complete analysis or research program in aphasia would have to include the data and methods of the neurologist.   Programs of research such as those developed by Wilder Penfield and Lamar Roberts (1959) will undoubtedly increase in number and add greatly to knowledge concerning aphasia in particular and language and speech behavior in general.

With obvious individual differences, the approaches considered here represent carefully reasoned thinking on aphasia.   There are, however, a number of other approaches to the study of aphasic language which, although not the result of fully developed theories, have much to recommend them. A few of these most recent approaches might be mentioned briefly to indicate the wide range of possibilities.   These new directions may well provide answers where previous methodologies have failed and perhaps even raise questions previously unasked.

STATISTICAL MEASURES. Both Osgood and Miron (1963) and Schuell, Jenkins, and Jiménez-Pabón (1964) stress the importance of research on the statistical properties of aphasic speech and language.   Some research on word frequency, word length, grammatical class, and redundancy may be used to illustrate the nature of this approach.

A number of different investigators have explored the relationship of word frequency and word length to aphasia.   For example, Schuell, Jenkins, and Landis (1961) found that as the frequency of a word decreased the difficulty aphasics had in comprehension increased.   Bricker, Schuell, and Jenkins (1964) found that spelling errors increased as the word frequency decreased and as the word length increased.   Normals will also find greater difficulty in comprehending words of low frequency and will also make more spelling errors on words which are longer and less frequent.   Because of this these findings may at first appear unimportant or of only peripheral interest to the study of aphasia.   They have, however, clear implications for theory building.   Specifically, they add support to the notion that aphasics appear to follow the same general laws of speech and language as do normals and only function in less efficient ways.   From evidence such as this, a quantitative rather than a qualitative difference appears to distinguish aphasic from normal speech and language.

Sefer and Henrikson (1966) investigated the relationship between word association and grammatical class in aphasics and normals.   Aphasics, they found, followed the same general pattern of word associations as normals. As the number of paradigmatic responses (same part of speech) increased the number of syntagmatic responses (completion) decreased.   This finding, according to the authors, supports the conclusions of Schuell and Jenkins on the unidimensionality of aphasia (as did the studies on word length and frequency) and argues against the distinction between selection and arrangement deficiencies proposed by Jakobson.

Jones and Wepman (1967), however, have found evidence from analyses of word frequency which supports not the unidimensionality theory but rather their own distinction between semantic and syntactic aphasia. These researchers found that when the speech samples of normals and aphasics were compared, aphasics could be divided into those who utilized a high proportion of the most frequently used words of normals and those who used a small proportion of these words, less than even the normals. This, they reason, supports the distinction between semantic and syntactic types. The semantic aphasic has difficulty in word finding and consequently relies heavily on the most frequently used terms; the syntactic aphasic has difficulty in combining terms and not in word finding and consequently uses a low proportion of high frequency terms. Furthermore, when the samples were factor analyzed one of the factors which emerged was one they call " descriptive specificity." This factor is characterized by a high proportion of articles, nouns, and adjectives especially. As expected, semantic aphasics were found to score extremely low on this factor using few articles, nouns, and adjectives while the syntactic aphasics scored high.

Similarly, research conducted by Davis Howes (1964, 1967) on speech rate and word association supports the distinction between what Wepman refers to as syntactic and semantic aphasia and which Howes prefers to label Types A and B. On the basis of words uttered per minute Howes' aphasic patients divided themselves into two classes: Type A (Wepman's syntactic) aphasics' rate decreased as the severity of their impairment increased; Type B (Wepman's semantic) aphasics, however, evidenced rates above those of normals. Furthermore, as the severity of the impairment increased their rate also increased—a pattern directly opposite to that followed by Type A aphasics. Measurements of word-association data likewise support this distinction. Type A patients give approximately the same associations as do normals whereas Type B aphasics give " associations that are quite eccentric by normal standards " (Howes, 1967, p. 195).

Fillenbaum and Jones (1962) investigated the free speech of aphasics in order to determine the degree to which it was redundant or predictable. Nine aphasics and three normals, serving as controls, responded to TAT cards. Utilizing cloze procedure (see Chapter 4), samples of approximately 250 words were drawn out and every fifth word deleted. These mutilated transcripts were then administered to college students who filled in the missing words from the context which remained. In scoring these tests the experimenters employed two methods. First, they scored as correct only verbatim fill-ins; all words filled in which were not exactly the same as the omitted words were considered incorrect. Second, they scored the tests on the basis of correct form class; any word which was of the same part of speech as the omitted word was scored as correct. The results from this cloze analysis indicate that aphasic speech is much less predictable than normal. Aphasic speech was less predictable when verbatim fill-ins were required, when the same form class was required, and when the subjects knew the form class but had to fill in the exact word omitted.

In information-theory terminology aphasic speech could be described as less predictable, less redundant, and of higher entropy than the speech of normals. In addition to demonstrating an important characteristic of aphasic speech these researchers also demonstrated that cloze procedure could distinguish passages of aphasic from normal speech where other methods such as sequential dependencies in speech and stereotypy in language could not. Continued application of cloze procedure to the speech of aphasics will probably enable researchers to specify in more precise terms the type of language impairment suffered by different patients. Cloze procedure would also provide a reliable and efficient method for measuring changes in the speech of aphasics as a result of therapy and/or time.

There are, of course, a number of other quantitative measures of speech and language which may prove useful in the analysis of aphasia. Some research has already been done on response latency and on speech rate, though much more remains to be done in this area. Diversity of vocabulary, as measured by the type-token ratio, merits more consideration than it has received. Various other " psychogrammatical factors " such as self-reference terms, allness terms, and terms indicative of consciousness of projection are obvious measures which should be explored in attempting to distinguish aphasic speech from that of normals and among different types of aphasias. Quantitative measures of abstraction level, readability, concreteness, realism, and various other " listenability " measures (see Klare, 1963) would probably distinguish the language processes of aphasics from normals where previously only subjective and impressionistic criteria were employed.

MEANING DIMENSIONS. Another direction for further research in aphasia is the investigation of the effects of aphasia on different dimensions of meaning, particularly on connotative as opposed to denotative meaning. Previous studies in aphasia have concentrated on losses in denotative meaning. The neglect of connotative meaning disturbances appears unwarranted.

The semantic differential (Chapter 3) would enable researchers to investigate this connotative meaning dimension and to determine whether losses in connotative meaning are independent of denotative meaning losses or whether they are positively correlated. Although a negative correlation would seem unlikely, it should not be dismissed as a possibility.

Osgood (Osgood and Miron, 1963) has suggested that a modified form of the semantic differential could be used with aphasics unable to handle the differential as generally administered. The aphasic would be shown pictures which differ from one another in one principal dimension, for example, a jagged versus a smooth line or a thick versus a thin line, and would be asked to select the picture which is more meaningful to the stimulus concept. Osgood and Miron (1963) administered this modified differential to two aphasics and found that the aphasic subjects selected the same pictures that normals selected despite the fact that one of them was unable to deal with normal word-finding tasks. It would appear profitable to pursue this line of research, investigating aphasics as opposed to normals, various different types of aphasics, as well as the influence of time and/or therapy on such responses.

Although the denotative and the connotative aspects of meaning are the easiest to quantify it need not be assumed that these are the only dimensions of language which could be studied. Utilizing a model of language functions such as that proposed by Jakobson (1960) one might investigate the abilities of various aphasics for dealing with each of the six language functions. Although all these aspects or functions of language have been studied they have been analyzed largely through the anecdotal evidence supplied by clinicians. More rigorous and objective measurements of the different language functions might well prove significant in the study of aphasia.

NONVERBAL COMMUNICATION CODES. One of the most interesting new directions suggested by Osgood and Miron (1963) is the investigation of aphasic disturbances in relation to the total communication code. Previous research has relied primarily on the oral code with some attention to writing. However, other channels by which information is communicated need also to be investigated. Particularly promising seems the gestural code.

In preliminary studies Goodglass and Kaplan (Osgood and Miron, 1963) administered a gestural communication test to twenty aphasic patients. This gestural test distinguished five levels of performance: pantomime interaction, natural expressive gestures, conventionalized gestures, simple pantomime, and complex pantomime. Goodglass and Kaplan found that the scores attained on the gestural test correlated highly with the severity of aphasia which supports the theory of unidimensional loss as argued by Schuell and Jenkins.

As Osgood and Miron (1963, p. 132) note, "the fact that deficiency in gestural communication has been shown to correlate highly with severity of aphasia, as ordinarily defined, clearly implies that lesions producing disturbances in symbolic communication processes are not restricted to the speech channel but also affect the visual-gestural channel."

If pursued to its logical conclusion research in aphasia would also be directed to the investigation of the proxemic code (see Chapter 4) as well as the kinesic or gestural (see Chapter 2). Proxemic codes, as has been mentioned, are learned in much the same way as are gestural codes. With the availability of an efficient and objective method of investigation, it appears that one could pursue answers to a number of pertinent questions. As in the case of gestural communication codes, if the proxemic code loss also correlated with severity of aphasia, added evidence for the unidimensional nature of aphasia would be supplied.

It would be fortunate, indeed, if we could conclude, as did Carl Wernicke almost one hundred years ago in his *Der Aphasische Symptomenkomplex* (1874) that everything needed for the understanding of aphasia was known.

Instead, however, the conclusion of Lamar Roberts (Penfield and Roberts, 1959, p. 81) is the more accurate: "None of the theories of the various types of aphasia have had general acceptance. Despite a century of study, the mechanisms of speech and aphasia remain as challenging problems." The principle questions facing aphasia research today, observes Hans-Lukas Teuber (Osgood and Miron, 1963) are the same questions which faced the earliest research: What is aphasia? Where are the lesions located which produce aphasia? How do aphasics recover?

Although they have not answered these questions, the approaches detailed here serve an extremely useful purpose in providing insight into normal language and speech behavior. At this stage of development this is all we can ask—actually it is probably a great deal.

STUTTERING

At one time in the history of communication there would have been little problem in detailing all that was known about stuttering. Aristotle, for example, reasoned that stuttering was due to an impaired tongue. The therapy was correspondingly simple—cut out pieces of the defective organ. In eighteenth-century France an equally simplistic theory of stuttering dictated that hot irons be administered to the troublesome tongue.

Today the situation is quite different. Of all the serious communication breakdowns, as Frank Robinson (1964, p. ix) recently noted, "none creates confusion, frustration, and discouragement more frequently or with greater impact than stuttering." The complexity of the actual stuttering event, the conflicting research findings, and the numerous differences and disagreements among the multitude of theories pose a seemingly insurmountable task for the student of communication breakdowns.

Yet despite the complexity, there seem to be only two basic questions which researchers have asked. The first and logically prior is, What is stuttered? Here research has centered on the properties of those linguistic elements where stuttering occurs or occurs most frequently. The second question and the one to which most researchers have addressed themselves is, What causes stuttering? Here attention has focused on various physiological and psychological reasons for stuttering. Each of these questions needs to be considered. Discussion of the first will rely heavily on the contributions of linguistic and communication theories; discussion of the second will draw most from the insights of learning theory.

Although many different definitions have been advanced, stuttering is most often regarded as disfluencies in speech production. Many disfluencies, however, occur in the speech of normals or nonstutterers. These normal nonfluencies, often referred to as primary stuttering, involve breaks in the natural rhythm of speech, false starts, vocalized pauses, and similar "hesitation phenomena." The unmodified term "stuttering" is, therefore, best reserved for the frequent and severe nonfluencies which are compounded by various psychological tensions, anxieties, fears, and by such physical accompaniments as facial distortions, excessive hand movements, foot pounding, etc.

The Properties of Stuttered Elements

One of the most obvious facts about stuttering is that it does not occur randomly.   Despite individual differences, stutterers, as a group, stutter more on certain linguistic units than on others.   A similar consistency is also evidenced in the same stutterer's behavior from one time to another.

The occurrence and frequency of stuttering has been related to four major linguistic factors: grammatical class, initial sound of the stuttered word, length of the word, and position of the word in the phrase or sentence. Each of these will be considered in turn.

GRAMMATICAL CLASS. In an early study S. F. Brown (1937) found that the order of stuttering frequency for the eight parts of speech was, from highest to lowest: adjective, noun, adverb, verb, pronoun, conjunction, preposition, and article.   The most striking feature here is that the list divides itself into content versus function words.   Content words are generally less predictable than function words and it would appear, at least from these data, that the relative predictability of words might provide a general theory as to which words are stuttered.

As with most things, however, general theories do not come so easily. Taylor (1966a, 1966b) has recently reviewed and re-analyzed the available data on the influence of grammatical class on stuttering and correctly concludes that in previous studies grammatical class has been confounded by a number of other factors which are considered below.   This same failure to isolate grammatical class is shown in the more recent study by Bloodstein and Gantwerk (1967).   When grammatical class is isolated (that is, is the only operating variable), it appears that it cannot be used to predict the stuttering event.

INITIAL SOUND OF THE WORD. A number of studies have attempted to investigate the sound of the word on which stuttering occurs (for example, Quarrington, Conway, and Siegal, 1962; Soderberg, 1962).   As in the case of grammatical class, however, these studies have not been completely successful in excluding the influence of other linguistic variables.   Yet despite the methodological shortcomings of these researches it is widely accepted (and correctly so) that more stuttering occurs on consonants than on vowels.   Taylor (1966b), in the most rigorous and sophisticated experiment on this question, found that the difference between stuttering frequency on vowels and on consonants was statistically significant at the .001 level.

Consonants, the more frequently stuttered sound type, are also less predictable; vowels, relatively infrequently stuttered on, are more predictable. Relative predictability is, however, not the only difference between consonants and vowels. The most obvious difference is in the manner of production. Whereas vowels involve relatively minor adjustments of the vocal mechanism, consonants involve considerably more complex adjustments. This observation is relatively easy to demonstrate to oneself by trying to articulate a string of consonants and then trying to articulate a string of vowels. With the vowels there is little difficulty but with the consonants it is impossible. This difference is also reflected in the fact that in all known languages there is a limitation on the number of consonants which can appear without an intervening vowel. There appears to be no such restriction on the number of vowels which may be used in sequence.

Relative predictability, then, is not the only factor which might account for the greater frequency of stuttering on consonants. It might be that the significant factor is the more sophisticated control of the vocal mechanism required for consonants. The stutterer, because of any number of psychological or physiological reasons, may have lost some of his control over these more complex adjustments.

LENGTH OF THE WORD. In her investigation of the influence of word length on stuttering Taylor (1966b) had nine male stutterers read a list containing both short words (five or less letters) and long words (six or more letters). The results support the intuitive conclusion that long words are stuttered on more than short words. Wingate (1967), comparing one-syllable and two-syllable words, also found more stuttering to occur on the long words.

Long words, however, are also less frequent. In fact, as Zipf (1949) has demonstrated, there is an inverse relation between the length of a word and its frequency. The relative influence of these two variables was recently investigated by Soderberg (1966). Nine ten-word lists were composed each of which contained three different word length levels (one-syllable, two-syllable, and three-to-four-syllable words) and three different frequency levels. The stress of the initial syllables, the grammatical class, and the initial sounds of the words were controlled.

From an analysis of the readings of twenty "fairly severe" stutterers Soderberg found that frequency of stuttering was significantly different in all three conditions of word length; there was significantly less stuttering on one-syllable words than on two-syllable words and significantly less stuttering on two-syllable words than on those of three or four syllables. Significant differences also appeared between high- and low-frequency terms. Words of medium frequency did not differ significantly from those of low or high frequency. Although Soderberg (1966, p. 586) concludes from this that "word length is a more potent variable than word frequency for differentiating the frequency of stuttering," it should be noted that the failure to find significant differences among all levels of frequency might have been a function of the frequency levels chosen by the experimenter. In this study "high-frequency words" occurred at least 100 times per million words, "medium-frequency words" from 50 to 99 times per million, and "low-frequency words" from 1 to 25 times per million. Had other frequency levels been chosen—levels which were more widely separated—significant differences might have been found. The fact that differences were found between the high and low conditions makes it highly probable that had other levels been selected other differences would have been found. Therefore, although this study does not in fact indicate which of the two variables was the more potent, it does demonstrate that both variables exert significant influence.

The investigation of Schlesinger, Forte, Fried, and Melkman (1965) on the relative influence of frequency and information load on stuttering relates directly to this issue. Transitional probabilities for each word in a particular text were first computed. That is, the relative amount of information carried by each word in a text was estimated and the frequency of of each word ascertained. Ten stutterers then read the passage and the words on which they stuttered were noted. It was found that most stuttering occurred on words which were low in transitional probability (that is, high in information) and frequency. When frequency was held constant, however, there was still more stuttering on words of low transitional probability than on those of high transitional probability. Since the authors do not analyze the influence of each factor separately, as they might have, it would be impossible to say which factor contributed more to stuttering. However, in normal speech transitional probability and frequency are positively correlated; as the frequency of a word increases so does its transitional probability. Recalling the findings on word length, it should be observed that since longer words usually contain more morphemes than shorter words they carry more information and are less predictable.

In other words, since word length bears an inverse relationship to word frequency and since the amount of information which a word carries increases as the length gets longer and as the frequency gets lower, the findings reviewed here might well be combined to support the tentative hypothesis that stuttering increases as the degree of predictability gets lower and the information load gets higher.

POSITION OF THE WORD. A number of studies (for example, Conway and Quarrington, 1963; Quarrington, 1965; Quarrington, Conway, and Siegel, 1962; Taylor, 1966b), have found that frequency of stuttering varies with the position of the word in the phrase or sentence. Taylor (1966b), for example, found that for both severe and mild stutterers there was a significant difference in stuttering as a result of sentence position. When all other variables are held constant less stuttering occurs on final words than on initial words and an intermediate amount of stuttering on medial words. For severe stutterers the probability of stuttering on the initial word of a sentence was .30, for the final word .12, and for the intermediate positions, when averaged, approximately .15. Relative probabilities for mild stutterers were similar. These findings likewise fit into the information-load hypothesis. Initial words are less predictable (carry more information) than medial words which in turn are less predictable than final words.

It is commonly held that with rereading of a passage stuttering decreases. This "adaptation phenomenon" has been attributed to a loss in what is referred to as propositionality, that is, with each rereading meaning is lost (cf. Eisenson, 1958a). As a result of these findings it has been hypothesized that the amount of meaning is positively correlated with stuttering. However, the findings just reviewed in regard to information load coincide rather neatly with this adaptation phenomenon without introducing the concept of meaning. Specifically, with rereading, the information carried by each word becomes less, that is, the words become more predictable. Therefore, the decrease in stuttering may be related to the increase in the transitional probabilities of the words rather than to any loss in meaning or propositionality. The advantage which this formulation provides is not merely terminological. Propositionality cannot be precisely quantified; information load and predictability can be.

A number of researchers (for example, Maclay and Osgood, 1959; Goldman-Eisler, 1968) have investigated the relationship between information load and hesitation phenomena in normal speech. These studies have found, for example, that more hesitations occur before content words and long words than before function words and short words. The evidence on this relationship provides substantial support for Lounsbury's (1954, p. 99) hypothesis that "hesitation pauses correspond to the points of highest statistical uncertainty in the sequencing of units of any given order."

That these studies have found the same relationship between hesitation phenomena and information load as has been found for stuttering and information load is significant from a number of points of view. First, they provide additional evidence for the importance of information load in accounting for the loci of stuttering. Second, they substantiate the relevance of hesitation phenomena in normal speech to stuttering since both appear to follow the same general pattern. Third, and perhaps most important, they suggest that stuttering may be viewed as quantitatively rather than qualitatively different from normally fluent speech. As Bloodstein, Alper, and Zisk (1965, p. 52) express it, "Stuttering appears to be essentially an intensification, an exaggeration, and ultimately, in its developed forms, a monstrification of certain kinds of normal disfluency."

The hypothesis that frequency of stuttering is positively correlated with information load seems well supported. This does not mean to say, however, that stuttering occurs because of information load. Correlations and relationships such as those considered here cannot be interpreted to signify causation. Yet a knowledge of such relations is essential if speech behavior in general and stuttering in particular are to be understood. The next question is what causes stuttering. The answers given to this question are considerably more varied, complex, and confusing.

Contemporary Theories of Stuttering

In an early attempt to put order into the area of stuttering theories Stanley Ainsworth (1945) proposed a three-fold classification. *Dysphemic theories*, while disagreeing on specifics, all hold that the stutterer is in some way different from the normal speaker and although there is no clear agreement as to what this difference is, it is assumed to be along physiological or biochemical lines. Robert West (West, Kennedy, and Carr, 1937), for example, proposed a dysphemic theory based on a series of studies in which he found that the blood of stutterers contained more inorganic phosphates, calcium, and sugar and less potassium and protein than did the blood of normally fluent speakers. Other theorists have advanced other reasons. Bryng Bryngelson (1935) proposed that stuttering was the result of an impairment in neural integration. Lee Edward Travis (1931) advanced an influential theory of cerebral dominance which holds that stuttering results from a failure of the left hemisphere of the brain to assume dominance as it does in normals. The organs of speech, located in the center of the brain, receive impulses from both sides of the brain which are not in harmony, with disfluency the result.

Neurotic theories, which also disagree in specifics, all claim that stuttering is a manifestation of some psychoneurotic condition which, as used by Ainsworth, refers to relatively mild neurotic states as well as to hysteria, anxiety, neurasthenia, and compulsive conditions. Isador Coriat (Hahn, 1956), for example, advanced the theory that stuttering is caused by a persistence of pregenital oral nursing, oral sadistic, and anal sadistic components into later life.

The third group, *developmental theories*, hypothesize that the stutterer is not physiologically different from the nonstutterer but rather that stuttering, due to various experiences, somehow developed. Current theorizing in stuttering is in sympathy with this general approach. Stuttering, in this view, is behavior that is learned in much the same way other behaviors are learned. How behaviors are learned is, of course, a controversial question with widely differing views prevailing in the psychology of learning. In stuttering research the approach which seems most useful and certainly the one most often employed is a behavioristic one, though even here there are individual differences and disagreements. A number of developmental theories will be examined here since they provide insight not only into stuttering but into general speech behavior as well.

SHEEHAN'S DOUBLE APPROACH-AVOIDANCE CONFLICT THEORY. Joseph Sheehan (1953, 1958) analyzes stuttering from a number of different, though not necessarily contradictory, points of view, and in his theory seeks to integrate the insights derived from personality and psychoanalytic theory as well as from learning theory. Two general hypotheses are advanced to account for stuttering: a conflict hypothesis and a fear-reduction hypothesis.

Conflict can take a number of different forms: in approach-avoidance conflict there is a tendency to both approach and to avoid a given object or event; in avoidance-avoidance conflict the subject is forced to make a choice between two alternatives both of which he desires to avoid; in approach-approach conflict the subject wishes to approach two incompatible or mutually exclusive objects or events. According to Sheehan, stuttering can be viewed as a double approach-avoidance conflict which includes avoidance-avoidance conflict and approach-avoidance conflict. More specifically, stuttering is a symptom of the conflict between speaking and not speaking and between being silent and not being silent. A stutterer desires to speak because of certain needs to communicate and at the same time desires not to speak because of a fear of stuttering. He therefore wishes to remain silent in order to escape from the fear of stuttering and not to remain silent in order to relieve the frustration which a failure to communicate creates. In other words, speech and silence each have both positive and negative characteristics. Consequently, the stutterer tends to approach (that is, speak) because of the positive characteristics and at the same time avoid (that is, not speak) because of the negative characteristics. It is this conflict which, according to Sheehan, produces stuttering.

The repetitions and prolongations of sounds are symptoms of the stutterer's attempt to approach speaking, at least part of the way, and then to stop or withdraw. This tendency to stop after going part of the way seems characteristic of all approach-avoidance conflicts; stuttering is simply the peculiar manifestation of such conflicts involving speech.

The fear-reduction hypothesis asserts that the occurrence of stuttering leads to a reduction of the fear which caused the stuttering behavior. Therefore, during the actual stuttering moment the conflict is resolved because of the reduction in fear. In this way Sheehan accounts for the eventual production of the stuttered or blocked word or sound.

According to the conflict hypothesis, when the avoidance drive is heightened or when the approach drive is lowered, there will be an increase in stuttering. On the other hand, when the avoidance drive is lowered or when the approach drive is heightened stuttering decreases. According to the fear-reduction hypothesis, stuttering behavior is followed by a reduction of the fear which brought on the stuttering.

In support of the conflict hypothesis Sheehan argues that attaching penalties to stuttering increases stuttering behavior. Sheehan also claims as support the studies showing that with repetition of a passage the amount of stuttering decreases. The reason for this decrease, says Sheehan, is that less punishment is contingent upon stuttering material which, through repetition, has lost some of its meaning. Sheehan also uses these studies as support for the fear-reduction hypothesis. The decrease in the frequency of stuttering, according to Sheehan, indicates that each reading of the passage reduces fear. Also, he notes that electromyographic measurements taken from the masseter muscles of stutterers while they are stuttering show that maximum tension occurs immediately preceding the stuttering moment (that is, when the fear is at its height).

In stuttering there are, according to Sheehan, five distinct levels of conflict.   (1) Stuttering, on the word level, represents a conflict between a desire to speak and not to speak a particular word which, as a result of previous experiences and conditioning, the stutterer has learned to fear. (2) At the situational level stuttering represents a conflict between entering and not entering a situation which elicits fear in the stutterer.   Many stutterers stutter in certain situations, for example, public speaking or interview situations, while remaining relatively fluent in others.   (3) Conflict may also arise from the emotional content of the speech or passage.   Some stutterers, for example, stutter a great deal when speaking of an object or event about which they have guilt feelings.   (4) Stuttering may increase as a result of a relationship conflict, particularly a superior-subordinate relationship.   Although many stutterers have no difficulty speaking to animals or with subordinates they have great difficulty speaking with those who are in authority.   (5) Stuttering conflict may center on the ego-protective level. Stuttering is viewed here as an unconscious means for protecting the ego; in effect, it serves to remove the subject from situations and experiences which may prove damaging to his self-concept.

This theory has two major weaknesses.   First, and most important, its predictions are directly contradicted by numerous experimental studies. These will be reviewed in considering the operant-conditioning theory. Second, it lacks the degree of predictability which would normally be expected of such a theory.   According to Sheehan, stuttering reduces fear; it leads to drive reduction.   This drive reduction then leads to increased fluency.   On the other hand, fluency increases fear and tension builds up; there is an increase in drive state.   This increased drive state then leads to an increase in stuttering.

As Sheehan (1958, p. 133) himself points out, ". . . we have a paradoxical relation—the stuttering produces the fluency and the fluency produces the stuttering."   Sheehan then uses this "paradoxical relation" to explain the tendency for stuttering to occur in waves.   The problem here is simply that the variables incorporated into the theory are not specifically defined so that definite predictions can be made and tested.   Consider a stutterer who speaks fluently for one sentence and then stutters.   The theory holds that the tension and fear built up during the fluency period led to the eventual stuttering.   However, consider a stutterer who speaks fluently for ten sentences and only after these does he stutter.   The theory again would hold that tension was building up during these ten fluent sentences and brought on the eventual stuttering.   The theory, however, provides no means for determining the level of tension necessary for stuttering.   Nor is the theory any more specific on fear reduction. Given a person who stutters and after this speaks fluently for the next few sentences, the theory claims that the stuttering reduced the fear which enabled the subject to speak fluently. However, stuttering which occurs on the first word of a sentence and then again on the second word is explained by hypothesizing that here the drive state or fear was not reduced sufficiently by the first stuttering act. But the theory provides no method of telling to what level the drive state must be reduced for fluent speech to occur.

This theory, then, is extremely difficult to test simply because it does not provide specific predictions. This "escape clause" demonstrates a major failing. If a theory is to be useful it must allow specific predictions to be made so that its adequacy as a theory may be tested; a theory which fails to do this fails because of it.

BLOODSTEIN'S ANTICIPATORY STRUGGLE REACTION THEORY. Oliver Bloodstein (1958, 1960, 1961) has proposed a theory which although not grounded in contemporary learning theory is nevertheless a developmental theory heavily dependent upon the assumption that stuttering is learned behavior. With some modification Bloodstein's theory derives from the theories of Wendell Johnson (1946, 1959) who first applied General Semantics principles to stuttering.

According to Johnson, stuttering is a disorder in fluency which arises from the normal nonfluencies of the child being diagnosed as stuttering by a layman, usually the mother, and the child's subsequent attempts to avoid such fluency failures. After being labeled a stutterer, the child develops a certain apprehension or anxiety about speaking which leads him to hesitate more. The increased hesitations in turn produce more anxiety which in turn produce more hesitations. The result is stuttering, nonfluencies complete with the various facial and bodily contortions designed to produce more fluent speech. Johnson's theory is often referred to as "semantogenic" or "diagnosogenic," indicating that the cause of stuttering is to be found in the semantic label or diagnosis.

Bloodstein's theory is quite similar though somewhat refined to take into consideration some of the more recent data. Specifically, the question of stuttering, according to Bloodstein, involves two assumptions on the part of the child. The first assumption is that he does not speak well and the second is that he should speak better.

Bloodstein does indicate that one of the reasons, although it is not given prominence, for the assumption that he does not speak well is the normal nonfluencies. These nonfluencies are characteristic of the speech of all children but in eventual stutterers they are perceived as failures. Other causes for this assumption may be specific language difficulties, pronunciation problems, delayed language development, or common defects of articulation. As can be appreciated from this list, failures of fluency are not the only possible causes for the child developing the feeling that he does not speak well: ". . . not hesitancy alone," says Bloodstein (1958, p. 36), "but anything at all which tends to shake a child's faith in his ability to speak may result in an appreciable danger that stuttering will arise sooner or later."

At this point, then, the child has acquired the attitude that he does not speak up to par; this alone, however, is not sufficient to produce stuttering. In addition to this attitude is needed an "exaggerated conscience about speech," which according to both Johnson and Bloodstein, is developed by the parents being overly perfectionistic, dominating, anxious, overprotective, and so on. In a world highly conscious of speech and in which achievement and excellence are often measured by speech behavior it is not surprising to these researchers that excessive pressures may be brought to bear upon the child to achieve a standard of speech which is, at his stage of development, beyond reach.

Research findings to support the corollaries of this theory are not difficult to come by. For example, of seventy cases for which a sufficient history was available to draw inferences and examined by Bloodstein (1958), forty-two evidenced parental pressures for improved speech. A family history of stuttering, found by many other researchers as well, was present in thirty-six cases. Here it appears logical to assume that where there is a history of stuttering there will also be anxious and perfectionistic attitudes concerning speech. Stuttering has also been found to be higher among groups who are socially upward-moving and here again it is logical to assume that in these groups there will be increased concern and anxiety over good speech and pressures to "correct" nonfluent or poorly articulated speech. These are only a few of the many findings which could be cited to illustrate the apparent logic of this approach.

Bloodstein's theory, however, does not enable one to account for those instances in which the same factors are present but in which stuttering does not develop. If these factors were actually causal in their operation then all cases in which these factors are present should exhibit the same symptoms or effects. This, however, does not appear to be the case. One of the "outs" for this theory, when so confronted, is to assume that the child's assumptions concerning his failures and his need to improve were not strong enough. That is, if cases were presented in which the individual feels that he speaks poorly and that he must improve and which may be coupled with parental pressure to improve, an atmosphere of general anxiety concerning speech, and perhaps even a family history of stuttering, and yet does not exhibit stuttering behavior, the theory would claim that such feelings of failure were not strong enough or that the need to improve was not intense enough to produce stuttering. In allowing for such an "out" the theory exhibits one of its inadequacies, as did Sheehan's. It does not allow for rigorous experimental testing as any adequate theory must. Just how one would go about determining the specific level of these needs, *necessary and sufficient* to produce stuttering, is difficult to imagine.

It should also be noted that any theory which attempts to put anything in the "black box" without clearly linking them to observable and measure-able antecedents is automatically suspect. Although it is not claimed that nothing should be put into the box, it is argued that it is undesirable and unscientific to speak in terms of "anticipation of failure" and the "acquisition of high standards" without clearly specifying the observables upon which these abstractions are based. Equally vague and abstract antecedents such as "parental pressure" or "climate of anxiety" will obviously not do. Such abstractions may conceivably include everything in the history of the organism with the result that the determination and measurement of the causal factors—whatever they may be—become impossible.

BRUTTEN AND SHOEMAKER'S NEGATIVE-REACTION THEORY. Brutten and Shoemaker (1967) have recently advanced a theory of negative reaction. In this approach stuttering is viewed as existing on a continuum which can be divided into three principal stages.

Stage 1 behavior is generally fluent; the occasional nonfluencies are unlearned. This is the speech behavior characteristic of the vast majority of speakers. Occasional nonfluencies result from stress rather than learning.

Stage 2 behavior is characterized as generally fluent but with more frequent and more severe nonfluencies than those at Stage 1. At this stage the individual experiences negative emotional reactions to the stimulus situation of speaking. This negative emotion is learned through a process of classical conditioning; the emotional reaction is learned because of its close or frequent association with the originally neutral stimulus (that is, the speaking situation). Negative emotional reactions disrupt the fine cordination required in the motor act of speech. The result is nonfluency. One way in which this theory differs from the one considered next is that Brutten and Shoemaker hold that not all learning is the result of reinforcement; emotional reactions are learned by classical conditioning. Furthermore, it differs in its assumption that the actual stuttering is not learned but rather that it is a simple reaction or disruption caused by the increase in negative emotion. At Stage 2 behavior, then, a stimulus situation, because of a pairing with negative emotion, gives rise to this emotion which in turn causes a disruption or fluency failure. This stage defines the onset of stuttering.

Stage 3 behavior is characterized by a further increase in nonfluency occasioned by a heightened emotional reaction and is what is normally referred to as stuttering. What happens here is relatively simple. The nonfluencies of Stage 2 produce in listeners negative reactions, for example, impatience or looks of disgust. Negative reactions may also come from the speaker himself as well as from the listener. Both types produce heightened emotionality. These reactions produce negative emotions which summate with the emotional reactions produced by the nonfluencies. This resulting emotionality leads to a further disorganization in the coordination required for speaking and the result is stuttering. The negative emotional reactions at this stage become conditioned to speaking in general or to various

and specific stimuli associated with a particular listener or with authority
figures or with certain words or sounds.

According to this approach, then, what are learned are the emotional
reactions (from stimuli associated with the speech act and from stimuli
emanating from listeners and from the speaker himself) which disrupt the
coordination necessary for fluent speech.

Although this theory seems logical there is at present no substantial
supportive experimental evidence. The reasons given by Brutten and
Shoemaker for rejecting the simpler operant-conditioning approach is that,
they claim, it does not account for the failure of punishment to decrease
stuttering. Their theory, like Sheehan's, claims that punishment, in producing negative emotions, increases stuttering. Two points need to be made
here. First, negative evidence fails to prove a case either way; when
researchers do not find a relationship it does not mean that a relationship
does not exist; it means only that it has not been found.

Second, the data on punishment and reinforcement, only some of which
was not available to Brutten and Shoemaker at the time of their writing,
seem to argue strongly that their rejection of the operant-conditioning
approach was premature and that it is their negative-reaction theory which
is in conflict with the experimental evidence.

SHAMES AND SHERRICK'S OPERANT-CONDITIONING THEORY. The theory of
operant conditioning has been implicit in much research on stuttering. It
was only recently, however, that its importance and relevance were fully and
thoughtfully articulated (Shames and Sherrick, 1963). Stuttering is
regarded as abnormal behavior which is learned in a relatively normal way,
in the same way that other behaviors are learned. The theory is an extension or application of Skinnerian conditioning theory reviewed in Chapter 3.

Operant behavior, it will be recalled, is emitted (rather than elicited)
and is modified and controlled by its consequences. Thus a rat, if rewarded
for pressing a lever, will press it again and again. The reward or positive
reinforcement serves to increase the lever pressing behavior. Likewise, if
the rat were subjected to a continual aversive stimulus, for example, shock,
and if the removal of this shock were made contingent upon its pressing the
lever, this lever-pressing behavior would increase. Here we have a case of
negative reinforcement. If, on the other hand, the rat were shocked (that
is, punished) for pressing the lever it would discontinue this behavior and
engage in behavior designed to avoid the painful stimulus. If the lever
press brought no rewards and no punishments—if it were not differentially
reinforced—the lever-pressing behavior would be inhibited. Stuttering,
according to Shames and Sherrick, is operant behavior and is to be viewed in
essentially the same manner.

As has been noted, hesitations or normal nonfluencies resemble stuttering in that both precede linguistic units of high information content. In
stuttering viewed as operant behavior there is naturally a strong relationship

or continuity postulated between these two forms of behavior. Nonfluency in children is normal and is probably the result of physiological limitations under which the child is operating; he has not developed sufficient muscular control to achieve what adults would regard as fluent speech and therefore speaks with various hesitations, vocalized pauses, prolongations of sounds, and so on. When there is no differential reinforcement for these nonfluencies such behaviors are inhibited, just as in the case of the rat's lever pressing which resulted in neither reward nor punishment. Since verbal behavior in general is positively dealt with, that is, rewarded, it is learned. In these cases the children pass from a normally nonfluent to a normally fluent stage which characterizes the speech of the adult community.

When, on the other hand, the listener punishes these normal non-fluencies, as many overanxious parents might easily do, trouble arises. There are a number of hypotheses which might be advanced to account for the reason punishment for nonfluency increases rather than decreases stuttering. Nonfluencies might increase because they enable the child to postpone the punishing conditions which he knows to be contingent upon the completion of the utterance. In cases such as lying or in admitting respon-sibility for some wrongdoing, where punishment is contingent on the com-pletion of the response, the child hesitates and thereby avoids or at least postpones the forthcoming punishment. There are, of course, other pos-sibilities. For example, repetitions are one way of maintaining attention. Silence, as noted earlier, is often a sign for the listener to begin talking. By repeating and pausing vocally the child prevents the listener from talking and maintains the floor. Also, the child has learned that if one response does not get what he wants he will succeed if he repeats himself. The parent, as Shames and Sherrick correctly point out, is not only giving the child what he wants but is at the same time teaching him to repeat since reward is made contingent upon repetition. The important thing to note in these examples is that in each instance the child derives reward from his nonfluencies; that is, he is reinforced.

When punishment becomes contingent upon nonfluent behavior the listener eventually acquires aversive properties and is seen as a threat. The child then approaches the speaking situation with this threat of punishment. In order to avoid this punishment he attempts to change or modify his behavior. One alternative is to remain silent but this is usually too difficult. The needs which speech serves are too many and too important for silence to develop as an effective defense. Rather, the child generally engages in some form of struggle, attempting to avoid the nonfluencies. Here the previously effortless repetitions come to involve muscular tensions, atypical facial and postural movements, and prolonged periods of silence.

The final stage in this developmental sequence is the incorporation of behaviors which are somewhat remote from those typically involved in speech activities such as closing one's eyes, pounding one's foot or hand, nodding one's head and so on—behaviors which generally characterize stuttering in its more advanced forms. Such behaviors are designed to terminate the listener's punishing consequences and to avoid the punishment contingent upon the original nonfluencies.

In summary, then, stuttering, when analyzed in these terms, is regarded as operant behavior which is dependent upon its contingencies or consequences. It is learned in essentially the same way as are other behaviors and develops and is maintained by reinforcement.

According to this position, stuttering, like all learned behaviors, can be controlled, modified, and changed. More specifically, punishment decreases stuttering frequency and reinforcement increases it. Flanagan, Goldiamond, and Azrin (1958) studied three stutterers, ages 15, 22, and 37. Each subject read from printed pages and each time he stuttered the experimenter pressed a microswitch to record the stuttering. In this way a curve of stuttering frequency was obtained for each of the three subjects under relatively normal conditions. After a smooth curve was obtained a thirty-minute response-contingent session began. Under these conditions each stutter had contingent upon it some consequence determined by the experimenters. After this thirty-minute session, the subjects read in a contingent-free condition for another thirty minutes so that any changes produced by the experimental manipulation could be observed.

The response-contingent sessions were of two kinds: aversive and escape. During the entire session a constant noise level of 60 decibels was maintained; this is an unpleasant though not painful sound. In the aversive condition each time the subject stuttered he was punished by receiving a one-second blast of a 6,000-cycle tone at 105 decibels. During the escape condition each time he stuttered he was rewarded by having the original constant noise of sixty decibels shut off for five seconds.

The results of this simple experiment showed that in the aversive periods all subjects' stuttering decreased; the stuttering behavior decreased in frequency for the thirty-minute aversive period as well as for the following session in which no contingencies were present. For the escape period the opposite result obtained.

This is a rather clear example of the application of operant-conditioning principles to the control of stuttering and provides experimental support for the theory as advanced by Shames and Sherrick. Other evidence might also be cited. Martin and Siegel (1966a, p. 351), studying the effects of response-contingent shock on the stuttering of three adult males, found that for all three subjects " the introduction of response-contingent shock resulted in an almost total reduction of stuttering behavior; removal of shock was followed by a return to base-rate frequency."

In another study Martin and Siegel (1966b) applied verbal punishment. For each stuttering event the punishing stimulus *not good* was administered. In even this extremely mild punishment situation a decrease in stuttering behavior was obtained. When the verbal contingency was removed the stuttering increased to near base-level frequency. Studies by Goldiamond

(1962, 1965) provide additional theoretical and experimental support for the effectiveness of reward and punishment in controlling stuttering behavior.

The results from studies on the nonfluencies of normal subjects show similar conditioning effects. Siegel and Martin (1966) investigated the influence of response-contingent punishment on the hesitations of sixty normal subjects and found essentially the same pattern evidenced by the stutterers. When the word *wrong* was made contingent on each repetition or hesitation the subjects' disfluencies decreased. When the contingency was removed the disfluencies increased. Siegel and Martin (1965) and Brookshire and Martin (1967) provide additional support for the effectiveness of verbal punishments in decreasing disfluencies in normal subjects.

It should be made explicit that there is no contradiction between the results of these studies and those on the operant conditioning of verbal behavior (see Chapter 3). It will be recalled that these latter results were considered questionable; there is considerable reason to doubt that verbal behavior can be conditioned and even more reason to doubt that verbal behavior is dependent upon and is maintained by reinforcement. Whereas verbal behavior in general does not seem learned by a process of conditioning, stuttering and hesitations do seem to evidence such learning history. Therefore, stuttering and hesitations can be controlled by the manipulation of their consequences. As the studies cited above illustrate, they can be increased by reinforcement and decreased by punishment.

Many linguists, in rejecting Skinner's position on verbal behavior, imply that the entire area of operant conditioning should likewise be rejected. This is both unnecessary and undesirable. That numerous forms of behavior can be controlled by conditioning seems incontrovertible.

When stuttering is viewed in terms of operant conditioning it is relatively easy to account for the data on what words are stuttered and the close connection between hesitation phenomena and stuttering. Hesitations, as has been pointed out, occur more frequently before units of high information and uncertainty. According to the operant conditioning theory, these hesitations are reinforced, are learned, and consequently occur more frequently and more severely. Such frequent and severe hesitations are simply given the new name "stuttering." In fairness to the other approaches it should be noted that any theory which considers stuttering as learned behavior would be able to incorporate such findings. Some, however, may have to introduce additional mechanisms or principles into already complex theoretical structures.

Operant conditioning leaves unanswered the question of why certain events function as reinforcers. Its claims are limited to the assertion that behavior can be controlled by the arrangement of consequences. As demonstrated by the studies cited, operant conditioning is an extremely powerful approach to the control of stuttering behavior. Such research will undoubtedly increase in the next few years and will probably answer many questions concerning the operation of different reinforcers, the degree to which nonfluencies and stuttering can be manipulated, the permanence of conditioning effects, the ways in which conditioning might be incorporated into therapy, and the implications for the prevention of stuttering.

Although there is a clear bias in favor of this approach it should not be assumed that operant conditioning has provided a complete theory of stuttering; research to date has only contributed some argument and some evidence for its usefulness.

Because of the many unanswered questions remaining it would seem premature to venture *a* theory of stuttering. The conclusion of Keith St. Onge and James Calvert (1964, p. 159) neatly summarizes the state of theorizing:

> What overwhelms the *critical reader* are the dogma-ridden, self-asserted theories and the inconsistent, contradictory studies and statistically insignificant results. The scholar who attempts to teach in the area of stuttering spends most of his time clarifying what the majority of experts disbelieve about stuttering, simply because the area of disbelief so greatly exceeds the consensus.

The state of present research on stuttering seems to demand not *a* theory but rather a set of facts and data which a preliminary theory would have to incorporate. Such a tentative theory of stuttering, I think, would have to account for findings such as the following:

1. Nonfluency is characteristic of the speech of normals and yet only a small proportion of these become stutterers.
2. Stuttering is not random but rather is associated with linguistic units which carry high information.
3. Stutterers appear normal in every respect except fluency.
4. Stuttering has been manipulated and controlled by contingency management, by the control of its consequences.
5. The manipulation of nonfluencies in normal subjects appears to follow the same pattern as found in stutterers.

These statements are suggestive, rather than exhaustive, of the types of "facts" which need to be recognized in theory construction. The student who reviews the literature on stuttering will have no difficulty adding other such statements to this list and will probably find reasons for rejecting some or all of those given here.

In this chapter we have considered two of the most complex language and speech pathologies. Clearly, little is known about either aphasia or stuttering. Yet, it is equally clear that great gains have been made in our understanding of these problems during the last few decades. These significant advances are largely due to the application of the methods and procedures of psycholinguistics. Further advances are sure to follow as this science progresses.

Chapter Seven

Speech and Language Differences: Differential Psycholinguistics

The concern in this chapter is not merely with differences in languages, nor merely with differences in behavior, but rather with the more complex issue of differences in speech and language which have some relationship to cognitive and/or behavioral differences.

The first section, *individual differences*, is concerned with what is more traditionally viewed as matters of style and stylistics. After providing some essential definitions attention is focused on the influence of psychological states of the source on differences in encoding behavior (source differences), the influence of differences in speech on decoding behavior (receiver differences), and the influence of the relationship between the source and receiver on speech behavior (source-receiver relationship differences). Only some of the essential variables in the communication act are singled out in this chapter. Others exist; others are important. The second section, *group differences*, focuses on the relationship between intralanguage and interlanguage differences and behavior. In the third section the broadest question, that of *system differences*, is explored through the comparison of human- and animal-communication systems.

Conveniently, this breakdown parallels the distinctions among speech, language, and communication. In focusing on individuals the concern is speech, in focusing on groups it is language, and in focusing on systems it is communication.

INDIVIDUAL DIFFERENCES

Before examining the topic of individual differences some essential definitions need to be introduced.

Some Preliminary Definitions

In the investigation of individual differences the concern is with what might be called style or, more specifically, with *the selection and arrangement of those linguistic features which are open to choice* (cf. Osgood, 1960b; Jakobson, 1957; DeVito, 1967e).

Style is concerned only with *linguistic features which are open to choice.* Style is not concerned with features which *must* be chosen and which *must* be arranged in a prescribed way.   The rules of the language have made many "choices" obligatory and these are matters of grammar.   The clearest example of this is probably the rule of English orthography which states that a *u* must be selected from the twenty-six possibilities and placed immediately after the *q*.   Put another way, concern is limited to those linguistic features which are not completely redundant.

As the freedom of choice increases so does the opportunity for individual differences.   There is, in other words, an inverse relationship between grammar on the one hand and style or individual differences on the other; as the rules of grammar fail to apply, individual freedom increases.   When a speaker is presented with a choice, that is, when the language rules do not specify the selection or arrangement which must be made, that choice is a stylistic one.

The amount of choice allowed the speaker bears a direct relationship to the size of the linguistic unit.   At the phonemic stage there are no real choices; the selections have already been made and constitute the phoneme inventory of the language.   Thus an English speaker, although capable physiologically of doing so, cannot choose the back /k/ of Arabic or the unrounded back vowels of Russian or the *ach-laut* of German.   Similarly, the arrangement of phonemes is prescribed by the particular language.   In English an /h/, for example, cannot occur in final position and /ŋ/ cannot occur in initial position; /k/ cannot immediately follow /d/ and /p/ cannot immediately follow /b/.   Al Capp, it might be noted, did break this rule for phoneme combination in naming one of his characters "Joe Btfsplk" and thereby made a choice on a level which normally allows none.

Where the rules of phoneme combination do not proscribe certain arrangements the speaker is still not completely free.   Many of the permissible phoneme combinations have already been made and constitute the morphemes of the language.   Those phoneme arrangements which are not proscribed by the language code and which are not already standard morphemes can be coined by the speaker.   He may, for example, coin the morphemes *stiz* or *kel* since these combinations do not violate the language code and are not established English morphemes.   This is, therefore, a matter of individual choice.   Cases of morpheme coinage and violations such as Capp's "Joe Btfsplk" are, of course, extremely rare and for the most part one could say that at the phonemic level, in regard to both selection and arrangement, there is no real choice and hence no individual differences.

At the morphophonemic level there is greater choice, though still not complete freedom.   The bound morpheme designating more than one *boy* which must be selected is {-z} and it must be placed at the end of the word. Here selection and arrangement are specified by the morphophonemic rules of the language, and are therefore not matters of individual variation.   Al Capp has also violated this rule; more than one *Shmoo*, said Capp, were

Shmoon (Brown, 1958a).   It is interesting to note that not even their creator could make this term acceptable; to everyone reading L'il Abner those little white creatures were *Shmoos*.

With free morphemes or words the choices are more numerous and the selection of linguistic features becomes more dependent upon the individual speaker than upon the grammar of the language.   After the word *the* the number of alternative morphemes which might be chosen is extremely large, though again there are some constraints.   One could not, for example, say *the predicts* except in very rare cases such as "The predicts it boy is an ungrammatical sentence."   Conceivably one might construct a grammatical sentence with this unit and more correctly one should say that the occurrence of such a sequence as *the predicts* has a probability approaching zero.

In the sentence "The _____ was good," to use Fries' (1952) example, the grammar of the language merely requires than a noun-word be used after *the*.   Semantics imposes a further restriction and requires that the noun-word make sense.   The remaining choice is then a matter of individual difference.   Thus the inclusion of *unicorn* would be grammatically correct but semantically or referentially doubtful.   The choice from among *man, prince, fellow, servant, drudge* and the like would depend upon the individual speaker, though, of course, semantic constraints are never entirely absent in connected discourse.   This, however, is not to imply that the manner of expression cannot be divorced from the content of expression.   Style, although operating within constraints imposed by both grammar and semantics, is independent of both.   As Paul Valéry (1966, p. 18) has observed, "style signifies the manner in which a man expresses himself, *regardless of what he expresses*, and it is held to reveal his nature, quite apart from his actual thought—for thought has no style."

On the level of constituents the choices become substantial.   For example, in the sentence "The young man lost his fortune" there are constituents at various levels.   The immediate constituents, as has been noted, would be the two parts of the sentence which native speakers feel can be most easily separated.   In English this generally corresponds to the division between subject and predicate, that is, between *the young man* and *lost his fortune*.   Other levels of constituents are obtained from finer sentence divisions, for example, between words.   After such constituents as *the young man* the choices are extremely great and would, as a minimum, consist of all the individual morphemes or morpheme combinations which could be substituted for *lost his fortune*, that is, any verb phrase.   As may be observed, as the constituents become smaller in size the number of choices become less.   On the sentence level the freedom becomes greater still and this needs no illustration.

Selection refers to the choice of a particular linguistic feature, say a word, from a number of possible alternatives provided by the language.   Selection can occur at the morphemic level, as has been pointed out, as well as on the suprasegmental level.   A choice between a rising and a falling intonation and between a high pitch and a low pitch is likewise a matter of individual difference. Somewhat less obvious, though equally important, is the selection of paralinguistic and kinesic features. Paralanguage, nonphonemic vocal characteristics such as intensity, rhythm, tempo, and kinesic motions need to be considered along with the other, more widely studied linguistic units such as words and sentences.

Arrangement refers to the placement of linguistic forms and the patterns which result. Although arrangement most often refers to the grouping of words and phrases it too can refer to the suprasegmental level, to such matters as intonational patterns, pitch patterns, and the like, and to paralinguistic and kinesic levels as well.

Source Differences

In an early and much publicized study, Fillmore H. Sanford (1942a) compared the speaking styles of two twenty-year-old college sophomores whom he called Merritt and Chatwell. These subjects responded orally to various stimuli, for example, they commented on well-known paintings, created narratives around given words, and described familiar scenes. In addition some written samples were obtained from semi-narratives they produced based on previous reading and from autobiographies. In all, eleven samples of discourse were secured for each subject and analyzed for 234 linguistic factors. A differentiation score for each factor was then computed. This score was obtained by totaling the number of samples on which Merritt scored higher, expressed as the first figure, and the number of samples on which Chatwell scored higher. Thus a score of 4-7 would mean that on the eleven samples Merritt scored higher on four and Chatwell scored higher on seven. A score which does not total eleven means that no differences occurred in certain samples.

Merritt's linguistic behavior was *complex*—much subordination (10-0), many relational and parenthetical clauses (8-2), and long sentences (9-1); *perseverative*—frequent repetition (7-0) and rephrasing (6-3), low type-token ratio (2-8), and much repetition of content (8-2); *thorough*—few implicit usages (2-9), many transitive (8-1) and intransitive (8-2) verbs, and few clauses without conjunction (1-8); *uncoordinated*—many hesitations (7-1), much grammatical awkwardness (8-1), and many repetitions (7-0); *static*— many infinitives (8-1), psychological verbs, that is, cognitive, sensory, and affective verbs (9-2), and few action verbs (3-7); *highly definitive*—many articles (7-4), restrictive adjectives (7-4), pointing words (7-4), concrete nouns (8-2), possessive pronouns (7-3), and verbs which are explicitly defined (6-2); *cautious*—many noun (9-2) and cause (9-1) clauses, modal auxiliaries, for example, *could, would, might* (7-3), and frequent use of static copula clauses such as *it seems that* (9-1); and *stimulus-bound*—frequent use of present tense (8-2), many concrete nouns (8-2), and few perfect (1-8) and progressive (2-7) tenses.

"If we go one step further toward synthesis and generalization," Sanford (1942a, p. 190) concludes,

we might conceive of his whole style as *defensive* and *deferent*. Most of his verbal behavior seems to reflect a *desire to avoid blame or disapproval*. He is cautious and indirect, rarely making a simple or bald statement. Once he makes a judgment he explains it and presents all aspects of it, leaving little to the auditor's imagination and little for the auditor to question. His concern for the adequacy of every response results in a re-examination of the response and this, in turn, brings about rough-nesses in his discourse. His disinclination to venture out "on his own" makes him feel more comfortable in the stimulus-bound situations.

Chatwell's linguistic behavior, on the other hand, was *colorful*—many rare words (10-1), high type-token ratio (8-2), many stylistic devices (9-0), and contractions (6-2); *emphatic*—many modified modifiers (6-3) and adverbs of degree (8-2); *direct*—little complexity (0-10) and subordination (0-10), many simple sentences (8-3), and pronouns used as direct objects (9-2); *active*—many verbs of action (7-3), few psychological verbs (2-9), modal auxiliaries (3-7), and static copulative expressions (1-9); *progressive*—many clauses of progressive relation (9-2), progressive tenses (7-2), and few rephrasings (3-6) and repetitions (2-7); *coordinated*—few hesitating sounds (2-7), little repetition (2-7), and no grammatical awkwardness (0-6); *evaluative*—many adjectival clauses (9-2) and "impressive" adjectives (9-2) and a high descriptive-pointing ratio (7-4); *inclusive*—many allness terms (8-2), impressive (9-2) and quantitative (9-1) adjectives, and frequent collective nouns (6-1); *implicit*—many implicit constructions (9-2), coordinate clauses without conjunction (8-1), and contractions (6-2); *connected*—many initial clauses coordinated with preceding sentence (7-2), infrequent rephrasing of single words (2-6), and few hesitating sounds between phrases (2-7); *confident* —few modal auxiliaries (3-7), noun clauses (1-9), and static copulative clauses (1-9); *autonomous*—many negatives (7-4) and unfavorable adjectives in his comments on the pictures (16.2 percent-0 percent); and *definite*—many definite articles (7-4), adverbs of place (7-4), and adverbial clauses of time (7-3).

Chatwell's style, Sanford (1942a, p. 197) summarizes,

is *colorful, varied, emphatic, direct, active, progressing always in a forward direction*. His responses are *well coordinated, closely interconnected,* more *evaluative* than *definitive*, and somewhat *enumerative* (that is, containing many "ands" beginning clauses, linking phrases, and within clauses, and many enumerating sentences). He covers *extensive* areas, verbally, and is *disinclined to consider details* or *precision of reference*. His speech is *confident, definite, independent*. In general he appears to use speech not so much to describe the external world and its relations as to *express his own individuality and to impress the auditor*.

Although in this particular study Sanford (1942a, p. 197) did not attempt to investigate the personalities of the subjects he does note that "the description of speech at many points reads like a description of the person. . . . The most frequent and most consummately human of human behaviors is speech. When we have characterized the person's speech we have gone a long way toward characterizing the person."

Sanford's study puts into focus the central concern of source differences or what might be termed "psychological stylistics." As Sanford expressed it, "we might well expect that the individual's verbal and nonverbal behaviors are all of a piece and that we can, if we are clever, see the latter in the former." This is precisely the business of psychological stylistics—to make inferences from linguistic data to psychological processes and behaviors.

Whereas Sanford was primarily concerned with linguistic factors as they served as indicants of personality variables, other researchers, such as Dieter (Sanford, 1942b), for example, attempted to correlate speech and types of thought processes. From an analysis of the compositions and speech of large numbers of students Dieter concluded that the styles revealed two principal types of thinkers. The *formalistic* thinker is abstract, static, perseverative, and repetitious. Causality is extremely important to him and his thought evidences continuity and closure. The *object-bound* thinker, on the other hand, is concrete and egocentric. Unlike the formalistic thinker who is static and perseverative, the object-bound thinker is dynamic and varied.

Inferences from the linguistic to the psychological are, in reality, much more difficult to make than these studies might at first indicate. Their limitations in terms of validity and reliability impose severe restrictions on the conclusions and generalizations one can legitimately draw. And although one may agree with Sanford that relationships between the style and the man do exist, it remains for these to be clearly defined. Preston and Gardner (1967), in a detailed factor analysis, attempted just such a task. Eighteen measures of oral and written language behavior, secured from seventy-two college students, were correlated with ten personality variables. The linguistic measures were: written type-token ratio, written mean-sentence length, written mean-type length, written productivity (total number of words), oral type-token ratio, oral mean-sentence length, oral mean-type length, oral productivity, *ah* speech-disturbance ratio, pause frequency, mean pause duration, verbal comprehension, grammar (the ability to identify the grammatical function of words and phrases), semantic spontaneous flexibility (the ability to name as many objects as possible which belonged to a certain class), ideational fluency (the ability to list the names of things that are similar in a specified way), controlled associations (the ability to produce words from a given area of meaning), word fluency I (the ability to write as many words as possible beginning with *s*), and word fluency II (the ability to write as many four-letter words as possible).

The personality variables were: attitude toward achievement, attitude toward change, attitude toward ambiguity and uncertainty, exhibitionism, impulsivity, need for organization and order, desire for social recognition, test anxiety, audience-sensitivity (predisposition to react in audience situations with anxiety), and manifest anxiety.

The data grouped themselves into seven classes or factors. Six of the factors consisted solely of language measures or solely of personality measures. Only one factor contained both language and personality variables. This factor, labeled social-approval, consisted of three personality variables (social recognition, test anxiety, and manifest anxiety) and one language measure (mean pause duration). Persons in need of social approval, according to these results, tend to pause longer than do those not in need of such approval. Such individuals appear more cautious in their speech behavior, their extra-long pauses probably reflecting a desire or need to select those words which they feel are appropriate and would meet with social approval. These same subjects also exhibited a dislike for ambiguity and uncertainty and a need for order and organization which likewise seem to reflect, at least in part, some desire for acceptance.

Persons who deviate widely from the normal population, say in terms of personality or motivational level, clearly reveal linguistic differences. Busemann (1925), for example, developed an action quotient, obtained by dividing the number of verbs by the number of adjectives, and found it to correlate highly with emotional stability. As the number of verbs increased so did emotional instability, as judged by the subjects' teachers. And Balken and Masserman (1940) were able to differentiate among conversion hysterics, obsessive compulsives, and anxiety hysterics solely on the basis of this verb-adjective ratio.

Recently a number of researchers have turned their attention to non-fluencies. George Mahl (1956), for example, defined two such measures. The "speech-disturbance ratio" is determined by dividing the total number of words into the total number of speech disturbances, for example, *ah*, sentence corrections, sentence incompletion, repetition, stutter, intruding incoherent sound, tongue-slip, and omission. Closely related is the "silence quotient," determined by dividing the number of seconds of silence by the total number of seconds available for talk. Mahl hypothesized that these measures would reflect degree of anxiety, specifically that scores from these two measures would be greater during the anxious and conflictful phases of discussion than they would be in the low-anxious or defensive phases. Fifteen phases of anxious or conflictful interviews and fifteen phases of low-anxious or defensive interviews were determined by a judge who had no knowledge of the quantitative indices to be employed. The ratios were then computed from typescripts by another judge who had no knowledge of how these phases had been categorized. Both hypotheses were supported at the .01 level of significance. Persons in anxious or conflictful states have a significantly greater percentage of speech disturbances and significantly more silent periods.

In what is probably the most impressive study in this area, Osgood and Walker (1959; Osgood, 1960b) attempted to clarify the relationship of the individual's motivational state to his encoding behavior. Osgood and Walker's study is particularly noteworthy for developing each hypothesis on the basis of specific theoretical principles. In this study suicide notes were compared with ordinary letters, written by others to their close friends and relatives. The assumption here was that when writing a suicide note the motivational or drive state will be high, certainly higher than when writing a normal letter. The increased motivational level will, in turn, influence encoding behavior, as it will influence behavior in predictable ways. Four specific hypotheses were formulated on the basis of this assumption. As compared with normal letters to friends and relatives, suicide notes should be characterized by: (1) *greater stereotypy*, since under increased drive those lexical and syntactic alternatives which are most familiar and most habitual will have an even greater probability of occurrence; (2) *greater frequency of those lexical and syntactic choices associated with the motives leading to self-destruction*, since behavior emitted under the influence of a particular drive state will make use of those choices which are appropriate to it; (3) *more conflict and compromise*, since suicide would logically involve competing motives; and (4) *greater disorganization*, since extreme increases in drive state (which are assumed to accompany suicide) generally result in the breakdown of behavior involving fine coordination, as would encoding.

The first hypothesis was supported; suicide notes did display more stereotypy. The writer of a suicide note tends to use shorter, simpler, and less diverse vocabulary. His writting is more repetitious, contains more simple action expressions (nouns and verbs) and few discriminative qualifiers (adjectives and adverbs). He uses more allness terms and his writing is more predictable, as measured by cloze procedure. This last result would follow from the fact that the writing was simpler, more repetitious, and less diverse in vocabulary. The second hypothesis was also supported; suicide notes contained more linguistic elements associated with self-destruction, for example, more distress-expressing phrases, less terms which were positively evaluated, and more mands. Third, suicide notes, as predicted, revealed more evidence of conflict. Verb phrases, for example, were qualified more often and there were significantly more evaluative assertions, referring to the writer himself or to those who were close to him, which were ambivalent in sign, that is, whether positive or negative.

The last hypothesis was not supported. Suicide notes did not reveal more structural disturbances, nor did they reveal shorter sentence lengths. This second measure was based on the assumption that encoding long sentences requires close attention which would not be typical of potential suicides.

Osgood and Walker also compared the suicide notes with notes produced by students instructed to assume the motivational state of a potential suicide and write suicide notes. As would be expected, the real suicide notes differed more widely from the letters to friends and relatives than did the simulated suicide notes. Although people can simulate a suicidal state, at least to some degree, they do not produce messages with demanding tone, reduced qualification, and evaluative ambivalence toward self and others.

This study would have been much improved had the researchers been able to obtain letters to friends written by the potential suicides themselves instead of using letters written by another group of persons. One might argue, for example, that the suicidal group differed from the other group on various personality variables and it was these differences, rather than their motivational states, which led to the observed linguistic differences. Though such arguments cannot be totally discounted, since the hypotheses were formulated on the basis of drive theory and since so many of the predictions were supported, it would seem that the results obtained here would not differ greatly from those which would have been obtained had both suicide and nonsuicide notes been written by the same individuals.

Excellent reviews of individual differences are available elsewhere (Mahl and Schulze, 1964; Nunnally, 1965). The few studies that were cited characterize the area of source differences or psychological stylistics and suggest some possible research approaches and strategies. It should be clear, however, even from such a brief discussion, that although "language most showeth a man," as Ben Jonson observed, it is not very easy to determine *how* and *in what manner* such connections manifest themselves. Linguistic differences are most pronounced when the psychological factors are extreme. When individuals differ in only small ways, whether from each other or from the norm, the language factors become difficult to pinpoint. Nevertheless, on the basis of available research one may well assume that such differences do exist and it remains for future research to specify them, however subtle and elusive they may be.

Receiver Differences

"Receiver differences" focuses on the effects of linguistic differences on the receivers' decoding of messages, an area which might be referred to as "rhetorical stylistics." The most frequently encountered work in this area is probably the familiar prescriptive chapter on style in the various speech and English composition texts. More typical of this area, however, are the studies concentrating on description.

A number of early studies focused on the speaking style of individual orators to provide insight on effectiveness or ineffectiveness. The long-range aim of such research is to determine how linguistic differences relate to differences in the effects of messages. These studies, however, did not attempt to deal directly with the relationship between linguistic factors and decoding. Rather, they provided descriptive data pertaining to certain speakers which could later be used to ascertain relationships between style and effect. Raymond Barnard (1932), for example, analyzed thirty-five speeches of Wendell Phillips, the abolitionist orator, for such factors as word length, type and length of sentences, and personal pronouns. In a similar study Howard Runion (1936) analyzed fifty speeches of Woodrow Wilson in terms of sentence type and length, figures of speech, and the length, quality, and rhetorical treatment of the introductions and conclusions.

Between the purely descriptive analysis of different speakers and the direct analysis of effects is a study conducted by Siegel and Siegel (1953). These researchers computed Flesch readability scores for four pre-election speeches of both Eisenhower and Stevenson in order to test the commonly held assumption that one of Stevenson's failures as a persuasive speaker was that he spoke above the level of his audience. Contrary to expectation Eisenhower's speeches were found to be significantly more difficult.

Most descriptive of current research in rhetorical stylistics are the studies which have manipulated linguistic factors and measured their differential effects on receivers, particularly in terms of comprehension and persuasion. One of the persistent notions in rhetorical theory is that the style of the speech should not be the same as the style of the written composition. Speech style must be "instantly intelligible" and contemporary rhetorics give much advice on how to achieve this goal. Gordon Thomas (1956) attempted to test experimentally the usefulness of such advice and composed two speeches, identical in all respects except style. One speech contained the elements of oral style advocated by current rhetorics and the other did not. The introductions and conclusions were identical for both speeches. As compared with the "nonoral style" speech, the "oral style" speech contained, for example, shorter, more colorful, and more concrete words and shorter and more personal sentences. In order to assess the influence that motivation might have, half the audience was told that they would be tested on the speech at the end of the period (motivated group) whereas the other half was not so informed (nonmotivated group). Also, half of the motivated group heard the speech delivered by a live speaker and half heard it from a tape recorder. Results from a multiple-choice comprehension test from over 1,400 college students showed that the "oral style" speech was approximately 10 percent more intelligible, an advantage which obtained regardless of whether the speech was delivered live or by tape or whether the audience was motivated or not motivated.

A major concern of rhetoric is the relationship between style and persuasion. One such example is provided by Weiss and Lieberman (1959) who investigated the effects of emotional language in arousing and changing opinions. In order to measure the arousal of opinions, groups of college students, after reading a series of eight negative statements on a fictitious person, responded to a like-dislike question and also rated the individual on twenty semantic differential scales, eight of which were evaluative and twelve of which were cognitive. Half of the group was given emotional statements and the other half nonemotional statements. Both, supposedly, contained the same informational content. For example, one emotional statement described the individual as "a selfish, greedy, money-mad person" whereas the nonemotional counterpart described him as "a person concerned only with his own best interests and welfare and exceedingly eager to gain monetary wealth." In order to measure opinion change these groups were next presented with an additional series of eight *positive* statements.

Half received emotional statements and half nonemotional statements. Again they were asked to rate the person in terms of like-dislike and on the semantic differential scales. This basic procedure was repeated on a somewhat smaller group whose members were given the positive assertions first. In addition to these opinion measures the researchers also obtained measures of two personality variables—"altruism" and "ease of emotional arousal."

No significant differences were obtained in terms of the arousal of opinions for those groups which received the negative statements first. For the group receiving the positive statements first, there was a tendency for the nonemotional statements to be more effective, that is, to arouse more favorable evaluative responses than did the emotional statements. Both altruism and ease of emotional arousal were found to be positively related to the arousal of negative opinions for those subjects receiving the negative statements first. This relationship was not found for those subjects receiving the positive statements first. Only ease of emotional arousal was found to be positively related to opinion change. The only significant difference with regard to change of opinion was obtained on the like-dislike question with those subjects exposed to the negative statements first; the favorable nonemotional counterstatements produced significantly greater change.

These results suggest that the effects of stylistic variation cannot be considered independent of the personalities of receivers nor of the order in which the messages are presented. There seems to be no simple relationship between emotional language and persuasion. Although one may conclude that emotional language has an effect different from nonemotional language, these effects cannot be separated from personality and other variables.

Language does not operate in isolation. Receivers differ and consequently do not all respond in the same way to the same linguistic stimulus. Similarly, the same person at different times and in different situations responds differently to the same linguistic stimulus and perhaps in the same way to different stimuli. What remains for research to elucidate is which variables influence differential decoding behavior and how they operate.

Source-Receiver Relationship Differences

The area of "sociological stylistics," is characterized by its primary concern with linguistic choices as they are determined by and serve as indicants of social relationships. Roger Brown and his associates, in their investigation of the pronouns of address in European languages (Brown and Gilman, 1960) and of the forms of address in English (Brown and Ford, 1961), provide excellent examples of the relationship between speech and source-receiver relationships. In many European languages there are two pronouns of address where English has only one, *you*. One pronoun would be used by a subordinate to a superior; for example, in French the servant speaking to his master would say *vous*, in Spanish *Usted*, in Italian *Lei*, and in German *Sie*. The other pronoun would be used by the superior addressing his subordinate; in French, Spanish, and Italian he would say *tu*, in German *du*.   Following Brown, V may be used to symbolize the pronoun of address used by a subordinate to a superior (upward communication) and T to symbolize the form used by a superior to a subordinate (downward communication) on the basis of the Latin *vos* and *tu* from which many of the modern forms derive.   When equals are communicating both use the same pronoun, that is, there is reciprocal usage.   If they have much in common or are very friendly T is used; if they have little in common or are strangers both use V.   During the Middle Ages, however, status determined which form would be used.   Reciprocal V was used by the nobility while reciprocal T was used by the lower classes.

There are two basic dimensions of social relationships: power versus equality (that is, status) and solidarity versus nonsolidarity (that is, friendship or intimacy).   Power relationships are established on the basis of a number of different criteria.   Age, wealth, social position, and occupation are probably the most obvious determinants.   Those who are older, richer, of higher social status, or in higher occupations use T in addressing those who are younger, poorer, lower in social status, or in lower occupations.   These latter persons in turn use V in addressing members of the former groups.   Similarly, solidarity relationships are established in a number of ways.   When, for example, persons work at the same job, have the same parents, attend the same school, or play on the same team, their relationship is one of solidarity and they would use T in addressing each other.   In the situations described there is no conflict; there is no doubt as to the correct pronoun to use.   There are situations, however, in which there is doubt as to the correct pronoun of address.   These conflicts appear in situations in which both power and solidarity or power and nonsolidarity exist.   For example, in the case of a younger brother addressing his older brother both power and solidarity are present and each dictates a different form.   The power relationship requires that the younger brother use V but the solidarity relationship requires T.   The conflict does not exist for the older brother since both power and solidarity dictate T.   In the other situation the conflict centers on the form to be used by the more powerful member.   For example, in the army the soldier says V to his officer since both power and nonsolidarity demand this form.   However, what does the officer say to his subordinate?   His superiority dictates T but his nonsolidarity relationship dictates V.

According to Brown and Gilman, these conflicts were resolved, at least up to the middle of the nineteenth century, on the basis of power.   Thus in the above examples the younger brother would have given V in addressing his older brother and the officer would have given T in addressing the soldier. More recently, however, solidarity has become the more significant, as judged from questionnaire results obtained from native speakers of various European languages.   Today the younger brother says T and the officer V—

the forms dictated by their solidarity and nonsolidarity relationships. This is not to say that power is no longer influential. In fact, as Brown and Gilman point out, power determines who may initially introduce reciprocal T. The suggestion to use reciprocal T or its first use cannot come from the less powerful; it can only come from the more powerful.

Use of the pronouns of power and solidarity has an interesting parallel in English. Similar social relationships are reflected in the use of the first name (FN) or a title plus the last name (TLN). Even more so than in the case of pronouns, the form of address used in English is not predictable from a knowledge of the addressor or addressee, however detailed that knowledge may be. The forms used can only be predicted from knowledge of the relationship existing between the two parties involved in the communication act.

In order to secure a reasonably large number of examples Brown and Ford (1961) analyzed the forms of address as they occurred in thirty-eight plays. All these plays were by American authors, performed since 1939, and set in contemporary America. Special care was taken to secure a broad spectrum of American life, involving different national groups, different geographical locations, and different social and occupational levels. Among those plays used were *Member of the Wedding*, *Picnic*, *The Rose Tattoo*, *Tea and Sympathy*, *Mister Roberts*, *The Solid Gold Cadillac*, *No Time for Sergeants*, and *Death of a Salesman*. In addition, examples were also obtained from those forms of address used in a Boston business firm, reported usages of business executives, and the forms appearing on various records from the Midwest. These three additional sources were used primarily as checks on the forms used in the plays.

As in the case of pronouns there are in English examples of both reciprocal and nonreciprocal patterns. Whether both use FN or both use TLN depends mainly on the degree of acquaintance or intimacy. With strangers TLN is used whereas with friends FN is used. The amount of time which must elapse before reciprocal use of FN, which seems to be shortening in recent years, is dependent primarily on the age of the persons involved. The time is shorter for younger than for older persons and also shorter for members of the same sex than for members of the opposite sex.

In the nonreciprocal pattern one member says FN and the other TLN. Differences in age and occupation account for most of the instances of nonreciprocal usage. Children say TLN to adults, but adults say FN to children. Even among adults differences in age are important and are observed in forms of address. When there is a difference of approximately fifteen years the junior members use TLN and the senior members FN.

Persons in higher occupational status give FN and receive TLN. For example, employers, teachers, and officers give FN but receive TLN from employees, students, and enlisted men. In cases of temporary subordination, as in the case of waiter and customer, the former says TLN and the latter FN. Even in cases in which no direct subordination is present differences in occupational status may similarly determine nonreciprocal forms of address. For example, occupations such as senator or congressman are clearly higher than policeman or fireman and in these cases the higher is given TLN and the lower FN.

Another similarity with the case of the pronouns is that at times the two criteria, age and occupation, are not correlated and a conflict as to the proper form of address develops. For example, a young boy and the family servant, a young lieutenant just out of officers training school and his much older, but lower in rank, enlisted men, and a young teacher and the members of an adult education class are just a few of the many cases in which differences in status and age do not match. In all of these cases there is a conflict. According to Brown and Ford these conflicts are generally resolved on the basis of occupation—the person of higher occupational status receives TLN regardless of the age of the addressor.

There are, of course, a number of other forms of address in English. In some cases just the title is used, for example, Sir, Madam, Miss. This is probably the least intimate form of address. Although it may be used reciprocally, it is most frequently used nonreciprocally especially when there is an obvious difference in social position and where the superior is not well known to the addressor. In other cases only the last name is used. At times this form indicates a degree of intimacy greater than TLN but less than FN as when an old professor or employer addresses younger colleagues or employees by just their last name. At other times the last name functions much as the first name but is preferred because it is shorter or somehow more distinctive. Greater social intimacy than even the first name is indicated by the use of multiple names, where at times the first name or a nickname, at times just the last name, and at other times the title plus last name is used.

There are still a number of situations in which the proper form of address is not clear. At times, it presents a real problem. One of the examples used by Brown and Gilman and which I still experience is the case of the student coming back to his college as a teacher. While a student there was no problem; the instructors were addressed with TLN. When I came back some four years later as a colleague they addressed me by FN. The problem was how to address them. If, on the one hand, I used TLN it might appear that I was still a subordinate and perhaps not ready to assume my role as an equal. On the other hand, if I used FN it might appear presumptious or pushy, especially since differences in age and rank were still clear-cut and often brought to the newcomers attention.

Now I see somewhat the same problem in reverse; some of my colleagues are also students in my graduate courses. As colleagues they should use FN but as students they should use TLN. Fortunately English provides a way out of such a dilemma by permitting us to avoid using any form of address. This, it appears, is the alternative some students and I have adopted.

GROUP DIFFERENCES

With "group differences" our focus shifts from speech to language and from the individual to the group. Our concern here is with differences within languages (intralinguistic) and between languages (interlinguistic).

One of the most provocative passages in George Orwell's *1984* concerns the creation of Newspeak, the language of the revolution designed to replace English. In this excerpt Syme, one of the compilers of the Eleventh Edition of the Newspeak dictionary, is talking with Winston Smith, the protagonist.

> Don't you see that the whole aim of Newspeak is to narrow the range of thought? In the end we shall make thought-crime literally impossible, because there will be no words in which to express it. Every concept that can ever be needed will be expressed by exactly *one* word, with its meaning rigidly defined and all its subsidiary meanings rubbed out and forgotten. Already in the Eleventh Edition, we're not far from that point. But the process will still be continuing long after you and I are dead. Every year fewer and fewer words, and the range of consciousness always a little smaller. Even now, of course, there's no reason or excuse for committing thought-crime. It's merely a question of self-discipline, reality-control. But in the end there won't be any need even for that. The Revolution will be complete when the language is perfect.

Here Orwell is expressing a notion over which men have theorized and argued for quite some time, namely, the relationship of language to thought and behavior. At one extreme is the belief that language and thought are completely separate and independent, that the language one speaks exerts no influence on thought whatever. At the other extreme is the belief that language and thought are essentially one, that the language one speaks determines the thoughts one has. Each of these extremes is probably incorrect; the truth seems to lie somewhere between these poles.

If language does influence thought and consequently behavior, at least to some extent, then a number of corollaries should follow. First, it should be possible to detect cognitive and behavior differences in regard to those aspects of the world which a language treats differently. Second, it should be possible to detect differences among speakers of the same language who use different "codes" or "sublanguages." In both of these cases comparisons are within one language or intralinguistic. A third corollary would predict that it should be possible to find cognitive and behavioral differences among persons speaking widely differing languages. Here the comparisons would be between languages or interlinguistic.

Intralinguistic Differences

The first prediction, that aspects of reality which are differently represented by language should be responded to differently, has, unfortunately, been the subject of only a few research efforts.   In one experiment, conducted by Brown and Lenneberg (1954) and replicated by Lantz and Steffler (1964), it was hypothesized that when a category has a highly "codable" name, that is, a short name, subjects would respond to it quickly and would agree with themselves from one trial to another and with other subjects more often than they would if the category had a less codable name.   Subjects were asked to name twenty-four colors from the Munsell *Book of Colors* and after a period of one month five of the subjects were recalled and put through the same basic procedure again.   From their responses four measures were taken: the length of the naming response in number of syllables (used as an index of codability), the average time it took to name the color, the degree of agreement from one trial to another for the five subjects who were retested, and the degree of agreement among the subjects.

Each of the three hypotheses was supported.   The average time it took to name a color increased with the length of the name; the degree of agreement of a subject from one trial to the next varied inversely with the length of the name; and the degree of agreement among subjects also varied inversely with the length of the name.

To a different group of subjects the experimenters exposed four colors for which codability scores had already been secured.   After a period of three minutes elapsed, during which time the subjects engaged in some unrelated task, they were asked to recover the four colors they had previously seen from a chart containing 120 colors.   It was predicted that the more highly codable colors would be recovered more easily than would those of lower codability.   The results supported this hypothesis; subjects were better able to recover the colors when they had short names than when they had long names.

It would appear from the results of this experiment that the semantic structure of a language may exert influence on such psychological processes as recognition and memory.   But before too many and too general conclusions are drawn some qualifications should be noted.   For example, Brown and Lenneberg found that when only a relatively short period of time elapsed between the initial presentation of the stimulus colors and the recovery task, there were no differences in the ability to recognize the colors from the chart.   Furthermore, in a study by Burnham and Clark (1955) it was shown that when the stimulus colors are presented in a circular array the same relations will not hold; contrary to Brown and Lenneberg, they found that codability and recognizability were negatively correlated. The reason for this "contradictory" finding appears to be that presenting the colors in a circular array made it easier for the subjects to recall colors which were on the border, say between X color and not-X color (which would be of low codability), and more difficult to recognize those colors which fell within borders (which would be of high codability) since there were so many of them.

A more reasonable conclusion is that the semantic structure of a language may exert influence on such psychological processes as recognition and memory only when the stimulus materials are of a certain kind and when the time intervening between initial presentation and recovery is relatively long, that is, when the task is difficult (cf. Lenneberg, 1957, 1961, 1967).

A second approach to intralanguage differences concerns the influence of what might be called "sublanguages" or "codes" on cognition and behavior. One of the most influential and insightful attempts to explicate this relationship has been developed by the British sociologist Basil Bernstein. In a series of publications Bernstein (1959, 1960, 1961, 1964) proposed that because of the different emphases placed on language potential by various social classes, different language forms or "codes" develop. The particular code a child learns exerts powerful influence on his interaction with the environment. By specifying or highlighting what in the environment is relevant or irrelevant, significant or insignificant, the code influences the nature of the individual's experiences. These experiences, in turn, affect the acquisition of various social and intellectual skills. More specifically, Bernstein has argued that members of the middle and lower working classes have different codes. The working-class code is a restricted one. It is "restricted" in that the linguistic alternatives are limited. The speaker of a restricted code has relatively few options; his choices are restricted to a narrow range of alternatives. Consequently, his language is relatively easy to predict or, in information-theory terms, of high probability. It is also restricted in the sense that his speech does not make explicit subjective intent. His intentions and meanings are seldom elaborated or explicit; most often they are only implicit. The middle class, on the other hand, speaks with an "elaborated" code. Here there are many alternatives available; the choices which these speakers make are drawn from a relatively large supply. Hence their language is more difficult to predict and of lower probability. Second, the speaker's intentions are more often made explicit.

Each of these codes has been analyzed and defined in terms of their specific linguistic characteristics and their cognitive and behavioral consequences. For example, in the restricted code one finds that the reasons and the conclusions for any behavior are often combined. When a child asks why he must do something middle- and working-class parents respond in different ways. The middle-class parent gives the child reasons why he should do as he was told—reasons which are generally logical and relevant—along with the conclusion. The working-class parent is more apt to give her conclusion as the reason. Thus when a child asks why he must go to bed the middle-class mother will more likely give him such reasons as "You need your rest" or "You have to get up early tomorrow." The working-class mother, on the other hand, is more likely to simply repeat her conclusion "Get to bed" as a response to the child's question. But patience soon wears thin with all parents, regardless of social class, and after a few minutes or so the conclusion "Get to bed" is repeated—probably more firmly and with greater authority. Normally, however, the dialogue between mother and child is longer for middle-class members. When reasons are given the child is exposed to sequences and connections among thoughts which facilitate learning and reinforce curiosity. The reasons given, in effect, expose the child to new and different language stimuli to which he can learn to respond. When reasons are omitted and only conclusions given, the child is not exposed to these sequences and connections, his curiosity is inhibited, and the range of language stimulation is severely restricted.

As has been noted there is in the restricted code of the working class little verbalizing of intent; in the elaborated code intent is frequently explicit. When a child does something wrong, for example, the working-class parent is less concerned with intent or the reasons why he did it and focuses on the act itself, on the immediate consequences of the behavior, promptly punishing it. The middle-class parent, on the other hand, concerns herself with the intentions motivating the act; she focuses on the processes underlying the act. And although she too punishes the child it is primarily for the intent rather than for the act itself. According to Bernstein, these differences have important consequences for the development of a sense of guilt in the child. The working-class child develops relatively little guilt and a high tolerance for guilt. His guilt feelings can easily be divorced from the idea of wrongness. The middle-class child, however, develops a low tolerance for guilt since his punishment is directed at the wrongness or bad intent and not so much at the act itself. These differences in turn influence the likelihood of wrong behavior recurring. Since the working-class child can easily divorce the guilt from the wrongness he is more apt to commit the same acts again; the middle-class child, who has had strong guilt feelings inculcated, is less likely to repeat this act.

Another characteristic of the restricted code is that its sentences are short and simple; they contain only simple conjunctions such as *so, then,* and *because* and make only limited use of modifying adjectives and adverbs. These features make it difficult, according to Bernstein, to express precisely various ideas and relationships. The elaborated code, containing the reverse of these characteristics, makes such precise formulation and expression relatively easy.

From both the theoretical and experimental research (cf. Bernstein, 1962a, 1962b; Lawton, 1963) it is not clear how powerful these differences are or how generalizable, to other languages and to other cultures, are the basic principles and assumptions. Bernstein has succeeded in raising an important question but it remains for future research to provide evidence.

Interlanguage Differences

The third prediction, that differences between languages result in cognitive and behavioral differences, goes under a number of different names —the Whorfian Hypothesis, the Sapir-Whorf Hypothesis, the Sapir-Whorf-

Korzybski Hypothesis, the Linguistic Relativity Hypothesis, the Linguistic Weltanschauung Hypothesis and probably others. Although this theory was considered by various philosophers, it owes most to the formulations of Edward Sapir and especially Benjamin Lee Whorf.

Sapir (Mandelbaum, 1949, p. 162) stated the issue clearly:

> Human beings do not live in the objective world alone, nor alone in the world of social activity as ordinarily understood, but are very much at the mercy of the particular language which has become the medium of expression for their society. It is quite an illusion to imagine that one adjusts to reality essentially without the use of language and that language is merely an incidental means of solving specific problems of communication or reflection. The fact of the matter is that the "real world" is to a large extent unconsciously built up on the language habits of the group. No two languages are ever sufficiently similar to be considered as representing the same social reality. The worlds in which different societies live are distinct worlds, not merely the same world with different labels attached.

Whereas Sapir contributed to this theory only incidentally, in his studies on the various Indian languages, his student Benjamin Lee Whorf devoted his entire energies to this one question and probably gave the theory its clearest and most provocative formulation. According to Whorf (Carroll, 1956, pp. 212–213):

> . . . the background linguistic system (in other words, the grammar) of each language is not merely a reproducing instrument for voicing ideas but rather is itself the shaper of ideas, the program and guide for the individual's mental activity, for his analysis of impressions, for his synthesis of his mental stock in trade. . . . We dissect nature along lines laid down by our native languages. The categories and types that we isolate from the world of phenomena we do not find there because they stare every observer in the face; on the contrary, the world is presented in a kaleidoscopic flux of impressions which has to be organized by our minds—and this means largely by the linguistic systems in our minds.

As can be appreciated, proving or disproving such an hypothesis is no easy task. A number of observations and experiments have been made which shed at least some light on this question.

Following Joshua Fishman (1960), a distinction may be made between those investigations concerned with "cultural reflections" and those concerned with nonlinguistic behavior. The former are clearly the less conclusive and might be reviewed first and only briefly. One of the most obvious differences among languages is that they differ in the number of vocabulary items they have for various aspects of reality. English, for example, has relatively few terms for horses—*horse, pony, mare, stallion,* and perhaps a few others. Arabic, on the other hand, has scores of terms, denoting the different kinds, breeds, and conditions of horses but no generic term corresponding to the English *horse*.   Similarly, Eskimo has no single term for snow but only numerous and distinct terms for different kinds of snow. Trobriand Islanders have dozens of terms for the different stages and qualities of yams.   From differences such as these—and many more examples could be cited—inferences are made concerning the cultures of the people speaking these differing languages.   Thus it seems reasonable to conclude that horses in Arabic culture, snow in Eskimo culture, and yams in the culture of the Trobriand Islanders are more important than they are in English-speaking cultures.   In fact, it now seems to be commonly accepted that the importance of a concept is directly related to the number of different terms the language has to express it.

There are also differences in grammatical structure of languages and their cultural reflections.   Edmund Glenn (Fishman, 1960), for example, has observed that in English the adjective precedes the noun, whereas in French it follows the noun.   In English one would say *the red wine* but in French *le vin rouge*.   This difference, Glenn notes, is reflected in differences in the thought processes of the two cultures.   English represents an inductive thought pattern; it begins with the particulars (the adjectives) and then works up to the general (the noun).   French, on the other hand, represents deductive thought; it begins with the general and from it deduces the particulars or details.   Glenn goes on to argue that there are a number of examples in which English speakers follow one thought pattern while French speakers follow another.   For instance, the English legal system is basically an inductive one in which generalizations are formulated on the basis of specific and particular precedents.   The French, on the other hand, have a deductive system in which general principles are formulated and then specific cases deduced from them.   Similarly, differences are reflected in English speakers' preference for details as opposed to general theoretical notions. The French, however, prefer broad theories and philosophical generalizations and care little for specific details.

Another such comparison has been made by Harry Hoijer (1951) who notes that Navaho does not separate actors, actions, and objects of actions as does English; in Navaho the clean division between subjects, predicates, and objects characteristic of English sentences does not exist.   According to Hoijer this difference is reflected in the Navaho's essentially passive and fateful attitude toward life.   To the Navaho, people somehow simply get involved in actions rather than initiate them.

Examples of this sort are not, as Fishman points out, to be confused with the " old wives' tales " that Italians are musical because of their language or that Germans are serious and rigid because of the heavy quality of their language.   These examples are clearly less scientific than those of say Glenn or Hoijer and are not based on any serious linguistic analysis of the language.

But even the examples adduced with some scientific rigor do not offer much evidence that people think or behave differently because of differences in their languages.   An English speaker can see all the distinctions among horses that an Arabic speaker sees.   It is simply that his language does not provide highly codable terms for these various nuances of difference. The important point is that the English speaker can make these distinctions (with adjectives, for example) but not as easily and as quickly. That is, rather than impose differences on abilities or competence these language differences refer primarily to the performance of speakers. With grammatical differences, such as those between English and French or between English and Navaho, the relationship to thought seems a bit more difficult to define. In the case of vocabulary it seems clear that cultural items such as horses, snow, or yams became important and vocabulary items were added to take into consideration the various differences which had to be noticed and communicated most frequently. With grammar, however, it is not so easy to say which came first since grammatical relationships such as those considered by Glenn and Hoijer operate below the level of consciousness.

In an attempt to investigate lexical differences and their influence on behavior differences John B. Carroll (Carroll and Casagrande, 1958) compared Hopi and English speakers on their perception of the similarity of various drawings. Hopi and English make a number of different distinctions among actions and objects. For example, a Hopi speaker must distinguish between whether the thing spilled is liquid or nonliquid and these two terms differ radically from the term for "drop." Similarly, in Hopi there is a word which means something like "to smear on a surface" and another term meaning "fine decorating."

Carroll presented English and Hopi subjects with three pictures from which they were to select the two they felt best went together. In one series the pictures were of (a) a man unloading a carton of fruit, (b) a man spilling milk, and (c) a man accidentally dropping a coin. Whereas English speakers most often grouped the two accidental actions (b and c), the Hopi speakers most often grouped pictures a and b. In Hopi, although the terms for these two actions are different (*wehekna* is used for solids and *wa:hokna* for liquids) they are more similar to each other than either is to the term for drop (*po:sna*). Another series contained pictures of (a) a woman frosting a cake, (b) a woman painting a wall, and (c) a woman painting or decorating a vase. English speakers grouped either the two pictures involving painting (b and c) or the two pictures involving decorating (a and c). The Hopi, however, most often grouped the two pictures which would be covered by their term meaning "to smear on a surface," namely, a and b. The twelve items which proved useful in this experiment yielded results which were in the expected direction but not statistically significant. One of the major problems with this experiment was that the Hopi were bilingual; had monolinguals been used the differences might have been more pronounced.

Probably the most rigorously conceived and executed experiment in this entire area was conducted by Joseph Casagrande (Carroll and Casagrande, 1958) who sought to explore the relationship between certain grammatical categories and behavior. For this purpose he compared English and Navaho speakers. In English we are forced, by the nature of our language, to make reference to time and number; with only few exceptions every sentence uttered must make some reference to whether the time is past, present, or future and to whether the subject and object are singular or plural.   These are termed "obligatory categories" and are probably used below the level of conscious awareness.   In Navaho there is an obligatory category referring to the form of the object.   That is, the form of the object referred to dictates the specific verb stem to be used.   For example, in requesting a long flexible object such as a piece of string the verb would be *sanleh*; in requesting a long rigid object such as a stick one must say *santiih*; and in requesting a flat flexible object such as a piece of paper the verb is *sanilcoos*.   The words which take a particular verb stem are not indentified linguistically in any way. That is, the various nouns denoting long and rigid objects, for example, do not have any common linguistic feature by which they can be identified.

English-speaking children, as many researchers have shown, give primary attention to color.   Similarities in color are noticed more frequently and would seem to have more importance attributed to them than noncolor similarities.   On the basis of the existence of the obligatory category in Navaho, however, Casagrande hypothesized that Navaho children's responses would give primary importance to form.

Navaho and English-speaking children were presented with two objects which differed from each other in both form and color, for example, a blue stick and a yellow rope.   They were then shown a third object which matched one of the original objects in color and the other in form, for example, a blue rope.   They were asked to select one of the two original objects which best matched this third object.   A number of such sets were used and the results confirmed the hypothesis.   Navaho children, in the example cited above, selected the yellow rope whereas English-speaking children selected the blue stick.

Although much theorizing and experimentation has been done on the question of interlanguage differences, the conclusions are at best tentative. What effects the language may have on thought and behavior, on the one hand, and how much language simply reflects the culture of which it is a part, on the other hand, are difficult matters to separate.   Carroll's experiment, although concerned with concrete behavioral and linguistic variables, failed to yield statistically significant results.   Only Casagrande was able to obtain statistically significant differences in a rigidly controlled experiment.   At best, these behavioral variations are minor.   Although conclusions in any area of language and behavior are premature, if we were forced to make one it would have to be that linguistic relativity, where it does exist, does not exert very profound influence on thought or behavior.

SYSTEM DIFFERENCES

Here we focus on the most pronounced and most obvious differences, those existing between systems of communication—between human language on the one hand and nonhuman "language" on the other.   In order to clarify some of these differences and, most importantly, to further understanding of the nature and function of human language, one animal-communication system is discussed and some of the similarities and differences between this system and human language are noted.

The "Language" of the Bee

Through the numerous writings of the Austrian zoologist Karl von Frisch, including *Bees, Their Vision, Chemical Senses and Language* (1950) and *The Dancing Bees* (1953), the "language" of the bees has become a familiar story—a story almost as popular and well known as that of Pavlov's dog. The "language" of the bee, one of the most interesting and possibly the most complex of all infrahuman communication systems, is particularly appropriate for discussion here since the differences between it and human language can be most easily appreciated.

It is, however, impossible to know with complete certainty how bees actually do communicate. The ideas discussed here are in reality only hypotheses, based largely on the work of Karl von Frisch (1950, 1953, 1962) and Martin Lindauer (1967).

Bees use both nonsymbolic and symbolic forms of communication. For example, when a forager bee returns to the hive after seeking new sources of food, the other bees smell the food clinging to its body and thereby learn the kind of food located. This is direct, nonsymbolic communication. Bees, however, communicate about a great deal more than the type of food located, utilizing an intricate symbolic system.

When the forager bee returns to the hive she performs a dance either on the vertical of the hive or on the horizontal platform outside the entrance to the hive. The duration and vitality of the dance indicate to the other bees the richness of the food supply located. If the dance continues for only a short time and if performed with little vigor the other bees "know" that the food supply is small; consequently only a limited number of bees go after it. If, on the other hand, the dance is vigorous and of long duration it means that a rich supply has been found to which a great number go.

Obviously, however, the worker bees must know where to go as well as how many should go. This they seem to learn from the type of dance the forager bee performs. When the food supply is relatively close to the hive, say within a radius of about 275 feet, the bee performs a round dance. For distances greater than 275 feet the bee does a wagging dance. The general pattern of these two dances is indicated in Figure 20(**A**) and (**B**).

More precise distances are communicated by the tempo of the dance. When the bee begins the wagging dance, for example, she runs a short distance in a straight line, returns to the starting point after completing a semicircle, runs up this line again, and returns to the starting place after completing another semicircle on the opposite side. The tempo of the dance, the number of complete cycles made in a given time, varies inversely with

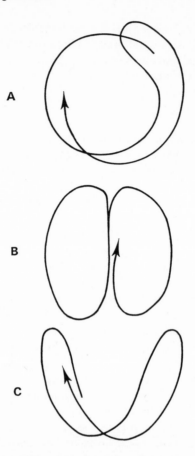

A

B

C

FIGURE 20. General Patterns of Bee Dances.   **(A)** the round dance used for distances up to approximately 275 feet; **(B)** the wagging dance used for distances longer than 275 feet; **(C)** the sickle dance used by some species for distances between 120 and 275 feet.

the distance of the food and thus communicates the distance in more precise terms.   Von Frisch has found, for example, that when the food is 1,000 feet away the bee will complete fifteen cycles in thirty seconds but when the food is 2,000 feet away the number of cycles completed in this same amount of time drops to eleven.

But it would be of little value for the bees to know the distance to the food supply if they did not also know the direction.   The first insight into this question came from learning that bees use sunlight for orientation.   In communicating direction the bee also uses sunlight.   On the horizontal the bee dances so that the line joining the two semicircles of the wagging dance forms the same angle with the rays of the sun that the imaginary line connecting the food and the hive form with the sun's rays.   An illustration is provided in Figure 21.

The dance on the vertical surface is somewhat more complex. Since there is no sunlight inside the hive the bee uses a somewhat different system. If the bee dances upward, that is, if the line connecting the two semicircles is traveled upward, it signifies that the food lies in the direction of the sun. If the bee runs this line in a downward direction it signifies that the food lies away from the sun. The number of degrees from the vertical which the line connecting the two semicircles forms indicates the angle of flight to the food. Thus if the bee dances upward and the line of the dance forms a 50° angle with the vertical, it signifies that the food lies toward the sun and that the line of flight and the sun's rays meet at an angle of 50°. If the bee dances downward and the dance line forms an angle of 110° with the vertical, it means that the bees must fly away from the sun with their line of flight forming an angle of 110° with the rays of the sun.

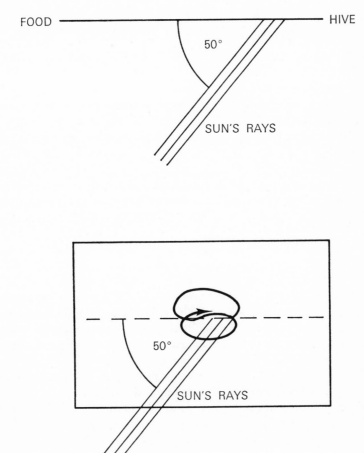

FIGURE 21. The Bee's Use of Sunlight for Orientation

These patterns have been based largely on research with the Austrian honey bee.   The Italian bee's communication system is somewhat different. Like her Austrian cousin the Italian bee does a round dance for short distances and a wagging dance for longer distances.   These, however, are not exactly the same among the two groups or "dialects" (Frisch, 1962). In indicating precise distances, for example, where the number of cycles per unit of time are crucial, the Italian bee uses a somewhat different timetable, dancing more slowly than the Austrian bee.   Although these bees can live together and interbreed they run into problems when they attempt to communicate.   If the Austrian bee, for example, takes her cues from the dance of the Italian bee she will consistently search for food too far away.   Another and more striking difference is that for intermediate distances the Italian bee performs a dance which resembles a bent figure eight.   This "sickle" dance, illustrated in Figure 20(**C**), does not appear in the communication system of the Austrian bee.

One of the major problems faced by these theories, which the reader may have already noticed, is how do the bees observe the dance in the hive where there is no light?   Some researchers have proposed that the bees touch the dancer with their antennae; in this way they detect the pattern, rate, and direction of the dance.

The major alternative hypothesis to communication by dance and touch is communication by sound.   In order to test this hypothesis Adrian Wenner (1962, 1964) recorded sounds made by dancing bees after returning from locating food.   From spectrographic analysis it was found that the sounds emitted during these dances are composed of trains, each of which is broken up into pulses.   During each straight run of the wagging dance the bee emits a train of sound.   The average length of the trains and of the pulses as well was found to be directly proportional to the distance the bee had traveled to the food supply.   Further, the rate of the pulses may also communicate information about the quality of the food found.   From preliminary investigations it appears that rate bears a strong correlation with the strength of the sugar concentration in the food supply.

Additional evidence for communication by sound comes from the research of Harald Esch (1967).   Esch noticed that when the bees returned to the hive many of them performed their dance without any accompanying sound.   These bees, for reasons unknown, simply performed a dance which was silent but normal in all other respects.   Although the other bees in the hive attended to and followed the silent dance, never once, in some 15,000 observations, did the bees go off to the food site.

It appears that some species of bees, particularly the stingless bee found in Brazil, communicate only by sound.   The forager bees of this species perform no dance upon returning to the hive but merely emit sounds by vibrating their wings.   In these cases the messages seem not as clear and precise as when accompanied by dancing.   These bees, for example, fly out with the forager in the general direction of the food but then go back to the hive and await the return of the forager. The forager must lead them out toward the food a number of times before they seem to "understand" the message. According to Esch, evidence such as this indicates that communication by sound is the more primitive process and that the dance gradually evolved out of this basic sound system.

From what we know now it appears that both dance and sound communicate the forager's message. However, as Wenner (1964, p. 118) notes, "it may conceivably turn out that the foraging bee's entire message is carried by sound signals."

Most of our information about the communication system of bees pertains to food sources. Bees, however, also communicate about other matters. Only one bee—the queen bee—can bear offspring. Whether a particular egg will develop into a queen, a worker, or a drone is determined in part by the queen herself and in part by the nurses attending the eggs and larvae. The queen determines sex by fertilizing some eggs, which become females (queens or workers), and by leaving others unfertilized, which become males (drones). If the nursing bees provide the female egg with a cell of greater than normal size and feed the larva special and greater quantities of food a queen develops; otherwise it develops into a worker. Each summer approximately half a dozen queen bees are born. But since the colony can have only one queen some adjustments are necessary and these provide interesting evidence for the existence of sound communication.

The queens do not all emerge at the same time—one develops and matures, becoming hard and steady, sooner than the others. Upon emerging from her cell the virgin queen emits a "tooting" sound and then attempts to destroy the other queen cells and sting their occupants to death. The workers, however, prevent her from destroying the premature queens. Throughout this attempt to destroy her rivals the queen who emerged first continues this tooting sound. As the other queens mature they attempt to come out of their cells. The workers, however, push them back in and reglue the cell shut. The queens still locked in their cells then begin to emit a "quacking" sound and are released one at a time. When released they duel with the first queen until one is killed. Then a second queen is released and the pattern continues. The tooting of the free queen and the quackings of the caged queens have different communicative functions. When these sounds were imitated it was found that the tooting sound led the caged queen to quack but the quacking sound produced no response in the caged queen. According to Wenner (1962) the tooting sound announces that a free queen is in the hive and the quacking sound announces that a caged queen is ready to come out of her cell. Both of these influence the behavior of the worker bees, for example, they release one and only one caged queen when the tooting and quacking sounds are present. The survivor of these duels then leaves the hive, mates with a number of drones while in flight, and returns to the hive to begin laying eggs. At this time the old queen must leave since the colony can have only one queen. (This is a particularly useful and adaptive measure since with more than one queen the birth rate would increase so rapidly that the hive would quickly become too small to house all the bees and the food supply in the area would soon prove insufficient.)

When the old queen together with her workers and drones, numbering in the thousands, leave the original hive—a practice called swarming—they settle on some tree or pole or wherever the queen happens to land, clinging to each other and resembling a large oval mass. Scouts then go out to look over possible living sites. When a possible home has been found they return to the swarm and perform dances similar to those of the forager bees. In addition to indicating the distance and direction of the possible new home it appears that the dance also gives the " arguments " in favor of adopting this new site—the more vigorous the dance the more highly the scout thinks of the place. At times a number of scouts return to the swarm, each of which dances and presents its arguments. Lindauer (1967) reports one case in which twenty-one scouts returned, each reporting on a different location. A bee who is particularly persuasive will in time attract the other scouts to also investigate this place and often they return doing the same dance as the first scout, adding their approval. These " debates " may last for hours, days, or even weeks. Hasty decisions are seldom made. Throughout this time scouts visit the various locations on a number of different occasions and in this way see the possible home at different times of day and under different weather conditions, providing added insurance that the selected home will be a suitable one. Among those factors the scouts consider are the size of the home, the protection it affords from the wind and rain, the available food sources in the vicinity, and the distance of it from the original home (cf. Lindauer, 1967). It appears that for a particular site to be selected there must be unanimous agreement; there is only one queen and consequently it is not possible for the swarm to split into two or three groups each finding its own home.

Although it is not clear exactly how these matters are communicated it might logically be expected that both sound and dance carry the information as is the case with food sources.

Obviously this is only a small part of what is known about bee communication and what is known is probably only a small part of their actual system. These few examples, however, should serve to make clear some of the ways in which animals communicate and some of the ways in which infrahuman systems differ from human. Some of these should be made explicit.

Characteristics of Human Language Systems

Although a number of approaches for defining the unique characteristics of human language have been proposed, the one most useful for our purposes is that advanced by the linguist Charles F. Hockett (1958, 1960a, 1960b, 1963). Hockett has defined sixteen features of human language—features which, when taken together, define human language and distinguish it from other nonhuman communication systems.   Throughout this discussion the ways in which these features differentiate human language from the communication system of the bee will be noted.   Following Hockett, the term *language* will be used though it should be clear that the concern here is with the abstract system as well as with the way in which this system is actually used.   We will not follow Hockett, however, in attributing or not attributing these features to bee communication; more recent research (for example, Sebeok, 1963; Frings and Frings, 1964; Wenner, 1962, 1964) seems to provide different answers.

VOCAL-AUDITORY CHANNEL.   To say that human language is vocal-auditory means that its signals are patterns of sound, produced by the respiratory system, and received by the auditory system.   Not all signals so produced, however, constitute language; paralinguistic features, for example, Hockett would exclude from the domain of language proper.

That human language makes use of the vocal-auditory channel is an obvious but not a necessary fact.   Gestural or tactile systems could conceivably have evolved to a point where they would serve many of the communicative functions now served by the vocal-auditory channel.   In point of fact, of course, they have not; as has been pointed out, these systems serve primarily to supplement the messages of the vocal-auditory channel. The advantage which this channel provides should be clear if one imagines what communication limited to other channels would be like.   With a gestural system, for example, communication in the dark, or around corners, or when working with our hands, or with someone not looking directly at us would be impossible.   Tactile systems are even more limiting.

Bee communication involves auditory reception but not vocal emission. The sounds of the bee are probably made by vibrating the wings.   The way in which they receive or "hear" the sounds, however, is not clear.   Some researchers have proposed that they "hear" through receiving organs on their legs and others have argued that the sounds are received by their antennae.   Possibly both organs serve as receivers.

BROADCAST TRANSMISSION AND DIRECTIONAL RECEPTION.   This feature follows from the nature of the channel used.   "Broadcast transmission" points to the public nature of language; sounds are emitted and can be received by anyone within earshot, by enemies as well as by friends.   "Directional reception" refers to the fact that the emitted sounds serve to localize the source; upon hearing a sound one can detect its location.   Although it is true that one can whisper so that others will not hear or "throw" one's voice so that receivers will not be able to tell where the sounds came from, in general, human language can be heard by anyone, regardless of the intended receiver, and indicates the location of the source.

Bee communication possesses this feature; any bee can receive the message and the dancing bee is located without any apparent problem.

RAPID FADING. Speech sounds fade rapidly; they are evanescent. They must be received immediately after they are emitted or else not received at all. Although mechanical devices now enable sound to be preserved much as writing is preserved, this is not a characteristic of human language. Rather, these are extralinguistic means of storing information, aiding memory, etc. Of course, all signals fade; written symbols and even symbols carved in rock are not permanent. Relatively, however, speech signals are probably the least permanent.

The signals provided by the dance and the accompanying sounds seem to fade just as rapidly as human speech. The odor of the nectar, however, probably fades less rapidly.

INTERCHANGEABILITY. Any human being can serve as both sender and receiver—the roles are interchangeable. Human beings are transceivers, as engineers put it. Exceptions to this property are not in the nature of language but in the nature of certain individuals. The person who cannot speak or hear obviously cannot exchange roles as can normal individuals. These limitations are not a function of language but of certain physiological or psychological peculiarities of the individual. Similarly, infants cannot function as both senders and receivers in the same way as adults. This, too, is not a function of language but of the maturational level of the individual. In some languages of the world there are different codes for men and women —certain morphemes are restricted to males and others to females. This, too, is not so much a linguistic as it is a cultural feature. Both men and women are capable of using the other's code; when directly quoting a member of the opposite sex, for example, the appropriate code is used.

The feature of interchangeability appears to be only partly realized in the language of the bee. Worker bees can serve as both sources and receivers, but queen bees and drones apparently do not. They do not, for example, perform the dances indicating food sources or possible new homes. Similarly there are sounds which only queen bees make. It is possible that the capacity for producing these sounds may exist in all bees but is actualized by only some.

TOTAL FEEDBACK. This feature enables a sender to receive his own messages. Primarily by auditory, though also through kinesthetic and proprioceptive, feedback a speaker receives what he sends. This is not to say that the source receives his message in the same way as do receivers or that he receives all and only what they receive. Because the sender also hears his voice through bone conduction, as well as by ear, he sounds different to himself than he does to others.

This feature combined with that of interchangeability, Hockett points out, makes it possible for human beings to act out the roles of other persons and to talk to themselves—features undoubtedly responsible for many improvements as well as for many problems.

Total feedback is realized to some extent in most bee communication. Although the dancing bee does not see the pattern of her dance she probably does get some feedback, from her own movements at least. In sound communication it seems that the sender should also receive her messages. Since so little is known about the way in which messages are "heard," however, it would be premature to venture any definite conclusion. It is possible, for example, that the receiving apparatus is "shut off" when messages are being sent or that the emission of messages interferes in some way with reception.

SPECIALIZATION. A specialized communication system, according to Hockett (1960b, p. 407) is one whose "direct energetic consequences are biologically irrelevant." Human language serves only one major purpose—to communicate; it does not aid any biological functions.

On the other hand, a dog panting communicates information as to his presence and perhaps about his internal state. But the panting serves the biological function of temperature regulation. The fact that communication accompanies or results from this behavior is only incidental. The dancing and sounds of the bees seem to function only to communicate information and hence theirs would be a specialized system.

SEMANTICITY. As already indicated, language signals refer to things in the real world; they have referents. Not all signals have such referents, of course; it would be difficult, for example, to find the referents of such terms as *mermaid* or *or*. Yet, for the most part, language symbols have some connection, however arbitrarily established, with the real world.

Bee communication is also semantic. Features of the dance, for example, its angle, and of the sounds, for example, their length, have referents in the real world.

ARBITRARINESS. Language signals are arbitrary; they do not possess any of the physical properties or characteristics of the things for which they stand. The word *wine* is no more tasty than the word *sand*, nor is the latter any less wet.

Opposed to arbitrariness is iconicity. Iconic signals do bear resemblance to their referents. A line drawing of a person is iconic in representing the body parts in proper relation to each other. It is arbitrary, however, in representing the texture and thickness of the anatomical structures.

Both arbitrariness and iconicity are relative. For example, a line drawing is more arbitrary than is a black and white photograph which is more arbitrary than a color photograph. Paralinguistic features are more iconic than are the features normally classified as belonging to language. Rate, for example, may vary directly with emotional arousal and hence would be iconic.

Bee communication appears to consist of both arbitrary and iconic features. Whether a wagging or a round dance is employed is arbitrary since neither is particularly descriptive of distance. The rate of the dance, being negatively correlated with distance, or the length of the sound trains, being proportional to distance, are iconic features.

DISCRETENESS. This feature can probably best be explained by first noting its opposite, continuousness. A continuous signal contains no sharp divisions; vocal volume is probably a good example. In reality there is no sharp break between loud and soft, for example, but rather only gradual changes. A discrete system does contain sharp divisions. For example, the sounds /t/ and /d/ differ in the feature of voiceness. Although voiceness is, in reality, a continuous variable, the sound is heard as either /t/ or /d/ and not as one midway between /t/ and /d/ regardless of how much voicing is used.

The communication system of the bee contains both discrete and continuous aspects. The types of dances, being either wagging or round, are discrete. In other respects the system is continuous, for example, the rate of the dance and the length of the sounds.

DISPLACEMENT. The feature of displacement has already been alluded to in the first chapter. Human language can be used to talk about things which are remote in both time and space; one can talk about the past and the future just as about the present. And one can talk about things one does not now, has not in the past, and will not in the future ever perceive—about mermaids and unicorns, about supernatural beings from other planets, about talking animals. One can talk about the unreal as well as the real, the imaginary as well as the actual.

Bee communication is most often displaced. The bee does not dance at the site of the nectar nor of the possible new home but returns to the hive and dances about what is no longer in her perceptual field. The tooting and quacking of the queen bees, however, are not displaced; they appear to pertain solely to the present time and place. Nor do bees communicate about matters very far removed in either time or place. There appears to be some limitation on their ability to communicate about the not-here and the not-now, limitations not existent in human language.

PRODUCTIVITY. Utterances in human language, with only trivial exceptions, are novel; each utterance is generated anew. However, as indicated in the first section of this chapter, the rules of the grammar have already imposed certain restrictions on the way in which sentences may be generated so complete productivity, in regard to form at least, does not exist. One can, however, talk about a vast number of different things and can even coin new words for new ideas and concepts. Whether human language imposes any restrictions on what can be communicated is an interesting, though probably unanswerable, question.

Bee communication possesses productivity since bees can communicate about sources of food and about sites for hives which are novel. Yet productivity, like displacement, seems limited. The bee cannot communicate about everything in its experience but only about certain things. This, of course, may well reflect a deficiency in our knowledge of their communication system rather than a limitation in the system itself.

DUALITY OF PATTERNING. Human language is composed of two levels— the level of the smallest differentiating, but meaningless, elements (called cenemes) and the level of the smallest meaningful combinations of these elements (called pleremes). In human language cenemes correspond to phonemes and pleremes to morphemes.

According to Hockett, it is characteristic of systems possessing significant duality of patterning to have a relatively small number of cenemes and an extremely large number of possible pleremes. Human language clearly evidences significant duality in this sense; there are relatively few phonemes but a great many morphemes.

It is not clear whether bee communication possesses dual patterning, even of a primitive sort. Conceivably, the sounds and the dance might be two levels of one basic code. Too little is known about the sound system and its relationship to the dance to state any definite conclusion with regard to duality.

CULTURAL OR TRADITIONAL TRANSMISSION. The form of any particular human language is traditionally transmitted. The child raised by English speakers learns English as a native speaker, regardless of the language of his biological parents. The genetic endowment pertains to human language in general rather than to any specific human language.

The communication system of the bee is not traditionally transmitted but rather genetically transmitted. An Italian bee, raised in an Austrian bee hive, will perform the dances characteristic of her biological parents.

REFLEXIVENESS. It has already been noted that human language can be used to refer to itself. Although a number of researchers (for example, Greenberg, 1961; Hockett, 1963) have suggested that this feature is absent from all animal communication systems, Sebeok (1963) has presented argument to the contrary. Rhesus monkeys, for example, have been observed to communicate messages which enable them to distinguish between playful and nonplayful activities. Reflexiveness might also be present in bee communication. When a worker bee leaves the hive she carries with her a sac of scent which is the same for all members of a particular colony. Upon returning the bee opens the sac as a sort of ticket of entry. This, according to Sebeok, functions to inform the other bees that further communication may take place. If it were an alien scent it would prevent further communication and, in all likelihood, initiate aggressive behavior in the colony.

These examples, however, seem to differ significantly from the reflexiveness of human language. In the case of the monkey the message does not refer so much to language as it does to nonlanguage behavior. In the case of the bee the scent functions primarily to identify the carrier as a member of the colony and makes reference not to language but rather to the bee itself. That the future communications of both monkeys and bees are influenced by these behaviors seems only an incidental by-product. Nevertheless, these examples do provide some cause to question the commonly held assumption that reflexiveness is solely a human language characteristic.

PREVARICATION. As a consequence of semanticity, displacement, and productivity, speakers of human languages can lie. In any system which does not possess these three features lying would be impossible. Although animal lovers are fond of telling about their pets who try to fool them, it appears that lying is extremely rare in animals.

In the bee lying seems totally absent; at least no reports could be found of bees giving false information. In all probability the bee cannot communicate about nectar that is not there nor about a possible home site that has not been found.

LEARNABILITY. Any human language can be learned by any normal human being. It might be added that this is only true at particular times in the history of the child. One cannot learn a language as a native after a certain age. This feature is best interpreted to refer to the equal learnability of all human languages—no one language should present any greater difficulty for the child than any other language.

Since this feature presupposes traditional transmission which is absent from the language of the bee, learnability is also absent.

This list neither exhausts all the characteristics of human language or what might be called "language universals," nor does it illustrate all the differences existing between human and infrahuman communication. It should, however, serve to clarify some of the major ways in which human language differs from at least one well-researched nonhuman communication system.

Despite the great quantity of research devoted to speech and language differences in individuals, in groups, and in systems, relatively little is known about the specific correlates of such variations. That the individual's psychological state influences his encoding behavior, that differences in speech have differential effects on receivers, and that different source-receiver relationships influence linguistic behavior seem clear. Yet the specific ways in which these differences operate has only been suggested. Likewise the behavioral correlates of intra- and inter-language differences have not been specified in any convincing detail and the postulated differential behaviors are hypotheses rather than facts. Even the consequences of differences among communication systems have not been rigorously defined. The important thing, however, is that the questions have been asked; the answers should not be long in coming.

Chapter Eight

Speech and Language Effects: Rhetorical Psycholinguistics

Currently in the central focus of this broad area of the effects of communication are the theories of attitude change and more specifically those theories based on the notion of psychological balance. Since these theories have clear and important implications for the entire area of communication influence, they may be legitimately singled out for discussion. Rather than attempting to provide coverage for all such theories and thus present only the skeleton of each, attention is focused on those which appear most significant and which are now dominating the field: the Principle of Congruity, the Psycho-logical Consistency Theory, and the Theory of Cognitive Dissonance.

Although each of the three theories is unique—each making different predictions and utilizing different conceptual frameworks—all show a close connection with the early formulations of Fritz Heider (1946, 1958) who first applied the notion of balance to attitude change. Certain central concepts in Heider's theory might, therefore, serve as a preface to the consideration of the three specific theories and as a general explanation of the concept of balance.

THE NATURE OF "BALANCE"

The nature of balance is best explained by developing a model of an individual's mind. An individual's mind is a storehouse of attitude objects, for example, persons, things, ideas, anything about which one can feel positively or negatively. This mind divides into a positive and a negative side; positively evaluated objects are stored on the positive side and negatively evaluated objects on the negative side.

Consider the mind pictured in Figure 22(**A**) as that of a student. This student is fond of or positively evaluates his teacher. The attitude object " teacher " can therefore be put into the positive side of his mind. Consider further that the student writes a term paper for this teacher's course. Since he thinks highly of the paper it too can be put into the positive side.

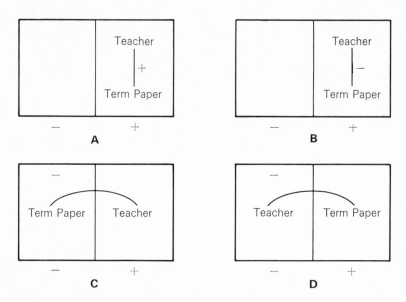

FIGURE 22.   The Hypothetical Characterization of the Mind of a Student.   **A**, **C**, and **D** are in a state of balance ; **B** is in a state of imbalance.

According to balance theory the mind " demands" that two positively evaluated objects be positively connected.   " Positively connected " means that the two objects somehow go together, like each other, agree with each other, and so on. (In the diagrams positive connections are symbolized as $+$ and negative connections as $-$.)   In other words, the mind would be in a state of balance if the teacher thought highly of the term paper (as in 22(**A**)). In this state of balance there would be no motivation for attitude change to take place.

Consider, however, the possibility that a positively evaluated teacher thinks badly of the term paper, as in Figure 22(**B**). By thinking negatively of the paper the teacher establishes a negative connection between himself and the paper; he dissociates himself from it.   Here there is imbalance; the situation is psychologically uncomfortable.   Some cognitive reorganization is necessary if balance is to be restored.

Reorganization for balance restoration can take a number of different forms.   First, the student could change his attitude towards his term paper. He might convince himself, for example, that this paper does not represent what he is really capable of doing or that there were too many other pressing problems to give full attention to it.   By changing his attitude toward the paper he restores balance; now there is a positively evaluated object negatively related to a negatively evaluated object (Figure 22(**C**)).   Second, the student could change his attitude toward his teacher, as in Figure 22(**D**). If the teacher were negatively evaluated balance would again be restored.

As in the case of the first alternative a negatively evaluated object is negatively connected to a positively evaluated object. A third alternative, beyond the power of the student, is to have the teacher change his attitude toward the paper. If this occurred balance would be restored by having two positively evaluated objects connected by a positive relationship, as in Figure 22(**A**).

The relationships of balance and imbalance merely express what most persons feel is "psychologically expected." For example, we expect persons we like to like each other, that is, two positively evaluated objects connected by a positive relationship. Also, we expect a person we like to dislike someone or something that we dislike, that is, a positive and a negative connected by a negative relationship.

More specifically, the mind is in a state of balance under the following conditions:

1. When two positively evaluated objects are positively related, for example, when a well-liked teacher (P, positively evaluated) likes (+, positive relationship) the student's term paper (P, positively evaluated);
2. When two negatively evaluated objects are positively related, for example, when two people who are disliked (both N) like (+) each other;
3. When a positively evaluated object dislikes a negatively evaluated object, for example, when a friend (P) dislikes (−) an enemy (N).

These three balanced states may be abbreviated as follows:

1. P + P
2. N + N
3. P − N

One's mind will be in a state of imbalance under the following conditions:

1. When two positively evaluated objects are negatively connected, for example, when a well-liked teacher (P) dislikes (−) one's term paper (P);
2. When two negatively evaluated objects are negatively related, for example, when two enemies (both N) dislike (−) each other;
3. When a positively evaluated object and a negatively evaluated object are positively related, for example, when a friend (P) likes (+) an enemy (N).

These three imbalanced states may be abbreviated as follows:

1. P − P
2. N − N
3. P + N

All three theories or models of attitude change make similar assumptions about the operation of balance and imbalance.   They differ, however, in a number of significant respects.   For example, given a state of imbalance the Principle of Congruity predicts that attitude change is almost automatic whereas Psycho-logical Consistency Theory predicts attitude change only under certain conditions.   Another difference concerns the nature of the predictions.   Congruity, for example, predicts not only which attitudes will change but also the amount of change; Psycho-logic and the Theory of Cognitive Dissonance do not make quantitative predictions about the amount of change.   Still another difference is that Congruity and Psycho-logic confine themselves to predictions concerning cognitive changes whereas Dissonance makes predictions about behavioral changes as well.

These and various other differences as well as the specific assumptions and processes implied in the three theories are examined in some detail. Examples of the experimental evidence which has been advanced in support of these theories' predictions and some evaluation of the theories are also included.   Since Congruity is the most specific, both in terms of its principles and its predictions, it is examined first.

THE PRINCIPLE OF CONGRUITY

The Principle of Congruity was developed by Charles Osgood (Osgood and Tannenbaum, 1955) and is an extension of his conception of meaning considered in the discussion of learning theory.

To understand this model we need first to visualize an individual's mind as we did previously, except that this time the concepts are distributed on a seven-point semantic differential scale (Table 7).   In order to force

TABLE 7.   A Hypothetical Mind As Viewed by the Principle of Congruity

+3	Apple Pie, Alfred Hitchcock
+2	*Reader's Digest*, New York
+1	Sophia Loren, Labor Unions
0	John Doe
−1	Soap Operas, Censorship
−2	Westerns, Cheating
−3	Communism, War

attention to the specific operations and predictions of the model rather than to what seems "logical" or "natural," the examples used here are deliberately peculiar ones.

In Congruity the attitude objects are of two general classes: sources of messages, for example, persons, magazines, newspapers, and concepts evaluated by sources, for example, other persons, ideas, physical things, and so on. Concepts in this hypothetical mind range from extremely favorable (+ 3) through neutral (0) to extremely unfavorable (− 3). The specific placement of any particular attitude object is revealed by the individual's ratings of that concept on the evaluative scales of the semantic differential (see Chapter 3). The neutral position (0) is extremely difficult to fill; in fact, it is probably impossible. "John Doe" has been put in to facilitate explaining some specific operations of the model. It should be clear, however, that there is very little, if anything, that one can feel truly neutral about. The relationships or bonds which connect two attitude objects can be either associative (+) or dissociative (−). For example, a positive (+) bond would be created by *Reader's Digest* endorsing labor unions; an endorsement associates the two attitude objects. A negative (−) bond, for example, Sophia Loren criticizing soap operas, dissociates the two attitude objects.

Because this theory quantifies attitudes the conditions under which the model is in a state of congruity or incongruity (similar to balance and imbalance) are somewhat complex. According to the theory the mind is in a state of congruity under only two conditions: (1) when two objects of the same scale position and sign are connected by an associative bond, for example, Alfred Hitchcock praising apple pie, or (2) when two objects of the same scale position but of opposite signs are connected by a dissociative bond, for example, labor unions fighting against censorship. Under these conditions no attitude change will take place; the attitude objects will remain at the same scale positions. Under all other conditions the mind is in a state of incongruity and forces are created to produce attitude change, that is, the attitude objects will change their scale positions.

The Principle of Congruity makes specific predictions concerning the objects that will change, the direction of the change, and the amount of the change. When the mind is in a state of incongruity the theory asserts that attitudes toward both source and concept will change. The total distance to be traveled, by either attitude object, is equal to the difference between the actual scale position of either object and its hypothetical position of equilibrium. Assume that one object (A) is at + 2, another object (B) is at −1, and that there is an associative bond between them. According to the formula the total scale distance to be traveled equals three units since the mind would be in a state of congruity if A was at −1 (a difference of three units) or if B was at + 2 (a difference of three units). The phrase "hypothetical position of equilibrium" simply refers to that scale position which would bring the mind to a state of congruity. If there was a dissociative bond between A (+ 2) and B (−1), the total distance to be traveled would equal one unit since the equilibrium position of A would be at +1 (a difference of one unit) and the equilibrium position of B would be at − 2 (a difference of one unit).

In deciding how much of the total distance each of the objects will move the first impulse might be to state that they each move half the distance.

However, experience tells us that extreme positions are more resistant to change than less extreme positions and that extremists are harder to persuade than middle-of-the-roaders. Osgood and Tannenbaum (1955) have postulated that the total distance to be traveled is divided between the two attitude objects in inverse proportion to their respective degrees of polarization. This formula states that the more polarized the object is (that is, the more removed it is from the neutral position), the less it will move or change and the less polarized the object is the more it will change.

Using the above example again, this would mean that if an associative bond connected A (+ 2) and B (−1) the total distance to be traveled would equal three units. These three units would be divided by the objects so that A will move less than will B. The part of the total distance A moves is the scale position of B without respect to sign and the part of the total distance B moves is the scale position of A without respect to sign. That is, A moves one part of the total distance (since B is at scale position 1) and B moves two parts of the total distance (since A is at scale position 2). A, therefore, will move one unit (that is, one part of three units) and B will move two units (that is, two parts of three units). The two objects would then meet at +1. Here there would be an associative relationship between two objects of the same scale position which is a congruity state.

Before moving on to the qualifications and exceptions to these general principles, some examples should be considered. Using the mind presented in Table 7 assume that Alfred Hitchcock in some way creates an associative bond between himself and westerns; for example, he directs a series of westerns. Since in this mind Hitchcock is at +3 and westerns is at −2, it is in a state of incongruity. Attitude change will result. The total scale distance to be traveled is five units since it would take a move of five units for westerns to come up to +3 (the position of Hitchcock) or for Hitchcock to fall to −2 (the position of westerns). Because Hitchcock is the more polarized object, he will move less—specifically, he will move 2 parts of the total distance (since 2 is the scale position of westerns) while westerns will move the greater distance, namely, 3 parts of the total distance (since 3 is the scale position of Hitchcock). Hitchcock then moves 2 units down to +1 while westerns moves up 3 units to +1. With these moves the mind reaches a state of congruity.

Consider an example involving a dissociative bond. Assume that labor unions (+1) in some way create a dissociative bond between themselves and communism (−3). The hypothetical position of equilibrium for labor unions is +3 while the hypothetical position of equilibrium for communism is −1. (Recall that when dissociative bonds are employed the hypothetical position of equilibrium is achieved when the two objects occupy the same scale position but of different signs.) Thus the total distance to be traveled equals two scale units. Communism, being the more polarized, will move less than will labor unions. Specifically, communism moves one part of the two units (since 1 is the scale position of labor unions) and labor unions move

3 parts (since 3 is the scale position of communism). (Since the two scale units consist of four parts, each part represents $\frac{1}{2}$ unit.) Therefore, communism moves $\frac{1}{2}$ unit up to $-2\frac{1}{2}$ while labor unions move $1\frac{1}{2}$ units up to $+2\frac{1}{2}$. The mind will then be in a state of congruity since there is a dissociative bond connecting two concepts of the same scale position but opposite signs.

Notice that although communism was criticized by a positively evaluated source it still made a favorable gain. In fact, "communism" and "war" cannot lose. They can stay where they are, for example, if Hitchcock criticizes them or if communism speaks in favor of war, but they cannot go any lower. Notice also that those attitude objects at $+3$ cannot gain; almost inevitably they lose. The only instances in which they do not lose are if associative bonds among $+3$ objects or dissociative bonds between $+3$ and -3 objects are created.

The one exception to this involves the case of a neutral object. According to Congruity a neutral object absorbs the full force of the change and does not exert a change on the other attitude object. So, if Hitchcock were to praise an unknown (John Doe) this person would move up to $+3$. Similarly, if communism were to create a dissociative bond between itself and John Doe, the latter would move to $+3$. If communism were to praise him or if Hitchcock were to denounce him, he would fall to -3.

To this basic model Osgood has added two modifications in order to make the theory's predictions more accurate. The first, an incredulity correction, covers instances in which such unlikely objects are associated or dissociated that the mechanical predictions of the theory are not followed. Rather, the person refuses to believe the assertions. For example, if Hitchcock were to praise communism, the theory implies that both objects would move to 0. What would actually happen, however, is that the statement would be disbelieved; the predictions of the theory would simply not hold. This correction for incredulity decreases as the associations and dissociations become less extreme or more believable.

The second correction, the assertion constant, adjusts the predictions of the theory so that the concept spoken about changes somewhat more than does the source. The assertion constant, set by Osgood at $\pm.17$ of one scale unit, is added to the distance to be traveled by the concept spoken about. The assertion constant carries the same sign as the sign of the predicted change for the concept. For example, if Hitchcock criticized censorship, censorship (the object spoken about), according to the basic formula, moves $-1\frac{1}{2}$ units. With the assertion constant added, censorship moves $(-1\frac{1}{2}) + (-.17)$ or -1.67 units.

The major test of the Principle of Congruity was conducted by Percy Tannenbaum (1953). First, Tannenbaum obtained six attitude objects. Three of these could logically serve as sources (labor leaders, *Chicago Tribune*, and Senator Robert Taft) and three could serve as concepts to be evaluated by sources (legalized gambling, abstract art, and accelerated college programs).   Four hundred undergraduate students rated each of these six attitude objects on semantic differential scales and the scores for each concept for each subject were computed.   Five weeks later these same students read "newspaper stories" in which the sources were related to the concepts, for example, Senator Taft favored accelerated college programs, labor leaders supported legalized gambling, Chicago Tribune disapproved of abstract art, etc.   These "newspaper stories" were extremely realistic in every detail and it is likely that the students did not question their authenticity.

Immediately after reading these stories the subjects were instructed to write short summaries of the articles and then rate these six concepts on the same scales they had used before.   Naturally, various "filler" items (additional sources and concepts) were included so as to obscure the real purpose of the experiment.

The object of the experiment was to determine the extent to which the predictions derived from the Principle of Congruity correlated with the obtained attitude changes as a result of the source-concept pairings appearing in these stories.   The obtained correlation was $+.91$ which is statistically highly significant.

In addition to serving the heuristic function of generating new hypotheses for research, the Principle of Congruity has also been used to provide a theoretical explanation of experimental findings in a number of different areas of attitude change.   Perhaps the area where Congruity is most directly relevant and where it has been most successful in accounting for obtained results is the area commonly referred to as "prestige suggestion" (cf. Insko, 1967).   Specifically, Congruity predicts that highly valued or high-status sources will exert more influence than will less-valued or lower-status sources.

In a study by Farnsworth and Misumi (1931) two groups of college students judged a series of eight paintings.   Of the paintings shown to the first group, four had well-known names attached (daVinci, Raphael, Rembrandt, and Rubens) and four had little-known names (Dewing, Doughty, Kensett, and Smibert).   For the second group the names were reversed; that is, the paintings which had well-known names attached for the first group here had the less known names and vice versa.   As hypothesized the paintings with well-known names attached were evaluated more highly than the same paintings when little-known names were attached.

In a similar study Saadi and Farnsworth (1934) constructed a questionnaire consisting of thirty dogmatic statements.   For each statement the subject was to indicate on a five-point scale the degree to which he agreed with it.   One of the statements, for example, was "There is nothing sacred about the constitution.   If it doesn't serve its purpose it should be changed as often as necessary."

One group of subjects received the statements with well-liked persons' names attached, a second group received them with disliked persons' names attached, and a third group received them without any names.   Some of the names used were Mark Twain, Thomas Edison, Will Rogers, Fatty Arbuckle, Boss Tweed, Al Capone, and even Clara Bow.

Although the results of this experiment are not as clear-cut as the theory would predict they are in the expected direction.   For fourteen of the thirty statements the order was as predicted: there was most agreement with the statements attributed to well-liked persons, less agreement with the statements with no names, and least agreement with the statements attributed to disliked persons.   For eight statements the order was well-liked, disliked, no name.   For the remaining eight the statements without names and those attributed to disliked persons were agreed with to a greater degree than were the statements attributed to well-liked persons.

It is possible and even probable that some subjects distinguished between liking a person and thinking the person credible on a given topic.   Clara Bow, for example, may have been well liked but it is doubtful that she would influence anyone on his attitude toward the constitution.   The Congruity model, however, does not distinguish among the ways in which sources are evaluated.   Nor does it enable one to separate relevant from irrelevant source-concept pairings.

Kerrick (1958) tried to test the ability of Congruity to deal with relevant and irrelevant relations.   Kerrick had newspaper stories linking sources (Henry Wallace, Director of the Museum of Modern Art, United States Department of Agriculture, and John Foster Dulles) and concepts (protective tariffs for farm products, abstract art, flexible price supports, and the recognition of Red China).   Some source-concept pairings were relevant whereas others were not.   For example, Wallace was relevant to the question of protective tariffs but not to modern art; similarly, the Director of the Museum of Modern Art was relevant to abstract art but not to protective tariffs. Each subject received two relevant and two irrelevant source-concept pairings.

The results from this study indicate that the predictions of Congruity are more accurate for relevant source-concept pairings than for irrelevant ones.   More specifically, Congruity was able to predict 83 percent of the source change and 97.5 percent of the concept change in the relevant situations but only 70.5 percent of the source change and 82.5 percent of the concept change in the irrelevant situations.

More recent studies seem to support the influence of prestige suggestion and the predictions of Congruity, in general.   Goldberg and Iverson (1965) for example, had subjects fill out questionnaires concerned with nutrition and health.   They then listened to three taped speeches each of which dealt with a different series of questionnaire items.   After listening to the speeches the subjects were told that they would again be asked to fill out the questionnaire.   But before they did, the experimenters introduced the prestige suggestion.   Half of the group witnessed the responses of a person introduced as a medical student who had graduated with honors and the other half witnessed the responses of a person introduced as a hospital orderly who had not graduated from high school.   The subjects then filled out the questionnaire again and the number of changes in their answers was scored. The results, as predicted, showed that the high-prestige source (the medical student) exerted more influence than did the low-prestige source (the hospital orderly).

Studies of this nature, however, support only one of Congruity's more general predictions. In a test of the more specific predictions Stachowiak and Moss (1965) obtained findings which differed in a number of significant ways from the theory's predictions. Subjects rated the objects "experimenter" and "Negro" on semantic differential scales. The subjects then heard the experimenter deliver a speech favorable to Negroes, thus creating an associative bond between himself and Negroes. Immediately after hearing the speech and again after two weeks the subjects again rated these objects. The initial ratings for "experimenter" were quite positive and for "Negro" slightly positive. The theory predicts that after hearing the speech in which the experimenter paired himself with Negroes that the rating for "experimenter" would become less positive and that the rating for "Negro" would become more positive. These predictions were supported when the initial ratings were compared with both the second and the third ratings. However, the theory also predicts that the change of the less polarized object (in this case "Negro") would be greater than the change of the more polarized object. Here the prediction was not supported; "experimenter" changed more. Further, the changes were not sufficient to produce congruity, as the theory predicts.

One possible reason for these nonsupportive findings, as both Osgood and the experimenters suggest (Stachowiak and Moss, 1965), is that the actual attitudes of the subjects and the attitudes they expressed on the test may not have been the same. They may not, for example, have felt as positive about Negroes as they indicated in their semantic differential ratings.

One of the great advantages of the Principle of Congruity over other theories of attitude change is that it makes precise predictions and can, therefore, be tested in specific detail. Given the scale positions of the attitude objects and the nature of the bond connecting them there is no doubt concerning the theory's predictions of the direction and the amount of the attitude change which will take place.

Furthermore, whereas the other attitude-change theories merely specify the direction of the change, Congruity also predicts the amount of change that will take place. Another virtue of Congruity is that it takes into consideration the obvious fact that attitudes, rather than being merely positive or negative, vary in strength and in reality exist on a continuum. In providing for attitude measurement on a seven-point scale Congruity more closely mirrors the real world.

And yet, perhaps because of its specificity, it is not difficult to find problems with this theory. One of its inadequacies is that the theory relies on two ad hoc corrections—the assertion constant and the correction for incredulity. Both of these are extraneous to the actual theory and are introduced to make the predictions square with the obtained results. When a theory resorts to such ad hoc adjustments, it is likely that the theory itself is in need of revision or some further refinement.   At the very least such corrections detract from the elegance and simplicity of the theory qua theory. Also, since the assertion constant was formulated on the basis of Tannenbaum's experiment, it is unlikely that this figure of $\pm.17$ would be applicable to all situations.

Congruity makes some predictions which seem intuitively unsatisfying. It asserts, for example, that the neutral object absorbs the full force of the bond and moves to the same scale position as the source.   This is a particularly troublesome prediction since it is denied by everyday experience. For example, when a friend introduces us to someone else and creates an associative bond between himself and this other person, we do not then evaluate this other person as highly as we evaluate our friend.   The person, in fact, may well be negatively evaluated as, for example, in cases of jealousy.

Another intuitively unsatisfying prediction is seen in the case of an associative bond connecting, for example, a $+3$ source with a $+2$ object. According to the theory the source becomes less positive and the concept more positive.   Martin Fishbein (1963) has advanced some experimental evidence which indicates that when an associative bond connects two positives both attitude objects become more positive.

A third prediction which intuition questions is the assertion that the attitude object spoken about changes more than the attitude source.   In computing the amount of change the assertion constant of $\pm.17$ must be added to the change predicted for the attitude object.   Although Brown (1962) states that this figure is probably too small, it appears that the basic assumption that objects change more than sources may be in need of rethinking.   Milton Rokeach (1968), for example, has argued and presented some experimental evidence for the amount of change depending on the relative importance of the beliefs aroused by the source and concept and not on whether the object is the source or the concept spoken about.   It seems unreasonable to predict that the object spoken about will always change more than the source when we consider such assertions as " God praises John Doe " and "John Doe praises God."

As has been noted, one of the advantages of Congruity is that it allows for the quantification of attitudes toward sources and concepts, rather than considering them as merely positive or negative.   Yet it does not permit the quantification of the relative strengths of associative or dissociative bonds. According to the theory the associative bond created by " likes " is as positive as one created by "loves passionately."   Similarly, one can " dislike " or " hate intensely " and yet the model deals with these equally as negative bonds. Or, to take a more extreme example, a positive bond created by a single assertion is treated in exactly the same way as one created by life-long friendship.

Another problem with the nature of the postulated bonds, as has been already implied in the discussion of Kerrick's (1958) study, is that the theory does not adequately deal with the question of relevance between source and concept.   Thus if a military leader were to argue in favor of a particular system of defense one may well be influenced by his prestige.   But if he were to speak on religion or correct diet his influence would probably not be as great.   A source, one might argue, is influential only when dealing with topics within his competence.

It seems that sources may be evaluated as both positive and negative depending on the particular attitude object with which they are associated. For example, one might have a positive evaluation for a particular teacher when he is dealing with questions of economics or political science.   At the same time, however, he might be negatively evaluated when dealing with questions concerning sports or child rearing or fashions.   In the studies which have been conducted on congruity the subjects have been instructed to rate sources without reference to any context.   This, it appears, may lead to somewhat false conclusions concerning the influence of the source; the model implies that the source, if positively evaluated, would exert influence regardless of the particular topic to which he addresses himself.

Yet one should not be too quick to conclude that the question of relevance is always important.   People have for some time been influenced by football players endorsing hair tonics and actresses endorsing dog foods. And although it is always dangerous to extend an analogy too far, the recent increase in the numbers of actresses and actors running (and successfully) for political office may well give pause to those who assume that relevance is always significant.   When dealing with college students and with an artificial experimental situation, relevance may logically be expected to play an important role.   But with the man in the street, in the real world, it may not be of great consequence.

An objection expressed by Brown (1962, 1965) and repeated by Insko (1967) is that the model deals only with attitude change as a means of resolving incongruity.   Yet as Rosenberg and Abelson (see below) have demonstrated there are a number of other alternatives, for example, the person could stop thinking, could redefine the concepts or the relation, or could simply tolerate the imbalance.   As a theory of attitude change, however, the Principle of Congruity is not obliged to deal with these other alternatives.   The theory does not deny that other ways of resolving incongruity may be employed; it is merely limited to predicting attitude change. On the other hand, as a theory of balance the Principle of Congruity, in omitting these alternatives, is clearly less complete than those which incorporate these other modes of balance restoration.

PSYCHO-LOGICAL CONSISTENCY THEORY

Differing from the Principle of Congruity primarily in the specificity of its predictions and in the alternatives it allows for dealing with imbalance is the Psycho-logical Consistency Theory, developed from the early work of

Rosenberg (1956) and modified by Rosenberg and Abelson (1960; Abelson and Rosenberg, 1958). Although this theory is sometimes grouped together with the balance theories of Heider (1946) and Newcomb (1953), the formulation of Rosenberg and Abelson is sufficiently distinct in its assumptions and predictions to merit separate consideration.

The theory is called "psycho-logical" or "affective-cognitive" because it assumes that attitudes consist of both psychological (or affective) and logical (or cognitive) components. An attitude, for Rosenberg and Abelson, is a composite of one's feelings for or against an object (affective dimension) as well as one's beliefs about the instrumentality of such attitudes (cognitive dimension). Balance is achieved when the affective and cognitive components are consistent and imbalance when these components are inconsistent.

Under certain conditions inconsistency leads to attitude change. According to this formulation attitude change can take place in two principal ways. First, a change in the affective component may lead to a change in the cognitive and second, a change in the cognitive may lead to a change in the affective. For example, an individual's negative attitude toward cheating on examinations, according to Rosenberg and Abelson, is a function of negative affect for cheating and also a function of his beliefs about the instrumental effects of cheating, for example, that it will destroy individual incentive, that it debases education, etc. This person's attitude toward cheating can, therefore, be changed in either of two ways. First, if he comes to feel positively about cheating he will also change his beliefs about the effects of cheating on individual incentive and on education. Second, if his beliefs about the effects of cheating are changed he will also change his negative affect for cheating, that is, come to feel positive or perhaps neutral about it.

In this theory there are three principal components: cognitive elements, cognitive relations, and cognitive units. A cognitive element, generally denoted by a noun or noun phrase, is anything, concrete or abstract, about which one can have an attitude. Elements include actors (persons or groups), means (instrumental activities for achieving some particular end), and goals. Cognitive relations, generally denoted by verbs or verb phrases, are the connections between cognitive elements and may be of four general types: positive (for example, "likes," "facilitates," "is compatible with"), negative (for example, "dislikes," "hinders," "is incompatible with"), null (for example, "does not influence," "has nothing to do with," "is unrelated to"), and ambivalent (that is, combinations of positive and negative relations). Cognitive units, generally denoted by sentences, are cognitive elements connected by a cognitive relation (for example, "The senator favors economic aid to underdeveloped countries," "The teacher criticized the textbook").

The mind is in a state of consistency or inconsistency under the conditions specified for general balance theory. That is, consistency is experienced when two positives or two negatives are connected by a positive relation or when a positive and a negative are connected by a negative relation.   Inconsistency results when two positives or two negatives are connected by a negative relation or when a positive and a negative are connected by a positive relation.

An example may help to clarify the theory.   Assume that an individual evaluates "high moral standards" and "making money" positively.   In his experience, however, he finds that these two cognitive elements are related negatively; that is, high moral standards do not lead to making money. The two cognitive elements, high moral standards and making money, are both positively evaluated, and since one does not lead to the other, there is a negative relation between them, that is, P — P.   This inconsistency is similar to that depicted in Figure 22(**B**).

Psycho-logical theory holds that attempts to achieve consistency are not automatic; rather, such attempts occur only when the person is motivated to think about the inconsistency and actually does think about it and when the inconsistency exceeds his level of tolerance.   Each individual has a different level of tolerance for inconsistency and therefore what will lead to activity designed to reduce inconsistency for one person may not lead to any activity for another.

Assuming that these conditions are met—that this individual does think about the inconsistency and that it does exceed his limits of tolerance—one of three general modes of consistency restoration will be employed.   First, he may choose to stop thinking either about the relation which exists between the elements or about the elements themselves or about both the relation and the elements.   This is an alternative which Congruity does not incorporate; intuitively, however, this seems to be a common, if not a logical, solution. The second alternative is that of attitude change, that is, he may change his evaluation of one or both of the elements or perceive a different relation between the objects.   In terms of the example, he may change his attitude toward "making money" and evaluate this negatively, or toward "high moral standards," or toward the relation, perceiving it as either null or positive.   Any one of these changes restores the mind to a state of consistency.   Consistency is also restored by changing attitudes toward both of the elements and the relation between them.   In this case there would be two negatives connected by a positive relation which would be a consistency state. This alternative, however, is unlikely.   The theory assumes, and correctly it seems, that consistency will be achieved in the most economical way possible, that is, by making the least number of changes.   The third alternative, probably the one most often adopted, is to differentiate or redefine one or both of the elements and in this way achieve a state of consistency.   For example, he may chose to differentiate the element "making money" into "making a great deal of money" and "making a comfortable living" and positively evaluate only the latter.   He may then perceive a null or even a positive relation between "high moral standards" and "making a comfortable living."   In so differentiating, he is saying, in effect, that although there is a negative relation between "high moral standards" and "making a great deal of money" it is not "a great deal of money" which is evaluated positively. Rather, only "making a comfortable living" is positively evaluated. This redefined cognitive element is not inconsistent with high moral standards since one can easily retain his standards and yet still earn a comfortable living. In a similar manner, he may have differentiated "high moral standards."

This process of differentiation or redefinition is extremely common and can be found quite easily in everyday behavior. If, for example, one positively evaluates high grades and knows that the only way to achieve this is by cheating which is evaluated negatively, cheating can easily be redefined. For example, one might "reason" that cheating is wrong but that a glance or two at someone's paper is not really cheating but merely checking. Or one may "reason" that although cheating is generally wrong, in this particular situation, where the instructor is obviously unfair in his testing, it is not wrong but a necessary safeguard against an unfair examination. The possibilities are almost unlimited.

In one experiment, conducted by Rosenberg and Abelson (1960), subjects were instructed to play the role of the owner of a large department store. They were further instructed to set high positive values on keeping sales at the highest possible volume in all departments of the store.

The subjects were then divided into three groups, each of which was given different instructions. Group 1 was instructed to place a positive evaluation on modern art and a positive evaluation on Fenwick, the manager of the rug department; Group 2 was to place a negative evaluation on modern art and a positive evaluation on Fenwick; Group 3 was to place a negative evaluation on both modern art and Fenwick.

In addition, all three groups were given the same set of beliefs: (1) displays of modern art reduce sales; (2) Fenwick plans to mount a modern art display in the rug department; and (3) Fenwick, as manager of the rug department, has increased sales. These beliefs, supported by alleged facts, established the relations between the cognitive elements.

In order to visualize the cognitive units more clearly, the minds of the subjects in the three groups are diagramed in Figure 23.

According to the general premises already explained, the minds of the subjects are in a state of inconsistency. In Group 1 all three cognitive elements are positively evaluated. For a state of consistency to exist there would have to be positive relations among all elements. Instead, however, sales and modern art are connected by a negative relation which causes the inconsistency. In Group 2 the inconsistency is caused by a positively evaluated element (Fenwick) and a negatively evaluated element (modern art) being connected by a positive relation. In Group 3 the inconsistency centers on the positive connection between a positively evaluated element (sales) and a negatively evaluated element (Fenwick). These inconsistent relations are indicated in the diagram by broken lines.

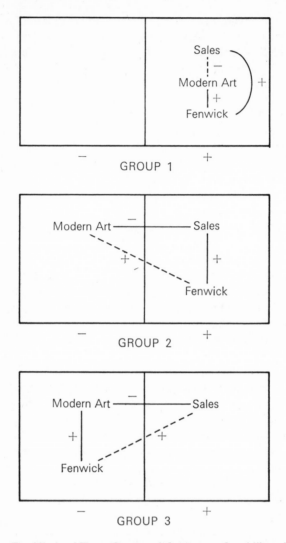

FIGURE 23. The Minds of Three Groups of Subjects. *See Milton Rosenberg and Robert Abelson, "An Analysis of Cognitive Balancing," in Milton Rosenberg, et al., eds.* Attitude Organization and Change *(New Haven: Yale University Press, 1960), pp. 112–163.*

All three groups were next given three communications relevant to the inconsistencies. The first communication argued that modern art does not decrease but rather increases sales; the second argued that Fenwick does *not* plan to mount a modern art display; and the third argued that Fenwick actually failed to increase sales. The subjects were then asked which communication was most acceptable (most logical, most pleasing, most persuasive).

According to the theory the minds of the subjects are in a state of inconsistency and there is, therefore, a tendency to seek consistency restoration. One way this can be accomplished is to take in information relevant to the inconsistency. Now which information does each group find most acceptable? The results, as predicted, showed that each group accepted the communication which allowed consistency restoration with the least amount of change. Specifically, Group 1, where the inconsistency was caused by a negative relationship connecting sales and modern art, accepted the argument that modern art actually increases sales and thereby was able to change the relation between sales and modern art and restore consistency. Subjects in Group 2 found the communication arguing that Fenwick does not plan to put up a modern art display most acceptable and were thereby able to change the positive relation between Fenwick and modern art to negative or null. Group 3 accepted the argument that Fenwick actually failed to increase sales. As in Groups 1 and 2, these subjects restored consistency by changing only one relation.

Probably the most provocative of all experiments on attitude change was conducted by Rosenberg (1960) as a test of Psycho-logical theory. Eleven graduate and professional-school students who could be deeply hypnotized constituted the experimental group and a comparable group, but whose members could not be easily hypnotized, constituted the control group. From these subjects three main types of information were secured. First, their attitudes and interests were obtained toward seven social issues: labor's right to strike, the city-manager plan, the United States being more conciliatory toward Russia, Negroes moving into white neighborhoods, the United States and Canada uniting to form one nation, comprehensive Federal medical insurance, and living in Los Angeles. Second, each subject rated thirty-one values, for example, all persons have equal rights, all people should be well educated, in terms of the degree of satisfaction or dissatisfaction they afforded him. Third, the subjects rated each of these thirty-one values in terms of the degree to which each would be attained or blocked by the attitude objects already rated; for example, to what degree would equal rights for all persons be attained or hindered by Negroes moving into white neighborhoods? In this way the experimenters obtained measures of attitudes toward various elements and values and the perceived relations between them. After these ratings were obtained members of the experimental group were hypnotized and were told to feel differently about a particular attitude element which they had previously indicated was of high-interest value. That is, the affective component of their attitude was changed. The control group subjects were given the same tests but instead of being hypnotized and given a suggestion to change an attitude were simply told to try to fall asleep.

For six of the experimental subjects the induced change was from negative to positive and for five it was from positive to negative. For example, one subject who was opposed to Negroes moving into white neighborhoods was given the following posthypnotic suggestion: "When you awake you will be very much in favor of Negroes moving into white neighborhoods. The mere idea of Negroes moving into white neighborhoods will give you a happy, exhilarated feeling.   Although you will not remember this suggestion having been made, it will strongly influence your feelings after you have awakened" (Rosenberg, 1960, pp. 26–27).   All of the induced changes were designed to create states of inconsistency.

After this suggestion the subjects were awakened and retested on their attitudes toward the objects and values and the relations they perceived between them.   The purpose of this retest, of course, was to see what corresponding changes in the values or in the relations would be brought about by the posthypnotic suggestion to change one of the attitudes.   The predictions that the changes would be greater for the experimental group than for the control group and that they would be in the direction of consistency restoration were well supported by the results of the experiment.

Some of the major types of changes may be indicated here.   One method to restore consistency is to change the relation from positive to negative or from negative to positive.   Assume, for example, that before hypnosis, one subject was opposed to the city-manager plan and saw it as facilitating "having power over people" for which he had a negative value. Here there is consistency: a negatively evaluated object (city-manager plan) is positively related ("facilitates") to a negatively evaluated object ("having power over people"), that is, $N + N$.   Under hypnosis he was instructed to feel positively toward the city-manager plan.   Now there is inconsistency $(P + N)$.   To restore consistency he could then perceive the relation as negative, that is, as blocking "having power over people."   Here there would be a positive (city-manager plan) negatively connected ("blocking") to a negative ("having power over people"), yielding the consistent cognitive unit $P - N$.

A second type of change occurred in the attitudes toward the values. For example, assume that a person felt negatively about Negroes moving into white neighborhoods and that he also rated negatively the value "people of different backgrounds getting to know each other better."   These two negatives would naturally be connected by a positive bond and the cognitive unit would be in a state of consistency $(N + N)$.   When he is instructed to feel positively about Negroes moving into white neighborhoods, inconsistency is generated $(P + N)$.   To restore consistency he then changes the value he had for "people of different backgrounds getting to know each other better" from the initially negative to positive.

A third means of restoring consistency is to redefine or differentiate one or both of the elements.   This has already been illustrated above in the example of "making money" and "high moral standards."

A fourth alternative is to change the instrumental relations between the elements.   For example, one subject negatively evaluated "abandoning foreign economic aid" and stated that this would hinder the positive value of "the economic development of ex-colonial nations." Here there was consistency since a negative bond ("hinder") connected a negative ("abandoning economic aid") and a positive ("the economic development of ex-colonial nations"), that is, $N - P$. During hypnosis, however, the suggestion to feel positively about "abandoning economic aid" produced the inconsistent unit $P - P$. When retested he was seen to have changed the connection between these two values and now asserted that the economic development of the ex-colonial nations would only be temporarily hindered and that the long range effects of abandoning economic aid would lead these nations to become more self-reliant.

In this experiment the inconsistency and the subsequent changes were brought about by an induced change in the affective component; the subjects were instructed to feel positively or negatively about a particular cognitive element. Other studies have obtained results to support the other half of the theory, namely, that a change in the beliefs about the instrumentality of various elements leads to a change in attitude.

DiVesta and Merwin (1960), for example, investigated student attitudes toward teaching as a career. They first measured the students' attitudes toward a teaching career, their need for achievement, and their beliefs concerning teaching as a means of attaining this achievement. Three groups of subjects were then exposed to different communications. The first group heard a discussion in which it was argued that a teaching career would satisfy the need for achievement and included such arguments as teaching provides opportunities for personal and civic contributions. The second group heard a discussion also in favor of teaching as a career but which did not relate to the need for achievement. The arguments this discussion stressed were, for example, that teachers have long vacations and that there is little competition in teaching. A third group heard a discussion favorable to teaching but which supposedly did not contain any need-fulfilling arguments.

The results of this study showed that the discussion related to the need for achievement produced significantly more attitude change toward teaching as a career than did the nonachievement discussion which, in fact, produced a negative change. The control-group subjects, who heard the discussion unrelated to any needs, did not change their attitudes significantly in either direction.

According to Insko (1967, p. 197), Rosenberg and Abelson's theory "is one of the most sophisticated and compelling statements of the consistency point of view" and the experimental evidence "is highly consistent and supportive" and "strong enough to produce considerable faith in the general adequacy of the formulation."

The theory still raises some questions. One problem is that the theory is extremely difficult to test. While it is relatively easy to test the prediction that a change in the cognitive component leads to a change in the affective component, it is not very easy to test the reverse, namely, that a change in the affective component leads to a change in the cognitive component. The experiments which have been done on this question are clearly among the most original and provocative of all attitude-change studies but they are difficult to devise and execute and hence few in number.

Psycho-logical Consistency Theory does not permit the scaling of attitude strength, as does the Principle of Congruity, nor does it make clear predictions concerning behavior responses as does the Theory of Cognitive Dissonance.

In allowing for so many possible ways to reduce inconsistency, the theory does not enable one to always predict which of the alternatives will be chosen. The general theory does state that the reorganization which involves the least number of changes will be employed, as illustrated in the role-playing experiment, and Abelson (1959) has proposed a hierarchy among the possible alternatives to consistency restoration. Neither of these two assumptions, however, has been conclusively supported.

THE THEORY OF COGNITIVE DISSONANCE

The Theory of Cognitive Dissonance, formulated by Leon Festinger and persuasively presented in his *A Theory of Cognitive Dissonance* (1957), is the most general and widely applicable and probably the most important theory in the field of communication research today.

"Dissonance" and "consonance" (similar, though not identical, to incongruity and congruity and consistency and inconsistency) refer to relations between elements. Unlike the other models in which "elements" refer to objects or persons, in Festinger's system elements are cognitions or "knowledges" about oneself, about other persons, or about one's environment and may refer to beliefs, attitudes, feelings, desires, behaviors, and so on. Elements are cognitions such as "The teacher likes the term paper," "I earn a high salary," "I am walking to work," "He will protest against discrimination."

Three possible relations may exist between elements: irrelevant, dissonant, and consonant. Irrelevant relations exist between elements which are unrelated to or unconnected with each other. For example, an irrelevant relation would exist between one's attitude toward television programing and postal rates or between postal rates and the proverbial price of tea. Relations such as these are of little concern in the theory; the theory is simply not applicable to them. At times, however, it is difficult to determine when relations are relevant and when they are irrelevant. Furthermore, relations which are at one time irrelevant may at another time become relevant. For example, if one wanted to send tea through the mail then postal rates and the price of tea would no longer be connected by an irrelevant relation.

The theory, of course, is concerned primarily with relevant relations and these may be either dissonant or consonant. The relation between two elements is said to be dissonant when the obverse of one element follows from the other. Elements A and B are dissonant if, given A, not-B would follow. For example, assume that I know that motorcycle riding is dangerous and that I also purchase a motorcycle. These two elements are dissonant since given one of them (say, my knowledge concerning the dangers of motorcycle riding) the obverse of the other element would follow. If I know that motorcycle riding is dangerous then it would be expected that I would *not* purchase a motorcycle. Of course, if I had a desire to injure myself then these elements would not be dissonant. In stating that these two elements are dissonant the assumption is made that I do not want to injure myself. In most instances such assumptions will not cause any great problem though it should be realized that assumptions of this nature are made throughout the research on dissonance theory and are at times not so obvious. The nature of a consonant relation should be clear by implication. Two elements are consonant when given one element the other element would follow. For example, if one enjoys writing letters and actually does write a letter the relation between these two elements is consonant.

Obviously not all dissonant relations are of equal strength. According to Festinger, there are two major determinants of dissonance magnitude: (1) the importance of the elements and (2) the number of elements that are dissonant with the given element. That the importance of the elements is related to the magnitude of the dissonance should be clear intuitively. For example, if a person eats a piece of candy between meals and yet knows that he should not eat between meals the dissonance would probably not be very great since neither element is of particularly great importance. On the other hand, the dissonance would be much greater if the person were a diabetic. Here the elements are much more important and the magnitude of the dissonance would be correspondingly greater.

The second factor influencing the magnitude of dissonance is the number of relevant elements which are dissonant with the one in question. For example, if a person changes jobs and if the new job involves additional travel time dissonance would be produced. The disadvantage of additional travel time would not "follow from" the taking of a new job. However, there would be greater dissonance if, in addition to increased travel time, this new job also paid less, was less enjoyable, had less status, and so on. In the former instance only one element (additional travel time) is dissonant with the new job whereas in the latter instance there are more dissonant elements.

When dissonance is present an individual can do a number of things to reduce this psychological discomfort. The pressure to reduce the dissonance will be a function of its magnitude. If there is little dissonance there will be little pressure; if there is great dissonance there will be much pressure. Probably one of the most frequent ways of reducing dissonance is to change the behavioral element. For example, if I stopped riding the motorcycle then the dissonance would be eliminated. In many instances changing one's behavior is not so easy. Persons who know that smoking is dangerous and yet continue to smoke experience dissonance; to change their behavior is not so simple.   Similarly, the boy in love with a girl who hates him may not be able to change his feelings for her.   Yet, in many instances, behavioral change can be accomplished and dissonance can thereby be reduced.

A second way of reducing dissonance is to change the environmental element.   This is generally more difficult since one seldom has control over the environment.   In the previous examples, this alternative would involve making motorcycle riding less dangerous, making smoking less harmful, and making the girl love the boy.   Festinger (1957) provides an example of successfully changing the environment which merits repeating.   An individual paces up and down his living room floor.   Every time he comes to a certain spot, instead of continuing his pacing, he leaps over it.   This behavior is clearly dissonant with his knowledge that this particular area of the floor is just as level and just as sturdy as the rest of the floor.   Obviously one way to reduce the dissonance would be to stop leaping over this area, that is, change the behavioral element.   But, he could also reduce dissonance by changing the environment, for example, by chopping a hole in that area of the floor he normally jumps over.   Now when he leaps over this area there will be no dissonance since, with a hole in the floor, there is good reason for his behavior.

A third way of reducing dissonance is to add new and relevant elements. For example, as a motorcycle rider I might acquire new elements relating to the dangers of automobile driving, plane travel, and the like and thus reduce the apparent danger of motorcycle riding.   That is, these other methods of travel are made to appear more dangerous or perhaps only slightly less dangerous than motorcycling.   In either case, motorcycling, by comparison with the other methods of travel, no longer appears so dangerous.   Similarly, the smoker may read about the biased nature of the research linking smoking to cancer or the contradictory evidence and the boy might look for faults in his girl.

At the same time that there are methods for reducing dissonance there are also resistances to be overcome.   For example, there may be difficulties involved in changing one's behavior; the change may involve pain or loss of some kind.   Not riding the motorcycle might involve a loss of money which would also produce dissonance.   Motorcycling might be enjoyable and giving up such enjoyment would produce dissonance.   And, of course, changing behavior is not always possible, as already noted.

With environmental elements resistance is much stronger.   When the environmental element corresponds with reality there is little hope of changing it.   Although one might be able to chop a hole in the floor, one cannot change the fact that today is Monday or that it is raining, despite the fact that this knowledge produces dissonance with a desire to go swimming or play baseball.

The magnitude of dissonance has a limit; dissonance cannot increase indefinitely.   The greatest amount of dissonance possible can be no greater than the resistance to change.   For example, assume that a person accepted a job which was lower in rank than he thought he deserved. The two elements (his accepting this job and his belief that the rank is lower than he deserves) are dissonant. To each of these elements there is resistance to change, for example, quitting his job would involve economic hardships and admitting that he made a mistake; changing his attitudes concerning the rank he deserves would involve ego conflicts and so on. However, if the dissonance gets too great, that is, greater than the resistance to change, then he will quit his job or admit that he is not worth more than the rank received. Naturally, the element changed will be the one with less resistance attached. Therefore, Festinger (1957, p. 28) postulates, more formally, that " *the maximum dissonance that can possibly exist between any two elements is equal to the total resistance to change of the less resistant element.*"

In *A Theory of Cognitive Dissonance* Festinger considers four major types of situations to which Dissonance is applicable: forced compliance, decision making, exposure to information, and social support. Discussion of these four situations and of the experimental support will help further clarify the theory of dissonance and give some indication of its scope and power of prediction.

FORCED COMPLIANCE. When public behavior contradicts private opinion, dissonance is experienced. This follows from the definition of dissonance already given; dissonance results if given two elements the obverse of one "follows from" the other. Given a private opinion, public behavior which contradicts it certainly does not follow from it and is, in fact, the obverse of this private opinion.

According to Festinger, public compliance without private acceptance may be forced by (1) a threat of punishment for noncompliance or (2) a promise of a reward for compliance. Under each of these conditions dissonance results. As has been noted the magnitude of the dissonance is related to the number and importance of the relevant cognitive elements. If an individual is asked to publicly renounce his religion or country or family for $10, this reward would clearly not be enough to get him to comply. Yet there would be some small amount of dissonance created by the loss of the $10. If, on the other hand, a person were asked to state publicly that he is a fool for a reward of a million dollars, he would, in all likelihood, readily comply. He would so state that he was a fool, confident in the knowledge that he had made a million dollars. Although there would be some dissonance, since he stated what he did not believe, it would not be a very significant amount and the reward would more than compensate. The same situations obtain in the case of punishments—threats of mild punishments seldom lead to overt behavior contrary to private opinions whereas threats of severe punishments do lead to compliance.

But what happens when compliance is brought about by a small reward or by the threat of a mild punishment? According to Festinger, these situations produce a great deal of dissonance. Here the person cannot take refuge in the fact that the reward or the avoidance of the punishment justified his compliance; consequently there is great pressure for dissonance reduction.

Two basic changes can reduce dissonance created by small rewards or mild punishments. First, the individual can change his private opinion and come to believe what his public behavior indicated; that is, he would come to believe in what he did. Second, he could magnify the reward or the punishment and thereby justify his behavior.

There are a number of examples and experiments which might be cited in support of this hypothesis. One of the most interesting studies appeared a few years ago in *The New York Times Magazine* in an article entitled "Try a Little Dissonance" by Elliot Aronson (1966). In this paper Aronson attempted to apply dissonance theory in general and the consequence of forced compliance in particular to child rearing.

According to Aronson, there are two basic goals in raising children: to prevent them from performing undesirable actions and to instill in them an enduring set of values or standards. With these goals in mind consider a boy of five or six who is hitting his younger brother and caught in the act by his father. The father has available to him a number of punishments—from extremely mild to extremely severe. Assuming that the father chooses the severe punishment it is likely that the boy will stop hitting his brother, at least while the father is present. However, this does nothing in terms of the child's value system—he still wants to beat up his brother but is prevented by the threat of severe punishment. In all probability, however, the child would resume hitting his brother after a week or so.

But what would happen if the father had chosen a mild punishment? According to Dissonance this punishment would be more effective both in deterring the child from hitting his brother and in instilling in him a set of values. A mild punishment, as already noted, creates dissonance; the child's private opinions and attitudes tell him that he wants to beat up his brother and these contradict his overt behavior of not hitting his brother. He must now reduce this dissonance. One possibility is to magnify the punishment and convince himself that he is not hitting his brother because of the punishment. But, if the punishment is mild enough he will find difficulty in convincing himself of this. The other way to reduce dissonance is to change his private opinions and attitudes; that is, to convince himself that he really does not want to beat up his brother. And this, it appears, is the choice that children normally take.

In order to test this theory four- and five-year-old children were asked to rate the attractiveness of a number of toys. The experimenters then chose one of the toys the children had rated as very attractive and told them that they could not play with it. To one group they applied mild punishment— "I would be a little annoyed." To the other group they applied severe punishment—"I would be very angry. I would have to take all the toys and go home and never come back again. I would think you were just a baby" (Aronson, 1966, p. 114). (Since the children were not the experimenters' this was about as severe a punishment as they were allowed to administer.)

After applying the threat of punishment they left the room, allowing the children to play with the other toys and to resist or succumb to the temptation to play with the forbidden toy. All of the children managed to resist the temptation. The children were then asked to re-evaluate the toys. Those children who received the severe threat rated the forbidden toy in the same way as they had initially. Here it seems that although the toy was attractive the threat was severe enough to prevent them from playing with it. Those children who received the mild threat, however, re-evaluated the toy as less attractive. These children lacked sufficient justification for not playing with the toy and consequently convinced themselves that they really did not want to play with it anyway, that it was not as attractive as they had originally thought.

In a similar study the experimenters returned twenty-three to sixty-four days after applying the threats of punishment and found that the children who received the severe threat were now playing with the forbidden toy but the children who received the mild threat, even after sixty-four days, still did not play with it.

In a study by Festinger and Carlsmith (1959), college students were asked to lie—to tell other students that the experiment they had just participated in was enjoyable when in fact it was extremely boring. The subjects in one group received $20 for lying whereas subjects in the other group received only $1. Upon rerating the experiment, the group receiving the large reward did not change their opinion; the task was still boring. The group receiving the small reward, however, rerated the task as more interesting and enjoyable. Here the small reward, like the mild punishment, was not enough to justify their lying so they changed their opinions. The large reward, like the severe punishment, was sufficient to justify their lying and so they had no need to reduce dissonance by changing their opinions.

In a later experiment (Cohen, 1960) high-school students were offered rewards for writing essays advocating a position with which they did not agree—shorter summer vacations. Here again the results supported the predictions of Dissonance. The group receiving the greatest reward showed the least attitude change; the group receiving the smallest reward showed the most change.

DECISION MAKING. According to Festinger (1957) dissonance is experienced after making a decision. The reason for this seems logical intuitively. Any decision involves a consideration of the advantages and disadvantages of the possible alternatives. Thus in choosing between X and Y and finally selecting X dissonance is experienced because of the advantages of Y which are rejected and the disadvantages of X which are accepted. Alternatively, if Y is selected dissonance is experienced because of the advantages of X which are rejected and the disadvantages of Y which are accepted. So regardless of which alternative is chosen dissonance results.

The theory also predicts that when one of the two alternatives is obviously the better choice then little dissonance is experienced. When, on the other hand, the alternatives are both of approximately the same value much dissonance is experienced.   The reason for this is that in the latter condition there are more advantages rejected and disadvantages accepted than in the former condition.

One way to reduce such dissonance is to seek out information which supports the decision made.   Ehrlich, Guttman, Schonback, and Mills (1957) subjected this prediction to experimental testing.   Their specific hypothesis was that new-car buyers, in having recently made a decision, would experience dissonance and that in order to reduce it would seek out information supporting their decision.   They predicted that new-car buyers would read more advertisements of the car they had purchased than of the cars they seriously considered but did not buy and that they would in fact avoid ads of these considered-but-rejected cars.   Reading advertisements for the car just purchased seems an excellent way of acquiring those cognitive elements which would reinforce one's decision; they would, in effect, tell the buyer that he had made the right choice.   On the other hand, reading advertisements of the rejected alternative would increase dissonance since these would present "evidence" that the buyer had made the wrong decision.   The best way to avoid such dissonance is to avoid this latter kind of information.   Their reading of advertisements for cars they had not seriously considered, the experimenters reasoned, would not be greatly influenced by dissonance and therefore should be read less than the purchased car and yet more than the rejected car.

The experimenters interviewed sixty-five males approximately four to six weeks after each had purchased a new car.   The interviews were ostensibly designed to ascertain reading habits.   During the interview the informant was shown the car advertisements which appeared in the magazines and newspapers he regularly bought and asked if he had noticed them and if he had read them.   He was then asked which cars he had seriously considered buying but rejected.   The results of this experiment were only in part supportive of the theory.   New-car buyers noticed approximately the same number of ads for the car they purchased and for the cars they rejected, 70 and 66 percent, respectively.   However, they read 65 percent of the ads they noticed for the cars they purchased but only 40 percent for the cars they rejected.   This result clearly supports the predictions of Dissonance.   However, there was no significant difference in the ads read for cars considered-but-rejected and for cars not seriously considered.   Therefore, it cannot be said that these buyers avoided the ads of the rejected cars as the theory predicts.   The reason for this discrepancy, according to Festinger (1957), is that these persons were still very sensitive to car advertisements and consequently may not yet have differentiated in their reading between ads of cars seriously considered and cars not seriously considered.   Another reason which, it seems, is more in line with the theory is that by reading advertisements for cars not considered and for cars considered-but-rejected they, in effect, grouped all the rejected alternatives together.   The seriously considered-but-rejected cars now acquired more similarity with the not seriously considered cars and thus this entire group becomes more differentiated from the selected car.

The possibility that dissonance had nothing to do with these reading practices cannot be overlooked. Since these car buyers did not read fewer advertisements of the cars considered-but-rejected than of cars not considered one cannot say that they avoided information. Similarly, since there is no indication of their advertisement reading habits before purchasing the car it cannot be concluded that the observed reading rate was higher than usual or that it was aimed at dissonance reduction. The preference for reading ads of their own cars may well have existed before the purchase or even before making the decision to buy a car. Many people, for example, read the Volkswagen ads simply because they are different and clever but have no intention of purchasing this or any car.

EXPOSURE TO INFORMATION. Ordinarily, individuals expose themselves to information when it is pertinent to future decisions. For example, academic departments annually hold "premajor conferences" at which the various opportunities for employment, requirements, and other information pertinent to selecting a particular major field of study are discussed. The students attending such meetings voluntarily expose themselves to this information since it is relevant to their future actions and decisions. Central to the theory, however, is information exposure related to dissonance. That is, when a person is in a state of dissonance how will he react to new information?

If a person experiences little or no dissonance he neither approaches nor avoids new information. The student who has already chosen his major and who experiences no dissonance will not be motivated to either attend or avoid such premajor meetings, for example.

When a moderate amount of dissonance is present, however, the individual seeks out information which will reduce dissonance and avoids information which will increase dissonance. For example, the student who has chosen to major in Astrology and who now hears that job opportunities in this field are scarce will probably experience dissonance and will be motivated to attend a lecture on "Career Opportunities in Astrology." At the same time he will be motivated to avoid exposing himself to information which would detail the small demand and the great supply of astrologers.

When a person experiences a great deal of dissonance the theory offers a somewhat different hypothesis, namely, that he will seek out information which will *increase* dissonance. Although this prediction may seem inconsistent with the general theory, it is actually quite logical. Recall that Festinger postulated that there is a maximum level to dissonance and that when dissonance becomes too great there is a change in one of the elements which leads to dissonance reduction. When a person experiences a great deal of dissonance and exposes himself to information which will increase this dissonance he is, in effect, allowing the dissonance to increase to the point where a change in one of the elements will take place.   Thus the student who is worried over having chosen to major in Astrology and who experiences a great deal of dissonance may expose himself to information which will increase this dissonance to the point where he will change his major or his career plans.   When he does change this element the dissonance will be reduced or possibly totally eliminated.   In other words, an individual who experiences great dissonance and exposes himself to information which increases dissonance is actually reducing the dissonance by forcing a change in one of the elements.

There are, as Festinger notes, a number of situations in which persons are involuntarily exposed to information which increases dissonance.   In cases of accidental exposure, for example, the individual may expect to hear a speaker praise the decision he has just made when it turns out that he severely criticizes it instead.   Sometimes persons expose themselves to information on an irrelevant basis.   Here they find that in addition to the information they intended to obtain they also expose themselves to information which increases dissonance.   Thus a person may, while driving, listen to the radio to hear some music but also hear about the increasing highway-accident rates which increases dissonance.   At other times there is forced exposure.   One cannot, for example, isolate himself from information on crime and war, information which almost invariably increases dissonance.   Also, in interaction with other persons one exposes oneself to potentially dissonance-increasing information.   Thus someone may remark that he did not make the right decision, hoping to have the other person say that indeed the decision was correct.   But when the person agrees with him, dissonance is increased.

Of course, there are many other ways in which one is involuntarily exposed to dissonance-increasing information.   Certainly this is not a complete catalog of all possibilities.   Rather, it suggests that often persons are not in control of the information they are exposed to and under these conditions their behavior does not follow the general predictions of Dissonance. When they are in control of the information they will be exposed to, however, they follow the road to dissonance reduction.   As has been noted, at times this road involves a detour during which dissonance is temporarily increased until one of the elements is changed.

Although the predictions of Dissonance with regard to information exposure are intuitively satisfying, convincing experimental support has been noticeably lacking.   The study conducted by Ehrlich, Guttman, Schonback, and Mills (1957) and discussed under " decision making" is clearly relevant here also but not particularly convincing.

A number of experiments on selective-exposure are likewise relevant but not fully convincing.   For example, Cannell and MacDonald (1956) found that 60 percent of nonsmoking males but only 32 percent of smoking males read articles on smoking and its connection with lung cancer.   Similarly,

Schramm and Carter (1959) report that twice as many Republicans watch a Republican-sponsored campaign as Democrats.   Klapper (1960, pp. 19–20), summarizing the results of these and other studies on information exposure, notes: "The tendency of people to expose themselves to mass communications in accord with their existing opinions and interest and to avoid unsympathetic material, has been widely demonstrated."   Although Klapper's statement is an accurate one, the evidence does not demonstrate that it is dissonance which motivates selective exposure.

SOCIAL SUPPORT. The social group serves both as a source for the creation of cognitive dissonance as well as for its reduction or elimination. Thus if the group disagrees with or holds opinions contrary to an individual he will experience dissonance.   Conversely, dissonance will be reduced if agreement with the group is found.   In addition to the two general factors determining the magnitude of dissonance there are, for social situations, two additional determinants.   First, the magnitude depends on the relative objectiveness of the elements.   For example, if someone were to hold that wood does not burn there would be little dissonance since this is an objective, testable assertion and past experience has proven that wood does in fact burn.   This contrary opinion is therefore given little weight, if any.   However, if someone were to hold that God does not exist much dissonance would be created in the believer since this is not an objective or testable statement.

Second, the magnitude of dissonance depends on the number of people who agree or disagree with an individual's opinions.   Thus if one group member were to disagree less dissonance would be experienced than if ten members disagreed.

As has been noted, the amount of dissonance created is, in part, a function of the importance of the elements.   In the case of social relations there are certain factors which determine importance and hence the magnitude of dissonance.   One such factor is the relevance of the person who disagrees.   If an elementary-school student disagreed with us about the value of a particular painting there would be less dissonance than if the person who disagreed were a noted art critic.   That is, when the person who disagrees is a noted expert or a high-credibility source, the disagreement produces great dissonance.   A low-credibility source produces only little dissonance, if any.

Another factor is the cohesiveness of the social group.   Disagreement among members of a close group creates more dissonance than disagreement among members of a less cohesive group.   Furthermore, if the person who disagrees is important to us for some particular reason then this creates more dissonance than disagreement with a person who is not important.

Finally, the magnitude of dissonance is a function of the extent of the disagreement; the greater the disagreement the greater the dissonance.   If, for example, someone were to say that an artist's painting techniques were completely inadequate and that he did everything from start to finish in the wrong way, this would create much more dissonance than would the assertion that one or two of his paintings were not particularly impressive.

According to Festinger, there are three principal ways in which dissonance originating from social disagreement may be reduced: by changing one's opinions, by changing the opinions of those who disagree, or by making those who disagree appear different.

Changing one's opinions so that they are in agreement with the opinions of the group members eliminates the source of the dissonance and hence restores consonance. By changing the opinions of those who disagree, the environment is, in effect, changed and made consonant with one's own opinions. By making those who disagree somehow different the individual makes their opinions less important and therefore less influential in producing dissonance. Most often, it seems, this takes the form of attributing to those who disagree some undesirable trait. Thus if someone disagrees with our attitudes toward a particular religious or racial group, it would reduce dissonance to separate ourselves from these persons by saying that they are prejudiced or bigoted or just downright stupid. In this way their opinions are seen as biased or unintelligent and not of any real importance.

In a major test of the theory, Festinger, Riecken, and Schachter (1956) studied a group which predicted the destruction of the world. The group was led by a Mrs. Keech who claimed to have received messages from the planet Clarion warning her that the world would be destroyed by flood on December 21. Mrs. Keech, however, along with her followers, were selected to be saved. The plan was to land a flying saucer on the eve of the impending flood and take the group to safety. The group was composed of students, faculty members from the near-by college, and town people. Many so fervently believed in the prophecy that they quit their jobs, sold their homes, and joined Mrs. Keech to await the saving saucer.

Festinger, quite convinced that the prophecy would fail, had here an ideal situation in which to study the operation of dissonance. Researchers were promptly dispatched to join the group and observe their behaviors at close range. According to Dissonance theory, when there is great commitment, such as there was on the part of these persons, and when their commitment is proven wrong, dissonance would result. Some changes would, therefore, be needed to restore consonance. But how would this be done?

On the eve of December 21, one part of the group gathered at the home of Mrs. Keech to await the saucer. The other members, oddly enough, were away at their respective homes since it was Christmas vacation. It was predicted that the members who were at their homes and isolated from the group would not have social support for their beliefs and hence would reduce dissonance by changing their own opinions, that is, by losing faith in the prophecy. By changing their beliefs they would bring their own opinions into agreement with their immediate and nonbelieving group and thereby eliminate or reduce dissonance. The members who stayed together at Mrs. Keech's home would, on the other hand, obtain social support. They would therefore not only not change their own beliefs but would actively attempt to change the beliefs of others.

On December 20 those with Mrs. Keech waited anxiously for the saucer, removed all metal objects from their clothing—metallic objects are dangerous on flying saucers—and rehearsed the necessary passwords. Some four hours after the scheduled landing time there was still no saucer. Having re-examined the messages and prophecies they gradually began to despair. Why hadn't the saucer come? Then, in the midst of this growing despair, Clarion sent a message to Mrs. Keech stating, in effect, that the faith of this small group had saved the earth from total destruction. The message was received gratefully and enthusiastically.

As had been predicted, the members separated from the group soon lost faith. But the members who stayed together amid social support not only retained their belief in the prophecy but became active proselytizers, seeking to convert those who disagreed. Here the predictions of Dissonance seem well supported.

However, Hardyck and Braden (1962), in a similar study, investigated twenty-nine Pentecostal families who had spent forty-two days in an underground shelter because of a predicted nuclear disaster. When the disaster failed to occur and these 135 people emerged from the shelter they made no attempt to change the opinions of others. Rather, they claimed that God was testing their faith and that they had misunderstood God's messages.

Differences between the two groups might account for the differences in their behaviors. The Pentecostal group was much larger than Mrs. Keech's and may have had sufficient social support from each other. There-fore, it was not as necessary for them to find additional outside support. Another difference was that whereas Mrs. Keech's group was under the strain of considerable ridicule from nonbelievers, the Pentecostal group was not. It seems reasonable that the former group would therefore have a greater need for support than would the latter.

The predictions of Cognitive Dissonance in regard to social support seem reasonable enough. The difficulty of finding appropriate situations in which to test the theory probably accounts for the many unanswered questions and the qualified conclusions.

Dissonance Theory has generated more research than any other theory of attitude change. It has clearly fulfilled its heuristic function. Its most significant virtue is its focus on behavior. The concentration on attitudes, opinions, and beliefs in this chapter should not obscure the fact that the ultimate aim of any psychological theory is to explain behavior. Although there are many predictions concerning behavior which can be derived from Congruity and from Psycho-logic, these are not immediately and directly concerned with behavioral responses. Rather, primary attention is given to the intervening variable called attitude, that is, with the predisposition to certain behaviors. In focusing his theory squarely on behavior Festinger comes to grips with the central concern of psychology.

In several ways Dissonance is less adequate than the other theories. For example, it does not permit the quantification of attitudes, nor does it predict the amount of attitudinal or behavioral change.   But perhaps it is too early for such a theory to attempt rigorous quantification.

Yet even if the necessity for only general predictions were granted, there are still a number of serious problems.   For example, the experiments on Cognitive Dissonance, although numerous, have not supported all the theory's predictions.   Particularly inconclusive are the predictions concerning information exposure and social support.   Freedman and Sears (1965), after reviewing the literature on selective exposure to information, conclude that the evidence is not supportive of Dissonance.   And, as already indicated, the predictions concerning social support and confirmed by Festinger, Reicken, and Schachter (1956) have not been replicated (Hardyck and Braden, 1962).

Chapanis and Chapanis (1964, p. 20), after reviewing the numerous dissonance experiments, conclude that "as a body of literature, it is downright disappointing."   Among their criticisms are that the experiments have been inadequately designed and the data improperly analyzed.   One of the peculiarities of dissonance experiments, for example, is that after the data are collected many subjects are, for various reasons, discarded.   Brehm and Cohen (1959), for instance, discarded 65 percent of their subjects and Cohen, Brehm, and Fleming (1958) eliminated 51 percent.   Generally the reason given is "to permit adequate test of the hypothesis" but it is seldom clear how discarding subjects, *after* the data are collected, helps permit adequate testing of anything.

Insko (1967) has criticized the theory because of the vagueness of its two central concepts.   Although Festinger (1957, p. 13) states specifically that "two cognitive elements are in dissonant relation if, considering these two alone, the obverse of one element would follow from the other," he does not make clear what "follow from" means and hence when the conditions for dissonance have been met.   "Logically follow," "psychologically expected to follow," "expected to follow on the basis of past experience," "following from cultural mores" are some of the meanings which this phrase has been given; but clearly these are quite different from one another.   Similarly, Festinger does not state explicitly when a cognitive element should be considered a single element or a cluster of elements.   As Insko (1967, p. 283) puts it, "we are therefore left with a peculiar situation in which an entire theory is erected on the foundation of two poorly conceptualized constructs, dissonance and cognitive elements."

Like Congruity, Dissonance Theory makes a number of predictions which seem to be contradicted by experience.   Take, for example, some of the classic plots in various novels or movies.   A husband believes he has murdered his wife only to be presented with evidence that he is really innocent and was brainwashed into thinking he committed the crime. Another familiar plot revolves around the woman who believes she is insane

TABLE 8. Summary of the Components and Assumptions of Balance Theories

	Elements	Relations	Balance	Imbalance	Resolution Modes
CONGRUITY	Attitude Sources Attitude Objects	Associative Dissociative	(Congruity) When source and object are of same scale position and sign and are associated When source and object are of same scale position and opposite signs and dissociated	(Incongruity) When any other condition prevails	Attitude change of both source and object
PSYCHO-LOGIC	Actors Means Ends	Positive Negative Null Ambivalent	(Consistency) Two positives positively connected Two negatives positively connected A positive and a negative negatively connected	(Inconsistency) Two positives negatively connected Two negatives negatively connected A positive and a negative positively connected	Stop thinking Attitude change of one or more of the elements or of the relation Differentiation of element(s) or of relation
DISSONANCE	Cognitions, that is, "knowledges," attitudes	Consonant Dissonant Irrelevant	(Consonance) When, given two cognitions, one "follows from" the other	(Dissonance) When, given two cognitions, the obverse of one "follows from" the other	Attitude change of one or more cognitions Behavioral change, that is, seeking converts, exposure to information

and only at the end of the movie does she find evidence that her husband was trying to make her think herself insane so that he could claim her fortune. In both of these situations, and many more like them, there are two elements which, given one, the obverse of the other would follow; in both situations, according to the theory, the new evidence should produce dissonance.   Yet it seems obvious that these are actually dissonance-reducing situations. Dissonance, it seems, would only be created if the initial belief was satisfying. For example, if the husband was pleased he had killed his wife evidence to the contrary would produce dissonance.

Dissonance Theory can probably get around such examples by stating that the intitial belief produced dissonance and that the cognition contradicting this belief was in fact dissonance reducing.   And here is perhaps the major problem with the theory.   How does one tell whether a given cognition produces dissonance?   Specifically, how does one tell if the husband's belief that he has killed his wife is dissonance producing?   This can be determined only by looking at other cognitions and behaviors.   Therefore, if the husband looks for support that he has not killed his wife, it is assumed that his initial belief was dissonant with some other cognition.   That is, the existence of a state of dissonance is inferred from "dissonant-reducing behavior" and a particular behavior is judged as an attempt to reduce dissonance by postulating a state of dissonance as the motivation.

As with almost every question raised in this book it is unfortunate that we cannot conclude with *the* answers.   With attitude change, as with language acquisition or language breakdown, for example, the data are far from conclusive and the theories only rough and general approximations. The principal components and assumptions of these three theories are summarized in Table 8.

Regardless of their possible shortcomings, however, all these theories have served useful and important purposes and will undoubtedly continue to do so.   They are generating research at an extremely rapid rate and raising questions concerning significant aspects of speech, language, and communication behavior.   If these were their only functions they would be of considerable value.   That they have also been able to organize at least part of the research data and to offer at least plausible explanations of why attitudes change is so much more to their credit.

For Further Reading

THE PSYCHOLOGY OF SPEECH
AND LANGUAGE (GENERAL WORKS)

General works covering the broad area of speech and language psychology include the definitional papers of Miller (1964, 1965) and DeVito (1967b); reviews of relevant research by Osgood and Sebeok (1954), Rubenstein and Aborn (1960), Kjeldegaard (1961), Lambert (1963), Osgood (1963c), Carroll (1964b), Diebold (1965), Ervin-Tripp and Slobin (1966), Samuels (1967), Rommetveit (1968), and Miller and McNeill (1969); and collections of articles by Saporta (1961), Lenneberg (1964c), Rosenberg (1965), Lyons and Wales (1966), DeCecco (1967), Hildum (1967), Jakobovits and Miron (1967), Miller (1967), Salzinger and Salzinger (1967), Oldfield and Marshall (1968), and Rosenberg and Koplin (1968).

SPEECH, LANGUAGE, AND BEHAVIOR

General Works

On the nature and importance of symbols and symbol systems see especially White (1949, 1960, 1962). Lotz (1956) and Hamp (1967) present discussions more closely related to the methods and procedures of contemporary linguistic science. Mead's (1922) discussion of the significant symbol is a classic with which the reader should be familiar.

Time-binding is presented in Korzybski (1921) and in most of the works on General Semantics referred to below.

The Nature of Speech and Language

In addition to those cited in the text other approaches to the definition of language include those by Sapir (1933), Francis (1958), Carroll (1959a), and Hockett (1963).

Though many writers distinguish between speech and language the classic discussion is to be found in Saussure (1959). Wells (1947) and

Dinneen (1967) both provide reviews and appraisals of Saussure's approach. A similar distinction—between competence and performance—is considered in Chapter 2.

Francis (1958) provides an excellent overview of some of the all-or-none differences between speaking and writing systems. Also see Hall (1964) for a brief discussion of graphemics and the relationship of sound to spelling. Pulgram's (1951) paper on the correspondence between phonemes and graphemes further clarifies the relationship between the linguistic units of speech and writing.

Quantitative studies on speech as opposed to writing have increased greatly in the last few years; recent studies include those by DeVito (1965a, 1966b, 1967c, 1967f), Driemann (1962), Gibson, et al. (1966), and Horowitz and Newman (1964).   Discussion of the reasons for these differences can be found in the papers cited above and more completely in DeVito (1966a).

The Semantic Dimension of Speech and Language

Introductions to semantics are provided by Ullmann (1962, 1966) and Schaff (1962). A short but excellent paperback by Salomon (1966) probably provides the best single introduction.

On meaning and semantics as viewed by linguists of different periods and schools of thought see Bloomfield (1933), Fries (1954), and Hill (1958). References to the approach of the generative grammarians are given in the section on "Linguistic Theory."

Ogden and Richards (1923) is the basic reference for the concept of meaning advocated by Richards. Sondel (1958) explains the principal implications of this approach and relates these to a general theory of communication.

In addition to the references cited in the text for the functions of speech and language see Hayakawa's (1964) provocative discussion and the excellent readings in Lee (1967). Hymes (1961) provides a somewhat different approach and attempts to clarify the functions of speech from the viewpoint of anthropology and evolutionary theory. The discussion of the levels of speech and language was based on the contributions of General Semantics to which references are given below. Also see DeVito (1965b). On the styles of speech and language, in addition to the references cited in the text, see the readings in Sebeok (1960) and Hymes (1964). Additional references to style and stylistics are provided in the section on "Speech and Language Differences." The approach of the readability researchers is thoroughly surveyed in Klare (1963).

The Pragmatic Dimension of Speech and Language

The General Semantics approach to language and speech behavior is set forth by Korzybski (1921 and especially 1933). These works, however, are difficult reading and the beginning student would be wise to start with some of the more readable and more basic introductions such as those by Hayakawa (1964), Johnson (1946), Bois (1966), and Weinberg (1959). Collections of significant articles have been edited by Hayakawa (1962) and Lee (1967).

The works of Charles Morris (1955, 1964) advance the concept of semiotics and its major concerns. Sondel (1958) provides a readable introduction to some of the more important issues.

LINGUISTIC THEORY

General Works

A number of texts thoroughly cover basic linguistic theory, for example, Hockett (1958), Gleason (1961), Hughes (1962), Hall (1964), Robins (1964), and Dinneen (1967). Whereas the first five are organized around the major areas of linguistic science, Dinneen discusses linguistic theory in terms of its principal contributors, for example, Saussure, Sapir, Bloomfield, Firth, Hjelmslev, and Chomsky. Sapir (1921) and Bloomfield (1933) are classics in linguistics and should be read by all interested in this general area.

English linguistics, although covered in the above works, is more thoroughly presented in Harris (1951), Trager and Smith (1957), Francis (1958), Hill (1958), and Gleason (1965).

In the last few years a number of collections of some of the more seminal papers in linguistics have been published. Two of the better ones should be noted explicitly. Allen (1964), containing sixty-two articles, emphasizes applied English linguistics. Wilson (1967), containing thirty-six articles, emphasizes basic issues in linguistic theory. The foreword by Paul Roberts is particularly valuable for clarifying some of the new directions in the study of language. Both of these readers are addressed to the beginning student though there is much in both for the more advanced student. Allen's (1966) bibliography, containing some 2,000 references, will prove particularly useful to all students of speech and language.

Carroll (1959a) surveys the entire field of linguistics and its relationship to other disciplines, for example, psychology, speech, philosophy, and education. Since this work was written in 1952, much of it is dated. Ivić (1965) provides an historical and bibliographical review of linguistic research with emphasis on twentieth-century contributions.

Some Basic Elements and Relationships

All the basic linguistic concepts are covered in the works listed above. Ebeling (1962) provides an excellent and detailed review of linguistic terminology.

For word analysis see Sanford (1942b) and Mahl and Schulze (1964) for reviews of the literature. Additional references are provided in the section "Speech and Language Differences."

Generative Grammar

Probably the best introduction to generative grammar is provided by Gleason (1961 and especially 1965). Thomas (1965) explains the basics for teachers of English and Bach (1964) provides a more thorough introduction addressed to linguists. Postal's (1964a) discussion of deep and surface structure clarifies many of the significant issues in generative grammar.

The basic theory of generative grammar with special reference to syntax was first presented in detail by Chomsky (1957) in his now famous *Syntactic Structures*. This work, however, has been superseded by more recent works. Syntax is most thoroughly presented in Chomsky (1964, 1965) and Postal (1964b). Lees (1960) presents the most extensive application of the theory; the first chapters clarify much of the basic theory. The relationship of generative grammar to more "traditional" views is covered in Chomsky (1966b).

The semantic component was first presented by Katz and Fodor (1963), integrated more closely with the theory of syntax by Katz and Postal (1964), and applied to problems in the philosophy of language by Katz (1966). For a criticism of this approach and for alternative models see Weinreich (1966).

The phonological component utilizes the distinctive features approach developed by Roman Jakobson and his colleagues (Jakobson, Fant, and Halle, 1952; Jakobson and Halle, 1956). The generative grammar approach to phonology is most thoroughly presented in Chomsky and Halle (1968). Postal (1968) provides the most extensive criticism of "autonomous" phonology and justification for a theory of phonology compatible with generative grammar.

The collection of articles edited by Fodor and Katz (1964) is probably the best single source for the broad area of generative grammar. Many of the papers included here have not been published elsewhere. Among those of particular importance are Klima's "Negation in English" and Katz' "Semi-Sentences." Bar-Hillel (1967), however, has severely criticized this collection.

For criticisms of generative grammar see, for example, Hill (1961), Reichling (1961), Dixon (1963), Harman (1963), and Uhlenbeck (1963). The most sophisticated and detailed criticism has come from Hockett (1967) who challenges Chomsky's assumption that language is a well-defined system. Chomsky has answered most of his critics in a number of publications; especially important are Chomsky (1961, 1966a).

For other types of grammars see Fries (1952) and Francis (1954), Lamb (1966), and especially Gleason (1965).

Special note should be made of Lounsbury's (1963) "Linguistics and Psychology," which provides an excellent statement of the points of contact between these two fields, as does the more recent paper by Miller and McNeill (1969).

LEARNING THEORY

General Works

A number of sources provide suitable overviews of learning theory, for example, Mowrer (1960a), Deese and Hulse (1967), and Hilgard (1956). This last work surveys the contributions of individual learning theorists. Osgood's (1953) discussion is somewhat complex but well worth the required effort. The most authoritative single source is probably Koch (1959).

B. F. Skinner's Functional Analysis

The foundations of Skinner's approach to learning are presented in his *Science and Human Behavior* (1965) and in his numerous articles, many of which have been reprinted in his *Cumulative Record* (1961). Particularly important is Skinner's "Are Theories of Learning Necessary?" (1950), reprinted in Skinner (1961). His model of language is presented in *Verbal Behavior* (1957). A brief overview and applications to speech are given in DeVito (1968a). Thorough reviews of verbal conditioning are presented by Krasner (1967) and Spielberger (1965).

Skinner's approach to verbal behavior has been criticized from a psychological viewpoint by Charles Osgood (1958), from a philosophical viewpoint by Charles Morris (1958), and most thoroughly from a linguistic viewpoint by Noam Chomsky (1959). This last review is particularly significant for clarifying the differences in approach between stimulus-response psychology and generative grammar. Osgood has repeated his criticisms and summarized those of others in a number of publications, for example, Osgood (1963b, 1963c, Osgood and Miron, 1963).

Skinner has chosen not to respond to his critics. When asked, for example, about Chomsky's review of *Verbal Behavior*, Skinner said: "I read a bit of it and saw that he missed the point, so I never read the rest. I never answer any of my critics. I generally don't even read them" (Rice, 1968, p. 90).

Mediational Theories

The elementary mediational models are presented by Mowrer (1954, 1960b) and by Osgood (1953, 1963c, 1968; Osgood and Miron, 1963; Osgood, Suci, and Tannenbaum, 1957; Osgood and Sebeok, 1954). The more complex three stage model is presented in Osgood (1957a, 1957b, 1963b, 1963c, 1968; Osgood and Miron, 1963). The major criticisms of these models have come from the viewpoint of generative grammar. Particularly important are criticisms by Fodor (1965), Bever (1968), McNeill (1968), Garrett and Fodor (1968), and Bever, Fodor, and Garrett (1968).

These criticisms are applicable to all learning-theory models based on stimulus-response bonds.   Osgood (1966) and Berlyne (1966) have responded to Fodor's (1965) criticism.   Remaining unconvinced of the value of S-R models, Fodor (1966a) has answered both Osgood and Berlyne.   More general defenses of learning-theory approaches have been made by Osgood (1963b, 1968) and Staats (1968).

Jenkins (1965 and especially 1968) has attempted to state the essential issues in the controversy in less extreme terms.

COMMUNICATION THEORY

General Works

Several valuable collections of articles on communication theory have recently been published and might well serve as a beginning library.   The proceedings of a number of communication conferences have been edited by Lee Thayer (1967a, 1967b, 1968b) and contain excellent papers by a wide variety of researchers.   A collection of previously unpublished papers on communication theory as viewed from different disciplines, for example, anthropology, neurophysiology, psycholinguistics, speech, sociology, and others has been edited by Dance (1967b).   Smith (1966) has edited a collection of fifty-five articles on communication arranged according to Morris's theory of semiotics—syntactics, semantics, and pragmatics.   Introductory sections on the mathematical, social psychological, and linguistic approaches to communication are especially valuable in providing a broad perspective for the study of communication.

A collection of a different type, edited by Matson and Montagu (1967), views communication as human dialog and contains fifty excellent and carefully chosen papers.

Communication Concepts

Since the mathematical theory of information has influenced the whole of communication theory and has served as the progenitor of so much research it would be profitable to begin with this approach.   Those with considerable training in mathematics might well begin with Shannon (Shannon and Weaver, 1949).   For most, however, this will prove too difficult.   Fortunately, a number of writers have attempted, with some success, to clarify this theory for the general reader.   Particularly important are Colin Cherry's (1957) *On Human Communication* and J. R. Pierce's (1961) *Symbols, Signals and Noise*.   These works provide thorough and clear discussions of information theory and its numerous and varied applications.   Briefer presentations of some of the essentials of the theory are available in a number of articles, for example, Broadhurst and Darnell (1965), Gleason (1961), Rapoport (1956), and Weaver (Shannon and Weaver, 1949).   Of special value are the papers by Schramm (1955) and Miller (1953, 1956). Miller's (1951) *Language and Communication*, though dated on many topics, is still valuable for clarifying many of the concepts of information theory and should be read by all students of communication.

Aranguren (1967) provides a broad, though basic, overview of human communication with numerous visual illustrations of the different forms and types of communication.

Hockett's (1953) perceptive review of Shannon and Weaver succeeds in clarifying some of the more difficult concepts and relates the theory to linguistics and language structure. Also see Jakobson (1961) for applications to linguistics. Papers in Quastler (1955) and the discussion by Attneave (1959) clarify the nature of information theory and its relation to psychology. Berlyne (1957) suggests some points of contact between information theory and behavior theory. The relationship of information theory and meaning is considered by Weaver and Weaver (1965) and more thoroughly by Bar-Hillel (1964). The Summer 1953 issue of *Etc.: A Review of General Semantics* was devoted entirely to information theory.

Communication Models

In addition to the specific models mentioned in our discussion the reader may wish to consult some more detailed reviews on the nature and functions of models. Especially appropriate are Bross (1953), Deutsch (1952), Johnson and Klare (1961), Ross (1967), and Thayer (1963).

Numerous writers have applied the basic concepts and processes of communication theory to various problems and questions. A few of the more important may be mentioned here. Berlo (1960) has applied communication theory to the general practice of effective speaking. Campbell and Hepler (1965) have edited a collection of both theoretical and applied articles related to communication as persuasion; special emphasis is placed on written communication. Thayer (1968a) and Haney (1967) have applied these concepts to business and industrial communication though both contain valuable and original discussions of basic theoretical questions and problems. Ruesch (1957, 1961), Ruesch and Bateson (1951), Shands (1960), Watzlawick, Beavin, and Jackson (1967), and Wiener and Mehrabian (1968) have utilized the theory of communication in explaining and clarifying the concerns of psychology and psychiatry. These works are particularly valuable for relating abstract theory to concrete communicative behaviors.

SPEECH AND LANGUAGE ACQUISITION

General Works

A number of review articles are available which might serve as a starting point for the study of speech and language acquisition. McCarthy's (1954) thorough summary, though failing to take into consideration the contribution of linguistics and rather dated, adequately reviews the research findings to 1954. Carroll's (1960a) brief summary and the more complete ones by Ervin and Miller (1963) and Ervin-Tripp (1966) give primary attention to the influence of linguistics. The last two are particularly useful for their lengthy bibliographies. Templin (1957) provides a useful summary of speech and language skills in children.

A number of books contain excellent sections on speech and language acquisition. Miller (1951), Osgood (1953), and Osgood and Sebeok (1954) are useful for summarizing research and theory prior to the advent of generative grammar. Brown (1958a), Church (1961), and Carroll (1964a) each provide basic overviews of some of the significant questions in this area. The best available discussion from a psycholinguistic point of view is contained in Brown's (1965) *Social Psychology*. A more recent overview, addressed to advanced students, is provided by Miller and McNeill (1969).

Piaget (1955) and Vygotsky (1962), particularly valuable for their discussions of research approaches and strategies, are two classics which should be read by all students of child language. Lewis's (1959, 1963) work should likewise be consulted for a readable and insightful view of the development of the child in general and of language in particular.

Bellugi and Brown (1964) and Riegel (1965) contain valuable papers and discussions from conferences on language acquisition. The papers in Smith and Miller's (1966) *The Genesis of Language* represent the best of contemporary thinking on language acquisition. This work also contains papers on animal communication and an appendix of abstracts on Soviet studies in child language. Significant papers from these works are mentioned below.

Berko and Brown (1960) provide a useful discussion of research approaches to child language. For references prior to 1952 see Leopold's (1952) extensive bibliography.

Factors Influencing Speech and Language Acquisition

Eisenson (Eisenson, Auer, and Irwin, 1963) provides an overview of those factors which influence the development of speech and language, though he fails to take into consideration much recent work in psycholinguistics. More authoritative on this subject is Lenneberg (1967). Both of these works provide adequate bibliographies. The January 1966 issue of *The Volta Review* is devoted entirely to language acquisition especially as it relates to the deaf.

Stages of Speech and Language Acquisition

Numerous writers have summarized the various stages of speech and language development. Particularly useful are Osgood (1953), Eisenson (Eisenson, Auer, and Irwin, 1963), and Lewis (1959, 1963).

Speech and Language Acquisition

For phonological development the studies by Irwin (for example, 1948a, 1948b), although referred to a great deal in the literature and endorsed by such researchers as Eisenson (Eisenson, Auer, and Irwin, 1963), are generally inadequate from the point of view of methodology. Nevertheless they are useful for certain questions. Jakobson's (1968) discussion of the distinctive features approach in the development of phonology, originally published in 1941, is a classic example of the application of linguistics to child language. Both Velten (1943) and Leopold (1953–1954) have utilized this general method. The more recent studies by Messer (1967) and Menyuk (1968), referred to in our discussion, are valuable for suggesting future directions in the study of the phonological system of the child. Ruth Weir's (1962) *Language in the Crib* is probably the most ambitious attempt to study the phonological system of the child.

Menyuk's (1963a, 1963b, 1964a, 1964b, 1967) series of studies on the development of syntax, although limited to performance, are useful examples of the application of generative grammar to the study of child language. These and other pertinent studies have recently been summarized by Menyuk (1969). Berko's (1958) study of morphology, Brown and Berko's (1960) work on word association, and Slobin's (1966) analysis of the acquisition of Russian illustrate a variety of methodological approaches to the study of child language. Perhaps most impressive are the studies on the development of transformations by Bellugi (1965), Klima and Bellugi (1966), and Brown (1968).

The area of semantic development has seen little research. McNeill (1967b) summarizes some hypotheses and is particularly useful for suggesting lines for future research.

Luria's (1959, 1961) studies of the development of the directive and regulatory functions are valuable for suggesting an approach to this relatively neglected question of child-language functions. Also see Piaget (1955), Vygotsky (1962), and Ervin-Tripp (1966) on language functions.

Theories of Speech and Language Acquisition

The autistic theory is presented by Mowrer (1950, 1960b). Fodor (1965) has insightfully attacked this view. The mediational theory is argued by Jenkins and Palermo (1964) and attacked by McNeill (1968). Contextual generalization is presented by Braine (1963a, 1963b, 1966), criticized by McNeill (1968) and Bever, Fodor, and Weksel (1965a), answered by Braine (1965), and counteranswered by Bever, Fodor, and Weksel (1965b). The criticisms of Fodor (1965), Bever, Fodor, and Weksel (1965a, 1965b), and McNeill (1968) are applicable to all learning-theory approaches to child-language acquisition.

Lenneberg's arguments for a biological approach are contained in Lenneberg (1960, 1964a). His case report (1962) of a child who understood language without having the ability to speak is valuable evidence illustrating the independence of the capacity for language acquisition from speech. Summary statements of the biological theory are given in Lenneberg (1964b, 1966) and most thoroughly and persuasively in Lenneberg's (1967) *Biological Foundations of Language*.   Useful appendices by Otto Marx on the history of the biological theory and by Noam Chomsky on generative grammar place the work of Lenneberg in historical perspective and clarify the theory of language upon which the biological approach rests.   The nativistic theory is presented by McNeill (1966a, 1966b, 1966c, 1966d, 1967a, 1967b, 1968). Fodor (1966b) contributes some highly abstract, though provocative, remarks on the structure of a general theory for language acquisition.

SPEECH AND LANGUAGE BREAKDOWN

General Works

Students of communication breakdowns should probably familiarize themselves with some general sources before pursuing the more detailed studies of specific breakdowns.   Three works which cover the broad range of breakdowns and which are yet detailed enough to provide more than surface treatment may be noted here.   Travis (1957), consisting of thirty-nine articles by twenty-seven contributors, will provide a reasonably good starting place.   Many of the articles, however, are outdated and for the most part fail to take into consideration the developments and contributions of linguistics.

Luchsinger and Arnold (1965) focuses primarily on implications for therapy.   Although revised in 1964 this work fails to unify and systematize the newer insights into language and speech breakdowns with the more traditional.   Since this is a translation from the German, the style is often awkward and the references are largely to German sources.   This work is valuable, however, because it does review much foreign research which might otherwise be inaccessible to the American student.   Its numerous diagrams are especially helpful.

Unlike the previous two works, Rieber and Brubaker (1966) carefully incorporates the latest developments in linguistics and learning theory. Though less comprehensive the works of deReuch and O'Connor (1964) and Rioch and Weinstein (1964) will prove helpful.   Lenneberg (1964d) provides an excellent overview of language disorders in children.

Aphasia

Travis (1957), Luchsinger and Arnold (1965), and Rieber and Brubaker (1966), mentioned above, all contain discussions of aphasia.   Those in Travis, by Eisenson and Myklebust, represent more traditional approaches than those discussed here and focus on the treatment of aphasia rather than on the nature of the language problem.   Luchsinger and Arnold's discussion is brief though it does highlight some of the more important concepts and processes necessary to an understanding of aphasia. The chapters in Rieber and Brubaker, by Kendell and Tikofsky, are particularly valuable for their review of pertinent and recent research.

Probably the most useful single source on aphasia is Osgood and Miron (1963), based on papers and discussions from an interdisciplinary seminar. Clear explanations of neurological, linguistic, and psycholinguistic points of view are provided along with reviews of recent research and theorizing. A comprehensive bibliography and an appendix of frequently used tests for aphasia, analyzed from the viewpoint of Osgood's psycholinguistic model, add to the value of this work.

Jakobson's approach to aphasia is most thoroughly presented in his *Child Language, Aphasia and Phonological Universals* (1968). Also see Jakobson and Halle (1956) and Jakobson (1957). A critique of this view of language and aphasia can be found in Martin Joos' (1957) review of Jakobson and Halle.

Brown's category theory is presented in his *Words and Things* (1958a) Other writers seem to have ignored this approach.

Skinner discusses aphasia in his *Verbal Behavior* (1957). A brief review and critique of Skinner's approach to language with particular reference to aphasia can be found in Osgood and Miron (1963).

Osgood's approach is presented in Osgood and Miron (1963).

Wepman's *Recovery from Aphasia* (1951) provides a clear and thorough discussion of his approach to the analysis and treatment of aphasia. This discussion, however, should be supplemented by the more recent research of Wepman and his associates. Particular mention should be made of the following papers: Jones and Wepman (1961, 1965, 1967), Spiegel, Jones, and Wepman (1965), and Wepman, Jones, Bock, and Van Pelt (1960).

Schuell and Jenkins' unidimensional theory developed with the aid of the Guttman scale analysis is presented in Schuell and Jenkins (1959) and further clarified with additional evidence and argument in Jenkins and Schuell (1964). Their factor analysis (Schuell, Jenkins, and Carroll, 1962) provides strong support for their hypothesis and illustrates the importance of this tool in the study of language behavior in general and of aphasia in particular. Schuell, Jenkins, and Jiménez-Pabón's *Aphasia in Adults* (1964) is probably the most detailed analysis of aphasia. Criticisms of this position can be found in Osgood and Miron (1963), Jones and Wepman (1961), and Spiegel, Jones, and Wepman (1965).

Lee's general semantic theory is presented in Lee (1958, 1959, 1961) and extended by Sies (1964).

Stuttering

Stuttering has been the subject of more research than any other single communication breakdown; the dearth of available material creates no small problem for the student.   Because of this it is probably best to begin with some general references such as those cited at the beginning of this section by Travis (1957), Luchsinger and Arnold (1965), and especially the article by Brutten and Bloodstein in Rieber and Brubaker (1966).   Another good starting place is Robinson's brief *Introduction to Stuttering* (1964).

Hahn's *Stuttering* (1956) provides brief overviews of twenty-five different approaches to stuttering.   Eisenson's *Stuttering: A Symposium* (1958b) provides detailed accounts of major theories proposed by Bloodstein, Glauber, Sheehan, West, and Eisenson and a thorough review of experiments on stuttering therapy by Van Riper.

Taylor's (1966a) review of the literature on the properties of stuttered words probably provides the best starting place for this topic.   Also see S. F. Brown (1945) for an earlier review.   The studies cited in the text supply additional support for Taylor's conclusions.

Sheehan's position is clearly explained in Sheenan (1953, 1958).

Consideration of Bloodstein's approach should begin with the earlier writings of Wendell Johnson (for example, 1946, 1959).   Bloodstein's theory is presented in Bloodstein (1958, 1960, 1961).   Further criticism of the theories of Sheehan and Bloodstein and a defense of operant conditioning are given in DeVito (1969b).

The negative-reaction theory is presented in Brutten and Shoemaker (1967) along with their objections to previous learning-theory approaches and suggestions for therapy.

The operant-conditioning approach is developed most fully by Shames and Sherrick (1963) and also argued by Goldiamond (1962, 1965), Siegel and Martin (1965, 1966), and Martin and Siegel (1966a, 1966b).   Wischner (1950) has presented a somewhat similar conditioning theory but based on principles of Hullian learning theory.

Wingate's (1966) arguments against a learning-theory approach to stuttering may be read to counterbalance the viewpoint presented here.

SPEECH AND LANGUAGE DIFFERENCES

General Works

Probably the best single source is Sebeok (1960) which contains the proceedings of a conference in which style was approached from psychological, linguistic, and literary points of view.   DeVito (1967e) has attempted to define style and organize the areas of stylistic research according to Jakobson's (1960) communication model.   Bailey and Burton (1968) provide a recent bibliography of stylistic research.

G. K. Zipf's *The Psycho-biology of Language* (1935) and *Human Behavior and the Principle of Least Effort* (1949) are classics which should be familiar to any student of style, however conceived or defined.

Individual Differences

On individual differences see the reviews by Sanford (1942b), Miller (1951), Mahl and Schulze (1964), Nunnally (1965), and Thompson (1967). Hertzler (1965) and Capell (1966) and the collections edited by Hymes (1964) and Fishman (1968), concerned with what is generally referred to as "sociolinguistics" or "language and culture," contain much that is relevant to this area.

Group Differences

The early and now classic study by Carmichael, Hogan, and Walter (1932) on the effects of naming on the reproduction of visually perceived stimuli and the replication by Herman, Marshall, and Lawless (1957) are often considered in discussions of intralanguage differences. Although they fall outside the scope of this chapter, they should be familiar to all students of speech, language, and behavior. Probably the best study in this area was conducted by Brown and Lenneberg (1954) and considered in this chapter. Also see the studies related to this experiment and referred to in our discussion.

The writings of Edward Sapir (1921, Mandelbaum, 1949, 1962) and especially Benjamin Lee Whorf (Carroll, 1956) should provide the starting place for the study of linguistic relativity. Papers contained in Hoijer (1954) clarify the many implications of this hypothesis, summarize the state of knowledge, and suggest future directions for research. The Spring 1952 issue of *Etc.: A Review of General Semantics* was devoted entirely to the Whorfian thesis. A number of attempts have been made to systematize and clarify the basic theory. Of special importance are those by Trager (1959) and Fishman (1960). Also see Miller and McNeill's (1969) discussion of what they call "anthropological psycholinguistics."

System Differences

Other attempts to define the characteristics of human language and distinguish it from animal communication systems include White (1949, 1960, 1962), whose approach was considered in Chapter 1, Lotz (1950), Marler (1961), Sebeok (1963, 1965b), and Bastian (1965).

Brown (1958a) provides an interesting overview of animal communication from the perspective of the psychologist. Frings and Frings (1964) present a more detailed analysis. Sebeok (1968) is probably the best single source on this topic. Sebeok (1965a) has attempted to organize much of the findings on animal communication in terms of Jakobson's (1960) communication model. Other general reviews are provided by Marler (1961), Collias (1960), and Marler and Hamilton (1966).

A topic of considerable interest but not touched upon in this chapter, largely because so little success has been achieved, is the learning of human language by animals.   The classic of Clever Hans, the horse who "learned" German has recently been reissued (Pfungst, 1965) and provides an excellent warning against crediting animals with too much ability before adequate analysis is made.   Other attempts to teach animals are discussed by Mowrer (1950), Hayes (1951), and Grosslight and Zaynor (1967).   Probably the most original and ambitious of all attempts to teach animals language is that proposed recently by Premack and Schwartz (1966).

SPEECH AND LANGUAGE EFFECTS

General Works

Jahoda and Warren (1966) and Fishbein (1967) both provide collections of articles on attitudes in general and attitude change in particular.   Zajonc (1960) presents a brief overview of congruity, dissonance, and Heider's theory of balance.   Cohen (1964) provides a similarly brief discussion of congruity, psycho-logic, and dissonance.   Brown (1962, 1965) covers the same ground as Cohen but in a more thorough fashion.   Osgood (1960a) reviews the similarities and differences among balance theories and applies the general principles to the thinking and behaving of groups.   McGuire (1966) surveys the current status of balance theories and Pepitone (1966) considers the various problems confronting these theories.

Feldman (1966) has edited a series of papers on various consistency approaches, many of them by leaders in the field.   The best single source is Insko's *Theories of Attitude Change* (1967).   Insko reviews and evaluates fourteen theories and the experimental evidence advanced in support or contradiction.

The Summer 1960 issue of *Public Opinion Quarterly* was devoted entirely to attitude change.

The Principle of Congruity

The Principle of Congruity was derived from Osgood's earlier work on learning and meaning to which references have already been given ("Learning Theory").   A thorough statement of the theory and a review of the experiment conducted by Tannenbaum (1953) is provided in Osgood and Tannenbaum (1955).   In his *An Alternative to War or Surrender* (1962) Osgood attempts to apply congruity to the problems of the arms race and eventual de-militarization.   Tannenbaum (1967) provides a comprehensive review of congruity theory and research.

A number of researchers have criticized the congruity principle and have developed alternative explanations while retaining much of the original framework developed by Osgood. Most notable are the summation theory of Martin Fishbein (1963, Fishbein and Raven, 1962) and the belief congruence theory of Milton Rokeach (1968).

The Psycho-Logical Consistency Theory

Rosenberg and Abelson's theory is derived in large measure from the earlier work of Fritz Heider (1946, 1958) who is rightly credited as the first to apply the notion of balance to a theory of attitude change.

In early work Rosenberg (1956) outlines a theory of consistency which, in collaboration with Abelson, he further refined. The theory as discussed here is presented in most detail in Rosenberg and Abelson (1960). A complete statement of the mathematical-logical assumptions and deductions of this theory is presented in Abelson and Rosenberg (1958).

The Theory of Cognitive Dissonance

Cognitive dissonance is most fully explained in Leon Festinger's *A Theory of Cognitive Dissonance* (1957). Additional explanation and experimental evidence is presented in Festinger (1964). Brehm and Cohen (1962) have reviewed the experimental evidence and offer an extension of the basic theory. Festinger, Riecken, and Schachter's *When Prophecy Fails* (1956) details the study of social support briefly reviewed in this chapter and suggests a number of examples where this theory may apply.

The most perceptive criticism of this theory is provided by Chapanis and Chapanis (1964).

Bibliography

Abelson, Robert P. "Modes of Resolution of Belief Dilemmas," *Journal of Conflict Resolution,* III (1959), 343–352.

Abelson, Robert P., and Milton J. Rosenberg. "Symbolic Psychologic: A Model of Attitudinal Cognition," *Behavioral Science,* III (1958), 1–13.

Ainsworth, Stanley. "Integrating Theories of Stuttering," *Journal of Speech Disorders,* X (1945), 205–210.

Allen, Harold B., ed. *Readings in Applied English Linguistics,* 2nd ed. New York: Appleton-Century-Crofts, 1964.

Allen, Harold B. *Linguistics and English Linguistics.* New York: Appleton-Century-Crofts, 1966.

Aranguren, J. L. *Human Communication,* trans. Frances Partridge. New York: McGraw-Hill, 1967.

Aronson, Elliot. "Try a Little Dissonance," *New York Times Magazine,* Part I, Section 6 (September 11, 1966), 109–119.

Attneave, Fred. *Applications of Information Theory to Psychology: A Summary of Basic Concepts, Methods, and Results.* New York: Holt, Rinehart and Winston, 1959.

Bach, Emmon. *An Introduction to Transformational Grammars.* New York: Holt, Rinehart and Winston, 1964.

Bailey, Richard W., and Dolores M. Burton, S. N. D. *English Stylistics: A Bibliography* Cambridge, Mass.: M.I.T. Press, 1968.

Balken, E. R., and J. H. Masserman. "The Language of Phantasy: III. The Language of the Phantasies of Patients With Conversion Hysteria, Anxiety State, and Obsessive-Compulsive Neuroses," *Journal of Psychology,* X (1940), 75–86.

Bar-Hillel, Yehoshua. *Language and Information.* Reading, Mass.: Addison-Wesley, 1964.

Bar-Hillel, Yehoshua. "Review of *The Structure of Language: Readings in the Philosophy of Language,* ed. Jerry A. Fodor and Jerrold J. Katz," *Language,* 43 (1967), 526–550.

Barnard, Raymond H. "An Objective Study of the Speeches of Wendell Phillips," *Quarterly Journal of Speech,* XVIII (1932), 571–584.

Bastian, Jarvis. "Primate Signalling Systems and Human Language," in I. DeVore, ed. *Primate Behavior: Field Studies of Monkeys and Apes.* New York: Holt, Rinehart and Winston, 1965, pp. 585–606.

Bateman, Barbara. *The Illinois Test of Psycholinguistic Abilities in Current Research: Summaries of Studies.* Urbana: Institute for Research on Exceptional Children, University of Illinois, 1965.

Bellugi, Ursula, and Roger Brown, eds. *The Acquisition of Language.* Monographs of the Society for Research in Child Development, XXIX, No. 1 (1964).

Bellugi, Ursula. "The Development of Interrogative Structures in Children's Speech," in Riegel (1965), pp. 103–137.

Bendig, A. W. "Twenty Questions: An Informational Analysis," *Journal of Experimental Psychology*, XLVI (1953), 345–348.

Berko, Jean. "The Child's Learning of English Morphology," *Word*, XIV (1958), 150–177.

Berko, Jean, and Roger Brown. "Psycholinguistic Research Methods," in Paul H. Mussen, ed. *The Handbook of Research Methods in Child Development.* New York: Wiley, 1960, pp. 517–557.

Berlo, David. *The Process of Communication.* New York: Holt, Rinehart and Winston, 1960.

Berlo, David, James B. Lemert, and Robert J. Mertz. "Dimensions for Evaluating the Acceptability of Message Sources," Research Monograph, Department of Communication, Michigan State University, 1966.

Berlyne, D. E. "Uncertainty and Conflict: A Point of Contact Between Information-Theory and Behavior-Theory Concepts," *Psychological Review*, LXIV (1957), 329–339.

Berlyne, D. E. "Mediating Responses: A Note on Fodor's Criticisms," *Journal of Verbal Learning and Verbal Behavior*, V (1966), 408–411.

Bernstein, Basil B. "A Public Language: Some Sociological Implications of a Linguistic Form," *British Journal of Sociology*, X (1959), 311–326.

Bernstein, Basil B. "Language and Social Class," *British Journal of Sociology*, XI (1960), 271–276.

Bernstein, Basil B. "Social Class and Linguistic Development: A Theory of Social Learning," in A. H. Halsey, J. Floud, and A. Anderson, eds. *Education, Economy and Society.* New York: Harcourt, Brace & World, 1961, pp. 288–314.

Bernstein, Basil B. "Linguistic Codes, Hesitation Phenomena, and Intelligence," *Language and Speech*, V (1962), 31–46. (a).

Bernstein, Basil B. "Social Class, Linguistic Codes, and Grammatical Elements," *Language and Speech*, V (1962), 221–240. (b).

Bernstein, Basil B. "Elaborated and Restricted Codes: Their Social Origins and Some Consequences," in J. Gumperz and Dell Hymes, eds. *The Ethnography of Communication, American Anthropologist* (Special Publication), LXVI, No. 6, Part 2 (1964), 55–69.

Berry, Mildred F., and Jon Eisenson. *Speech Disorders: Principles and Practices of Therapy.* New York: Appleton-Century-Crofts, 1956.

Bever, Thomas G. "Associations to Stimulus-Response Theories of Language," in Dixon and Horton (1968), pp. 478–494.

Bever, Thomas G., Jerry A. Fodor, and Merrill Garrett. "A Formal Limitation of Associationism," in Dixon and Horton (1968), pp. 582–585.

Bever, Thomas G., Jerry A. Fodor, and W. Weksel. "On the Acquisition of Syntax: A Critique of 'Contextual Generalization'," *Psychological Review*, LXXII (1965), 467–482. (a).

Bever, Thomas G., Jerry A. Fodor, and W. Weksel. "Is Linguistics Empirical?" *Psychological Review*, LXXII (1965), 493–500. (b).

Birdwhistell, Ray L. *Introduction to Kinesics: An Annotation System for Analysis of Body Motion and Gesture.* Washington, D.C.: Foreign Service Institute, Department of State, 1952.

Birdwhistell, Ray L. "Kinesics and Communication," in Edmund Carpenter and Marshall McLuhan, eds. *Explorations in Communication.* Boston: Beacon Press, 1960, pp. 54–64.

Birdwhistell, Ray L. "Some Body Motion Elements Accompanying Spoken American English," in Thayer (1967), pp. 53–72. (b)

Block, Bernard, and George L. Trager. *Outline of Linguistic Analysis.* Baltimore: Linguistic Society of America, 1942.

Bloodstein, Oliver. "Stuttering as an Anticipatory Struggle Reaction," in Eisenson (1958), pp. 1–69. (b)

Bloodstein, Oliver. "The Development of Stuttering: I. Changes in Nine Basic Features. II. Developmental Phases," *Journal of Speech and Hearing Disorders*, XXV (1960), 219–237, 366–376.

Bloodstein, Oliver. "The Development of Stuttering. III. Theoretical and Clinical Implications," *Journal of Speech and Hearing Disorders*, XXVI (1961), 67–82.

Bloodstein, Oliver, Janice P. Alper, and Paulette Kendler Zisk. "Stuttering as an Outgrowth of Normal Disfluency," in Dominick A. Barbara, ed. *New Directions in Stuttering: Theory and Practice.* Springfield, Illinois: Charles C. Thomas, 1965, pp. 31–54.

Bloodstein, Oliver, and Barbara F. Gantwerk. "Grammatical Function in Relation to Stuttering in Young Children," *Journal of Speech and Hearing Research*, X (1967), 786–789.

Bloomfield, Leonard. *Language* New York: Holt, Rinehart and Winston, 1933.

Blumenthal, Arthur L., and Robert Boakes. "Prompted Recall of Sentences," *Journal of Verbal Learning and Verbal Behavior*, VI (1967), 674–676.

Bodor, David P. "The Adjective-Verb Quotient: A Contribution to the Psychology of Language," *Psychological Record*, III (1940), 309–344.

Bois, J. Samuel. *The Art of Awareness.* Dubuque, Iowa: William C. Brown, 1966.

Braine, Martin D. S. "The Ontogeny of English Phrase Structure: The First Phase," *Language*, XXXIX (1963), 1–13. (a)

Braine, Martin D. S. "On Learning the Grammatical Order of Words," *Psychological Review*, LXX (1963), 323–348. (b)

Braine, Martin D. S. "On the Basis of Phrase Structure: A Reply to Bever, Fodor, and Weksel," *Psychological Review*, LXXII (1965), 483–492.

Braine, Martin D. S. "Learning the Positions of Words Relative to a Marker Element," *Journal of Experimental Psychology*, LXXII (1966), 532–540.

Bram, Joseph. *Language and Society.* New York: Random House, 1955.

Brehm, Jack W., and Arthur R. Cohen. "Re-evaluation of Choice Alternatives as a Function of Their Number and Qualitative Similarity," *Journal of Abnormal and Social Psychology*, LVIII (1959), 373–378.

Brehm, Jack W., and Arthur R. Cohen. *Explorations in Cognitive Dissonance*. New York: Wiley, 1962.

Bricker, Amy L., Hildred Schuell, and James J. Jenkins. "Effects of Word Frequency and Word Length on Aphasic Spelling Errors," *Journal of Speech and Hearing Research*, VII (1964), 183–192.

Broadhurst, Allan R., and Donald K. Darnell. "Introduction to Cybernetics and Information Theory," *Quarterly Journal of Speech*, LI (1965), 442–453.

Brookshire, Robert H., and Richard R. Martin. "The Differential Effects of Three Verbal Punishers on the Disfluencies of Normal Speakers," *Journal of Speech and Hearing Research*, X (1967), 496–505.

Bross, Irwin D. J. *Design for Decision*. New York: Macmillan, 1953.

Brown, Roger. "Language and Categories," in Jerome S. Bruner, Jacqueline J. Goodnow, and George A. Austin, *A Study of Thinking*. New York: Wiley, 1956, pp. 247–312.

Brown, Roger. *Words and Things*. New York: Free Press, 1958. (a)

Brown, Roger. "How Shall a Thing Be Called?" *Psychological Review*, LXV (1958), 14–21. (b)

Brown, Roger. "Models of Attitude Change," in *New Directions in Psychology*. New York: Holt, Rinehart and Winston, 1962, pp. 1–85.

Brown, Roger. *Social Psychology*. New York: Free Press, 1965.

Brown, Roger. "The Development of Wh Questions in Child Speech," *Journal of Verbal Learning and Verbal Behavior*, VII (1968), 279–290.

Brown, Roger, and Ursula Bellugi. "Three Processes in the Child's Acquisition of Syntax," in Lenneberg (1964c), pp. 131–161.

Brown, Roger, and Jean Berko. "Word Association and the Acquisition of Grammar," *Child Development*, XXXI (1960), 1–14.

Brown, Roger, and Margarite Ford. "Address in American English," *Journal of Abnormal and Social Psychology*, LXII (1961), 375–385.

Brown, Roger, and Colin Frazer. "The Acquisition of Syntax," in Charles N. Cofer and Barbara S. Musgrave, eds. *Verbal Behavior and Learning: Problems and Processes*. New York: McGraw-Hill, 1963, pp. 158–201.

Brown, Roger, and Albert Gilman. "The Pronouns of Power and Solidarity," in Sebeok (1960), pp. 253–276.

Brown, Roger, and Eric H. Lenneberg. "A Study in Language and Cognition," *Journal of Abnormal and Social Psychology*, IL (1954), 454–462.

Brown, S. F. "The Influence of Grammatical Function on the Incidence of Stuttering," *Journal of Speech Disorders*, II (1937), 207–215.

Brown, S. F. "The Loci of Stuttering in the Speech Sequence," *Journal of Speech Disorders*, X (1945), 181–192.

Brutten, Eugene J., and Donald J. Shoemaker. *The Modification of Stuttering*. Englewood Cliffs, New Jersey: Prentice-Hall, 1967.

Bryngelson, Bryng. "Sidedness as an Etiological Factor in Stuttering," *Journal of Genetic Psychology*, XLVII (1935), 204–217.

Burnham, R. W., and J. R. Clark. "A Test of Hue Memory," *Journal of Applied Psychology*, XXXIX (1955), 164–172.

Busemann, A. *Die Sprache der Jugend als Ausdruck der Entwicklungsrhythmik*. Jena, 1925.

Campbell, James H., and Hal W. Hepler, eds. *Dimensions in Communication: Readings*. Belmont, California: Wadsworth, 1965.

Cannell, Charles F., and James C. MacDonald. "The Impact of Health News on Attitudes and Behavior," *Journalism Quarterly*, XXXIII (1956), 315–323.

Capell, A. *Studies in Socio-Linguistics*. The Hague: Mouton, 1966.

Carmichael, L., H. P. Hogan, and A. A. Walter. "An Experimental Study of the Effect of Language on the Reproduction of Visually Perceived Forms," *Journal of Experimental Psychology*, XV (1932), 73–86.

Carroll, John B. "Diversity of Vocabulary and the Harmonic Series Law of Word-Frequency Distribution," *Psychological Record*, II (1938), 379–386.

Carroll, John B., ed. *Language, Thought, and Reality: Selected Writings of Benjamin Lee Whorf*. New York: Wiley, 1956.

Carroll, John B. *The Study of Language*. Cambridge, Mass.: Harvard University Press, 1959. (a)

Carroll, John B. "Review of Charles E. Osgood, George Suci, and Percy Tannenbaum's *The Measurement of Meaning*," *Language*, XXXV (1959), 58–77. (b)

Carroll, John B. "Language Development in Children," *Encyclopedia of Educational Research*. New York: Macmillan, 1960, pp. 744–752. (a)

Carroll, John B. "Vectors of Prose Style," in Sebeok (1960), pp. 283–292. (b)

Carroll, John B. *Language and Thought*. Englewood Cliffs, New Jersey: Prentice-Hall, 1964. (a)

Carroll, John B. "Linguistics and the Psychology of Language," *Review of Educational Research*, XXXIV (1964), 119–126. (b)

Carroll, John B., and Joseph B. Casagrande. "The Function of Language Classifications in Behavior," in Eleanor E. Maccoby, Theodore M. Newcomb, and Eugene L. Hartley, eds. *Readings in Social Psychology*, 3rd ed. New York: Holt, Rinehart and Winston, 1958, pp. 18–31.

Chapanis, Natalia P., and Alphonse Chapanis. "Cognitive Dissonance: Five Years Later," *Psychological Bulletin*, LXI (1964), 1–22.

Cherry, Colin. *On Human Communication: A Review, a Survey, and a Criticism*. New York: Wiley, 1957.

Church, Joseph. *Language and the Discovery of Reality*. New York: Random House, 1961.

Chomsky, Noam. *Syntactic Structures*. The Hague: Mouton, 1957.

Chomsky, Noam. "Review of B. F. Skinner's *Verbal Behavior*," *Language*, XXXV (1959), 26–58.

Chomsky, Noam. "Some Methodological Remarks on Generative Grammar," *Word*, XVII (1961), 219–239.

Chomsky, Noam. *Current Issues in Linguistic Theory.* The Hague: Mouton, 1964.

Chomsky, Noam. *Aspects of the Theory of Syntax.* Cambridge, Mass.: M.I.T. Press, 1965.

Chomsky, Noam. *Topics in the Theory of Generative Grammar.* The Hague: Mouton, 1966. (a)

Chomsky, Noam. *Cartesian Linguistics.* New York: Harper, 1966. (b)

Chomsky, Noam. "The Formal Nature of Language," in Lenneberg (1967), pp. 397–442.

Chomsky, Noam. *Language and Mind.* New York: Harcourt, Brace & World, 1968.

Chomsky, Noam, and Morris Halle. *The Sound Pattern of English.* New York: Harper, 1968.

Cohen, Arthur R. "Attitudinal Consequences of Induced Discrepancies Between Cognitions and Behavior," *Public Opinion Quarterly,* XXIV (1960), 297–318.

Cohen, Arthur R. *Attitude Change and Social Influence.* New York: Basic Books, 1964.

Cohen, Arthur R., Jack W. Brehm, and W. H. Flemming. "Attitude Change and Justification for Compliance," *Journal of Abnormal and Social Psychology,* LVI (1958), 276–278.

Collias, N. E. "An Ecological and Functional Classification of Animal Sounds," in W. E. Lanyon and W. N. Tavolga, eds. *Animal Sounds and Communication.* Washington, D.C.: American Institute of Biological Sciences, 1960, pp. 368–387.

Conway, J. K., and B. Quarrington. "Positional Effects in the Stuttering of Contextually Organized Verbal Material," *Journal of Abnormal and Social Psychology,* LXVII (1963), 299–303.

Dance, Frank E. X. "The Functions of Speech Communication as an Integrative Concept in the Field of Communication," *XV Convegno Internazionale delle Comunicazioni.* Genoa, Italy: Istituto Internazionale delle Comunicazioni, 1967, pp. 1–15. (a)

Dance, Frank E. X., ed. *Human Communication Theory: Original Essays.* New York: Holt, Rinehart and Winston, 1967. (b)

Darley, Frederic L., and Harris Winitz. "Age of First Word: Review of Research," *Journal of Speech and Hearing Disorders,* XXVI (1961), 272–290.

Darnell, Donald K. "Concept Scale Interaction in the Semantic Differential," *Journal of Communication,* XVI (1966), 104–115.

DeCecco, John P., ed. *The Psychology of Language, Thought, and Instruction.* New York: Holt, Rinehart and Winston, 1967.

Deese, James, and Stewart H. Hulse. *The Psychology of Learning,* 3rd ed. New York: McGraw-Hill, 1967.

deReuch, A. V. S. and M. O'Connor, eds. *Ciba Foundation Symposium: Disorders of Language.* Boston: Little, Brown, 1964.

Deutsch, Karl. "On Communication Models in the Social Sciences," *Public Opinion Quarterly,* XVI (1952), 356–380.

DeVito, Joseph A. "Comprehension Factors in Oral and Written Discourse of Skilled Communicators," *Speech Monographs,* XXXII (1965), 124–128. (a)

DeVito, Joseph A. " Levels of Abstraction and Listenability," *Today's Speech*, XIII (1965), 12–14. (b)

DeVito, Joseph A. " The Encoding of Speech and Writing," *Speech Teacher*, XV (1966), 55–60. (a)

DeVito, Joseph A. " Psychogrammatical Factors in Oral and Written Discourse by Skilled Communicators," *Speech Monographs*, XXXIII (1966), 73–76. (b)

DeVito, Joseph A. " Cloze Procedure," *Today's Speech*, XV (1967), 31–32. (a)

DeVito, Joseph A. " The Meaning of Psycholinguistics," *Today's Speech*, XV (1967), 19–22. (b)

DeVito, Joseph A. "A Linguistic Analysis of Spoken and Written Language," *Central States Speech Journal*, XVIII (1967), 81–85. (c)

DeVito, Joseph A. " Oral and Written Style: Directions for Research," *Southern Speech Journal*, XXXIII (1967), 37–43. (d)

DeVito, Joseph A. " Style and Stylistics: An Attempt at Definition," *Quarterly Journal of Speech*, LIII (1967), 248–255. (e)

DeVito, Joseph A. " Levels of Abstraction in Spoken and Written Language," *Journal of Communication*, XVII (1967), 354–361. (f)

DeVito, Joseph A. " The Teacher as Behavioral Engineer," *Today's Speech*, XVI (1968), 2–5. (a)

DeVito, Joseph A. " Kinesics: Other Codes, Other Channels," *Today's Speech*, XVI (1968), 29–32. (b)

DeVito, Joseph A. " Some Psycholinguistic Aspects of Active and Passive Sentences," *Quarterly Journal of Speech*, LV (1969), 401–406. (a)

DeVito, Joseph A. "Are Theories of Stuttering Necessary?" *Central States Speech Journal*, XX (1969), 170–177. (b)

Diebold, A. Richard. "A Survey of Psycholinguistics Research, 1954–1964," in Osgood and Sebeok (1965 ed.), pp. 205–291.

Dinneen, Francis P., S. J. *An Introduction to General Linguistics*. New York: Holt, Rinehart and Winston, 1967.

DiVesta, F., and J. Merwin. " The Effects of Need-Oriented Communications on Attitude Change," *Journal of Abnormal and Social Psychology*, LX (1960), 80–85.

Dixon, R. M. W. *Linguistic Science and Logic*. The Hague: Mouton, 1963.

Dixon, Theodore R., and David L. Horton, eds. *Verbal Behavior and General Behavior Theory*. Englewood Cliffs, New Jersey: Prentice-Hall, 1968.

Dollard, John, and O. Hobart Mowrer. "A Method of Measuring Tension in Written Documents," *Journal of Abnormal and Social Psychology*, XLII (1947), 3–32.

Driemann, G. H. J. "Differences Between Written and Spoken Language," *Acta Psychologica*, XX (1962), 36–57.

Ebeling, C. L. *Linguistic Units* The Hague: Mouton, 1962.

Ehrlich, D., I. Guttman, P. Schonbach, and J. Mills. " Post-decision Exposure to Relevant Information," *Journal of Abnormal and Social Psychology*, LIV (1957), 98–102.

Eisenson, Jon. "A Perseverative Theory of Stuttering," in Eisenson (1958b), pp. 223–271. (a)

Eisenson, Jon, ed. *Stuttering: A Symposium.* New York: Harper, 1958. (b)

Eisenson, Jon. "Historical Highlights in the Study of Aphasia During the Past Fifty Years," in Robert T. Oliver and Marvin G. Bauer, eds. *Re-establishing the Speech Profession: The First Fifty Years.* New York: Speech Association of the Eastern States, 1959, pp. 40–46.

Eisenson, Jon, J. Jeffery Auer, and John V. Irwin. *The Psychology of Communication.* New York: Appleton-Century-Crofts, 1963.

Ervin, Susan M., and Wick R. Miller. "Language Development," in H. Stevenson, ed. *Child Psychology,* 62nd Yearbook, National Society for the Study of Education. Chicago: University of Chicago Press, 1963, pp. 108–143.

Ervin, Susan M., and Charles E. Osgood. "Second Language Learning and Bilingualism," in Osgood and Sebeok (1954), pp. 139–146.

Ervin-Tripp, Susan M. "Language Development," in Lois Wladis Hoffman and and Martin L. Hoffman, eds. *Review of Child Development Research,* Vol. II. New York: Russell Sage Foundation, 1966, pp. 55–105.

Ervin-Tripp, Susan M., and Dan Slobin. "Psycholinguistics," *Annual Review of Psychology,* XVII (1966), 435–474.

Esch, Harald. "The Evolution of Bee Language," *Scientific American,* CCXVI (1967), 96–104.

Fairbanks, Grant, and N. Guttman. "Effects of Delayed Auditory Feedback Upon Articulation," *Journal of Speech and Hearing Research,* I (1958), 12–22.

Farnsworth, P., and I. Misumi. "Further Data on Suggestion in Pictures," *Journal of Abnormal and Social Psychology,* XLIII (1931), 632.

Fearing, Franklin. "Toward a Psychological Theory of Human Communication," *Journal of Personality,* XXII (1953), 71–78.

Feldman, Shel, ed. *Cognitive Consistency: Motivational Antecedents and Behavioral Consequents.* New York: Academic Press, 1966.

Festinger, Leon. *A Theory of Cognitive Dissonance.* Stanford, California: Stanford University Press, 1957.

Festinger, Leon. *Conflict, Decision, and Dissonance.* Stanford, California: Stanford University Press, 1964.

Festinger, Leon, and J. Carlsmith. "Cognitive Consequences of Forced Compliance," *Journal of Abnormal and Social Psychology,* LVIII (1959), 203–210.

Festinger, Leon, Henry W. Riecken, and Stanley Schachter. *When Prophecy Fails: A Social and Psychological Study of a Modern Group That Predicted the Destruction of the World.* New York: Harper, 1956.

Fillenbaum, Samuel. "Verbal Satiation and the Exploration of Meaning Relations," in Salzinger and Salzinger (1967), pp. 155–165.

Fillenbaum, Samuel, and Lyle V. Jones. "An Application of 'Cloze' Technique to the Study of Aphasic Speech," *Journal of Abnormal and Social Psychology,* LXV (1962), 183–189.

Fishbein, Martin. "An Investigation of the Relationships Between Beliefs About an Object and the Attitudes Toward That Object," *Human Relations*, XVI (1963), 233–239.

Fishbein, Martin, ed. *Readings in Attitude Theory and Measurement*. New York: Wiley, 1967.

Fishbein, Martin, and B. H. Raven. "The AB Scales: An Operational Definition of Belief and Attitude," *Human Relations*, XV (1962), 35–44.

Fishman, Joshua. "A Systematization of the Whorfian Hypothesis," *Behavioral Science*, V (1960), 323–339.

Fishman, Joshua, ed. *Readings in the Sociology of Language*. The Hague: Mouton, 1968.

Flanagan, Bruce, Israel Goldiamond, and Nathan Azrin. "Operant Stuttering: The Control of Stuttering Through Response-Contingent Consequences," *Journal of the Experimental Analysis of Behavior*, I (1958), 173–177.

Flesch, Rudolf. *How to Write, Speak and Think More Effectively*. New York: New American Library, 1963.

Fodor, Jerry A. "Could Meaning Be an r_m?" *Journal of Verbal Learning and Verbal Behavior*, IV (1965), 73–81.

Fodor, Jerry A. "More About Mediators: A Reply to Berlyne and Osgood," *Journal of Verbal Learning and Verbal Behavior*, V (1966), 412–415. (a)

Fodor, Jerry A. "How to Learn to Talk: Some Simple Ways," in Smith and Miller (1966), pp. 105–122. (b)

Fodor, Jerry A., and Merrill Garrett. "Some Reflections on Competence and Performance," in Lyons and Wales (1966), pp. 133–154.

Fodor, Jerry A., James J. Jenkins, and Sol Saporta. "Psycholinguistics and Communication Theory," in Dance (1967), pp. 160–201. (b)

Fodor, Jerry A., and Jerrold J. Katz, eds. *The Structure of Language: Readings in the Philosophy of Language*. Englewood Cliffs, New Jersey: Prentice-Hall, 1964.

Francis, W. Nelson. "Revolution in Grammar," *Quarterly Journal of Speech*, XL (1954), 299–312.

Francis, W. Nelson. *The Structure of American English*. New York: Ronald, 1958.

Freeman, J., and D. Sears. "Selective Exposure," in Leonard Berkowitz, ed. *Advances in Experimental Social Psychology*, Vol. II. New York: Academic Press, 1965, pp. 58–97.

Fries, Charles C. *The Structure of English: An Introduction to the Construction of English Sentences*. New York: Harcourt, Brace & World, 1952.

Fries, Charles C. "Meaning and Linguistic Analysis," *Language*, XXX (1954), 57–68.

Frings, Hubert, and Mable Frings. *Animal Communication*. New York: Blaisdell, 1964.

Frisch, Karl von. *Bees: Their Vision, Chemical Senses, and Language*. Ithaca, New York: Cornell University Press, 1950.

Frisch, Karl von. *The Dancing Bees: An Account of the Life and Senses of the Honey Bee*, trans. Dora Ilse. New York: Harcourt, Brace & World, 1953.

Frisch, Karl von. "Dialects in the Language of the Bees," *Scientific American*, CCVII (1962), 78–87.

Fry, D. B. "The Development of the Phonological System in the Normal and the Deaf Child," in Smith and Miller (1966), pp. 187–206.

Garrett, Merrill, and Jerry A. Fodor. "Psychological Theories and Linguistic Constructs," in Dixon and Horton (1968), pp. 451–476.

Gerbner, George. "Toward a General Model of Communication," *Audio-Visual Communication Review*, IV (1956), 171–199.

Gibson, James W., Charles R. Gruner, Robert J. Kibler, and Francis J. Kelly. "A Quantitative Examination of Differences and Similarities in Written and Spoken Messages," *Speech Monographs*, XXXIII (1966), 444–451.

Gibson, Walker. *Tough, Sweet, and Stuffy: An Essay on Modern American Prose Styles.* Bloomington: Indiana University Press, 1966.

Gleason, Henry A., Jr. *An Introduction to Descriptive Linguistics*, rev. ed. New York: Holt, Rinehart and Winston, 1961.

Gleason, Henry A., Jr. *Linguistics and English Grammar.* New York: Holt, Rinehart and Winston, 1965.

Goldberg, H., and M. Iverson. "Inconsistency in Attitude of High Status Persons and Loss of Influence: An Experimental Study," *Psychological Reports*, XVI (1965), 673–683.

Goldiamond, Israel. "The Maintenance of Ongoing Fluent Verbal Behavior and Stuttering," *Journal of Mathetics*, I (1962), 57–95.

Goldiamond, Israel. "Stuttering and Fluency as Manipulable Operant Response Classes," in Leonard Krasner and Leonard P. Ullman, eds. *Research in Behavior Modification.* New York: Holt, Rinehart and Winston, 1965, pp. 106–156.

Goldman-Eisler, Frieda. *Psycholinguistics: Experiments in Spontaneous Speech.* New York: Academic Press, 1968.

Goldstein, Kurt. *The Organism.* New York: American Book, 1939.

Goldstein, Kurt. *Language and Language Disturbances.* New York: Grune and Stratton, 1948.

Goodglass, Harold, and J. Hunt. "Grammatical Complexity and Aphasic Speech," *Word*, XIV (1958), 197–207.

Goodglass, Harold, and J. Mayer. "Agrammatism in Aphasia," *Journal of Speech and Hearing Disorders*, XXIII (1958), 99–111.

Greenberg, Joseph H. *Essays in Linguistics.* Chicago: University of Chicago Press, 1957.

Greenberg, Joseph H. "Review of Charles F. Hockett's *A Course in Modern Linguistics*," *American Anthropologist*, LXIII (1961), 1140–1145.

Greenberg, Joseph H., ed. *Universals of Language.* Cambridge, Mass.: M.I.T. Press, 1963.

Greenspoon, J. "The Reinforcing Effect of Two Spoken Sounds on the Frequency of Two Responses," *American Journal of Psychology*, LXVIII (1955), 409–416.

Grosslight, Joseph H., and Wesley C. Zaynor. "Verbal Behavior and the Mynah Bird," in Salzinger and Salzinger (1967), pp. 5–19.

Hahn, E. F., ed. *Stuttering: Significant Theories and Therapies*, 2nd ed. Stanford, California: Stanford University Press, 1956.

Hall, Edward T. *The Silent Language.* Garden City, New York: Doubleday, 1959.

Hall, Edward T. "A System for the Notation of Proxemic Behavior," *American Anthropologist,* LXV (1963), 1003–1026.

Hall, Edward T. *The Hidden Dimension.* Garden City, New York: Doubleday, 1966.

Hall, Robert A., Jr. *Introductory Linguistics.* New York: Chilton, 1964.

Hamp, Eric P. "Language in a Few Words: With Notes on a Rereading, 1966," in DeCecco (1967), pp. 5–23.

Haney, William V. *Communication and Organizational Behavior: Text and Cases,* 2nd ed. Homewood, Illinois: Irwin, 1967.

Hardyck, J., and M. Braden. "Prophecy Fails Again: A Report of a Failure to Replicate," *Journal of Abnormal and Social Psychology,* LXV (1962), 136–141.

Harman, G. H. "Generative Grammars Without Transformation Rules: A Defense of Phrase Structure," *Language,* XXXIX (1963), 597–616.

Harris, Zellig. *Structural Linguistics.* Chicago: University of Chicago Press, 1951.

Hayakawa, S. I., ed. *The Use and Misuse of Language.* Greenwich, Conn.: Fawcett, 1962.

Hayakawa, S. I. *Language in Thought and Action,* 2nd ed. New York: Harcourt, Brace & World, 1964.

Hayes, Cathy. *The Ape in Our House.* New York: Harper, 1951.

Head, Henry. *Aphasia and Kindred Disorders of Speech.* New York: Macmillan, 1926.

Hebb, Donald O. *The Organization of Behavior: A Neurophysiological Theory.* New York: Wiley, 1949.

Heider, Fritz. "Attitudes and Cognitive Organization," *Journal of Psychology,* XXI (1946), 107–112.

Heider, Fritz. *The Psychology of Interpersonal Relations.* New York: Wiley, 1958.

Herman, David T., Richard H. Lawless, and Richard W. Marshall. "Variables in the Effect of Language on the Reproduction of Visually Perceived Forms," *Perceptual and Motor Skills,* VII, Monograph Supplement 2 (1957), 171–186.

Hertzler, Joyce O. *A Sociology of Language.* New York: Random House, 1965.

Hildum, Donald C., ed. *Language and Thought.* Princeton, New Jersey: Van Nostrand, 1967.

Hilgard, Ernest R. *Theories of Learning,* 2nd ed. New York: Appleton-Century-Crofts, 1956.

Hill, Archibald A. *Introduction to Linguistic Structures: From Sound to Sentence in English.* New York: Harcourt, Brace & World, 1958.

Hill, Archibald A. "Grammaticality," *Word,* XVII (1961), 1–10.

Hockett, Charles F. "Review of Claude E. Shannon and Warren Weaver's *The Mathematical Theory of Communication,*" *Language,* XXIX (1953), 69–93.

Hockett, Charles F. *A Course in Modern Linguistics.* New York: Macmillan, 1958.

Hockett, Charles F. "The Origin of Speech," *Scientific American,* CCIII (1960), 89–96. (a)

Hockett, Charles F. "Logical Considerations in the Study of Animal Communication," in W. E. Lanyon and T. N. Tavolga, eds. *Animal Sounds and Communication*. Washington, D.C.: American Institute of Biological Sciences, 1960, pp. 392–430. (b)

Hockett, Charles F. "The Problem of Universals in Language," in Greenberg (1963), pp. 1–22.

Hockett, Charles F. *Language, Mathematics, and Linguistics*. The Hague: Mouton, 1967.

Hoijer, Harry. "Cultural Implications of Some Navaho Linguistic Categories," *Language*, XXVII (1951), 111–120.

Hoijer, Harry, ed. *Language in Culture, Proceedings of a Conference on the Interrelations of Language and Other Aspects of Culture*. Chicago: University of Chicago Press,1954.

Homans, George C. *The Human Group*. New York: Harcourt, Brace & World, 1950.

Horowitz, Milton W., and John B. Newman. "Spoken and Written Expression: An Experimental Analysis," *Journal of Abnormal and Social Psychology*, LXVIII (1964), 640–647.

Howes, Davis H. "Application of the Word-Frequency Concept to Aphasia," in deReuck and O'Connor (1964), pp. 47–75.

Howes, Davis. H. "Some Experimental Investigations of Language in Aphasia," in Salzinger and Salzinger (1967), pp. 181–196.

Hughes, John P. *The Science of Language: An Introduction to Linguistics*. New York: Random House, 1962.

Hymes, Dell H. "Functions of Speech: An Evolutionary Approach," in Frederick C. Gruber, ed. *Anthropology and Education*. Philadelphia: University of Pennsylvania Press, 1961, pp. 55–83.

Hymes, Dell H., ed. *Language in Culture and Society: A Reader in Linguistics and Anthropology*. New York: Harper, 1964.

Insko, Chester A. *Theories of Attitude Change*. New York: Appleton-Century-Crofts, 1967.

Irwin, Orvis C. "Infant Speech: Development of Vowel Sounds," *Journal of Speech and Hearing Disorders*, XIII (1948), 31–34. (a)

Irwin, Orvis C. "Infant Speech: The Effect of Family Occupational Status and of Age on Sound Frequency," *Journal of Speech and Hearing Disorders*, XIII (1948), 320–323. (b)

Ivić, Milka. *Trends in Linguistics*. The Hague: Mouton, 1965.

Jackson, Hughlings. *The Selected Writings*. Vol. II. *Speech*. New York: Basic Books, 1958.

Jahoda, Marie, and Neil Warren, eds. *Attitudes: Selected Readings*. Baltimore, Maryland: Penguin, 1966.

Jakobovits, Leon A., and Murray S. Miron, eds. *Readings in the Psychology of Language*. Englewood Cliffs, New Jersey: Prentice-Hall, 1967.

Jakobson, Roman. *Child Language, Aphasia and Phonological Universals*, trans. Allan R. Keiler. The Hague: Mouton, 1968.

Jakobson, Roman. "The Cardinal Dichotomy in Language," in Ruth Nanda Anshen, ed. *Language: An Enquiry into Its Meaning and Function.* New York: Harper, 1957, pp. 155–173.

Jakobson, Roman. "Closing Statement: Linguistics and Poetics," in Sebeok (1960), pp. 350–377.

Jakobson, Roman, ed. *Structure of Language and Its Mathematical Aspects.* Providence, Rhode Island: American Mathematical Society, 1961.

Jakobson, Roman, Gunnar Fant, and Morris Halle. *Preliminaries to Speech Analysis: The Distinctive Features and Their Correlates.* Cambridge, Mass.: M.I.T. Press, 1952.

Jakobson, Roman and Morris Halle. *Fundamentals of Language.* The Hague: Mouton, 1956.

Jenkins, James J. "Mediation Theory and Grammatical Behavior," in Rosenberg (1965), pp. 66–96.

Jenkins, James J. "The Challenge to Psychological Theorists," in Dixon and Horton (1968), pp. 538–549.

Jenkins, James J., and David S. Palermo. "Mediation Processes and the Acquisition of Linguistic Structure," in Bellugi and Brown (1964), pp. 141–169

Jenkins, James J., and Hildred M. Schuell. "Further Work on Language Deficit," *Psychological Review,* LXXI (1964), 87–93.

Johnson, F. Craig, and George R. Klare. "General Models of Communication Research: A Survey of the Developments of a Decade," *Journal of Communication,* XI (1961), 13–26.

Johnson, Wendell. *People in Quandaries: The Semantics of Personal Adjustment.* New York: Harper, 1946.

Johnson, Wendell. "The Spoken Word and the Great Unsaid," *Quarterly Journal of Speech,* XXXVII (1951), 419–429.

Johnson, Wendell. *The Onset of Stuttering.* Minneapolis: University of Minnesota Press, 1959.

Jones, Lyle V., and Joseph M. Wepman. "Dimensions of Language Performance in Aphasia," *Journal of Speech and Hearing Research,* IV (1961), 220–232.

Jones, Lyle V., and Joseph M. Wepman. "Language: A Perspective from the Study of Aphasia," in Rosenberg (1965), pp. 237–253.

Jones, Lyle V., and Joseph M. Wepman. "Grammatical Indicants of Speaking Style in Normal and Aphasic Speakers," in Salzinger and Salzinger (1967), pp. 169–180.

Joos, Martin. "Review of Roman Jakobson and Morris Halle's *Fundamentals of Language,*" *Language,* XXXIII (1957), 408–415.

Joos, Martin. *The Five Clocks. International Journal of American Linguistics,* XXVIII, No. 2 (1962).

Katz, Elihu. "The Two-Step Flow of Communication: An Up-to-Date Report on an Hypothesis," *Public Opinion Quarterly,* XXI (1957), 61–78.

Katz, Jerrold J. *The Philosophy of Language.* New York: Harper, 1966.

Katz, Jerrold J., and Jerry A. Fodor. "The Structure of a Semantic Theory," *Language,* XXXIX (1963), 170–210.

Katz, Jerrold J., and Paul Postal. *An Integrated Theory of Linguistic Descriptions.* Cambridge, Mass.: M.I.T. Press, 1964.

Kelman, Herbert C. "Processes of Opinion Change," *Public Opinion Quarterly*, XXV (1961), 57–78.

Kerrick, J. "The Effect of Relevant and Non-Relevant Sources on Attitude Change," *Journal of Social Psychology*, XLVII (1958), 15–20.

Kjeldegaard, Paul M. "The Psychology of Language," *Review of Educational Research*, XXXI (1961), 119–129.

Klapper, Joseph T. *The Effects of Mass Communication.* New York: Free Press, 1960.

Klare, George R. *The Measurement of Readability.* Ames: Iowa State University Press, 1963.

Klima, Edward S., and Ursula Bellugi. "Syntactic Regularities in the Speech of Children," in Lyons and Wales (1966), pp. 181–208.

Knower, Franklin H. "A Model for a Communicology," *Ohio Speech Journal*, II (1963), 181–187.

Koch, Sigmund, ed. *Psychology: A Study of a Science.* Vol. II. *General Systematic Formulations, Learning, and Special Processes.* New York: McGraw-Hill, 1959.

Korzybski, Alfred. *Manhood of Humanity.* New York: Dutton, 1921.

Korzybski, Alfred. *Science and Sanity: An Introduction to Non-Aristotelian Systems and General Semantics.* Lakeville, Conn.: The International Non-Aristotelian Library, 1933.

Krasner, Leonard. "Verbal Operant Conditioning and Awareness," in Salzinger and Salzinger (1967), pp. 57—76.

Lackowski, Peter. "Review of Jerrold J. Katz's *The Philosophy of Language*," *Language*, 44 (1968), 606–616.

Lamb, Sydney M. *Outline of Stratificational Grammar.* Washington, D.C.: Georgetown University Press, 1966.

Lambert, Wallace E. "Psychological Approaches to the Study of Language. Part I. On Learning, Thinking and Human Abilities. Part II. On Second-Language Learning and Bilingualism," *Modern Language Journal*, XLVII (1963), 51—62, 114–121.

Lambert, Wallace E., and Leon A. Jakobovits. "Verbal Satiation and Changes in the Intensity of Meaning," *Journal of Experimental Psychology*, LX (1960),376–383.

Lantz, D., and V. Steffler. "Language and Cognition Revisited," *Journal of Abnormal and Social Psychology*, XXXVI (1964), 472–481.

Lasswell, Harold D. "The Structure and Function of Communication in Society," in Lyman Bryson, ed. *The Communication of Ideas.* New York: Harper, 1948, pp. 37–51.

Lawton, D. "Social Class Differences in Language Development," *Language and Speech*, VI (1963), 120–143.

Lee, Irving J., ed. *The Language of Wisdom and Folly: Background Readings in Semantics.* San Francisco: International Society for General Semantics, 1967.

Lee, Laura L. "Two Kinds of Disturbed Communication," *General Semantics Bulletin*, XXII and XXIII (1958), 47–50.

Lee, Laura L. "Brain Damage and the Process of Abstracting: A Problem in Language and Learning," *Etc.*, XVI (1959), 154–162.

Lee, Laura L. "Some Semantic Goals for Aphasia Therapy," *Etc.*, XVIII (1961), 261–274.

Lees, Robert B. *The Grammar of English Nominalizations.* Bloomington: Indiana University Research Center in Anthropology, Folklore, and Linguistics, 1960.

Lees, Robert B. "Transformation Grammars and the Fries Framework," in Allen (1964), pp. 137–146.

Lenneberg, Eric H. "A Probabilistic Approach to Language Learning," *Behavioral Science*, II (1957), 1–13.

Lenneberg, Eric H. "Language, Evolution and Purposive Behavior," in S. Diamond, ed. *Culture in History: Essays in Honor of Paul Radin.* New York: Columbia University Press, 1960, pp. 869–893.

Lenneberg, Eric H. "Color Naming, Color Recognition, Color Discrimination: A Reappraisal," *Perceptual and Motor Skills*, XII (1961), 376–382.

Lenneberg, Eric H. "Understanding Language Without Ability to Speak: A Case Report," *Journal of Abnormal and Social Psychology*, LXV (1962), 419–425.

Lenneberg, Eric H. "The Capacity for Language Acquisition," in Fodor and Katz (1964), pp. 579–603. (a)

Lenneberg, Eric H. "A Biological Perspective of Language," in Lenneberg (1964c), pp. 65–88. (b)

Lenneberg, Eric H., ed. *New Directions in the Study of Language.* Cambridge, Mass.: M.I.T. Press, 1964. (c)

Lenneberg, Eric H. "Language Disorders in Childhood," *Harvard Educational Review*, XXXIV (1964), 152–177. (d)

Lenneberg, Eric H. "The Natural History of Language," in Smith and Miller (1966), pp. 219–252.

Lenneberg, Eric H. *Biological Foundations of Language.* New York: Wiley, 1967.

Leopold, Werner F. *Bibliography of Child Language.* Evanston, Illinois: Northwestern University Press, 1952.

Leopold, Werner F. "Patterning in Children's Language Learning," *Language Learning*, V (1953–54), 1–14.

Levine, J. M., and G. Murphy. "The Learning and Forgetting of Controversial Material," *Journal of Abnormal and Social Psychology*, XXXVIII (1943), 507–517.

Lewis, M. M. *How Children Learn to Speak.* New York: Basic Books, 1959.

Lewis, M. M. *Language, Thought and Personality in Infancy and Childhood.* New York: Basic Books, 1963.

Lieberman, Philip. *Intonation, Perception, and Language*, Research Monograph No. 38. Cambridge, Mass.: M.I.T. Press, 1967.

Lindauer, Martin. *Communication Among Social Bees.* New York: Atheneum, 1967.

Lotz, John. "Speech and Language," *Journal of the Acoustical Society of America*, XXII (1950), 712–717.

Lotz, John. "Linguistics: Symbols Make Man," in Lynn White, Jr., ed. *Frontiers of of Knowledge*. New York: Harper, 1956, pp. 207–231.

Lounsbury, Floyd G. "Pausal, Juncture, and Hesitation Phenomena," in Osgood and Sebeok (1954), pp. 98–101.

Lounsbury, Floyd G. "Linguistics and Psychology," in Sigmund Koch, ed. *Psychology: A Study of a Science*. Vol. VI. New York: McGraw-Hill, 1963, pp. 552–582.

Luchsinger, Richard, and Godfrey E. Arnold. *Voice-Speech-Language: Clinical Communicology: Its Physiology and Pathology*. Belmont, California: Wadsworth, 1965.

Luria, Alexander R. "Brain Disorders and Language Analysis," *Language and Speech*, I (1958), 14–34.

Luria, Alexander R. "The Directive Function of Speech in Development and Dissolution. Part I. Development of the Directive Function of Speech in Early Childhood. Part II. Dissolution of the Regulative Function of Speech in Pathological States of the Brain," *Word*, XV (1959), 341–352, 453–465.

Luria, Alexander R. *The Role of Speech in the Regulation of Normal and Abnormal Behavior*. New York: Liveright, 1961.

Lyons, J., and R. J. Wales, eds. *Psycholinguistic Papers, Proceedings of the Edinburgh Conference*. Chicago: Aldine, 1966.

Maclay, Howard, and Charles E. Osgood. "Hesitation Phenomena in Spontaneous English Speech," *Word*, XV (1959), 19–44.

Mahl, George F. "Disturbances and Silences in the Patient's Speech in Psychotherapy," *Journal of Abnormal and Social Psychology*, LIII (1956), 1–15.

Mahl, George F., and Gene Schulze. "Psychological Research in the Extralinguistic Area," in Thomas A. Sebeok, Alfred S. Hayes, and Mary Catherine Bateson, eds. *Approaches to Semiotics, Transactions of the Indiana University Conference on Paralinguistics and Kinesics*. The Hague: Mouton, 1964, pp. 51–124.

Malinowski, Bronislaw. "The Problem of Meaning in Primitive Languages," in Ogden and Richards (1923), pp. 296–336.

Mandelbaum, David G., ed. *Selected Writings of Edward Sapir in Language, Culture, and Personality*. Los Angeles: University of California Press, 1949.

Mandelbaum, David G., ed. *Edward Sapir: Culture, Language and Personality*. Los Angeles: University of California Press, 1962.

Marler, Peter. "The Logical Analysis of Animal Communication," *Journal of Theoretical Biology*, I (1961), 295–317.

Marler, Peter, and William J. Hamilton, III. *Mechanisms of Animal Behavior*. New York: Wiley, 1966.

Martin, Richard R., and Gerald M. Siegel. "The Effects of Response Contingent Shock on Stuttering," *Journal of Speech and Hearing Research*, IX (1966), 340–352. (a)

Martin, Richard R., and Gerald M. Siegel. "The Effects of Simultaneously Punishing Stuttering and Rewarding Fluency," *Journal of Speech and Hearing Research*, IX (1966), 466–475. (b)

Matson, Floyd W., and Ashley Montagu, eds. *The Human Dialogue: Perspectives on Communication*. New York: Free Press, 1967.

McCarthy, Dorothea. "Language Development in Children," in Leonard Carmichael, ed. *A Manual of Child Psychology*, 2nd ed. New York: Wiley, 1954, pp. 492–630.

McGuire, William J. "The Current Status of Cognitive Consistency Theories," in Feldman (1966), pp. 1–46.

McLuhan, Marshall. *Understanding Media: The Extensions of Man*. New York: McGraw-Hill, 1964.

McLuhan, Marshall, and Quentin Fiore. *The Medium Is the Massage: An Inventory of Effects*. New York: Bantam, 1967.

McNeill, David. "The Capacity for Language Acquisition," *The Volta Review*, LXVIII (1966), 5–21. (a)

McNeill, David. "The Creation of Language," *Discovery*, XXVII (1966), 34–38. (b)

McNeill, David. "Developmental Psycholinguistics," in Smith and Miller (1966), pp. 15–84. (c)

McNeill, David. "The Creation of Language by Children," in Lyons and Wales (1966), pp. 97–115. (d)

McNeill, David. "The Capacity for Grammatical Development in Children," unpublished paper, 1967. (a)

McNeill, David. "Development of the Semantic System," unpublished paper, 1967. (b)

McNeill, David. "On Theories of Language Acquisition," in Dixon and Horton (1968), pp. 406–420.

Mead, George H. "A Behavioristic Account of the Significant Symbol," *Journal of Philosophy*, XIX (1922), 157–163.

Menyuk, Paula. "Syntactic Structures in the Language of Children," *Child Development*, XXXIV (1963), 407–422. (a)

Menyuk, Paula. "A Preliminary Evaluation of Grammatical Capacity in Children," *Journal of Verbal Learning and Verbal Behavior*, II (1963), 429–439. (b)

Menyuk, Paula. "Syntactic Rules Used by Children from Preschool Through First Grade," *Child Development*, XXXV (1964), 533–546. (a)

Menyuk, Paula. "Alternation of Rules in Children's Grammar," *Journal of Verbal Learning and Verbal Behavior*, III (1964), 480–488. (a)

Menyuk, Paula. "Acquisition of Grammar by Children," in Salzinger and Salzinger (1967), pp. 101–110.

Menyuk, Paula. "The Role of Distinctive Features in Children's Acquisition of Phonology," *Journal of Speech and Hearing Research*, XI (1968), 138–146.

Menyuk, Paula. *Sentences Children Use*, Research Monograph 52. Cambridge, Mass.: M.I.T. Press, 1969.

Messer, Stanley. "Implicit Phonology in Children," *Journal of Verbal Learning and Verbal Behavior*, VI (1967), 455–460.

Miller, George A. *Language and Communication*. New York: McGraw-Hill, 1951.

Miller, George A. "What Is Information Measurement?" *American Psychologist*, VIII (1953), 3–11.

Miller, George A. "The Magical Number Seven, Plus or Minus Two: Some Limits on Our Capacity for Processing Information," *Psychological Review*, LXIII (1956), 81–97.

Miller, George A. "Some Psychological Studies of Grammar," *American Psychologist*, XVII (1962), 748–762.

Miller, George A. "The Psycholinguists: On the New Scientists of Language," *Encounter*, XXIII (1964), 29–37.

Miller, George A. "Some Preliminaries to Psycholinguistics," *American Psychologist*, XX (1965), 15–20.

Miller, George A. *The Psychology of Communication: Seven Essays*. New York: Basic Books, 1967.

Miller, George A., and Noam Chomsky. "Finitary Models of Language Users," in R. D. Luce, R. Bush, and E. Galanter, eds. *Handbook of Mathematical Psychology*. Vol. II. New York: Wiley, 1963, pp. 419–492.

Miller, George A., and David McNeill. "Psycholinguistics," in Gardner Lindzey and Elliot Aronson, eds. *The Handbook of Social Psychology*, 2nd ed., Vol.III. Reading, Mass.: Addison-Wesley Publishing Co., 1969, pp. 666–794.

Morris, Charles. *Signs, Language and Behavior*. New York: George Braziller, 1955.

Morris, Charles. "Words Without Meaning: Review of B. F. Skinner, *Verbal Behavior*," *Contemporary Psychology*, III (1958), 212–214.

Morris, Charles. *Signification and Significance*. Cambridge, Mass.: M.I.T. Press, 1964.

Mowrer, O. Hobart. "On the Psychology of Talking Birds—A Contribution to Language and Personality Theory," in O. Hobart Mowrer, *Learning Theory and Personality Dynamics*. New York: Ronald, 1950, pp. 688–726.

Mowrer, O. Hobart. "The Psychologist Looks at Language," *American Psychologist*, IX (1954), 660–692.

Mowrer, O. Hobart. *Learning Theory and Behavior*. New York: Wiley, 1960. (a)

Mowrer, O. Hobart. *Learning Theory and the Symbolic Processes*. New York: Wiley, 1960. (b)

Newcomb, Theodore M. "An Approach to the Study of Communicative Acts," *Psychological Review*, LX (1953), 393–404.

Nielsen, J. M. *Agnosia, Apraxia, Aphasia: Their Value in Cerebral Localization*, 2nd ed. New York: Paul B. Hoeber, 1947.

Nunnally, Jum C. "Individual Differences in Word Usage," in Rosenberg (1965), pp. 203–234.

Ogden, C. K., and I. A. Richards. *The Meaning of Meaning: A Study of the Influence of Language Upon Thought and of the Science of Symbolism*. New York: Harcourt, Brace & World, 1923.

Oldfield, R. C., and J. C. Marshall, eds. *Language: Selected Readings*. Baltimore, Maryland: Penguin, 1968.

Osgood, Charles E. *Method and Theory in Experimental Psychology*. New York: Oxford, 1953.

Osgood, Charles E. "Behavior Theory and the Social Sciences," *Behavioral Science*, I (1956), 167–185.

Osgood, Charles E. "A Behavioristic Analysis of Perception and Language as Cognitive Phenomena," in *Contemporary Approaches to Cognition*. Cambridge, Mass.: Harvard University Press, 1957, pp. 75–118. (a)

Osgood, Charles E. "Motivational Dynamics of Language Behavior," in Marshall R. Jones, ed. *Nebraska Symposium on Motivation, 1957*. Lincoln: University of Nebraska Press, 1957, pp. 348–424. (b)

Osgood, Charles E. "A Question of Sufficiency: Review of B. F. Skinner, *Verbal Behavior*." *Contemporary Psychology*, III (1958), 209–212.

Osgood, Charles E. "Semantic Space Revisited: A Reply to Uriel Weinreich's Review of *The Measurement of Meaning*," *Word*, XV (1959), 192–200. (a)

Osgood, Charles E. "The Representational Model and Relevant Research Methods," in Ithiel De Sola Pool, ed. *Trends in Content Analysis*. Urbana: University of Illinois Press, 1959, pp. 33–88. (b)

Osgood, Charles E. "Cognitive Dynamics in the Conduct of Human Affairs," *Public Opinion Quarterly*, XXIV (1960), 341–365. (a)

Osgood, Charles E. "Some Effects of Motivation on Style of Encoding," in Sebeok (1960), pp. 293–306. (b)

Osgood, Charles E. *An Alternative to War or Surrender*. Urbana: University of Illinois Press, 1962.

Osgood, Charles E. "Language Universals and Psycholinguistics," in Greenberg (1963), pp. 236–254. (a)

Osgood, Charles E. "On Understanding and Creating Sentences," *American Psychologist*, XVIII (1963), 735–751. (b)

Osgood, Charles E. "Psycholinguistics," in Sigmund Koch, ed. *Psychology: A Study of a Science*. Vol. VI. New York: McGraw-Hill, 1963, pp. 244–316. (c)

Osgood, Charles E. "Meaning Cannot Be an r_m?" *Journal of Verbal Learning and Behavior*, V (1966), 402–407.

Osgood, Charles E. "Toward a Wedding of Insufficiencies," in Dixon and Horton (1968), pp. 495–519.

Osgood, Charles E., and Murray S. Miron, eds. *Approaches to the Study of Aphasia: A Report of an Interdisciplinary Conference on Aphasia*. Urbana: University of Illinois Press, 1963.

Osgood, Charles E., and Thomas A. Sebeok, eds. *Psycholinguistics: A Survey of Theory and Research Problems. Journal of Abnormal and Social Psychology*, IL (1954) and *International Journal of American Linguistics*, X (1954). Reissued: Bloomington: Indiana University Press, 1965.

Osgood, Charles E., George Suci, and Percy Tannenbaum. *The Measurement of Meaning*. Urbana: University of Illinois Press, 1957.

Osgood, Charles E., and Percy Tannenbaum. "The Principle of Congruity in the Prediction of Attitude Change," *Psychological Review*, LXII (1955), 42–55.

Osgood, Charles E., and Evelyn G. Walker. "Motivation and Language Behavior: A Content Analysis of Suicide Notes," *Journal of Abnormal and Social Psychology*, LIX (1959), 58–67.

Pei, Mario. *Language for Everybody*. New York: Pocket Books, 1956.

Penfield, Wilder, and Lamar Roberts. *Speech and Brain Mechanisms*. Princeton, New Jersey: Princeton University Press, 1959.

Pepitone, Albert. "Some Conceptual and Empirical Problems of Consistency Models," in Feldman (1966), pp. 257–297.

Pfungst, Oskar. *Clever Hans: The Horse of Mr. Von Osten*, trans. C. L. Rahn, ed. Robert Rosenthal. New York: Holt, Rinehart and Winston, 1965.

Piaget, Jean. *The Language and Thought of the Child*, trans. Marjorie Gabain. New York: World, 1955.

Pierce, J. R. *Symbols, Signals and Noise: The Nature and Process of Communication*. New York: Harper, 1961.

Pittinger, Robert E., and Henry Lee Smith, Jr. "A Basis for Some Contributions of Linguistics to Psychiatry," *Psychiatry*, XX (1957), 61–78.

Poole, Irene. "Genetic Development of Articulation of Consonant Sounds in Speech," *Elementary English Review*, II (1934), 159–161.

Postal, Paul M. "Underlying and Superficial Structure," *Harvard Educational Review*, XXXIV (1964), 246–266. (a)

Postal, Paul M. *Constituent Structure: A Study of Contemporary Models of Syntactic Description*. The Hague: Mouton, 1964. (b)

Postal, Paul M. *Aspects of Phonological Theory*. New York: Harper, 1968.

Premack, David, and Arthur Schwartz. "Preparations for Discussing Behaviorism with Chimpanzee," in Smith and Miller (1966), pp. 295–335.

Preston, Joan M., and R. C. Gardner. "Dimensions of Oral and Written Language Fluency," *Journal of Verbal Learning and Verbal Behavior*, VI (1967), 936–945.

Pulgram, Ernst. "Phoneme and Grapheme: A Parallel," *Word*, VII (1951), 15–20.

Quarrington, B. "Stuttering as a Function of the Information Value and Sentence Position of Words," *Journal of Abnormal Psychology*, LXX (1965), 221–224.

Quarrington, B., J. K. Conway, and N. Siegel. "An Experimental Study of Some Properties of Stuttered Words," *Journal of Speech and Hearing Research*, V (1962), 387–394.

Quastler, H., ed. *Information Theory in Psychology: Problems and Methods*. New York: Free Press, 1955.

Rapoport, Anatol. "What Is Semantics?" *Etc.*, X (1952), 12–24.

Rapoport, Anatol. "The Promise and Pitfalls of Information Theory," *Behavioral Science*, I (1956), 303–309.

Reichling, Anton. "Principles and Methods of Syntax: Cryptanalytical Formalism," *Lingua*, X (1961), 1–17.

Rice, Berkeley. "Skinner Agrees He Is the Most Important Influence in Psychology," *New York Times Magazine*, Part I, Section 6 (March 17, 1968), 27ff.

Rieber, R. W., and R. S. Brubaker, eds. *Speech Pathology: An International Study of the Science*. Amsterdam: North-Holland, 1966.

Riegel, Klaus F., ed. *The Development of Language Functions* (Report No. 8). Ann Arbor: University of Michigan, Center for Human Growth and Development, 1965.

Rioch, D. M., and E. A. Weinstein, eds. *Disorders of Communication: Proceedings of the Association for Research in Nervous and Mental Disease*. Baltimore: Williams and Wilkins, 1964.

Robins, R. H. *General Linguistics: An Introductory Survey*. Bloomington: Indiana University Press, 1964.

Robinson, Frank B. *Introduction to Stuttering*. Englewood Cliffs, New Jersey: Prentice-Hall, 1964.

Rokeach, Milton. *Beliefs, Attitudes, and Values*. San Francisco: Jossey-Bass, Inc., 1968.

Rommetveit, Ragnar. *Words, Meanings, and Messages: Theory and Experiments in Psycholinguistics*. New York: Academic Press, 1968.

Rosenberg, Milton. "Cognitive Structure and Attitudinal Affect," *Journal of Abnormal and Social Psychology*, LIII (1956), 367–372.

Rosenberg, Milton. "An Analysis of Affective-Cognitive Consistency," in Milton Rosenberg, *et al.*, eds. *Attitude Organization and Change: An Analysis of Consistency Among Attitude Components*. New Haven: Yale University Press, 1960, pp. 15–64.

Rosenberg, Milton, and Robert P. Abelson. "An Analysis of Cognitive Balancing," in Milton Rosenberg, *et al.*, eds. *Attitude Organization and Change: An Analysis of Consistency among Attitude Components*. New Haven: Yale University Press, 1960, pp. 112–163.

Rosenberg, Sheldon, ed. *Directions in Psycholinguistics*. New York: Macmillan, 1965.

Rosenberg, Sheldon, and James H. Koplin, eds. *Developments in Applied Psycholinguistics Research*. New York: Macmillan, 1968.

Ross, Raymond S. "Fundamental Processes and Principles of Communication," in Keith Brooks, ed. *The Communicative Arts and Sciences of Speech*. Columbus, Ohio: Charles E. Merrill, 1967, pp. 107–128.

Rubenstein, Herbert, and Murray Aborn. "Psycholinguistics," *Annual Review of Psychology*, XII (1960), 291–322.

Ruesch, Jurgen. "Synopsis of the Theory of Human Communication," *Psychiatry*, XVI (1953), 215–243.

Ruesch, Jurgen. *Disturbed Communication: The Clinical Assessment of Normal and Pathological Communicative Behavior*. New York: Norton, 1957.

Ruesch, Jurgen. *Therapeutic Communication*. New York: Norton, 1961.

Ruesch, Jurgen, and Gregory L. Bateson. *Communication: The Social Matrix of Psychiatry*. New York: Norton, 1951.

Runion, Howard L. "An Objective Study of the Speech Style of Woodrow Wilson," *Speech Monographs*, III (1936), 75–94.

Saadi, M., and P. Farnsworth. "The Degree of Acceptance of Dogmatic Statements and Preferences for Their Supposed Makers," *Journal of Abnormal and Social Psychology*, XXIX (1934), 143–150.

St. Onge, Keith R., and James J. Calvert. "Stuttering Research," *Quarterly Journal of Speech*, L (1964), 159–165.

Salomon, Louis B. *Semantics and Common Sense*. New York: Holt, Rinehart and Winston, 1966.

Salzinger, Kurt, and Suzanne Salzinger, eds. *Research in Verbal Behavior and Some Neurophysiological Implications*. New York: Academic Press, 1967.

Samuels, S. Jay. "The Psychology of Language," *Review of Educational Research*, XXXVII (1967), 109–119.

Sanford, Fillmore H. "Speech and Personality: A Comparative Case Study," *Character and Personality*, X (1942), 169–198. (a)

Sanford, Fillmore H. "Speech and Personality," *Psychological Bulletin*, XXXIX (1942), 811–845. (b)

Sapir, Edward. *Language: An Introduction to the Study of Speech*. New York: Harcourt, Brace & World, 1921.

Sapir, Edward. "Language," *Encyclopedia of the Social Sciences*, IX (1933), 155–169.

Saporta, Sol, ed. *Psycholinguistics: A Book of Readings*. New York: Holt, Rinehart and Winston, 1961.

Saussure, Ferdinand de. *Course in General Linguistics*, ed. Charles Bally and Albert Sechehaye in collaboration with Albert Reidlinger, trans. Wade Baskin. New York: Philosophical Libary, 1959.

Schaff, Adam. *Introduction to Semantics*. New York: Pergamon Press, 1962.

Schlesinger, I. M., Moshe Forte, Baruch Fried, and Rachel Melkman. "Stuttering, Information Load, and Response Strength," *Journal of Speech and Hearing Disorders*, XXX (1965), 32–36.

Schramm, Wilbur. "How Communication Works," in Wilbur Schramm, ed. *The Process and Effects of Mass Communication*. Urbana: University of Illinois Press, 1954, pp. 3–26.

Schramm, Wilbur. "Information Theory and Mass Communication," *Journalism Quarterly*, XXXII (1955), 131–146.

Schramm, Wilbur, and Richard F. Carter. "Effectiveness of a Political Telethon," *Public Opinion Quarterly*, XXIII (1959), 121–126.

Schuell, Hildred, and James J. Jenkins. "The Nature of Language Deficit in Aphasia," *Psychological Review*, LXVI (1959), 45–67.

Schuell, Hildred, James J. Jenkins, and John B. Carroll. "A Factor Analysis of the Minnesota Test for Differential Diagnosis of Aphasia," *Journal of Speech and Hearing Research*, V (1962), 349–369.

Schuell, Hildred, James J. Jenkins, and Edward Jiménez-Pabón. *Aphasia in Adults: Diagnosis, Prognosis, and Treatment*. New York: Harper, 1964.

Schuell, Hildred, James J. Jenkins, and Lydia Landis. "Relationship Between Auditory Comprehension and Word Frequency in Aphasia," *Journal of Speech and Hearing Research*, IV (1961), 30–36.

Sebeok, Thomas A., ed. *Style in Language*. Cambridge, Mass.: M.I.T. Press, 1960.

Sebeok, Thomas A. "Review of Martin Lindauer's *Communication Among Social Bees*, Winthrop N. Kellogg's *Porpoises and Sonar*, and John C. Lilly's *Man and Dolphin*," *Language*, XXXIX (1963), 448–466.

Sebeok, Thomas A. "Animal Communication," *Science*, CXLVII (1965), 1006–1014. (a)

Sebeok, Thomas A. " Coding in Animals and Man," *Etc.*, XXII (1965), 330–349. (b)

Sebeok, Thomas A., ed. *Animal Communication: Techniques of Study and Results of Research*. Bloomington: Indiana University Press, 1968.

Sefer, Joyce W., and Ernest H. Henrikson. "The Relationship Between Word Associations and Grammatical Classes in Aphasia," *Journal of Speech and Hearing Research*, IX (1966), 529–541.

Shames, George H., and Carl E. Sherrick, Jr. "A Discussion of Nonfluency and Stuttering as Operant Behavior," *Journal of Speech and Hearing Disorders*, XXVIII (1963), 3–18.

Shands, Harley C. *Thinking and Psychotherapy: An Inquiry into the Process of Communication*. Cambridge. Mass.: Harvard University Press, 1960.

Shannon, Claude E., and Warren Weaver. *The Mathematical Theory of Communication*. Urbana: University of Illinois Press, 1949.

Sheehan, Joseph G. "Theory and Treatment of Stuttering as an Approach-Avoidance Conflict," *Journal of Psychology*, XXXVI (1953), 27–49.

Sheehan, Joseph G. "Conflict Theory of Stuttering," in Eisenson (1958b), pp. 121–166.

Shriner, Thomas H., and Lynn Miner. "Morphological Structures in the Language of Disadvantaged and Advantaged Children," *Journal of Speech and Hearing Research*, XI (1968), 605–610.

Siegel, A. E., and E. Siegel. "Flesch Readability Analysis of the Major Pre-Election Speeches of Eisenhower and Stevenson," *Journal of Applied Psychology*, XXXVII (1953), 105–106.

Siegel, Gerald M., and Richard R. Martin. "Verbal Punishment of Disfluencies in Normal Speakers," *Journal of Speech and Hearing Research*, VIII (1965), 245–251.

Siegel, Gerald M., and Richard R. Martin. "Punishment of Disfluencies in Normal Speakers," *Journal of Speech and Hearing Research*, IX (1966), 208–218.

Sies, Luther F. "Aphasia and General Semantics," *Etc.*, XXI (1964), 116–118.

Skinner, B. F. "Are Theories of Learning Necessary?" *Psychological Review*, LVII (1950), 193–216.

Skinner, B. F. *Verbal Behavior*. New York: Appleton-Century-Crofts, 1957.

Skinner, B. F. *Cumulative Record*, enlarged edition. New York: Appleton-Century-Crofts, 1961.

Skinner, B. F. *Science and Human Behavior*. New York: Free Press, 1965.

Slobin, Dan I. "The Acquisition of Russian as a Native Language," in Smith and Miller (1966), pp. 129–148.

Slobin, Dan I. "Imitation and Grammatical Development in Children," in N. S. Endler, L. R. Boulter, and H. Osser, eds. *Contemporary Issues in Developmental Psychology*. New York: Holt, Rinehart and Winston, 1968, pp. 437–443.

Smith, Alfred G., ed. *Communication and Culture: Readings in the Codes of Human Interaction*. New York: Holt, Rinehart and Winston, 1966.

Smith, Frank, and George A. Miller, eds. *The Genesis of Language: A Psycholinguistic Approach*. Cambridge, Mass.: M.I.T. Press, 1966.

Smith, Raymond G. "Development of a Semantic Differential for Use With Speech Related Concepts," *Speech Monographs*, XXVI (1959), 263–272.

Smith, Raymond G. "A Semantic Differential for Theatre Concepts," *Speech Monographs*, XXVIII (1961), 1–8.

Smith, Raymond G. "A Semantic Differential for Speech Correction Concepts," *Speech Monographs*, XXIX (1962), 32–37.

Smith, William M., John W. McCrary, and Karl U. Smith. "Delayed Visual Feedback and Behavior," *Science*, CXXXII (1960), 1013–1014.

Snider, James G., and Charles E. Osgood, eds. *Semantic Differential Technique: A Sourcebook*. Chicago: Aldine, 1969.

Soderberg, George A. "Phonetic Influences Upon Stuttering," *Journal of Speech and Hearing Research*, V (1962), 315–320.

Soderberg, George A. "The Relations of Stuttering to Word Length and Word Frequency," *Journal of Speech and Hearing Research*, IX (1966), 584–589.

Sondel, Bess. *The Humanity of Words*. New York: World, 1958.

Spiegel, Douglas K., Lyle V. Jones, and Joseph M. Wepman. "Test Responses as Predictors of Free-Speech Characteristics in Aphasia Patients," *Journal of Speech and Hearing Research*, VIII (1965), 349–362.

Spielberger, Charles D. "Theoretical and Epistemological Issues in Verbal Conditioning," in Rosenberg (1965), pp. 149–200.

Staats, Arthur W. *Learning, Language, and Cognition: Theory, Research, and Method for the Study of Human Behavior and Its Development*. New York: Holt, Rinehart and Winston, 1968.

Stachowiak, J., and C. Moss. "Hypnotic Alterations of Social Attitudes," *Journal of Personality and Social Psychology*, II (1965), 77–83.

Taft, R. "Selective Recall and Memory Distortion of Favorable and Unfavorable Material," *Journal of Abnormal and Social Psychology*, XLIX (1954), 23–28.

Tannenbaum, Percy. "Attitudes Toward Source and Concept as Factors in Attitude Change Through Communications." Unpublished doctoral dissertation. Urbana: University of Illinois, 1953.

Tannenbaum, Percy. "The Congruity Principle Revisited: Studies in the Reduction, Induction, and Generalization of Persuasion," in Leonard Berkowitz, ed. *Advances in Experimental Social Psychology*. Vol. III. New York: Academic Press, 1967, pp. 271–320.

Taylor, Insup K. "What Words Are Stuttered?" *Psychological Bulletin*, LXV (1966), 233–242. (a)

Taylor, Insup K. "The Properties of Stuttered Words," *Journal of Verbal Learning and Verbal Behavior*, V (1966), 112–118. (b)

Taylor, Wilson L. "'Cloze' Procedure: A New Tool for Measuring Readability," *Journalism Quarterly*, XXX (1953), 415–433.

Taylor, Wilson L. "Recent Developments in the Use of 'Cloze' Procedure," *Journalism Quarterly*, XXXIII (1956), 42–48, 99.

Taylor, Wilson L. "'Cloze' Readability Scores as Indices of Individual Differences in Comprehension and Aptitude," *Journal of Applied Psychology*, XLI (1957), 19–26.

Templin, Mildred C. *Certain Language Skills in Children.* Institute of Child Welfare Monograph, Series No. 26. Minneapolis: University of Minnesota Press, 1957.

Thayer, Lee O. "On Theory Building in Communication: Some Conceptual Problems," *Journal of Communication,* XIII (1963), 217–235.

Thayer, Lee O., ed. *Communication: Theory and Research, Proceedings of the First International Symposium.* Springfield, Illinois: Charles C. Thomas, 1967. (a)

Thayer, Lee O., ed. *Communication: Concepts and Perspectives.* Washington, D.C.: Spartan Books, 1967. (b)

Thayer, Lee O. *Communication and Communication Systems.* Homewood, Illinois: Irwin, 1968. (a)

Thayer, Lee O., ed. *Communication—Spectrum '7, Proceedings of the 15th Annual Conference of the National Society for the Study of Communication.* Lawrence, Kansas: National Society for the Study of Communication, 1968. (b)

Thomas, Gordon L. "The Effect of Oral Style on Intelligibility of Speech," *Speech Monographs,* XXIII (1956), 46–54.

Thomas, Owen. *Transformational Grammar and the Teacher of English.* New York: Holt, Rinehart and Winston, 1965.

Thompson, Wayne N. *Quantitative Research in Public Address and Communication.* New York: Random House, 1967.

Trager, George L. "The Systematization of the Whorf Hypothesis," *Anthropological Linguistics,* I (1959), 31–35.

Trager, George L., and Henry Lee Smith, Jr. *An Outline of English Structure.* Washington, D.C.: American Council of Learned Societies, 1957.

Travis, Lee Edward. *Speech Pathology.* New York: Appleton-Century-Crofts, 1931.

Travis, Lee Edward, ed. *Handbook of Speech Pathology.* New York: Appleton-Century-Crofts, 1957.

Uhlenbeck, E. M. "An Appraisal of Transformational Theory," *Lingua,* XII (1963), 1–18.

Ullmann, Stephen. *Semantics: An Introduction to the Science of Meaning.* New York: Barnes & Noble, 1962.

Ullmann, Stephen. *Words and Their Use.* New York: Hawthorn, 1966.

Valéry, Paul. "Style," in J. V. Cunningham, ed. *The Problem of Style.* Greenwich, Conn.: Fawcett, 1966, pp. 18–19.

Velten, H. V. "The Growth of Phonemic and Lexical Patterns in Infant Language," *Language,* XIX (1943), 281–292.

Vygotsky, Lev Semenovich. *Thought and Language,* ed. and trans. Eugenia Hanfmann and Gertrude Vakar. Cambridge, Mass.: M.I.T. Press, 1962.

Watzlawick, Paul, Janet Helmick Beavin, and Don D. Jackson. *Pragmatics of Human Communication: A Study of Interactional Patterns, Pathologies, and Paradoxes.* New York: Norton, 1967.

Weaver, Carl H., and Garry L. Weaver. "Information Theory and the Measurement of Meaning," *Speech Monographs,* XXXII (1965), 435–447.

Weinberg, Harry L. *Levels of Knowing and Existence: Studies in General Semantics.* New York: Harper, 1959.

Weinreich, Uriel. "Travels Through Semantic Space: Review of Charles E. Osgood, George Suci, and Percy Tannenbaum's *The Measurement of Meaning,*" *Word,* XIV (1958), 346–366.

Weinreich, Uriel. "Explorations in Semantic Theory," in Thomas A. Sebeok, ed. *Current Trends in Linguistics,* III (The Hague: Mouton, 1966), pp. 395–477.

Weir, Ruth Hirsch. *Language in the Crib.* The Hague: Mouton, 1962.

Weiss, Walter, and Bernhardt Lieberman. "The Effects of 'Emotional' Language on the Induction and Change of Opinions," *Journal of Social Psychology,* L (1959), 129–141.

Wells, Rulon S. "DeSassure's System of Linguistics," *Word,* III (1947), 1–31.

Wenner, Adrian M. "Communication with Queen Honey Bees by Substrate Sound," *Science,* CXXXVIII (1962), 446–448.

Wenner, Adrian M. "Sound Communication in Honeybees," *Scientific American,* CCX (1964), 116–124.

Wepman, Joseph M. *Recovery from Aphasia.* New York: Ronald, 1951.

Wepman, Joseph M., Lyle V. Jones, R. Darrell Bock, and Doris Van Pelt. "Studies in Aphasia: Background and Theoretical Formulations," *Journal of Speech and Hearing Disorders,* XXV (1960), 323–332.

West, Robert, L. Kennedy, and Anna Carr. *The Rehabilitation of Speech.* New York: Harper, 1937.

Westley, Bruce H., and Malcolm S. MacLean, Jr. "A Conceptual Model for Communications Research," *Journalism Quarterly,* XXXIV (1957), 31–38.

Whatmough, Joshua. *Language: A Modern Synthesis.* New York: New American Library, 1956.

White, Leslie A. "The Symbol: The Origin and Basis of Human Behavior," in Leslie A. White, *The Science of Culture, A Study of Man and Civilization.* New York: Farrar, Straus, and Cudahy, 1949, pp. 22–39.

White, Leslie A. "Four Stages in the Evolution of Minding," in Sol Tax, ed. *Evolution After Darwin.* Vol. II. Chicago: University of Chicago Press, 1960, pp. 239–253.

White, Leslie A. "Symboling: A Kind of Behavior," *Journal of Psychology,* LIII (1962), 311–317.

Wiener, Morton, and Albert Mehrabian. *Language Within Language: Immediacy, a Channel in Verbal Communication.* New York: Appleton-Century-Crofts, 1968.

Wiener, Norbert. *The Human Use of Human Beings: Cybernetics and Society.* Garden City, New York: Doubleday, 1954.

Wilson, Graham, ed. *A Linguistics Reader.* New York: Harper, 1967.

Wingate, M. E. "Stuttering Adaptation and Learning. I. The Relevance of Adaptation Studies to Stuttering as 'Learned Behavior'. II. The Adequacy of Learning Principles in the Interpretation of Stuttering," *Journal of Speech and Hearing Disorders,* XXXI (1966), 148–156, 211–218.

Wingate, M. E. "Stuttering and Word Length," *Journal of Speech and Hearing Research*, X (1967), 146–152.

Wischner, George J. "Stuttering Behavior and Learning: A Preliminary Theoretical Formulation," *Journal of Speech and Hearing Disorders*, XV (1950), 324–335.

Zajonc, Robert B. "The Concepts of Balance, Congruity, and Dissonance," *Public Opinion Quarterly*, XXIV (1960), 280–296.

Zipf, George Kingsley. *The Psycho-biology of Language*. Boston: Houghton Mifflin, 1935.

Zipf, George Kingsley. *Human Behavior and the Principle of Least Effort: An Introduction to Human Ecology*. Cambridge, Mass.: Addison-Wesley, 1949.

Subject Index

AB (attitude/belief) scales, 74
Abstraction, levels of, 15–18, 16 (fig.)
Acquisition of speech and language, 111–
150, *259–262* *
 age and, 122
 autistic theory of, 141–142
 babbling stage, 118
 bilingualism and, 115–116
 biological-nativistic approach, 145–150
 comfort sounds, 120–122, 121 (fig.)
 communication stage, 119
 consonants, distinctive features, matrix
  for, 123
 contextual generalization theory of,
  143–145
 corpus, role of, 140–145
 data, inadequacy of, 119–120
 differentiation, 120, 136, 137
 discomfort sounds, 120–122, 121 (fig.)
 distinctive features hypothesis, 123–124,
  123 (fig.)
 echolalia, 119
 factors influencing, 111–117
 first sounds, 117–118
 gradual differentiation process, 120, 136,
  137
 heredity and, 147
 history within species, lack of, 148–149
 intelligence and, 116–117
 lallation stage, 118–119
 learning theory approaches to, 141–145
 mediational theory of, 142–143
 morphological rules, 131–133
 names, 136–137
 phonemes, 122–126

 phonological, naming distinguished
  from, 137
 phonological competence, 124–126
 phonological level, 120–126, 121 (table),
  122 (table), 123 (fig.)
 phrase and structure rules, 126
 physiological condition and, 112–113
 reflexive and random vocalization, 118
 semantic level, 133–137, 135 (fig.)
 semantic markers, 133–136
 semantic structure, role of, 200–201
 sex differences and, 113
 siblings, number of, and, 113–114
 socioeconomic level and, 114–115
 specific organic correlates, 146–148
 stages in, 117–119, 260
 syntactic level, 126–134, 131 (fig.)
 naming distinguished from, 137
 theories of, 137–150, 261–262
 task faced by, 137–141
 transformational rules, 127–131, 144
 variations in, 146, 148
 vocabulary items, 136–137
Affective-Cognitive Consistency Theory,
 230–238, 234 (fig.), 251 (table)
Agnosia, 161
Allomorphs
 acquisition of, 131–133
 defined, 35
Allophones, defined, 29–30
Animal communication, 8–9
 bees, 207–212, 208 (fig.), 209 (fig.)
 see also Bee language, human compared
  with
Anomia, 157

* Italicized numbers refer to the For Further Reading section, pp. 253–268.

Name Index